Human Rights, Race, and Resistance in Africa and the African Diaspora

Africans and their descendants have long been faced with abuse of their human rights, most frequently due to racism or racialized issues. Consequently, understanding shifting conceptualizations of race and identity is essential to understanding how people of color confronted these encounters. This book addresses these issues and their connections to social justice, discrimination, and equality movements. From colonial abuses or their legacies, black people around the world have historically encountered discrimination, and yet they do not experience injustice opaquely. The chapters in this book explore and clarify how Africans, and their descendants, struggled to achieve agency despite long histories of discrimination. Contributors draw upon a range of case studies related to resistance, and examine these in conjunction with human rights and the concept of race to provide a thorough exploration of the diasporic experience. *Human Rights, Race, and Resistance in Africa and the African Diaspora* will appeal to students and scholars of Ethnic and Racial Studies, African History, and Diaspora Studies.

Toyin Falola is the Jacob and Frances Sanger Mossiker Chair in the Humanities and University Distinguished Teaching Professor at the University of Texas at Austin, US.

Cacee Hoyer is an Assistant Professor in the Department of History at the University of Southern Indiana, US.

Routledge African Studies

11 **Pan-Africanism, and the Politics of African Citizenship and Identity**
Edited by Toyin Falola and Kwame Essien

12 **Securing Africa**
Local Crises and Foreign Interventions
Edited by Toyin Falola and Charles Thomas

13 **African Youth in Contemporary Literature and Popular Culture**
Identity Quest
Edited by Vivian Yenika-Agbaw and Lindah Mhando

14 **Indigenous Discourses on Knowledge and Development in Africa**
Edited by Edward Shizha and Ali A. Abdi

15 **African Culture and Global Politics**
Language, Philosophies, and Expressive Culture in Africa and the Diaspora
Edited by Toyin Falola and Danielle Porter Sanchez

16 **Urbanization and Socio-Economic Development in Africa**
Challenges and Opportunities
Edited by Steve Kayizzi-Mugerwa, Abebe Shimeles and Nadège Désirée Yaméogo

17 **Continuity and Change in Sub-Saharan African Demography**
Edited by Clifford O. Odimegwu and John Kekovole

18 **Sexual Violence in Conflict and Post-Conflict Societies**
International Agendas and African Contexts
Edited by Doris Buss, Joanne Lebert, Blair Rutherford, Donna Sharkey and Obijiofor Aginam

19 **Land Reforms and Natural Resource Conflicts in Africa**
New Development Paradigms in the Era of Global Liberalization
Edited by Tukumbi Lumumba-Kasongo

20 **Cultural Entrepreneurship in Africa**
Edited by Ute Röschenthaler and Dorothea Schulz

21 **The New African Diaspora in the United States**
Edited by Toyin Falola and Adebayo Oyebade

22 **Human Rights, Race, and Resistance in Africa and the African Diaspora**
Edited by Toyin Falola and Cacee Hoyer

Human Rights, Race, and Resistance in Africa and the African Diaspora

Edited by
Toyin Falola and
Cacee Hoyer

Routledge
Taylor & Francis Group
NEW YORK AND LONDON

First published 2017
by Routledge
711 Third Avenue, New York, NY 10017

and by Routledge
2 Park Square, Milton Park, Abingdon, Oxon OX14 4RN

Routledge is an imprint of the Taylor & Francis Group, an informa business

© 2017 Taylor & Francis

The right of Toyin Falola and Cacee Hoyer to be identified as the authors of the editorial matter, and of the authors for their individual chapters, has been asserted in accordance with sections 77 and 78 of the Copyright, Designs and Patents Act 1988.

All rights reserved. No part of this book may be reprinted or reproduced or utilized in any form or by any electronic, mechanical, or other means, now known or hereafter invented, including photocopying and recording, or in any information storage or retrieval system, without permission in writing from the publishers.

Trademark notice: Product or corporate names may be trademarks or registered trademarks, and are used only for identification and explanation without intent to infringe.

Library of Congress Cataloging in Publication Data
Names: Falola, Toyin, editor. | Hoyer, Cacee, editor.
Title: Human rights, race, and resistance in Africa and the African diaspora / Edited by Toyin Falola and Cacee Hoyer.
Other titles: Routledge African studies ; 22.
Description: New York, NY : Routledge, 2016. | Series: Routledge African studies ; 22 | Includes bibliographical references and index.
Identifiers: LCCN 2016009875| ISBN 9781138679887 (hardback) | ISBN 9781315543819 (ebook)
Subjects: LCSH: Africa–Race relations. | Blacks–Civil rights–Africa. | Human rights. | African diaspora–Social conditions. | Race relations.
Classification: LCC DT15 .H86 2016 | DDC 302.896–dc23
LC record available at http://lccn.loc.gov/2016009875

ISBN: 978-1-138-67988-7 (hbk)
ISBN: 978-1-315-54381-9 (ebk)

Typeset in Times New Roman
by Wearset Ltd, Boldon, Tyne and Wear

To Cherno Njie, for struggles to transform the Gambia.
—Toyin Falola

To my family for their support and love.
—Cacee Hoyer

Contents

Notes on Contributors	ix
Introduction	1
TOYIN FALOLA AND CACEE HOYER	

PART I
Human Rights   15

1 **Human Rights as Natural Rights: The Quest for Theoretical Grounding**   17
WANJALA S. NASONG'O

2 **Exploring the Social Protection Rights of the African Child**   32
RACHAEL OJIMA AGARRY

3 **Untangling Discursive Reproduction: *Negras*, Sterilization, and Reproductive Rights in Brazil**   47
UGO FELICIA EDU

4 **Human Rights and Physical Capital: Panacea to Sustainable Development in Africa**   64
JONATHAN ALI OGWUCHE

PART II
Race, Racism, and Discrimination   83

5 **Yearning for Whiteness: Racial Identification Among the Coloureds of Antigua, 1660s–1860s**   85
NSAKA SESEPKEKIU

viii *Contents*

6 *The African Drum, Bantu World* and South Africa–United
   States Transnational Linkages, 1949–1954   109
   DEREK CHARLES CATSAM

7 Organized Labor and the Struggle for Black and
   Working-Class Citizenship in Cienfuegos, Cuba, 1899–1902   126
   BONNIE A. LUCERO

PART III
Discrimination and Resistance   149

8 State Violence, Radical Protest and the Black/African
   Female Body   151
   KANYINSOLA O. OBAYAN

9 Revolution at the Crossroads: Re-Framing the Haitian
   Revolution from the Heights of Platons   170
   MICHAEL BECKER

10 Uprooted: African Americans in Mexico; International
   Propaganda, Migration, and the Resistance against US
   Racial Hegemony   188
   ALFREDO AGUILAR

11 Re-Membering Samson Other*Wise*: Resistance, Revolution,
   and Relationality in a Rastafari Reading of Judges 13–16   210
   A. PAIGE RAWSON

   Index   232

Contributors

Editors

Toyin Falola, past President of the African Studies Association, occupies the Jacob and Frances Sanger Mossiker Chair in the Humanities. He has written widely on Africa, including books on contemporary issues and is a recipient of over 20 life-time distinguished career awards.

Cacee Hoyer is an Assistant Professor in the Department of History at the University of Southern Indiana, US. Her current research examines cross-cultural opposition to apartheid in post-World War II Durban, South Africa; her work challenges the accepted historiography of the early anti-apartheid movement in South Africa by arguing that non-white elites were unable to gain a broad base of support from their working class constituents. Her teaching and research interests are human rights and social justice, Africa and the Indian Ocean world, race relations in southern Africa, ethnicity and identity formation, apartheid politics, and oral histories. Cacee earned her PhD from the University of Texas at Austin. She also graduated with with a Master's in Social Studies Education from the University of Iowa, and a Bachelor of Science in History Education from the University of Northern Iowa.

Authors

Rachael Ojima Agarry is a Lecturer in Kwara State University, Malete, Nigeria. She specializes in Early Childhood Education. She is an advocate for children, particularly less privileged ones. She is very passionate about children, their education and general well-being. She had organized various advocacy programs for young children and had also authored several journal articles on issues relating to children.

Alfredo Aguilar is a doctoral student in the Department of History at Texas Tech University. He holds a BA and MA in History from the University of Texas-Pan American. His research focuses on race and ethnicity, transnationalism, and borderlands. His current research is focused on the international relationship of African Americans and Mexico.

x *Contributors*

Michael Becker is a PhD student in Caribbean history at Duke University. His research examines the relationship between enslaved peoples' resistance, the abolitionist movement, and the process of state formation in colonial Jamaica. He also researches and writes on marronage and rural protest movements in Haiti before, during, and after the revolution.

Derek Charles Catsam is Professor of History and the Kathlyn Cosper Dunagan Fellow in the Humanities at the University of Texas of the Permian Basin. He is the author of three books, including *Freedom's Main Line: The Journey of Reconciliation and the Freedom Rides* (2009, paper 2011), *Beyond the Pitch: The Spirit, Culture, and Politics of Brazil's 2014 World Cup* (2014) and *Bleeding Red: A Red Sox Fan's Diary of the 2004 Season* (2005). He is currently working on a book on bus boycotts in the United States and South Africa in the 1940s and 1950s. He has contributed numerous columns and articles on American and African politics and sports to many publications.

Ugo Felicia Edu is the Science, Justice, and Health Equity Postdoctoral Fellow for the Health Equity Institute at San Francisco State University. She received her PhD in Medical Anthropology with a Designated Emphasis in Women, Gender, and Sexuality from the University of California, San Francisco/ University of California, Berkeley. A California native, she received her BS in Physiological Sciences from the University of California, Los Angeles and her MPH in International Health from Morehouse School of Medicine. Using interdisciplinary approaches, her scholarship focuses on reproductive and sexual health, gender, sexuality, race, reproduction, and social justice. Her dissertation traces the intersections of race, reproduction, gender, and esthetics as they relate to black women's decisions regarding tubal ligations.

Bonnie A. Lucero is Assistant Professor of Latin American history at the University of Texas-Rio Grande Valley, where she has worked since earning her doctorate from the University of North Carolina at Chapel Hill in 2013. She teaches courses on the histories of Latin America, the Caribbean, and the African Diaspora, with special emphasis on issues of social justice. Her most recent research centers on the intersections of race and gender in Cuba and appears in *Transnational American Studies*, *Atlantic Studies* and in her edited volume, *Voices of Crime: Constructing and Contesting Criminality in Modern Latin America* (co-edited, forthcoming). Her forthcoming book *Revolutionary Masculinity and Racial Inequality: Gendering War and Politics in Cuba, 1895–1902*, explains how Cuban men employed ideas of masculinity to construct and contest racial inequality amidst a nationalist discourse of racial democracy at the turn of the twentieth century.

Wanjala S. Nasong'o is Stanley J. Buckman Professor of International Studies and chair of the Department of International Studies, Rhodes College, Memphis, Tennessee. Professor Nasong'o has previously taught at the University of Nairobi, Kenyatta University, and the University of Tennessee at Knoxville. He has published widely on issues of governance, democratization, and identity conflict in Africa. His latest publication is a volume

Contributors xi

entitled *The Roots of Ethnic Conflict in Africa: From Grievance to Violence* (2015). Professor Nasong'o is the 2012 recipient of Rhodes College's Clarence Day award for excellence in research and creative activity.

Kanyinsola O. Obayan is a PhD Student in Africana Studies at Cornell University. Her research focuses primarily on coloniality and violence; gender, feminism and sexuality; globalization, transnationalism and Diaspora. She hopes to use these dynamic conceptualizations as a way to read meaning into the socio-political environment of post-independence Nigeria, and imagine alternative possibilities for its future.

Jonathan Ali Ogwuche is an Associate Professor of Environmental Management, in the Department of Geography, Benue State University, Makurdi, Nigeria. He has published over 50 papers in reputable international journals, and has attended several local and international conferences. His research interests include environment, gender, and development. He is a Registered Surveyor of the Federal Republic of Nigeria, and a member of Professional bodies, including Nigerian Institution of Surveyors (NIS), Nigerian Environmental Society (NES), and Institute of Development Administration of Nigeria (IDAN).

A. Paige Rawson is a PhD candidate in biblical studies and women and gender studies at Drew University in Madison, New Jersey. She is an adjunct professor of religious studies at Seton Hall University in South Orange. Paige currently teaches religion, philosophy, and biblical studies and her research includes folktales and wisdom literatures, various poststructuralist theories, orality theory, and Africana studies with particular interest in the discursive potentialities in/at their intersections. When not teaching or writing in New Jersey, Paige enjoys traveling around the world, but especially when it involves solidarity and justice work. She has taught and served in Jamaica, Southeast Asia, Uganda, Rwanda and the Philippines.

Nsaka Sesepkekiu presently works as a senior researcher for the government of Antigua and Barbuda and as private consultant senior policy analyst. Dr. Nsaka is a native of Antigua and Barbuda, West Indies where he is a well-known campaigner against calls for reparations for slavery in the region. He attained a BA in African and Asian Studies and History at the University of the West Indies (St. Augustine Campus) in 2005. He was the winner of a Cambridge Commonwealth Scholarship to Cambridge University where he obtained both an M. Phil and a D. Phil (PhD). Dr. Nsaka has taught for a number of institutions including the St. Francois Girls College, Trinity College, and the University of the West Indies Open Campus in the areas of Sociology, History, Caribbean Studies, Legal History, Historical Jurisprudence and Law. Dr. Nsaka has also worked as a consultant to the Immigration Department of Antigua and Barbuda. The author's main areas of research include the African Diaspora in the Caribbean and Latin America, Legal History and Jurisprudence of Non-White Citizenship in the Leeward Islands, Immigration, Citizenship and Employment Law in the Leeward Islands and Anti-Reparations.

Introduction

Toyin Falola and Cacee Hoyer

Africans and those in the African diaspora have long histories of facing human rights abuses. All too often, race and racism coincide with these various instances of injustice, ranging from colonial abuses to their contemporary off-shoots. Academics have thoroughly discussed such notorious examples as South African apartheid or the Rwandan genocide. However, new scholarship explores emerging trends in discrimination, with special emphasis on gendered rights and the rights of vulnerable and minority populations in the African diaspora. This volume addresses these emerging themes as they intersect with notions of race and methods of resistance.

Discussions regarding discrimination experienced by Africans or those living in the African diaspora are almost exclusively focused around racial and ethnic constructs. As a result, understanding changing notions of race and identity is essential to understanding how people of color negotiated colonial encounters, independence movements, and post-colonial experiences. This volume seeks to address these ideas and their connections to social justice, discrimination, and movements for equality. The contributors further intend to explore various ways Africans, and their descendants, achieved agency despite the long history of discrimination.

People of African descent frequently experience racial discrimination and disadvantage. However, Africans do not experience injustice opaquely. Ample evidence exists that illustrates their ability to work within these discriminatory frameworks to limit the control of their oppressors or even discard it completely. Africans employ their agency in a diverse set of situations and under a variety of conditions, displaying tenacity of spirit and the resiliency of the human condition. By examining human rights and race in conjunction with case studies of resistance, a more robust and complete picture of the diasporic experience becomes evident.

The novelty of this volume is the juxtaposition of these three themes within the context of Africa and its diaspora. Several works have addressed these themes, but not all three in conjunction and not including an analysis of all people of African descent. Manning Marable's 2006 collection of previously published works has an extensive range covering Africa and the diaspora.[1] Chapter topics discuss race, class, and gender, in addition to ethnicity. However, its goal is to create an all-inclusive, local *American* coalition that engages

2   T. Falola and C. Hoyer

democratic strategies to change society, with emphasis on creating a common forum through which to address issues of economic oppression. Our volume differs significantly from Marable's in that it sees the intersections of the geographic regions where people of African heritage live, rather than discontiguous categories of "American" and "Third World." Additionally, our volume addresses the ways in which a variety of different rights movements, besides the economic focus of Marable, intersect with issues of race and methods of resistance.

Similarly, Curtis Stokes' 2009 collection of essays, *Race and Human Rights*, brings together scholars discussing race in relationship to human rights.[2] Stokes' main focus is people of African heritage, but he also discusses other populations in Iraq and the United States. Stokes' volume differs significantly from our collection, in that he focuses on the War on Terror, immigration, and affirmative action. Stokes' goal was to examine the debate between individualistic and collective notions of human rights. Our volume pushes past this debate to deal with case studies of race and resistance within their particular social justice contexts.

Faye Harrison's 2005 volume shares our volume's goal of illuminating the connections between race and human rights; however, our volume extends this analysis by discussing ways in which people have challenged oppression.[3] Additionally, Harrison's volume heavily emphasizes gender and the ramifications of 9/11, a significant difference from our more broadly-themed volume that focuses on the intricacies of human rights, racist oppression, and the ways people of African descent confront them. Likewise, Obioma Nnaemeka and Joy Ngozi Ezeilo's 2005 edited volume heavily focuses on gendered rights issues.[4] This volume seeks to stretch beyond this boundary to broaden the discourse on discrimination against people of African descent.

The intention is not to dissect the debates surrounding human rights, race, or resistance, but rather to integrate these three themes in order to reveal overlapping and intersecting points. By examining these concepts simultaneously in one volume, we can begin to see emerging themes of resistance as it has existed and evolved over time throughout Africa and the diaspora.

Vulnerable Populations and Human Rights

The first section of this volume addresses contemporary human rights issues in Africa and throughout its diaspora. It especially highlights protective and legal rights for women, children, and vulnerable populations. The emerging scholarship in this field of human rights work reflects movements in larger transnational bodies to advocate more awareness of these populations by local governments and civil societies. Such discussions are taken up in this volume to question this agenda and its efficacy.

Scholarship surrounding the rights and protections of children vary widely, but several main themes connect distinctly to discussions of human rights and vulnerable populations in this volume. Scholars perhaps most frequently center their discussion of the rights of the child on critiques of United Nations proposals, and other international accords, especially highlighting the lack of efficacy

Introduction 3

and challenges to local implementation.[5] For example, Aisling Parkes' in-depth analysis of Article Twelve of the 1989 UN Convention on the Rights of the Child lays out the groundwork that has developed as a result of this Article, how it has been implemented since 1989, and then suggests recommendations for future better practices.[6] Though such work is productive in understanding where things have been, the challenge lies with suggesting effective ways to implement the Convention in diverse locations in the world. Similarly, another trend is global and regional comparative studies in the implementation and effectiveness of particular human rights legislation targeting children.[7] Jacqueline Bhabha conducts her global comparative analysis by examining stateless children, who often experience multiple deprivations, and questions how various States handle this vulnerable population. Her work compares various locales across the globe, seeking a summative solution to the problem of stateless children. Perhaps most interesting, and pertinent to our interests here, is more targeted research on vulnerable African and diasporic populations. For example, Barbara Stark's work on the "Lost Boys" and "Forgotten Girls," questions the specific gender considerations, that are often overlooked, when discussing African children, especially in diaspora.[8] Her discussion centers on the more precarious position of the "Forgotten Girls" of Sudan (and African refugee girls in general), because of their gender they have lost their ability to lobby for refugee status as a group resulting in their subsequent vulnerability. As evidenced by existing literature, a wide gulf exists between objectives toward rights recognition and acquisition by African children and children of the diaspora.

While much of the recent research concerning women in Africa and the diaspora securing individual rights, perhaps the most contentious discussions recently have focused on reproductive rights. Reproductive rights for women in the African Diaspora often centers on criticisms of sterilization programs, highlighting the vulnerable position of many women of African descent in the diaspora.[9] Specifically, Joao Costa's work on the "genocide" of the black populations of Brazil, where he argues the state-sanctioned sterilization campaigns target Brazilians of African descent is indeed a genocide based on Patterson's 1951 definition.[10] While his contentions are widely debated, significant research exists on Rights-Based family planning. In 2015, the WHO clarified its position on Rights-Based Family Planning, claiming

> For societies to reap the many benefits of family planning, both at the individual and macro levels, all methods of family planning, reversible *and* permanent, should be widely—indeed universally—available. Provision of these methods must include free choice, discontinuation on demand, and comprehensive counseling that proactively focuses on the WHO tiers of effectiveness. Until then, we are failing to accurately inform women with rights-based family planning programs.[11]

Their discussion highlighted vulnerable populations in both the developing and developed world who are denied rights-based family planning, including the sterilization techniques discussed by Vargas, based on a range of factors from

4   T. Falola and C. Hoyer

doctor bias to affordability. Their global health initiative supports the work discussed here and seeks to problematize what is often treated as a strict dichotomy between institutionalized racism and individual basic rights.

The WHO statement was in response to the 2012 Family Planning Summit in London, where important stakeholders met and established the goal to provide "effective family planning information and services to 120 million additional women and girls by the year 2020,"[12] increasing initiatives examining critical family planning practices have commenced. Such discussions frequently revolve around vulnerable populations, often those lacking access to family planning resources or those living in countries whose politics or culture strongly discourage such efforts. For this reason, it is important to discuss specific methods used to limit the rights of women in family planning, especially women of color around the globe. Brazil is perhaps the best documented example of this struggle between race and rights to family planning. As Felicia Ugo Edu discusses in her contribution to this volume,

> paying attention to race allows us to see the ways that things have in fact remained relatively the same, albeit shifting in some ways the mechanisms by which they work. We must pay attention to race, racism, and the role it plays in the process of social and physical reproduction, those moments at which the anatomo-political and bio-political axes intersect.[13]

She believes understanding the direct connection between race and reproductive rights is essential, because

> we cannot afford to focus only on the economic aspect of the issue or think of it in terms of citizenship in Brazil or only speak about it in terms of rights, sexual freedom, and individual choice, to which blacks were never meant to be included.[14]

By engaging race in the rights-based approach to family planning, Edu is pushing the paradigm and encouraging a more stringent and accurate portrayal of the prohibition of these rights for many women of the African diaspora.

Race and Resistance

Much of this work is centered on understanding how Africans and those in the diaspora identify themselves. The process of understanding the wide variety of terms such identification elicits requires an additional layer of recognizing the various ways these populations have resisted discrimination and subjugation over time.

Essential to conceptualizing race and resistance in human rights discussions is our understanding of the various definitions of *race* itself. Historians have argued about the specifics of change, but most agree that Enlightenment notions of *race* differed from colonial/scientific notions of race, which differed still from our recent belief in *race* as a social construct. David Goldberg explains *race* as

Introduction 5

one of the "central conceptual inventions of modernity," defining modernity as developing out of the post-sixteenth-century Western world.[15] In his work, he uses *race* to understand designations of different groups which are a result of a variety of discursive values placed on subjects in a variety of ways. Goldberg believes the "prevailing conceptual order" is responsible for how people understand themselves and others and influences relations between them.[16] This includes perceptions of one's self, which can be created external or internal to the self, but dictates a person or groups' normative rules of behavior, acceptable methods of interaction and ways of organizing. The concept of race has developed as a result of a combination of such factors as violence, "technologies of surveillance," and "internalized constraint."[17]

There is significant criticism for the general failure of scholars of globalization to centralize race and racialization in their discussions.[18] Deborah Thomas and Kamari Clarke claim that racial prejudice is so entrenched in society that a failure to include them in globalization discourses means to misinterpret our understanding of the historical forces behind contemporary distributions of wealth and power. They argue that analysis of existing global developments can only be understood within a historical context that sees the evolutions of global processes as both responsible for establishing race while also being formed by it. Thomas and Clarke's work desires to "recuperate the power of race as a central category of social analysis without either falling into essentialisms or forestalling the possibility of developing a critical analysis that overarches the specificities of location."[19]

African notions of race and ethnicity differ significantly from Western developments of these ideas; however, several major themes emerge, such as the reactionary and oppositional tendencies of race, black consciousness and black nationalism movements, and identity politics. Historically, Africans' understanding of race, when confronted with imperialism, often took on aspects of opposition and resistance. According to Bush, race consciousness in Africa and its diaspora increased significantly due to black nationalism and pan-Africanist movements.[20] This was especially evident in the 1930s where race theories and black consciousness were confronted with Marxism, fascism, liberal democracy and "new" notions discrediting scientific racism. *Racism* was first used by Africans during the 1930s and it became clear that racial issues were firmly placed in the political sphere.

Wallerstein raises several issues that problematize Western understandings of African notions of race.[21] First, he highlights the challenges and fluidity of terminology, which often leads to confusion. This is largely because of conceptual challenges, where Western understandings of social groupings are not equipped to express such African notions, or when employed they often create misunderstandings. Literature on Africa often refers to *tribes* or *ethnic groups* when attempting to explain group affiliations and identities, rather than *race*.[22] When *race* is used, it is primarily in conjunction with discussions of *white* Europeans and *black* Africans, usually in a colonial or post-colonial context, often because of conflict between the two *racial* groups. However, Wallerstein argues that *race* is rarely used to differentiate various indigenous groups of

6 T. Falola and C. Hoyer

African populations.[23] For example, he explains that most Africans would deny that the "conflict between the lighter-skinned Arabs of northern Sudan and the dark-skinned Nilotes of southern Sudan is a racial conflict," because they are using the term *race* for instances of "particular international social tension."[24] Wallerstein explains that though the conflict has the same characteristics as those understood in the West as *racial*, Africans differentiate this with conflicts between Africans and Europeans on the continent. Wallerstein argues that

> as a status-group category, race is a blurred collective representation for an international class category, that of the proletarian nations. Racism, therefore, is simply the act of maintaining the existing international social structure, and is not a neologism for racial discrimination.[25]

Black Consciousness inserted a new perspective on racial theories in Africa during the 1960s and 1970s.[26] Steve Biko, one of its biggest supporters, clarifies the recodification of *black* and *white* into new racial terms with distinctly different, and non-biological or cultural, underpinnings.[27] Steve Biko conceptualized black as a level of consciousness or a "reflection of mental attitude," which has nothing to do with the color of your skin (excepting whites).[28] In addition, being black meant you had to endure racial discrimination and oppression, as well as fight against it. This meant that you must be aware of white oppression against you, your complicity in this system of oppression, and willing to stand up and struggle against it. Therefore, being African is not a determinate for being black, so Biko opened the door to other "nonwhite" racialized categories to claim "blackness," which denotes a positive affirmation of character while still grappling with issues of race.[29] Biko's emphasis on action and psychological consciousness of oppression signaled the meaning behind the racial category of black. It was meant to empower subjugated people into modes of action. Likewise, however, black Africans who failed to achieve consciousness and refused to fight racial discrimination were not considered *black*. So previous notions of black were flipped around; being African did not automatically determine you as black. The important element was the "particular subjectivity about race and power, to recognize that blacks, because oppressed by reason of their blackness, must affirm themselves as black."[30]

Race as a Contemporary Issue

Recent understandings of race, especially among the general public, is that we live in a post-racial society, where racism and racial issues no longer exist because they have been replaced by other issues, such as class. Goldberg warns against this perspective, claiming instead that it is important to continue to understand the role race and racism play in contemporary culture.[31] Goldberg believes we inherently understand people in racial terms and that due to the historical flexibility of this term that modernity is largely responsible for the transformations of these notions.

Introduction 7

Grant Farred discusses Paul Gilroy's analysis of the "currency of race," in *Against Race.*[32] Farred extends Gilroy's discussion to question the epistemological foundations of race and racism. Farred argues that race cannot be "transcended," that in order to be "against race" one is inherently "doing race," which ultimately, he argues, displays the inconsistencies and possibly harmful nature of nonracialism.[33] He claims it is impossible to have sustainable communities, because either they are subjugated or their identities are tied to the historical development of racialization. Farred identifies the existence of this contradiction between an antiracist campaign in a highly racialized society in South Africa, where he highlights the essential role race plays in political thinking. He expresses this as the

> two-phase paradox: transforming the foundational element of the society, race and racism, from the defining trauma (apartheid) into a public speakability (this was the task of the Truth and Reconciliation Commission), and then into a (post-apartheid) discourse outmoded by the transcendent, incorporative commonality of national identity—the nonracially imaged community.[34]

Notions of nonracialism or the possibilities of living in a post-racial society, Goldberg argues, are entrenched in contemporary society due to its "renewable currency throughout modernity."[35] He examines the way race and racism is understood at various significant historical points in order to illustrate that the different ways race has been conceptualized means that it is perpetuated and therefore normalized. Goldberg argues that culture has been especially adopted to "mask" race in recent decades.[36] More specifically, Goldberg describes class, culture, ethnicity and race as "masks of race."[37]

He explains that this concept includes "identifying race with language group, religion, group habits, norms, or customs: a typical style of behavior, dress, cuisine, music, literature, and art."[38] What is argued as problematic with this concept is essentializing all cultural group members to display specific behaviors or values. Despite this, cultural emphasis (or multiculturalism) over race enjoyed vast support, primarily due to its lack of ordered placement of inferior or superior values or inclusions and exclusions. Goldberg claims the most significant problem with placing emphasis on culture rather than race is that most culturalists emphasize the biological nature of race without acknowledging the historical and social implications that race carries. As a result, culture acts to "mask" the same symptoms and issues that race previously held and distances racism and racialized acts in the guise of culture. As an example, he cites Margaret Thatcher's fear in 1978 of native Britain's being "swamped by people with a different culture"[39]—where her racialized ideas were essentially being couched in more politically and socially acceptable terms.

Several other issues became evident within the political and economic spheres of multi-culturalism. Large corporations began using the ideology as a marketing tool; the education system claimed multicultural curricula while failing to dismantle nationalist concepts or address class structures. Most importantly, multiculturalism diluted the political economy of postcolonial projects, especially

8   T. Falola and C. Hoyer

concerning articulations of race and imperialism. Too often multiculturalism "risked becoming the feel-good diversity pabulum," of the twentieth century.[40]

Additionally, a significant problem with claiming multiculturalism was that it diverted attention from racialized issues. As a result a new racism developed, which distanced itself from old tropes of superiority and biological distinctions to discussing cultural differences as natural to discrimination.[41] Different cultures were different, had evidence of long histories of being different and although this does not place superiority or inferiority anywhere, it perpetuates divisions and supported divisive political policies which were in fact more subtle versions of earlier racisms.

Cashmere and Troyna argue against notions that racism has disappeared following World War II, instead claiming that is has "transmuted: like baser metals turned to gold, racism and discrimination have become nationalism and cultural inviolability."[42] They claim this was especially so during the 1980s where movements claiming to be "national" or "cultural" were in actuality racial at its base. For example, they highlight a campaign in 1980s Britain that asserted "there were no 'blacks,' no 'whites,' just people."[43] However, Cashmere and Troyna highlight that this disregards those that want to identify as white or black without struggle or violence. Therefore, stressing nationalisms or non-racialism actually perpetuates notions of race. They argue this is also evident in the movement toward multiculturalism in public education as a way to address the needs of minority students.[44] They believe that by highlighting multiculturalism it gives precedence to it and therefore disregards or ignores or invalidates racial issues. They argue that recent ethnographic approaches and methods are uniquely situated to facilitate the global inclusion of racial relationships.

Part I: Human Rights

The first section of this volume begins with an exploration into the theoretical frameworks used in grounding human rights in Africa. Chapter 1 examines the philosophical debate between the Universalist and Relativist schools of thought. The remainder of this section focuses on various current "hot button" topics related to human rights in Africa and the diaspora. Chapter 2 includes an examination of the rights and responsibilities of foreign governments toward children in the diaspora, questioning authentic efforts toward social protection rights of African children in the diaspora. The next chapter in this section highlights reproductive rights and protections affecting women. It examines the efficacy of diasporic governments in protecting women, such as in Brazil, where the federal law is questioned as to whether it truly protects female reproductive rights or in reality inhibits them, especially for black women. The final chapter of this section delves into the challenges to accessing physical capital in regards to sustainable development in Africa. Taken as a whole, this section enhances the reader's understanding of current challenges and obstacles in securing rights by vulnerable African populations, both at home and abroad. By examining these various case studies, the existing debates and complex nature of securing human rights for Africans become clear.

Introduction 9

Part II: Race, Racism, and Discrimination

The second section centers on notions of race and how Africans and those in the diaspora understand and identify themselves along ethnic and racial lines. These ideas intersect with issues of human rights by engaging with various methods of resistance used in the struggle to gain or maintain basic human dignity.

This section consists of a diverse collection of diasporic communities grappling with issues of race and racism. The first two chapters address issues of race and identity in the United States among Africans and African-Americans. These works call for a re-examination of these relationships using an Afrocentric lens. Sam Tenorio explores the impact of the middle passage as a divisive tool propagated throughout American pop culture, while Derek Catsam provides a comparative analysis of American civil rights struggles as viewed by the South African readership of the African newspaper, *Bantu World*. Two case studies round out this section's collaborative efforts to elaborate the racial paradigm. The first argues that the mixed race population in Antigua has historically desired to be identified as white and collectively rejected their African heritage, while the other examines claims of citizenship based on ideas of dignity that failed to create a racially inclusive Cuba. These essays connect issues of rights, dignity, and worth in Africans and the diaspora to forms of resistance, which are expounded on in the final section of this volume.

Part III: Discrimination and Resistance

The third section discusses vulnerable populations conceptually and explores these populations' agency through various forms of resistance. This section provides several case studies addressing issues of race, racism, and equality in Africa and its diaspora. It highlights specific examples of protest, violence, and revolution as manifestations of agency held by Africans and those living throughout the diaspora against the issues of race, racism, and injustice so often experienced throughout the colonial and post-colonial periods.

The third section starts with an examination of the black female body as used to protest British colonial control of Nigeria. It emphasizes the clash between knowledge structures and understanding the indigenous practice of nude protest. This chapter is followed by Michael Becker's criticism of the scholarship on the Haitian revolution. Becker argues that the scholarship intended to uplift the historical positioning of the Haitian revolution has instead perpetuated marginalization of others involved in the conflict, such as the maroon community of Platons. As a result, Becker places this marginalized group at the forefront of his discussion, charging that the Haitian revolution was indeed a crossroads of the Atlantic world, political and economic exchange, and colonial modernity. The next chapter in this section is a case study that provides a unique historical examination of African Americans in Mexico. Alfredo Aguilar discusses the African American struggle against US racial hegemony, encouraging many African Americans to migrate to Mexico.

10   *T. Falola and C. Hoyer*

The final chapter examines biblical hermeneutics. A. Paige Rawson assesses the relation of Judges 13–16, the story of Samson, to the Rastafari movement, questioning the need to develop a diasporic Africana hermeneutic.

Conclusion

This volume seeks to tie together three themes that often appear as disparate topics. Although race, racism, and resistance movements are frequently associated, rarely is a human rights approach taken in conjunction with these discussions. By combining contemporary notions of human rights, which are shifting increasingly to include vulnerable populations, with race, a new range of abuses have come to the fore. As evidenced by the work in this volume, race indeed impacts the extent to which human rights legislation is enforced, primarily due to lasting institutionalized racism in many States. By incorporating such discussions with historical and contemporary instances of resistance, our hope is to expose injustice and create avenues for activism. For the essence of resistance against racial oppression is the desire for equitable access to basic human rights and protections.

Notes

1 Manning Marable, *Speaking Truth To Power: Essays on Race, Resistance and Radicalism* (Boulder, CO: Westview Press, 2006).
2 Curtis Stokes, *Race and Human Rights* (East Lansing: Michigan State University Press, 2009).
3 Faye Harrison, *Resisting Racism and Xenophobia: Global Perspectives on Race, Gender, and Human Rights* (Walnut Creek, CA: AltaMira Press, 2005).
4 Obioma Nnaemeka and Joy Ngozi Ezeilo, *Engendering Human Rights: Cultural and Socioeconomic Realities in Africa* (New York: Palgrave Macmillan, 2005).
5 See for example: Uche Ewelukwa Ofodile, "Universal Declaration of Human Rights and the African Child Today: Progress or Problems," *American University International Law Review* 25.1 (2010): 37–76; Michael Gill and Cathy J. Schlund-Vials, *Disability, Human Rights and the Limits of Humanitarianism* (Farnham: Ashgate, 2014); Yves Beigbeder, *New Challenges for UNICEF: Children, Women, and Human Rights* (New York: Palgrave, 2001); Aisling Parkes London, *Children and International Human Rights Law: The Right of the Child to be Heard* (New York: Routledge, 2013).
6 Aisling Parkes London, *Children and International Human Rights Law.*
7 See for example: Jacqueline Bhabha, ed., *Children Without a State: A Global Human Rights Challenge* (Cambridge, MA: MIT Press, 2011).
8 Barbara Stark, "Lost Boys and Forgotten Girls: Intercountry Adoption, Human Rights, and African Children," *St. Louis University Public Law Review*, 22, no. 275 (2003).
9 See for example: Mark Largent, *Breeding Contempt: The History of Coerced Sterilization in the United States* (New Brunswick, NJ: Rutgers University Press, 2007); Kevin Begos, *Against Their Will: North Carolina's Sterilization Program and the Campaign for Reparations* (Apalachicola, FL: Gray Oak Books, 2012); Jennifer Nelson, *Women of Color and the Reproductive Rights Movement* (New York University Press, 2003); Ophra Leyser-Whalen and Abbey B. Berenson, "Control and Constraint for Low-Income Women Choosing Outpatient Sterilization," *Qualitative Health Research*, 23, no. 8 (2013): 1114–1124.
10 Vargas, João H. Costa, "Genocide in the African Diaspora: United States, Brazil, and the Need for a Holistic Research and Political Method," *Cultural Dynamics*, 17, no. 3 (2005).

Introduction 11

11 John Stanback, Markus Steiner, Laneta Dorflinger, Julie Solo, and Willard Cates, Jr., "WHO Tiered-Effectiveness Counseling Is Rights-Based Family Planning," *Global Health Science Practitioners*, 3, no. 3 (2015): 352–357.

12 K. Hardee, J. Kumar, K. Newman, L. Bakamjian, S. Harris, M. Rodríguez, and W. Brown, "Voluntary, Human Rights-Based Family Planning: A Conceptual Framework," *Studies in Family Planning*, 45 (2014): 1–18.

13 See Felicia Ugo Edu, "Untangling Discursive Reproduction: Negras, Sterilization, and Reproductive Rights in Brazil," in the present volume.

14 Ibid.

15 David Goldberg, *Racist Culture: Philosophy and the Politics of Meaning* (Oxford: Blackwell Publishers, 1993), 3.

16 Ibid., 2.

17 Ibid., 2. He is referencing Foucault's "anguish of responsibility" which Foucault argues was a result of the emergence of scientific epistemologies.

18 Kamari Maxine Clarke, and Deborah A. Thomas, eds., *Globalization and Race: Transformations in the Cultural Production of Blackness* (Durham: Duke University Press, 2006).

19 Clarke and Thomas *Globalization and Race*, 3.

20 Barbara Bush, *Imperialism, Race and Resistance: Africa and Britain, 1919–1945* (New York: Routledge, 1999), 43.

21 Etienne Balibar and Immanuel Wallerstein, *Race, Nation, Class: Ambiguous Identities* (New York: Verso, 1991), 187.

22 Peter Kivisto and Paul Croll break down the differences between race and ethnicity. They present three theoretical frameworks for understanding the relationship between race and ethnicity; the first model presents both groups as distinctly different, the second presents them as typically distinct but at times overlapping, and last they claim that a racial group is a subset of a larger ethnic group. They do highlight that despite the problems of both terms, ethnicity is often easier for scholars to employ because it lacks the long history that race has of abuse and biological emphasis, which is now firmly discredited. Additionally, they support beliefs that scholars who focus on racial aspects of ethnicity, such as race relations, are essentially analyzing racism. Peter Kivisto and Paul R. Croll, *Race and Ethnicity: The Basics* (New York: Routledge, 2012).

23 Balibar and Wallerstein *Race, Nation, Class*, 188.

24 Ibid., 199.

25 Ibid., 199.

26 Michael MacDonald, *Why Race Matters in South Africa* (Cambridge: Harvard University Press, 2006), 115–122. Anthony Marx further develops these ideas, although they align with MacDonald's approach. Anthony Marx, *Making Race and Nation: A Comparison of South Africa, the United States, and Brazil* (Cambridge: Cambridge University Press, 1998).

27 Steve Biko wrote many articles and books explaining his various ideas on race and Black Consciousness. Perhaps his most quoted is *I Write What I Like*, which was published shortly after his murder in 1977. Steve Biko, *I Write What I Like* (San Francisco: Harper and Row, 1978).

28 Biko, *I Write What I Like*, 48–50.

29 By the 1970s, apartheid South Africa had four legal categories for racial classification: White, Bantu (black African), Indian and Coloured. Biko's theory allowed all black Africans, Indians and Coloured to claim blackness rather than non-white status, which is a significant divergence from contemporary racial understandings.

30 Macdonald *Why Race Matters*, 120.

31 David Theo Goldberg, *Racist Culture: Philosophy and the Politics of Meaning* (Oxford: Blackwell Publishers, 1993), viii and 1.

32 Clarke and Thomas *Globalization and Race*, 226. Citing Paul Gilroy, *Against Race: Imagining Political Culture beyond the Color Line* (Cambridge: Harvard University Press, 2000).

12 T. Falola and C. Hoyer

33 Ibid., 229.
34 Ibid., 231.
35 Ibid., 89.
36 Goldberg, *Racist Culture*, 70.
37 Ibid., 61–84.
38 Ibid., 70.
39 Ibid., 73.
40 Robert Stam and Ella Shohat, *Race in Translation: Culture Wars Around the Postcolonial Atlantic* (New York: New York University Press, 2012), 85.
41 Phil Cohen, ed., *New Ethnicities, Old Racisms* (New York: St. Martin's Press, Inc., 1999), 4.
42 Ernest Cashmore and Troyna, Barry, *Introduction to Race Relations* (Bristol, PA: The Falmer Press, Taylor and Francis Inc., 1990), 5.
43 Ibid., 8.
44 Ibid., 12.

References

Balibar, Etienne, and Immanuel Wallerstein. *Race, Nation, Class: Ambiguous Identities*. New York: Verso, 1991.
Begos, Kevin. *Against Their Will: North Carolina's Sterilization Program and the Campaign for Reparations*. Apalachicola, FL: Gray Oak Books, 2012.
Beigbeder, Yves. *New Challenges for UNICEF: Children, Women, and Human Rights*. New York: Palgrave, 2001.
Bhabha, Jacqueline, ed. *Children Without a State: A Global Human Rights Challenge*. Cambridge, MA: MIT Press, 2011.
Biko, Steve. *I Write What I Like*. San Francisco: Harper and Row, 1978.
Bush, Barbara. *Imperialism, Race and Resistance: Africa and Britain, 1919–1945*. New York: Routledge, 1999.
Cashmore, Ernest, and Barry Troyna. *Introduction to Race Relations*. Bristol, PA: Falmer; Taylor and Francis, 1990.
Clarke, Kamari Maxine, and Deborah A. Thomas, eds. *Globalization and Race: Transformations in the Cultural Production of Blackness*. Durham: Duke University Press, 2006.
Cohen, Phil ed., *New Ethnicities, Old Racisms*. New York: St. Martin's, 1999.
Gill, Michael and Cathy J. Schlund-Vials. *Disability, Human Rights and the Limits of Humanitarianism*. Farnham: Ashgate, 2014.
Gilroy, Paul. *Against Race: Imagining Political Culture beyond the Color Line*. Cambridge, MA: Harvard University Press, 2000.
Goldberg, David. *Racist Culture: Philosophy and the Politics of Meaning*. Oxford: Blackwell, 1993.
Hardee, K., J. Kumar, K. Newman, L. Bakamjian, S. Harris, M. Rodríguez, and W. Brown, "Voluntary, Human Rights-Based Family Planning: A Conceptual Framework," *Studies in Family Planning*, 45 (2014): 1–18.
Harrison, Faye. *Resisting Racism and Xenophobia: Global Perspectives on Race, Gender, and Human Rights*. Walnut Creek, CA: AltaMira Press, 2005.
Kivisto, Peter, and Paul R. Croll. *Race and Ethnicity: The Basics*. New York: Routledge, 2012.
Largent, Mark. *Breeding Contempt: The History of Coerced Sterilization in the United States*. New Brunswick, NJ: Rutgers University Press, 2007.
Leyser-Whalen, Ophra and Abbey B. Berenson. "Control and Constraint for Low-Income Women Choosing Outpatient Sterilization." *Qualitative Health Research*, 23, no. 8 (2013): 1114–1124.

MacDonald, Michael. *Why Race Matters in South Africa*. Cambridge, MA: Harvard University Press, 2006.

Marable, Manning. *Speaking Truth to Power: Essays on Race, Resistance and Radicalism*. Boulder, CO: Westview Press, 2006.

Marx, Anthony. *Making Race and Nation: A Comparison of South Africa, the United States, and Brazil*. Cambridge: Cambridge University Press, 1998.

Nelson, Jennifer. *Women of Color and the Reproductive Rights Movement*. New York: New York University Press, 2003.

Nnaemeka, Obioma, and Joy Ngozi Ezeilo. *Engendering Human Rights: Cultural and Socioeconomic Realities in Africa*. New York: Palgrave Macmillan, 2005.

Ofodile, Uche Ewelukwa. "Universal Declaration of Human Rights and the African Child Today: Progress or Problems." *American University International Law Review* 25, no. 1 (2010): 37–76.

Parkes London, Aisling. *Children and International Human Rights Law: The Right of the Child to Be Heard*. New York: Routledge, 2013.

Stam, Robert, and Ella Shohat. *Race in Translation: Culture Wars Around the Postcolonial Atlantic*. New York: New York University Press, 2012.

Stanback, John, Markus Steiner, Laneta Dorflinger, Julie Solo, and Willard Cates, Jr. "WHO Tiered-Effectiveness Counseling Is Rights-Based Family Planning." *Global Health Science Practitioners*, 3, no. 3 (2015): 352–357.

Stark, Barbara. "Lost Boys and Forgotten Girls: Intercountry Adoption, Human Rights, and African Children." *St. Louis University Public Law Review*, 22 (2003): 275.

Stokes, Curtis. *Race and Human Rights*. East Lansing: Michigan State University Press, 2009.

Vargas, João H. Costa, "Genocide in the African Diaspora: United States, Brazil, and the Need for a Holistic Research and Political Method," *Cultural Dynamics*, 17, no. 3 (2005).

Part I
Human Rights

1 Human Rights as Natural Rights

The Quest for Theoretical Grounding

Wanjala S. Nasong'o

Introduction

There is something deeply attractive in the idea that every person anywhere in the world, irrespective of citizenship or territorial legislation, has some basic rights that others should respect. The moral appeal of human rights has been used for a variety of purposes, from resisting torture and arbitrary incarceration to demanding the end of hunger and medical neglect. At the same time, the central idea of human rights as something that people have, even without any specific legislation, is seen by many as foundationally dubious and lacking in cogency. A recurrent question is: where do these rights come from? It is not usually disputed that the invoking of human rights can be politically powerful. Rather, the worries relate to what is taken to be the "softness" or "mushiness" of the conceptual grounding of human rights. Many philosophers and legal theorists see the rhetoric of human rights as just loose talk—perhaps kindly and well-meaning forms of locution—but loose talk nevertheless. More ardent critics of the notion of human rights argue that it is no more than "bawling upon paper."[1] So, where do human rights come from? Are human rights universal or are they relative? What is the basis of the belief that people have unconditional rights simply by virtue of being humans rather than contingent on the basis of certain qualifications? This chapter grapples with these questions by tracing the trajectory of philosophical debates about the theoretical grounding of the concept of human rights with particular focus on two dialectical schools—the Universalists and the Relativists. The overall purpose is to establish justification for the high moral ground occupied by human rights in contemporary societies.

Human Rights: The Contested Nature of a Hallowed Concept

The end of the Cold War at the turn of the 1990s marked the emergence of a period of proliferation of non-governmental organizations within the realm of civil society. These organizations are devoted to advocacy work in the fields of social, economic, and political empowerment. Despite the contested nature of the meaning of the concept of civil society, social formations have emerged within its ranks to push the case for the protection and observation of human

18   *W. S. Nasong'o*

rights however defined.[2] Indeed, according to scholars such as Issa Shivji, few concepts are as frequently invoked in contemporary political discussions as human rights.[3] For Amartya Sen, there is something deeply attractive in the idea that every person anywhere in the world, irrespective of citizenship or territorial legislation, has some basic rights, which others should respect.[4] Sen argues that the concept of human rights has been used for a variety of purposes including the notions that everyone across the globe is entitled not only to civil liberties and political freedoms unencumbered by the state, but, even more importantly, that everyone has the right to food, health, education, shelter, and a minimum environmental standard. Given the hallowed nature of the concept, its invocation remains politically potent. Yet there are many, especially among conservative legal theorists, who question the inherent validity of its claims, especially the position that people are entitled to these rights by virtue of being human beings, not contingently upon some qualification such as citizenship, cultural context, or express legislation. Critics thus point to the "softness," or "mushiness" of human rights to argue that they are foundationally dubious and lacking in essence. Accordingly, as observed above, many philosophers and legal theorists see the rhetoric of human rights as just loose talk—perhaps kindly and well-meaning forms of locution—but loose talk nevertheless.[5]

Amartya Sen goes on to contend that the contrast between the widespread use of the idea of human rights and the intellectual skepticism about its conceptual soundness is not new. The US Declaration of Independence of 1776 took it to be "self-evident" that everyone is "endowed by their Creator with certain inalienable rights, among them the right to life, liberty and the pursuit of happiness" and 13 years later, the French Declaration of "The Rights of Man and the Citizen" asserted that "men are born and remain free and equal in rights." But it did not take Jeremy Bentham long to propose the total dismissal of all such claims. Bentham insisted that the notion of "natural rights" "is simple nonsense: natural and imprescriptible rights, rhetorical nonsense, [and] nonsense upon stilts."[6]

Bentham's skepticism and dismissal of the notion of natural and thus universal human rights, in Sen's view, remains very alive today. Despite persistent use of the idea of human rights in practical affairs, there are some who see the idea of human rights as no more than "bawling upon paper," to use another of Bentham's barbed portrayals of natural right claims. Some critics, however, propose a discriminating rejection: they accept the general idea of human rights, but exclude from the acceptable list specific classes of proposed rights, in particular the so-called economic and social rights, or welfare rights. These rights, which are sometimes referred to as second generation rights, such as a common entitlement to subsistence or to medical care, or to a minimum environmental standard, have mostly been added relatively recently to earlier enunciations of human rights, thereby vastly expanding the claimed domain of human rights.[7] These additions have certainly taken the contemporary literature on human rights well beyond the eighteenth-century declarations that concentrated on a narrower class of "rights of man," including such demands as personal liberty and political freedom. These newer inclusions have been subjected to more specialized

Human Rights as Natural Rights 19

skepticism, with the critics focusing on their feasibility problems and their dependence on specific social institutions that may or may not exist.[8]

Hans Schmitz and Kathryn Sikkink conceptualize human rights as a set of principled ideas about the treatment to which all individuals are entitled by virtue of being human.[9] The two scholars posit that over time, these ideas have gained widespread acceptance as international norms defining what is necessary for humans to thrive, both in terms of being protected from abuses, and provided with the elements necessary for a life in dignity. Toward this end, human rights norms create a relationship mainly between individual rights holders and other entities, mostly states. Any human rights discourse, they argue, must have the essential requirements of equality and non-discrimination. In their view, belief systems in which rights are granted only in exchange for the performance of duties, or where different categories of people have different categories of rights, contradict the basic idea that all people are entitled to equal rights.[10]

Accordingly, Andrew Heard contends that human rights are almost a form of religion in the contemporary world.[11] They are the fundamental ethical standard that is used to measure a government's treatment of its people. Heard rightly notes that a broad consensus has emerged in the world today on the rhetoric that frames judgment of nations against an international moral code, prescribing certain benefits and treatment for all humans simply because they are human. Political debates rage within many nations over the denial or abuse of human rights. Even in prosperous, democratic countries like Canada, Heard points out, much public discourse is phrased in the rhetoric of rights. Legal documents to protect human rights have proliferated in Canada, culminating in the 1982 entrenchment of the Charter of Rights in the Canadian constitution. Especially since the advent of the Charter, many Canadians have claimed that particular benefits they desire are a matter of human rights and must be provided. Indeed, according to Heard, the claim that the desired benefit is a human right "is often meant to undercut any opposition as unprincipled or even immoral."[12]

Lost in much of the discussion is any justification for the high moral ground occupied by human rights. Most human rights activists and political commentators are content just to look at the United Nations' ever-growing body of human rights agreements as proof that these rights exist universally and therefore have to be respected by everyone. Domestic human rights legislation is assumed to represent the local implementation of internationally recognized rights that are universal and inalienable. However, what are the theoretical origins and basis of this conceptualization of human rights? According to Heard, any inquiry into the origin, nature, and content of human rights reveals tremendous conceptual hurdles that need to be overcome before one can accept their pre-eminent authority. The bottlenecks that encumber such analysis are, to some scholars, enough evidence that the concept of human rights is a misnomer, and that the rhetoric of human rights is really a description of a controversial set of ideals.

Arguably, however, the invoking of human rights is usually the province of those whose intention is to change the world rather than to interpret it. It is understandable, therefore, that this category of people is unwilling to spend time trying to provide conceptual justification, given the great urgency to respond to

20   *W. S. Nasong'o*

global deprivations. This proactive stance has had its practical rewards, since it has allowed immediate use of the colossal appeal of the idea of human rights to confront intense oppression or great misery, without having to wait for the theoretical air to clear.[13] However, as Sen rightly argues, the conceptual doubts must also be satisfactorily addressed, if the idea of human rights is to command reasoned loyalty and establish a secure intellectual standing. In Sen's view, it is critically important to see the relationship between the force and appeal of human rights, on the one hand, and their reasoned justification and scrutinized use, on the other.[14]

According to Andrew Heard, human rights are a product of a philosophical debate that has raged for over two millennia within European societies and their colonial descendants.[15] This debate centers on a search for moral-ethical standards of political organization and behavior that is independent of the contemporary society. In other words, many people are not content with the idea that what is right or good is simply what a particular society or ruling elite feels is right or good at any given time. This unease has led to a quest for enduring moral imperatives that bind societies and their rulers across the space of time and place. Fierce debates raged among political philosophers as these issues were argued through that led to two trajectories. While a path was paved by successive thinkers that led to contemporary human rights, a second lane was laid down at the same time by those who resisted this direction.

Human Rights: The Quest for Theoretical Grounding

Are rights truly the product of a particular vision and laws of a society? Or, are human rights so inherent in humanness that their origins and foundations are incontestable? Two competing schools of thought are linked to the notion of human rights. First is the Universalist school, which holds that human rights derive from our very essence as human beings, are universal in character, and thus, are equally applicable across geographic and cultural spaces. Second is the Relativist school, which believes that while human rights are necessary, they may nevertheless vary from one culture to another. Such variance across cultural spaces is viewed as normal and acceptable. To human rights relativists, a standard of human rights need not be universal; it can be adapted to fit into a given culture. A fundamental premise of the relativist school of thought is that all cultural practices have a purpose in the culture and thus fulfill some essential goal and, ipso facto, should be accepted prima facie. Let us focus on each of these schools separately.

The Universalist School of Thought

The concept of human rights has its first theoretical roots in the idea of natural rights developed by classical Greek philosophers, such as Aristotle, but that was much more comprehensively developed and elaborated by the Catholic theologian, Thomas Aquinas.[16] According to Aquinas, there were behaviors that are naturally right and naturally wrong because God ordained it so. What was

Human Rights as Natural Rights 21

naturally right could be ascertained by humans through "right reason" (by thinking properly). Hugo Grotius further expanded on this notion by declaring the immutability of what is naturally right and wrong. He contended:

> Now the Law of Nature is so unalterable, that it cannot be changed even by God himself. For although the power of God is infinite, yet there are some things, to which it does not extend ... Thus two and two must make four, nor is it possible otherwise; nor, again, can what is really evil not be evil.[17]

This naturalist theory of law stands for the proposition that there is some objective standard or 'higher law' against which positive (man-made) law can and should be measured. According to Hart, there are certain principles of human conduct, awaiting discovery by human reason, with which man-made law must conform if it is to be valid.[18] Similarly, Henry Maine argued that the Roman doctrine of *Jus Gentium* (law of nations) entailing principles of law common to all peoples is a basis for the development of international law.[19] Complementing *Jus Gentium* was the Roman doctrine of *Jus Naturale* (law of nature), which recognized certain human rights—e.g., the right to life—as inherent. This naturalist school stands on two pillars: (1) universally held principles of law, and (2) a philosophical commitment to human rights. Natural law theorists are thus mainly concerned with the substantive content of positive law and its congruence with morality. Law that does not conform to justice and morality is not proper law at all, but simply naked force.

The notion that natural rights were rooted in moral authority that was divinely ordained survived for several centuries. It was secured by the understanding that it is God who decided what limits should be placed on human political activity. Nevertheless, as Heard posits, the long-term difficulty for this train of political thought lay precisely in its ecclesiastical foundations. A challenge to this divine basis of human rights came with the age of reformation and the emergence of rationalism, which questioned and shook ecclesiastical authority. The first challenge was posed by Thomas Hobbes in the mid seventeenth century.[20] Hobbes not only postulated a state of nature in which God seemed to have no role to play, he also shifted the discourse from "natural rights" to "a natural right." In this Hobbesian conception, there was no longer just a list of behavior that was deemed naturally right or wrong, but the only claim to a natural entitlement was the right to one's self-preservation.

Despite the Hobbesian efforts to civilianize the theoretical basis of natural rights, John Locke revived the link between natural rights and God with his generous references to "what God had ordained or given" to humankind.[21] For his part, Immanuel Kant, reacting to Hobbes' postulation later in the eighteenth century, helped further reinforce the idea of natural rights, though he too, like Hobbes, shifted from postulating such rights as emanating from divine origin. In Kant's view, the congregation of humans into a state-structured society resulted from a rational need for protection from each other's violence found in a state of nature. Nonetheless, the basic requirements of morality required that each treat another according to universal principles. Kant's political doctrine was derived

22   W. S. Nasong'o

from his moral philosophy, and as such he argued that a state had to be organized through the imposition of, and obedience to, laws that applied universally; nevertheless, these laws should respect the equality, freedom, and autonomy of the citizens. In this way, Kant prescribed that basic rights were necessary for civil society: "A true system of politics cannot therefore take a single step without first paying tribute to morality.... The rights of man must be held sacred, however great a sacrifice the ruling power must make."[22] Interestingly, however, Kant did not believe that the citizenry could revolt against the sovereign for misuse of power. Accordingly, as Andrew Heard rightly notes, the rights of individuals in a Kantian society would lack the ultimate in political enforcement.[23]

It was in an effort to repudiate this renewed divine link between God and human rights that Jean Jacques Rousseau opened the floodgates of a virulent critique of the Universalist school by the Relativist school that forcefully emerged following the French revolution.

The Relativist School of Thought

Writing in the immediate pre-revolutionary period in France, Rousseau castigated attempts at tying religion to the foundations of political order and sought to disentangle the rights of society from natural rights. Rousseau argued that people agree to live in common if society protects them. The purpose of the state is to protect those rights that individuals cannot defend on their own. In his view, the rights in a civil society are hallowed: "But the social order is a sacred right which serves as a basis for other rights. And as it is not a natural right, it must be one founded on covenants."[24] Such covenants, Rousseau postulated, delineate the rights of citizens and the limits on the power of the sovereign. The rights of civil society thus emanate from such covenants and are thus relative and cannot be universal.

Rooted in the relativist school is the positivist theory of law. As a legal positivist, John Austin defines law in terms of imperativism: law is seen as the command of a 'sovereign' endorsed by the fact of habitual obedience.[25] Legal positivists view law as a social phenomenon, as a decision or a process of authoritative decisions that require authoritative enforcement by a political authority. Positive law is thus a set of rules designed by political superiors for the management of society. Hence, law is what a particular society decides for itself. Entitlements under such law cannot be universal but specific to each society. Legal positivists focus on the legal process, arguing that it is naive and illegitimate to deal with "principles" of law in a sociological vacuum. Law is a process, a system run by people. We must thus examine each system to see what law is about.

Nonetheless, it was France's Declaration of the Rights of Man and the Citizen, passed by the Republican Assembly after the French Revolution of 1789 that unleashed the most scathing attacks on the concept of natural rights and amplified the emphasis on the relativist perspective. The French Declaration proclaimed 17 rights as "the natural, inalienable, and sacred rights of man." This declaration provoked two scathing attacks on the notion of natural rights. The

Human Rights as Natural Rights   23

first critique was by Jeremy Bentham, already alluded to above. Bentham's clause-by-clause critique of the French Declaration forcefully argued that there can be no natural rights, since rights are created by the law of a society:

> *Right*, the substantive *right*, is the child of law: from *real* laws come *real* rights; but from laws of nature, fancied and invented by poets, rhetoricians, and dealers in moral and intellectual poisons come *imaginary* rights, a bastard brood of monsters, "gorgons and chimeras dire"... *Natural rights* is simple nonsense: natural and imprescriptible rights, rhetorical nonsense— nonsense upon stilts.[26]

The second critique came from Edmund Burke who wrote a stinging attack on the French Declaration's assertion of natural rights. In Burke's view, rights were those benefits fought for and won within each society. The rights held by the English and French, he asserted, were different, since they were the product of different political struggles through history.[27]

For his part, Thomas Paine, writing after Bentham's and Burke's critiques, was more nuanced in his approach. He did recognize the notion of natural rights but linked them to the rights of particular societies at particular historical junctures. Paine went so far as to distinguish between natural rights and civil rights, though in his view, the two were connected:

> Natural rights are those which appertain to man in right of his existence. Of this kind are all the intellectual rights, or rights of the mind, and also all those rights of acting as an individual for his own comfort and happiness, which are not injurious to the natural rights of others. Civil rights are those which appertain to man in right of being a member of society. Every civil right has for its foundation, some natural right pre-existing in the individual, but to the enjoyment of which his individual power is not, in all cases, sufficiently competent. Of this kind are all those which relate to security and protection.[28]

The works of Rousseau and Paine laid the groundwork for modern human rights theorists to elaborate a notion of natural rights that is not inspired by divine origin. As a result, various theories of rights have emerged that are humanist and rationalist. The "natural" element in this conception is determined from the prerequisites of human society, which are said to be rationally ascertainable. Thus, there are constant criteria, which can be identified for peaceful governance and the development of human society. Contemporary notions of human rights draw very deeply from this natural rights tradition. Human rights are now often viewed as arising essentially from the nature of humankind itself. The ideas that all humans possess human rights simply by existing and that these rights cannot be taken away from them are direct descendants of natural rights. However, a persistent opposition to this view builds on the criticisms of Burke and Bentham, and even from the social contractual views of Rousseau's image of civil society. In this perspective, rights do not exist independently of human

24   *W. S. Nasong'o*

endeavor; they can only be created by human action. Rights are viewed as the product of a particular society and its legal system.

Human Rights: Contemporary Theorization

In the contemporary sense, Amartya Sen argues that for a theory of human rights to be viable, it is necessary to clarify what kind of a claim is made by a declaration of human rights, how such a claim can be defended, and how the diverse criticisms of the coherence, cogency, and legitimacy of human rights encompassing first generation (civil and political), second generation (social and economic), and third generation (environmental and group/minority) rights, can be adequately addressed.[29] In Sen's view, a theory of human rights must address a number of critical questions, such as "what makes human rights important?" or "what duties and obligations do human rights generate?"[30]

Interest Theory vs. Choice Theory

Overall, contemporary discourse on human rights is framed by interest and choice theories. According to George Rainbolt, the interest theory was first proposed by Jeremy Bentham and has been defended and elaborated by scholars such as David Lyons, Joseph Raz, and Neil MacCormick.[31] These proponents of interest theory argue that a person has a right when others have duties that protect one of that person's interests. The main strength of interest theory is that it has the potency to account for the relational aspect of rights. There is an important difference between failing to respect someone's rights and failing to fulfill an obligation, which is not part of a right. In this sense, Rainbolt invites us to consider the difference between failing to pay a debt and failing to give to charity. In failing to pay the debt, one wrongs the debt-holder. In failing to give to charity one does something wrong, but one does not wrong anyone in particular. The first case involves what Amartya Sen calls a "perfect obligation" while the second one involves an "imperfect obligation."[32] From this, Rainbolt concludes that rights are relational in the sense that the obligations implied by rights are owed *to* someone.[33] According to interest theory therefore, the obligation implied by a right is an obligation *to* the right-holder because it is the right-holder's interest, which is protected by the right. Of course, this raises further critical questions—what if, by paying the debt, one can no longer feed one's family? What if the lending was predatory? Would one still be morally and ethically obligated to pay the debt?

Perhaps the central weakness and limitation of the interest theoretic approach to human rights is that there exist rights that are not in the interest of the right-holder. Consider another Rainbolt example: one might inherit some property, which is bound up in complex legal proceedings that prevent its sale or profitable utilization but require a great deal of time and attention. In the same vein, the rights of public officials also pose a difficulty for interest theorists. A judge's right to impose sentence seems to be justified by the public's interest in a well-functioning criminal justice system, not by a judge's personal interests. In a

Human Rights as Natural Rights   25

particular case under different circumstances, however, it might well be in a judge's own interest not to impose sentence as the said judge might be the target of an angry mob of the accused person's supporters.

The choice theory, on the other hand, was first proposed by Herbert Hart and has been defended by scholars such as Phillip Montague and Hillel Steiner.[34] Defenders of choice theory argue that a person has a right when others have duties, which protect one of that person's choices. Choice theory has no problem accounting for the relational nature of rights either. According to the choice perspective, the obligation implied by a right is an obligation *to* the right-holder because it is the right-holder's choice that is protected by the right.[35] A major limitation of choice theory is that there seem to be rights that do not protect the right-holder's choices. Rainbolt argues, for instance, that assume a police officer is ordered by a judge to arrest an individual. Apparently, the police officer has a right to arrest the individual. Nonetheless, the officer has no choice, because he has a duty to perform the arrest based on the judge's order, whether the arrest is lawful or not. Similarly, the rights of beings, which cannot choose, like animals and human newborns, pose another problem for choice theorists. If rights necessarily protect an individual's choices then individuals who cannot choose cannot have rights.[36]

Additionally, available scholarship on rights distinguishes institutional rights from non-institutional rights.[37] Institutional rights are created by institutions such as states, corporations, associations, clubs, and other forms of social organization. The law is the institution that has the most complex and subtle rights and it is with legal rights that most research and theorizing on rights begin. Non-institutional rights are all those rights, which exist independent of institutions. Such non-institutional rights are subdivided into a number of groups. In the first group are conventional rights, which are rights conferred largely by custom. The rules about lining up before a bank teller or a movie or bus ticket counter for instance, create conventional rights. The traditional customs of a culture also generate conventional rights, such as the conventional right of a Muslim man to marry up to four wives. In the second group are moral rights, which are those rights created by moral rules and principles. Many believe that Jim Crow legislation in the US was a violation of the moral rights of Blacks. Third, human rights are said to be an important category of moral rights. Traditionally, human rights are defined as those moral rights held by all humans on the basis of their being human. However, as pointed out above, this universalistic position is contested by relativists who posit that human rights are contingent upon a given cultural context, geographic space, and historical epoch.

Furthermore, as Rainbolt shows, rights could be active or passive.[38] Active rights are rights to do something oneself, such as the right to drive one's car or the right to vote. Passive rights, on the other hand, are rights that another person do or not do something. Such passive rights may be positive or negative. A positive right is a right that another person do something. For example, employees have a positive right that their employers pay them their wages. A negative right is a right that another person not do something. An example here is the right of each person not to be hit by another. Some scholars posit a further classification comprising

26   W. S. Nasong'o

"complex rights." This, however, has remained a matter of dispute among scholars of different persuasions. Libertarians, for example, hold that the right to life is a purely negative right (the right that one's life cannot be taken away). Others contend that this right is at least partly positive for it involves the right to work and the right of movement. Yet others aver that it is not only a passive right but involves some active aspects as well, hence the notion of "complex rights."[39]

Back to the Problematic: Are Human Rights Relative or Universal?

As demonstrated by the foregoing exposition, theoretical contestation over the concept of natural rights has raged for many centuries. Human rights, the offspring of this theoretical debate, have emerged to occupy a powerful position in the political consciousness of the world today. Yet, as Andrew Heard contends, neither preponderant belief in, nor even a consensus of support for human rights provides answers to the concerns raised by the earlier thinkers—are rights truly the product of a particular vision and laws of a society? Or, are human rights so inherent in humanness that their origins and foundations are incontestable?[40] As shown above, two competing schools of thought are linked to this notion of human rights. The first school, rooted in the positivist theory of law, is made up of Relativists who believe that while human rights are necessary, they may nevertheless vary from one culture to another. Such variance across cultural spaces is viewed by relativists as normal and acceptable. To human rights Relativists, a standard of human rights need not be universal; it can be adapted to fit into a given culture.[41] A fundamental premise of the Relativist school of thought is that all cultural practices have a purpose in the culture and thus fulfill some essential goal and, ipso facto, should be accepted prima facie. Nothing illustrates this perspective more than the contested nature of the rights of homosexuals around the world. Whereas Western industrial societies have increasingly recognized homosexual rights as inherently human rights that qualify for universal application, many non-Western societies, including countries such as Russia, Uganda, and Nigeria have resisted this idea, with the latter two going so far as legislating against homosexuality in 2014.

The second school of thought, rooted in the naturalist theory of law, is made up of Universalists who hold that human rights derive from our very essence as human beings, are universal in character, and thus are equally applicable across geographic and cultural spaces. Universalists are thus fervent supporters of the international human rights regime from the perspective that an international paradigm on human rights needs to be applied uniformly across the world. Followers of this persuasion strongly support the efforts of the United Nations in developing international covenants and treaties that work to develop an international dialogue and consensus on the universality of human rights. For them, the United Nations' 1948 Universal Declaration of Human Rights was a landmark development that was effectively reinforced by the coming into force of the 1998 Rome Statute and the 2002 inauguration of the International Criminal Court (ICC) to dispense justice to those who, in their private or official capacities, commit atrocious violations of fundamental human rights. These include crimes of genocide, crimes against humanity, and war crimes.

Human Rights as Natural Rights   27

In the final analysis, it is evident from the practical achievements of the human rights advocacy network and the institutionalization of an international regime of human rights that the Universalist school has trumped the Relativist school. Accordingly, three "generations" of human rights have emerged. The first generation, sometimes referred to as "Blue Rights," consists of political freedoms and civil liberties whose purpose is to protect individuals' participation in the civil and political life of their political systems from discrimination and repression by the state. Among these are the freedoms of association, assembly, religion, the press, conscience, and movement, as well as the right to life, a fair trial, due process, right to vote, and to non-discrimination on the basis of gender, race, class, or creed. These are essentially "negative" rights for they stop governments from interfering in individuals' enjoyment of their civil and political entitlements.

Social and economic rights constitute the second generation rights, popularly known as "Red Rights." These focus on socio-economic equality and guarantee citizens the right to a livelihood, to education, housing, healthcare, and social security. Third generation human rights, commonly referred to as "Green Rights," are environmental and group or collective rights that include the right to self-determination, economic and social development, right to a cultural heritage as well as to a healthy environment and sustainable natural resource use to ensure intergenerational equity. There is, evidently, a fourth generation of rights emerging in the global system. Whether this will be called "Pink Rights" or some other color, I am not sure; but it has to do with gender and sexual rights, especially the rights of the LGBTQ community. This emergent rights domain was particularly brought into focus by the enactment of laws in Nigeria and Uganda in 2014 outlawing same sex relationships. In counter position, the US passed the Marriage Equality bill in June 2015, underscoring the recognition and legality of same-sex relationships. Overall, there seems to be general agreement on the veracity of the first generation human rights and some general agreement on the second generation rights. However, the third and fourth generation rights remain largely contested terrains. Indeed, at the international level, it has remained overtly impossible to enact legally binding instruments in regard to third generation rights, leave alone the emergent fourth generation.

Conclusion

There is no gainsaying the fact that the debate over the nature of human rights and the question as to whether they are universal or relative has a long and checkered pedigree. Contestations between the Universalists and their Relativist interlocutors has raged fast and furious for centuries if not millennia. Yet, at the end of the day, as illustrated by the foregoing exposition, the Universalists seem to have triumphed over the Relativists. Some countries and sections of particular societies may resist and denounce certain aspects of human rights, but the trend in the contemporary international system is toward universalism as progressively illustrated by the Universal Declaration of Human Rights in 1948, the operationalization of the 1998 Rome Statute via the 2002 coming into force of the

28 *W. S. Nasong'o*

International Criminal Court (ICC), and the newly emergent international law popularly known as R2P (Responsibility to Protect).

The ICC was established for purposes of administering international criminal law and justice; ending the culture of impunity on the part of perpetrators of mass atrocity crimes including genocide, war crimes, and crimes against humanity; and effectively protecting human rights; as well as efficiently upholding the rule of law. The R2P, on the other hand, proposes that: (1) a state has a responsibility to protect its population from genocide, war crimes, crimes against humanity, and ethnic cleansing; (2) the international community has a responsibility to assist the state to fulfill its primary responsibility; and (3) if the state manifestly fails to protect its citizens from the aforementioned four mass atrocities and peaceful measures have failed, the international community has the responsibility to intervene through coercive measures such as economic sanctions with military intervention as a last resort. This trend toward grounding human rights in a universalistic ethos is derived from the powerful moral force invoked by the concept.

Notes

1 See Jeremy Waldron, ed. *Nonsense Upon Stilts: Bentham, Burke and Marx on the Rights of Man* (New York: Methuen, 1987).
2 See, Mahmood Mamdani, "A Critique of the State and Civil Society Paradigm in Africanist Studies," in Mahmood Mamdani and Earnest Wamba-dia-Wamba, eds., *African Studies in Social Movements and Democracy* (Dakar: CODESRIA, 1995); Shadrack Nasong'o, *Contending Political Paradigms in Africa: Rationality and the Politics of Democratization in Kenya and Zambia* (New York: Routledge, 2005).
3 Issa Shivji, *The Concept of Human Rights in Africa* (Dakar: Codesria, 1989).
4 Amartya Sen, "Elements of a Theory of Human Rights," *Philosophy and Public Affairs* 32, no. 4 (2004): 315–356.
5 Ibid.
6 See Jeremy Bentham, *Anarchical Fallacies*; *Being an Examination of the Declaration of Rights Issued during the French Revolution* (1792); republished in J. Bowring, ed. *The Works of Jeremy Bentham*, vol. II (Edinburgh: William Tait, 1843), 501.
7 See Shivji, *The Concept of Human Rights in Africa*; Sen, "Elements of a Theory of Human Rights"; Ivan Hare, "Social Rights as Foundational Human Rights," in *Social and Labour Rights in Global Context*, ed. Bob Hepple (Cambridge: Cambridge University Press, 2002); William F. Felice, *The Global New Deal: Economic and Social Human Rights in World Politics* (Lanham: Rowman & Littlefield, 2003); Cass R. Sunstein, *After the Rights Revolution: Reconceiving the Regulatory State* (Cambridge, MA: Harvard University Press, 1990); Thomas W. Pogge, *World Poverty and Human Rights: Cosmopolitan Responsibilities and Reforms* (London: Polity Press, 2002); James W. Nickel, "Rawls' Theory of Human Rights in Light of Contemporary Human Rights Law and Practice," http://Homepages.Law.Asu.Edu/~Jnickel/Rawlsessay.pdf.
8 See Maurice Cranston, "Are There any Human Rights?" *Daedalus* (1983) 1–17; Onora O'Neill, *Towards Justice and Virtue* (Cambridge: Cambridge University Press, 1996); Michael Ignatieff, *Human Rights as Politics and Idolatry* (Princeton: Princeton University Press, 2001).
9 See Hans Peter Schmitz and Kathryn Sikkink, "Human Rights," in Walter Carlsnaes *et al.*, eds. *Handbook of International Relations* (London: Sage Publications, 2002), 517–537.
10 Ibid.
11 See Andrew Heard, "Human Rights: Chimeras in Sheep's Clothing?" (1997) www.sfu.ca/~aheard/intro.html.

Human Rights as Natural Rights   29

12 Ibid.
13 Sen, "Elements of A Theory of Human Rights," 317; see also Nicholas Onuf, *World of Our Making: Rules and Rule in Social Theory and International Relations* (New York: Routledge, 2012).
14 Sen, "Elements of a Theory of Human Rights," 317.
15 Heard, "Human Rights: Chimeras in Sheep's Clothing?"
16 See Thomas Aquinas, *Summa Theologica* (Teddington, UK: Echo Library Publisher, 2007).
17 Hugo Grotius, *De jure belli et paci* [*The Law of War and Peace*] (Cambridge: Cambridge University Press, 2012), 22.
18 H.L.A. Hart, *The Concept of Law* (Oxford: Oxford University Press, 1961).
19 Henry Main, *International Law* (London: John Murray, 1890); see also, James H. Wolfe, *Modern International Law* (Upper Saddle River, NJ: Pearson, 2002), 1–2.
20 See Thomas Hobbes, *The Leviathan* (New York: Penguin Books, 1982).
21 See John Locke, *Two Treatises of Government* (Cambridge, UK: Cambridge University Press, 1988).
22 Immanuel Kant, "Perpetual Peace," in *Kant: Political Writings*, ed. Hans Reiss, 2nd edn. (Cambridge: Cambridge University Press, 1991), 125.
23 Heard, "Human Rights: Chimeras in Sheep's Clothing?"
24 Jean Jacques Rousseau, *The Social Contract*, Maurice Cranston [trans.] (Baltimore: Penguin, 1968), p. 50.
25 John Austin, *The Province of Jurisprudence Determined and the Uses of the Study of Jurisprudence* (London: John Murray, 1832 [New York: Noonday, 1954]).
26 Jeremy Bentham, "Anarchical Fallacies: Being an Examination of the Declaration of Rights issued during the French Revolution," in *Nonsense Upon Stilts: Bentham, Burke and Marx on the Rights of Man*, ed. Jeremy Waldron (New York: Methuen, 1987), 53 and 69.
27 See Edmund Burke, *Reflections on the Revolution in France* (Cambridge, MA: Hackett Publishing Company, 1987).
28 Thomas Paine, *The Rights of Man* (New York: Penguin Books, 1985), 68.
29 Sen, "Elements of a Theory of Natural Rights."
30 Sen, "Elements of a Theory of Human Rights," 318–319.
31 George Rainbolt, "Human Rights Theory," *Philosophy Compass* 1, no. 3 (2006): 3; Jeremy Bentham, "Anarchical Fallacies," in Jeremy Waldron, ed. *Nonsense Upon Stilts* (New York: Methuen, 1987). David Lyons, *Rights, Welfare, and Mill's Moral Theory* (Oxford: Oxford University Press, 1994). Joseph Raz, *The Morality of Freedom* (Oxford: Oxford University Press, 1986). Neil MacCormick, *Legal Rights and Social Democracy: Essays in Legal and Political Philosophy* (New York: Clarendon Press, 1982).
32 Sen, "Elements of a Theory of Human Rights," 318.
33 Rainbolt, "Human Rights Theory," 3.
34 Herbert L.A. Hart, *Essays on Bentham* (New York: Clarendon Press, 1982); *Essays in Jurisprudence and Philosophy* (New York: Clarendon Press, 1983); Phillip Montague, "Two Concepts of Rights," *Philosophy and Public Affairs*, 9 (1980), 372–384; Hillel Steiner, *An Essay on Rights* (Oxford: Blackwell, 1994).
35 Rainbolt, "Human Rights Theory," 3.
36 Ibid., 4.
37 Ibid., 3; see also, Joel Feinberg, *Rights, Justice, and the Bounds of Liberty* (Princeton: Princeton University Press, 1980).
38 Rainbolt, "Human Rights Theory," 4.
39 Wanjala S. Nasong'o, *The Human Rights Sector in Kenya: Key Issues and Challenges* (Nairobi: Kenya Human Rights Institute, 2009).
40 Heard, "Human Rights: Chimeras in Sheep's Clothing?"
41 Laura Rowe, "Basic Theory of Human Rights," http://iml.jou.ufl.edu/projects/Spring03/Rowe/theory.htm.

30   *W. S. Nasong'o*

References

Aquinas, Thomas. *Summa Theologica*. Teddington, UK: Echo Library Publisher, 2007.

Austin, John. *The Province of Jurisprudence Determined and the Uses of the Study of Jurisprudence*. London: John Murray, 1832 [New York: Noonday, 1954].

Bentham, Jeremy. "Anarchical Fallacies; Being an Examination of the Declaration of Rights Issued during the French Revolution," in *Nonsense Upon Stilts: Bentham, Burke and Marx on the Rights of Man*, edited by Jeremy Waldron, 29–76. New York: Methuen, 1987.

Burke, Edmund. *Reflections on the Revolution in France*. Cambridge, MA: Hackett Publishing Company, 1987.

Cranston, Maurice. "Are There any Human Rights?" *Daedalus* (1983): 1–17.

Feinberg, Joel. *Rights, Justice, and the Bounds of Liberty*. Princeton: Princeton University Press, 1980.

Felice, William F. *The Global New Deal: Economic and Social Human Rights in World Politics*. Lanham: Rowman and Littlefield, 2003.

Grotius, Hugo. *De jure belli et paci* [*The Law of War and Peace*]. Cambridge: Cambridge University Press, 2012.

Hare, Ivan. "Social Rights as Foundational Human Rights," in *Social and Labour Rights in Global Context*, edited by Bob Hepple, 153–181. Cambridge: Cambridge University Press, 2002.

Hart, Herbert L.A. *The Concept of Law*. Oxford: Oxford University Press, 1961.

Hart, Herbert L.A. *Essays on Bentham*. New York: Clarendon Press, 1982.

Hart, Herbert L.A. *Essays in Jurisprudence and Philosophy*. New York: Clarendon Press, 1983.

Heard, Andrew. "Human Rights: Chimeras in Sheep's Clothing?" www.sfu.ca/~aheard/intro.html, 1997.

Hobbes, Thomas. *The Leviathan*. New York: Penguin Books, 1982.

Ignatieff, Michael. *Human Rights as Politics and Idolatry*. Princeton: Princeton University Press, 2001.

Kant, Immanuel. "Perpetual Peace," in *Kant: Political Writings*, 2nd edn., edited by Hans Reiss. Cambridge: Cambridge University Press, 1991.

Locke, John. *Two Treatises of Government*. Cambridge: Cambridge University Press, 1988.

Lyons, David. *Rights, Welfare, and Mill's Moral Theory*. Oxford: Oxford University Press, 1994.

MacCormick, Neil. *Legal Rights and Social Democracy: Essays in Legal and Political Philosophy*. New York: Clarendon Press, 1982.

Main, Henry. *International Law*. London: John Murray, 1890.

Mamdani, Mahmood. "A Critique of the State and Civil Society Paradigm in Africanist Studies," in *African Studies in Social Movements and Democracy*, edited by Mahmood Mamdani and Earnest Wamba-dia-Wamba. Dakar: CODESRIA, 1995.

Montague, Phillip. "Two Concepts of Rights," *Philosophy and Public Affairs*, 9 (1980): 372–384.

Nasong'o, Shadrack. *Contending Political Paradigms in Africa: Rationality and the Politics of Democratization in Kenya and Zambia*. New York: Routledge, 2005.

Nasong'o, Wanjala S. *The Human Rights Sector in Kenya: Key Issues and Challenges*. Nairobi: Kenya Human Rights Institute, 2009.

Nickel, James W. "Rawls' Theory of Human Rights in Light of Contemporary Human Rights Law and Practice," http://Homepages.Law.Asu.Edu/~Jnickel/Rawlsessay.pdf.

O'Neill, Onora. *Towards Justice and Virtue*. Cambridge: Cambridge University Press, 1996.

Human Rights as Natural Rights   31

Onuf, Nicholas. *World of Our Making: Rules and Rule in Social Theory and International Relations*. New York: Routledge, 2012.

Paine, Thomas. *The Rights of Man*. New York: Penguin Books, 1985.

Pogge, Thomas W. *World Poverty and Human Rights: Cosmopolitan Responsibilities and Reforms*. London: Polity Press, 2002.

Rainbolt, George. "Human Rights Theory," *Philosophy Compass*, 1, no. 3 (2006): 11–21.

Raz, Joseph. *The Morality of Freedom*. Oxford: Oxford University Press, 1986.

Rousseau, Jean Jacques. *The Social Contract*, trans. Maurice Cranston. Baltimore: Penguin, 1968.

Rowe, Laura. "Basic Theory of Human Rights," http://iml.jou.ufl.edu/projects/Spring03/Rowe/theory.htm.

Sen, Amartya. "Elements of A Theory of Human Rights," *Philosophy and Public Affairs* 32, no. 4 (2004): 315–356.

Shivji, Issa. *The Concept of Human Rights in Africa*. Issa. Dakar: Codesria, 1989.

Schmitz, Hans Peter and Kathryn Sikkink. "Human Rights," in *Handbook of International Relations*, edited by Walter Carlenaes, 517–537. London: Sage Publications, 2002.

Steiner, Hillel. *An Essay on Rights*. Oxford: Blackwell, 1994.

Sunstein, Cass R. *After the Rights Revolution: Reconceiving the Regulatory State*. Cambridge, MA: Harvard University Press, 1990.

Wolfe, James H. *Modern International Law*. Upper Saddle River, NJ: Pearson, 2002.

2 Exploring the Social Protection Rights of the African Child

Rachael Ojima Agarry

Introduction

Children are key members of any society whose existence cannot be ignored. By nature, they are so tender and could barely help or defend themselves in times of tough situations. They are characterized by their formative years and vulnerability. They are growing future adults who have no means to protect themselves in any way. As a result, each community is expected to consider the children to be of paramount interest wherein adults and the government protect the interest or rights of the child on every side. In Africa, children are cherished by all; that is why their upbringing and well-being is a communal affair. Every adult member of the community takes the responsibility of caring for the child; most of the time they give up their pleasure to ensure that children are all right.[1] As good as the intentions of many African adults are, they oftentimes violate the rights of children, especially the social protection right, consciously or unconsciously. It is therefore important to consider some key issues that will inform and guide against further infringement of children's social protection right in Africa.

The Concept of Social Protection

Vulnerability comes from the notion that certain groups in society are more exposed than others to shocks that threaten their livelihood or survival. Other groups are so defenseless that they live in a chronic state of impoverishment in which their livelihood is constantly at risk. Even a small decline in welfare for such people could be life threatening or could have permanent consequences for human capital. It is important to observe at the outset that the vulnerable include not only those who are already poor, but also those who are currently above the poverty line but who are potentially in danger of being affected by severe shocks and have little ability to manage risk—people who are most likely to "sink into poverty after a shock has occurred."[2]

There is a strong relationship between human rights and development. Human rights and sustainable human development are interdependent and mutually reinforcing. For example, human rights are enhanced when poverty reduction programs empower people to claim their rights. The links between human rights and development are clearly shown in the people-centered, poverty eradication, human rights mainstreaming, good governance and globalization.

Across Africa, the social protection agendas have gained increasingly significant political attention over the last decade, as governments pursuing the Millennium Development Goals (MDGs) and other development initiatives have sought to reduce population vulnerabilities in the face of emerging global challenges, shifting demographic patterns, and persistent drivers of inequality and exclusion.[3] The term "social protection" is a set of interventions whose objective is to reduce social and economic risk and vulnerability, and to alleviate extreme poverty and deprivation.[4] Social protection or assistance programs are ubiquitous in developed countries and are becoming more common in developing countries. It is fundamentally about the nature of the social contract between the state/country and its citizens, and each country's responsibility to provide a minimum level of well-being to its citizens.

In addition, social protection is increasingly seen as an important component of poverty reduction strategies and efforts to reduce vulnerability to economic, social, natural, and other shocks and stresses. It can play an important role in strengthening access to and demand for quality basic services and social welfare services by the poorest through childhood and beyond. Social protection can also facilitate a better balance between care-giving and productive work responsibilities which is critical for the achievement of the Millennium Development Goals, particularly MDGs 4 and 5.[5]

Among some development partners, social protection is considered as part of the essential package of basic social services that each country is expected to provide for its citizens. However, the term social protection is used in different ways by different countries and organizations, hence, it has no single definition. The United Nations Children's Fund outlines the definition of social protection according to different bodies as follows:[6]

- The World Bank defines social protection as informal, market-based and public interventions that assist poor individuals, households, and communities to reduce their vulnerability by managing risks better.
- The Department for International Development (DFID) defines social protection as interventions that strengthen the capacity of the poor to protect their consumption and to support household investment in the assets required to manage and overcome their situation.
- The ILO refers to social protection as mechanisms that provide access to health care and protect citizens against the stoppage or reduction of earnings resulting from sickness, maternity, employment injury, occupational diseases, unemployment, invalidity, old age and death.
- As an example of a National Government's definition, the Malawi National Social Protection Strategy defines social protection as "policies and actions that protect and promote the livelihood and welfare of poor and vulnerable people."[7]
- The UNDP Poverty Centre defines social protection as interventions from public, private, voluntary organizations and informal networks to support

34 R. Ojima Agarry

communities, households and individuals in their efforts to prevent, manage, and overcome a defined set of risks and vulnerabilities. Other development partners, including NGOs, also have their definitions.

- UNICEF in a global conference on social protection refers to social protection as a set of transfers and services that help individuals and households confront risk and adversity (including emergencies), and ensure a minimum standard of dignity and well-being throughout the lifecycle.

The Livingstone Accord represents a major political landmark for social protection in 13 countries in Eastern and Southern African regions, under the auspices of the African Union, that have committed themselves to developing national social protection strategies, and integrating them into national development plans and budgets.[8] Consequently, the commitment creates new opportunities for working with governments on the fulfillment of children's rights to survival, development and protection.

The Child-Sensitive Social Protection

Children are more at risk, vulnerable, and are more sensitive to an array of economic, social, and environmental shocks and stresses than adults in a number of ways. The long- and short-term effects of this irregularity will directly tell on the economies and total development of the country. Hence, there is a need for a deeper understanding of the range of existing social protection policies and programs in Africa and their impacts, both direct and indirect, on children.

Child-sensitive social protection is an approach that aims to improve opportunities and development outcomes for children through a multi-dimensional understanding of their well-being, with sensitivity to the manner in which risks facing children differ from those of adults and those in distinct stages of child and adolescent development.[9] The approach is not limited to children alone, but also includes the households, communities, and individual caregivers who play crucial roles in determining children's socio-economic vulnerability.

The following approaches to child-sensitive social protection based on the transformative social protection framework were proposed.[10]

- *Protective:* Child-sensitive social protection aims to safeguard household income and consumption levels so that children's basic well-being can be maintained. In other words, the basic elements for the child's livelihood such as provision and access to good health facilities, nutrition, security and shelter from hazards need to be in place for the child's well-being.
- *Preventative:* When children are not properly care for by adults and government of a country, they turn out to become nuisance and problematic to the society. Child-sensitive social protection therefore seeks to provide households with alternatives to potentially negative coping strategies, which might otherwise increase child risk, such as dropping out of school, child labor or inadequate adult care.

Social Protection Rights of the African Child   35

- *Promotional:* Due to the vulnerability of children, child-sensitive social protection supports active investment on the path of government, organizations, and philanthropic individuals in critical aspects of children's development, including schooling and health.
- *Transformative:* Children like any other human being deserve to be treated with dignity and respect. As a result, child-sensitive social protection addresses structural and societal power imbalances that might otherwise create or sustain child vulnerabilities, while also encouraging greater equity and empowerment.

Children's Right to Social Protection in Africa

Children as human beings equally have rights to live a meaningful life maximizing their potentials. According to the United Nations Universal Declaration of Human Rights (UDHR), all human beings are born free and equal in status and rights.[11] People understand instinctively that everybody irrespective of one's status is born with the same rights and that we all have an obligation to protect those rights. The link between social protection and the realization of people's rights is specifically enshrined in the constitution of virtually all the African countries, and is backed up by a range of international human rights instruments, including the Universal Declaration of Human Rights, and the International Covenant on Economic, Social, and Cultural Rights.

Nevertheless, it is important that the authorities know their human rights obligations and should implement them in order to give their citizens the good life they deserve. Under the International Human Rights Law, countries are legally obligated to establish social protection systems, which flow directly from the right to social security, which is articulated in Article 22 of the Universal Declaration of Human Rights and in Article 9 of the International Covenant on Economic, Social and Cultural Rights (ICESCR). This is in line with the Part 1 Article 1 of African Charter on the Rights and Welfare of the Child (ACRWC) of 1999. The Charter clearly states the obligations of States as follows:

- Member States of the Organization of African Unity Parties to the present Charter shall recognize the rights, freedoms and duties enshrined in this Charter and shall undertake to the necessary steps, in accordance with their Constitutional processes and with the provisions of the present Charter, to adopt such legislative or other measures as may be necessary to give effect to the provisions of this Charter.
- Nothing in this Charter shall affect any provisions that are more conductive to the realization of the rights and welfare of the child contained in the law of a State Party or in any other international Convention or agreement in force in that State.
- Any custom, tradition, cultural or religious practice that is inconsistent with the rights, duties and obligations contained in the present Charter shall to the extent of such inconsistency be discouraged.

36 *R. Ojima Agarry*

The African Charter on the Rights and Welfare of the Child (ACRWC) defines a "child" as a human being below the age of 18. The idea through this definition is that the child is a human being with rights and dignity. The charter recognizes the child's unique and privileged place in African society and that African children need social protection and special care. It also acknowledges that children are entitled to the enjoyment of freedom of expression, association, peaceful assembly, thought, religion, and conscience.

In addition, the ACRWC aim is to protect the private life of the child and safeguard the child against all forms of economic exploitation and against work that is hazardous, interferes with the child's education, or compromises his/her health or physical, social, mental, spiritual, and moral development. It also calls for protection against abuse and bad treatment, negative social and cultural practices, all forms of exploitation or sexual abuse, including commercial sexual exploitation, and illegal drug use. It also aims to prevent the sale and trafficking of children, kidnapping, and begging of children

Children in Africa are affected by many different types of abuse, including economic and sexual exploitation, gender discrimination in education and access to health, and their involvement in armed conflict. Other factors affecting African children include migration, early marriage, differences between urban and rural areas, child-headed households, street children and poverty. Furthermore, child workers in Sub-Saharan Africa account for about 80 million children or 4 out of every 10 children under 14 years old, which is the highest child labor rate in the world.[12]

It is a common saying that children are the future leaders in the society, and they therefore deserve to be cared for and protected. As promising as children are to the continuous existence of the society, they are the most vulnerable members of the society. Millions of children in Africa have no access to education, work long hours under hazardous conditions, are forced to serve as soldiers in armed conflict, or languish in institutions or detention centers where they endure inhumane conditions and assaults on their dignity as humans.[13]

As a result, there is need for intervention programs that will promote the well-being and interest of the African child. Hence, demand for social protection programs especially for children within more empowered segments of the poor population in African societies is on the increase due to the historically high levels of poverty, faster economic growth, rapid urbanization, and increasingly open, pluralistic political systems. Resources required to meet this demand are substantial and bound to compete with investments required to accelerate and broaden the current economic recovery process. However, countries that fail to address the demand are likely to face social as well as political unrest.

International Food Policy Research Institute revealed that African governments are spending substantial and increasing amounts of resources on health and education, but efforts need to be made to noticeably improve access to these public services for the poor and vulnerable.[14] It added that governments of African countries can and must make significant progress in developing functional social protection schemes as stability and growth of their economies depends largely on the extent to which progress is achieved in the well-being of their citizens, which invariably affects their productivity.

For centuries, the rights of children have been argued and the concept touches raw nerves when adult decisions and actions are put to the test.[15] In addition, rights are entitlements, valuable commodities we do not have to beg to get.[16] In other words, children are entitled to certain things in life, which will make their existence valuable and meaningful to them, and they are not supposed to struggle to get these benefits. Melton declares that in Africa, children's rights have not received general public or political support.[17] He added that the rights of children are being perceived to be jeopardized rather than advancing them.

UNICEF revealed that in 1989 governments worldwide promised all children the same rights by adopting the United Nation Convention on the Rights of the Child.[18] These rights are based on what the child needs to survive, develop, participate and to fulfill their potential. These rights apply equally to every child, regardless of who they are, or where they come from.

Children have rights as humans. The child's rights protect the child as a human being. The Convention on the Rights of the Child states clearly in 2003 that all children have rights that are inherent human rights, and that these should not be perceived as optional, as a question of favor or kindness to children, or as an expression of charity. These rights generate obligations and responsibilities. More than acknowledging the vulnerable nature of the child and the social responsibility to provide special assistance and protection, the Convention promotes the value of the child as a citizen, a partner in decision-making and in the broader process of social change.

The CRC thus envisions the "whole child" as a full, valuable, participating member of society. Children's rights are constituted by fundamental guarantees and essential human rights which state that children's rights recognize fundamental guarantees to all human beings—the right to life, the non-discrimination principle, the right to dignity through the protection of physical and mental integrity.[19] Also, children's rights are civil and political rights, that is, the right to identity, the right to a nationality. In addition, children's rights are economic, social and cultural rights—the right to education, the right to a decent standard of living, the right to health. Children's rights include individual rights such as the right to live with his/her parents, the right to education, and the right to benefit from a protection. It also includes collective rights—e.g., rights of refugee and disabled children, rights of minority children.

The devastating effects of poverty, ill health, under nutrition, and poor education affect the physical, emotional, and cognitive development of millions of children in Africa who are overrepresented among the poor.[20] Indeed while poverty denies opportunities to people of all ages, there are several key reasons for a child-oriented approach in social protection. First, children have a right to social protection and to have their interests pronounced in policy. Second, children are at a higher risk of poverty because they are not independent economic actors and rely on the distribution of resources within their households or communities. In addition, children experience poverty in distinctly different ways from adults because poverty in childhood has immediate effects that influence a child's well-being. These can be sustained into adulthood (life course poverty

38   R. Ojima Agarry

transmission) and also facilitate the transmission of disadvantage into the next generation (intergenerational transmission of poverty).

Children are key actors who often make huge contributions to the economic and social lives of their households. Yet there is still far too little understanding of how children experience poverty and vulnerability and what impoverishment means to them, or how their perceptions and priorities interact with those of local communities and the agendas of local, national and international agencies. The extent of generalized child vulnerability in Africa calls for evidence-based social protection measures to address poverty among children, households and communities.

Studies revealed that the West and Central African region (WCA) have the highest aggregate poverty and vulnerability levels in the world, as well as some of the most challenging governance environments. Demographically, children make up a very high percentage of the population (an average of 50 percent), but most countries in the region are significantly off-track in terms of meeting the child-related MDGs. This underscores the urgency of a child-sensitive approach to social protection interventions.

A child-sensitive approach to social protection needs to be informed by an understanding of the multiple and often intersecting vulnerabilities and risks that children and their caregivers encounter and how the ways in which experience of these vulnerabilities changes throughout childhood. Social protection can be conceptualized not only as being protective but also as preventative (preventing households from resorting to negative coping strategies that are harmful to children such as pulling them out of school and involving them in child labor), and promotional (promoting children's development through investments in their schooling, health and general care and protection).[21]

In addition, social protection can also be transformative, helping to tackle power imbalances in society that encourage, create and sustain vulnerabilities, and to support equity and empowerment.[22] In the case of children, this can include measures that protect their rights as well as ensuring that all children have a voice and agency in their families, schools and communities, irrespective of gender, religion, ethnicity, race, class, ability or disability.

Operationally, Overseas Development Institute (ODI) refers the framework of social protection as a set of initiatives, formal and informal, that provide:

- Social assistance to poor children and households, including regular, predictable transfers (e.g., cash or in-kind, school scholarships, school feeding programs, health service fee waivers) from governments and non-governmental entities. These aims to reduce poverty and vulnerability, increase access to basic services and, in some cases, promote asset accumulation.
- Social services for marginalized groups of children who need special care, including child fostering systems, child-focused violence prevention and protection services, rehabilitation services after trafficking, and basic alternative education for child laborers.
- Social insurance to protect children and their families against the risks and consequences of livelihood, health and other shocks. Such insurance typically takes the form of subsidized risk-pooling mechanisms, with potential

Social Protection Rights of the African Child 39

contribution payment exemptions for the poor; and social equity measures to protect children and their families against social risks such as discrimination or abuse, including anti-discrimination legislation (e.g., laws to protect children from trafficking, early child marriage, harmful traditional practices or to ensure special treatment and rehabilitation services for young offenders). Such measures also include affirmative action measures (e.g., scholarships for children of ethnic minority or indigenous communities) to try to redress past patterns of discrimination.[23]

Specific Vulnerable Conditions Affecting the African Child

Countries in Africa, specifically in west and central Africa, are highly vulnerable to a variety of economic, environmental, and socio-political shocks and stress, but there is also much diversity between countries. Countries in the region span different levels of economic development, ranging from high-income in Equatorial Guinea to middle-income in Congo, low-income to middle-income in Ghana and Senegal and least developed in Mali and Niger. There is also a diverse range of governance contexts including recent conflict (Congo, Niger), political fragility (Equatorial Guinea), and relatively open and vibrant democratic political cultures (Ghana, Mali and Senegal). Poverty rates also differ, from 29 percent in Ghana to 76.8 percent in Equatorial Guinea.

Taken as a whole, however, the region has the highest under-five mortality rate; accounts for more than 30 percent of global maternal deaths; lags far behind in universal primary education (with a net enrolment rate of just 62 percent); and has high child stunting indicators at 36 percent.[24] Children in WCA are exposed to the risks of exploitation, including child labor and trafficking, which can be particularly aggravated in the context of violence and conflict. In countries such as these, children are recruited as fighters, cooks, porters and so forth, which exposes them to a host of risks, including psychological trauma, drug addiction, and social stigma, in addition to the obvious risks posed by extreme violence.

Social and cultural factors also influence high rates of poverty and vulnerability. Vulnerability is often a complex interplay of different factors, including gender relations, discrimination and power imbalances. Gender inequality is pervasive in the region: the 2007/08 Gender-related Development Index (GDI) finds 12 WCA countries in the 20 lowest ranking countries.[25] Girls grow up vulnerable to male violence, ill-health, early marriage and maternal death, and face limited work opportunities and persistent poverty due to lack of education.

Domestic violence is also believed to be widespread and a number of harmful gendered traditional practices persist in the region. The most widespread is Female Genital Mutilation (FGM) or Cutting (FGC). Prevalence varies widely between countries, from less than 10 percent in Ghana, Niger and Cameroon to over 90 percent in Guinea and Mali. Other practices include various forms of indentured labor and exploitation, ranging from the tradition of *talibe* (a form of indentured labor of boys to local mosques) in countries such as Mali and Senegal, to that of *troski* (a form of indentured sexual slavery) in northern Ghana.

40 R. Ojima Agarry

These vulnerabilities impact children in ways such that social protection policy and programming must remain particularly sensitive, given the impacts that child deprivation can have both present effect but across children's life-courses and inter-generationally.[26] Consequently, there is a pressing need for a more detailed understanding of the wide variety of social protection policies and programs that presently exist throughout the continent, and the impacts they have on children—whether they directly target children or affect them indirectly. An understanding of the central challenges and opportunities facing social protection systems can help to inform current and future efforts to extend social protection to the most marginalized and vulnerable children on the continent.

Challenges of Child-Sensitive Social Protection in Africa

In Africa, there are challenges that affect the effectiveness, accessibility, and sustainability of existing social protection efforts, and the introduction of new initiatives aiming to tackle the multi-dimensional risks and vulnerabilities affecting the African child. These challenges are: the political economy of social protection, fiscal space constraints, socio-cultural attitudes, and weak evidence generation and dissemination systems.

The *political economy* of many African states poses serious limitations to social protection policy and programming across the continent. Governance systems are often characterized by neo-patrimonial patronage structures manifested in political and fiscal centralization, which directly impedes both legal rule and human development objectives.[27] Many African states also suffer from political instability as a result of ongoing violent conflicts. Such instability not only puts households and communities directly at risk, but also creates dysfunctions in governance and accountability, which limit the state's ability to provide for children's security from abuse and poverty.

Second, most African states face serious *fiscal space constraints*, which although varied between sub-regions nonetheless remain a consistent challenge for most governments. The ILO estimates that universal social assistance demands roughly 3 percent of a country's GDP, while 1 percent is required for a social pension, and 1–2 percent for child-related transfers and roughly 3–4 percent for basic health insurance.[28] In the poorest African countries, these necessary fiscal resources may not exist, while even in middle-to-higher income states, fiscal space is routinely limited by governance and administrative capacity deficits, exacerbated by downturns in government revenue during times of economic challenge.[29]

Moreover, many countries rely heavily on expensive food and energy subsidies, which are often regressive and disproportionally limited to high-income households, yet which have simultaneously become entrenched behind difficult-to-remove institutional barriers.[30] Fiscal space constraints, in turn, typically presage the need for heavy involvement from multilateral and bilateral donors in the design, implementation, promotion and evaluation of social protection policy and programming. This support can, however, often result in limited government ownership and control over program objectives. Donors may also hold distinct

Social Protection Rights of the African Child   41

or even conflicting social protection agendas, hampering more harmonized policy and programming inputs. The result is often reduced high-level political buy-in for social protection approaches.[31]

Third, tensions between the wider aims and principles of social protection and those of traditional *socio-cultural attitudes*, beliefs, and practices toward children and gender often impede broader progress toward transformative child-sensitive social protection programs. At the governmental level, African political traditions typically downplay the importance of the state as a provider of fundamental security and well-being, while fears persist of the role of social transfers in fostering cultures of dependency among populations.

Broader social values and attitudes toward child vulnerability and protection are, as noted above, also often at odds with the goals of child-sensitive social protection, particularly regarding traditional harmful practices such as female genital mutilation/cutting (FGM/C), early child marriage, and the discriminatory treatment of children by gender, age, ethnicity, and/or disability. Such attitudes may impair progress toward social protection and social equity in the household and the wider community, and increase risks and inequalities to children in terms of both their basic livelihoods and the achievement of wider justice for children.[32]

Finally, the absence of an institutionalized evidence-based political culture presents a challenge to effective social protection policy development and programming. This should not be under-estimated. Reliable data on poverty and vulnerability, and related social spending, disaggregated by gender and age, is very limited in most countries in African. This makes it difficult to tailor social protection initiatives in a child-sensitive way. Data constraints are further compounded by limited capacity of many government institutions, NGOs and national legislatures to oversee and effectively use data, even when data exist. Monitoring, evaluation and learning mechanisms to track progress and promote knowledge sharing about ongoing social protection initiatives are also very rudimentary and poorly coordinated in most contexts.

How to Improve Child-Sensitive Social Protection in Africa

With the above challenges in mind, African governments and their development partners wishing to improve the effectiveness of their social protection efforts should heed the following suggestions.

Avoid a narrow approach to child-sensitive social protection: As highlighted above, an array of potentially complementary social protection instruments are available, and should be selected on the basis of a carefully considered child-sensitive vulnerability assessment. The popularity and ubiquity of cash transfers as a centerpiece of African social protection programming throughout the last decade too often obscures opportunities to advance broader, multidimensional protection agendas. Cash transfers can indeed be critical in reducing household insecurity and poverty, and promoting human capital development. However, in pursuing these approaches exclusively, governments risk failing to take into account the deeper social dimensions of child vulnerability, such as its inter-generational origins or roots in embedded discrimination or harmful practices. They can also fail to make

42   R. Ojima Agarry

use of the wider array of improved social protection mechanisms, such as social insurance, social equity measures and legislation, in-kind transfers, and subsidized services. Given the many socio-cultural impediments to improving child-sensitive social protection agendas, it is also important to expand the horizons of social protection systems beyond strict social service delivery and transfers, to a more ambitious agenda of transformative change aimed at redressing the power inequalities in societies that lead to child vulnerabilities in the first place. At the same time, the design and rollout of formal social protection initiatives needs to be informed by an understanding of more informal social protection mechanisms, in order to identify potential synergies and avoid undermining more indigenous safety net approaches for children.

Avoid overly complex program design: In light of the serious limitations to administrative and coordination capacity that are present throughout many African governments, careful thought should be given to avoiding unnecessary complexity in social protection programs and mechanisms for eligibility. A cost-benefit calculation must be made regarding universal versus targeted approaches based on the fiscal space and political economy of the country in question. Pursuing a targeted approach may reduce overall costs in comparison to a universal approach, and therefore represent the better choice for fiscally constrained states; however, it is important to keep in mind that targeted approaches can also often require costly investments in skilled staff and sophisticated monitoring and conditionality mechanisms.[33]

Do not overlook short-term stop-gap measures while developing longer-term social protection systems: Developing new, efficient social protection systems and/or improving existing systems are important, but such efforts can also prove to be lengthy undertakings. Until well-functioning systems are in place, governments must also retain the ability to provide short-term responses to vulnerabilities facing their populations in the present. Growing evidence regarding the potentially regressive and cost-ineffective nature of universal subsidies compared to more targeted approaches, for instance, may point to the need for reform; however, rapidly dismantling popular programs such as food subsidies in response can increase vulnerability in the interim. If political leaders do not introduce such measures properly, with good public communication, they can provoke popular backlash against otherwise-needed social protection reforms.

Improve the evidence base, knowledge management and lesson sharing around child-sensitive social protection policy and programming: It is imperative to enhance current understanding of existing child-sensitive social protection efforts, through expanded and better-coordinated research efforts, monitoring and evaluation. A stronger evidence base could greatly improve existing understanding of how child-sensitive program design and implementation may best be tailored to existing social protection policies and programming. At the same time, better data could equip policymakers with a powerful tool, skills needed to equip these ministries with the ability to present and defend their budget proposals with confidence when dealing with more-powerful finance ministries. Greater capacity-building and training in key ministries charged with child-sensitive social protection policy—particularly for allocating limited resources and advancing their social protection agendas through the use of persuasive evidence that shows the advantages of child-sensitive social protection for governments and communities, both in the short-term and inter-generationally.

Conclusion

The vulnerability of children in the African continent is very alarming. Many children are exposed to life-threatening situations with little or no defense, but over the last decade across Africa, the governments have been pursuing the Millennium Development Goals (MDGs) and other development initiatives in order to reduce the population of vulnerable members. One of the interventions is the social protection whose objective is to reduce social and economic risk and vulnerability, and to alleviate extreme poverty and deprivation among the people of Africa. This initiative is meant to inform the authorities about their human rights obligations and how to implement them in order to give their citizens the good life they deserve.

However, there are challenges that affect the effectiveness, accessibility, and sustainability of existing social protection efforts, as well as the introduction of new initiatives aiming to tackle the multi-dimensional risks and vulnerabilities affecting the African child. These challenges range from the political economy of social protection, fiscal space constraints, socio-cultural attitudes, and weak evidence generation and dissemination systems. To tackle these problems, avoiding a narrow approach to child-sensitive social protection, avoiding overly complex program design, not overlooking the short-term stop-gap measures while developing longer-term social protection systems and improving the evidence base, knowledge management and lesson sharing around child-sensitive social protection policy and programming were suggested ways to improve the effectiveness of their social protection efforts.

Notes

1 Oduolowu Akinbote and Lawal, *Pre-primary and Primary School in Nigeria: A Basic Text* (Nigeria: Sterling Housing Publishers, Ltd., 2001).
2 J. Ogoola, "The Right to Social Protection in Africa: The Role of Governments, Political Leaders and the Judiciary," A paper presented during the International Conference on Social Protection (September 8–10, 2008).
3 I. Ortiz, G. Fajth, J. Yablonski, and A. Rabi, *Social Protection: Accelerating the MDGs with Equity*. UNICEF Social and Economic Policy Working Briefs (New York: UNICEF, 2010).
4 UNICEF, *State of the World's Children 2009: Maternal and Newborn Health* (New York: UNICEF, 2008).
5 N. Jones and R. Holmes, *Gender-sensitive Social Protection and the MDGs*. ODI Briefing Paper 61. (London: Overseas Development Institute (ODI), 2010).
6 UNICEF, *A Joint Statement on Advancing Child Sensitive Social Protection*. Draft, July 28, 2008.
7 R. Sabates-Wheeler and L. Haddad, *Reconciling Different Concepts of Risk and Vulnerability: A Review of Donor Documents* (Institute of Development Studies (IDS), University of Sussex, Brighton, 2005), www.oecd.org/dataoecd/33/60/36570676.pdf.
8 UNICEF, *Social Protection in Eastern and Southern Africa: A Framework and Strategy* (New York: UNICEF, 2006), www.unicef.org/socialpolicy/files/Social_ Protection_ Strategy%281%29.pdf.

44 R. Ojima Agarry

9 Africa Child Policy Forum (ACPF) and Overseas Institute (ODI) (2013). *Child-sensitive Social Protection in Africa: Challenges and Opportunities*. Retrieved from www.africanchildforum.org.

10 S. Devereux and R. Sabates-Wheeler, *Transformative Social Protection*, IDS Working Paper 232 (Brighton: Institute of Development Studies, University of Sussex, 2004).

11 J. Ogoola, "The Right to Social Protection in Africa."

12 UNICEF, *UNICEF Data: Monitoring the Situation of Children and Women* (2015), Retrieved from http://data.unicef.org/child-protection/child-labour.html#sthash.bUjQqlFV.dpuf.

13 Human Rights Watch, *Children's Rights* retrieved from www.hrw.org/topic/*children-rights* on February 20, 2014.

14 International Food Policy Research Institute (IFRI)—West and Central Africa Office, *Social Protection in West Africa: The Status Quo, Lessons from Other Regions, Implications for Research* (2012), Retrieved from http//www.ifpri-copyright@cgiar.org on March 2, 2014.

15 Rogers W. Stainton, "Promoting Better Childhoods: Constructions of Child Concern," in M. J. Kehily (ed.), *An Introduction to Childhood Studies* (Maidenhead: Open University Press, 2004), 125–144.

16 M. Freeman, "Children's Rights in a Land of Rites," in B. Franklin (ed.), *The Handbook of Children's Rights* (London: Routledge, 1995), 70–88.

17 G. B. Melton, "Treating Children like People: A Framework for Research and Advocacy," *Journal of Clinical Child and Adolescent Psychology*, 34(4) (2005).

18 UNICEF, *Children's Rights*, 2009, retrieved from www.unicef.org.uk/UNICEFs-Work/Our-mission/Children's-rights/ on February 20, 2014.

19 Humanium, *Rights of the Child*, 2014, retrieved from www.humanium.org/en/child-rights/ on February 22, 2014.

20 Council for the Development of Social Science Research in Africa (CODESRIA), *2013 Child and Youth Institute*, 2013, retrieved from www.codesria.org/spip.php?article on February 23, 2014.

21 S. Guhan, "Social Security Options for Developing Countries," *International Labor Review* 133(1) (1995): 35–53.

22 S. Devereux and R. Sabates-Wheeler, "Transformative Social Protection," IDS Working Paper 232 (Brighton: Institute of Development Studies, University of Sussex, 2004).

23 N. Jones and R. Holmes, *Tackling Child Vulnerabilities Through Social Protection: Lessons from West and Central Africa* (London: Overseas Development Institute (ODI) and UNICEF, 2010).

24 UNICEF, *State of the World's Children 2009: Maternal and Newborn Health* (UNICEF: New York, 2008).

25 UNDP, *Human Development Report 2009. Overcoming Barriers: Human Mobility and Development* (UNDP: New York, 2009).

26 N. Jones and R. Holmes, *Tackling Child Vulnerabilities through Social Protection: Lessons from West and Central Africa*, Background Note. (London: Overseas Development Institute (ODI) and UNICEF, 2010).

27 D. Booth, R. Crook, E. Gyimah-Boadi, T. Killick, and R. Luckham, with N. Boateng, *What Are the Drivers of Change in Ghana?* (Legon and London: CDD/ODI policy brief no. 1, 2005); D. Kaufmann, A. Kraay, and M. Mastruzzi, *Governance Matters V: Governance Indicators for 1996–2005*, World Bank Policy Research Working Paper No. 4654 (Washington, DC: World Bank, 2006).

28 K. Pal, C. Behrendt, F. Léger, M. Cichon and K. Hagemejer, *Can Low Income Countries Afford Basic Social Protection? First Results of a Modelling Exercise* (2005). Retrieved from http://papers. ssrn.com/sol3/papers.cfm?abstract_id=807366.

29 H. Handa, S. Devereux, and D. Webb, (eds.), *Social Protection for Africa's Children* (London: Routledge, 2012).

Social Protection Rights of the African Child   45

30 B. Fatouh, "Energy Subsidies in the Middle East: Issues and Implications," Paper presented at the Conference on Increasing the Momentum of Fossil Fuel Subsidy Reform, Geneva, October 14, 2010.
31 A. Barrientos and D. Hulme, "The Future of Social Protection in the Developing World: Actors, Bottlenecks and Politics," in *Social Protection for the Poor and Poorest: Reflections on a Quiet Revolution*, A. Barrientos, and D. Hulme, (eds.), Brooks World Poverty Institute. (Manchester: University of Manchester, 2008); IDS, ODI, University of East Anglia School of International Development, and the Regional Hunger and Vulnerability Programme, *Social Protection for Africa: Where Next?* Joint Statement (2010). Online at: www.ids.ac.uk/go/news/social-protection-in-africa-where-next.
32 B. Ras-Work, *Legislation to Address the Issue of Female Genital Mutilation* (FGM). (2009). Retrieved from www.un.org/womenwatch/daw/egm/vaw_legislation_2009/Expert%20Paper%20EGMGPLHP%20_Berhane%20Ras-Work%20revised_pdf.
33 R. Marcus and P. Pereznieto, *Child and Social Protection in the Middle East and North Africa* (London: Overseas Development Institute (ODI), 2011).

References

Africa Child Policy Forum (ACPF) and Overseas Institute (ODI). *Child-sensitive Social Protection in Africa: Challenges and Opportunities*. 2013. Retrieved from www. africanchildforum.org.

Akinbote, Oduolowu and Lawal. *Pre-primary and Primary School in Nigeria: A Basic Text*. Nigeria: Sterling Housing Publishers, lLd., 2001.

Barrientos, A. and Hulme, D. "The Future of Social Protection in the Developing World: Actors, Bottlenecks and Politics." In *Social Protection for the Poor and Poorest: Reflections on a Quiet Revolution*. Barrientos, A. and Hulme, D., eds. Brooks World Poverty Institute. Manchester: University of Manchester, 2008.

Booth, D., Crook R., Gyimah-Boadi, E., Killick, T., and Luckham, R., with Boateng, N. *What Are the Drivers of Change in Ghana?* Legon and London: CDD/ODI policy brief no. 1, 2005.

Council for the Development of Social Science Research in Africa (CODESRIA). *2013 Child and Youth Institute.* 2003. Retrieved from www.codesria.org/spip. php?article 1787 on February 23, 2014.

Devereux, S. and Sabates-Wheeler, N. "Transformative Social Protection." IDS Working Paper 232, Brighton: Institute of Development Studies, University of Sussex, 2004.

Fatouh, B. "Energy Subsidies in the Middle East: Issues and Implications." Paper presented at the Conference on Increasing the Momentum of Fossil Fuel Subsidy Reform, Geneva, October 14, 2010.

Guhan, S. "Social Security Options for Developing Countries." *International Labor Review*. 133, no. 1 (1995): 35–53.

Handa, H., Devereux, S. and Webb, D., eds. *Social Protection for Africa's Children*. London: Routledge, 2012.

Handley, G. *Fiscal Space for Strengthened Social Protection in West and Central Africa*. Regional Thematic Report 2 for the Study on Social Protection in West and Central Africa. London: Overseas Development Institute (ODI), 2009.

Human Rights Watch. *Children's Rights*. 2014. Retrieved from www.hrw.org/topic/children-rights on February 20, 2014.

Humanium. *Rights of the Child*. Retrieved from www.humanium.org/en/child-rights/ on February 22, 2014.

IDS, ODI, University of East Anglia School of International Development, and the Regional Hunger and Vulnerability Programme. *Social Protection for Africa: Where*

46 R. Ojima Agarry

Next? Joint Statement, 2010. Online at: www.ids.ac.uk/go/news/social-protection-in-africa-where-next.

IFRI- West and Central Africa Office. *Social Protection in West Africa. International Food Policy Research Institute West and Central Africa Office.* 2012. Retrieved from http//www.ifpri-copyright@cgiar.org on March 2, 2014.

Jones, N. and Holmes, R. "Gender-sensitive Social Protection and the MDGs." ODI Briefing Paper 61. London: Overseas Development Institute (ODI), 2010.

Jones, N., and Holmes, R. *Tackling Child Vulnerabilities through Social Protection: Lessons from West and Central Africa.* London: Overseas Development Institute (ODI) and UNICEF, 2010.

Kaufmann, D., Kraay, A., and Mastruzzi, M. "Governance Matters V: Governance Indicators for 1996–2005." World Bank Policy Research Working Paper No. 4654. Washington, DC: World Bank, 2006.

Marcus, R. and Pereznieto, P. with Cullen, E., and Jones, N. *Child and Social Protection in the Middle East and North Africa.* London: Overseas Development Institute (ODI), 2011.

ODI. "Linking Social Protection and the Productive Sectors," Briefing Paper, London: Overseas Development Institute (ODI), 2007.

Ogoola, J. "The Right to Social Protection in Africa: The Role of Governments. Political Leaders and the Judiciary." A paper presented during the International Conference on Social Protection. September 8–10, 2008.

Ortiz, I., Fajth, G., Yablonski, J., and Rabi, A. *Social Protection: Accelerating the MDGs with Equity.* UNICEF Social and Economic Policy Working Briefs. New York: UNICEF, 2010.

Tabor, S. "Assisting the Poor with Cash: Design and Implementation of Social Transfer Programs." Social Protection Discussion Paper Series. Washington, DC: The World Bank, 2002.

Taylor, E., Kagin, J., Filipsky, M. and Thome, K. *Evaluating General Equilibrium Impacts of Kenya's Cash Transfer Programme for Orphans and Vulnerable Children* (CT-OVC). Rome: FAO, 2013. Retrieved from: www.fao.org/fileadmin/user_upload/p2p/Publications/Kenya_LEWIE_2013.

Taylor, V. *Social Protection in Africa: An Overview of the Challenges.* Cape Town: University of Cape Town, 2009.

Temin, M. "Expanding Social Protection for Vulnerable Children and Families: Learning from an Institutional Perspective." Working Paper, United Nations Inter-Agency Task Team on Children and HIV and AIDS, Working Group on Social Protection, New York: March, 2008.

Thomson, R. and Posel, D. "The Management of Risk by Burial Societies in South Africa." *South African Actuarial Journal*, no. 2 (2002): 83–128.

UNICEF. *State of the World's Children 2009: Maternal and Newborn Health.* New York: UNICEF, 2008.

UNICEF. *A Joint Statement on Advancing Child Sensitive Social Protection.* Draft, July 28, 2008.

UNICEF. *Children's Rights.* 2009. Retrieved from www.unicef.org.uk/UNICEFs-Work/Our-mission/Children's-rights/ on February 20, 2004.

UNDP. *Human Development Report 2009: Overcoming Barriers: Human Mobility and Development.* New York: UNDP, 2009.

3 Untangling Discursive Reproduction

Negras, Sterilization, and Reproductive Rights in Brazil

Ugo Felicia Edu

Despite a stressful start to the day, I had been able to make my trek up to the contraceptive clinic for their lectures.... As the instructor moved along to talk about sterilizations, a bronzed brunette, whom I will call Ivete, had a question early on. She was 41, separated, a mother of one and currently using the IUD. She wanted to get sterilized as she didn't want more children, but was having a hard time getting one. The instructor told her and the rest of the class, that even if she was 50, if she only had one child, she would not be able to get a sterilization. The same went for men with only one child. They too wouldn't be able to get sterilized ... Ivete (the bronzed brunette) was now thinking of using the hormonal implant since it was likely that she wouldn't be able to get sterilized.[1]

Despite being illegal and in the absence of any national family planning program, sterilization ranked as the method most popularly employed by Brazilian women for contraception in 1996. A full 40.1 percent of married women between the ages of 15–49 had been sterilized.[2] In some of the poorer regions, it had reached rates as high as 59.9 percent and as low as 29 percent in some parts of the South.[3] In the Northeast of Brazil, 70 percent of sterilizations were arranged and paid for by politicians and doctors.[4] The percentage of sterilized women who had undergone the procedure before the age of 30 had reached 57 percent.[5] This reliance in part on sterilization by women as a form of contraception had influenced a reduction of Brazil's total fertility rate (TFR) by 45 percent between 1970–1990, to a TFR of 2, something that had taken Sweden and England more than half a century to do.[6] This Brazilian story of over access is shared among demographers and family planning program officers. This excerpt pulled from my field notes tells an unexpectedly different story of access to sterilization in Brazil.

Ivete's case reveals that after legalization of the method of sterilization and the implementation of a national family planning program, sterilizations are not easily accessible for all. Women who have tried other contraceptive methods and do not want to have more children find it difficult to permanently end their fertility. Ivete went to the clinic to find out if she could get a tubal ligation—or other options—since her IUD had expired and she did not want more children. One analysis of Ivete, and other women's stories similar to this one, would be that of class—those that are poor have less access when the public health system fails. I draw our attention beyond class, to the question of race, which so often has been

48   U. Felicia Edu

ignored in studies about sterilization in Brazil. In my interrogation of a reading that is reluctant to see race, I ask us to examine the connections between legality, race, and poverty more generally.

At the same clinic where I met Ivete, *Centro de Pesquisa e Assistência em Reprodução Humana* (CEPARH), I interviewed a gynecologist.[7] When asked about the criteria for a woman to get a tubal ligation and whether a woman of 30 years of age with one or no children could get sterilized, she responded with the following:

> The criteria. She has to have a stable union. She has to have... Because here you have the Brazilian laws. It's not just us that do, right? You have the law.
>
> You have to have a stable union. You have to have sixty days from the date that one chooses for the surgery. So that, so that you don't have the chance of regretting. Think well and she has to have at least two children. Here, if she were to be twenty-five years old with three or two children and be thirty. If a girl arrives here, nineteen years of age and two children we don't tie because she's not adequate, right? Now, if a thirty year old woman or a thirty-five year old woman with two children arrives, there, she is within our criteria.[8]

This account of the law did not mention how class and race influence the practice of the law. I am interested in examining who gets constrained by laws, and the mechanisms by which this occurs in spite of language of freedom, choice, and exercising rights, through the procedure of tubal ligation. In other words, despite the law spelling out the criteria for the granting of a tubal ligation and increased contraceptive options, what makes it so that some women are able to escape the constraints of the law and others cannot?

An important document for understanding what reproductive rights are and what they would look like materialized, is ascertainable from the International Conference on Population and Development (ICPD) Programme of Action, initially drafted in 1994 at the conference in Cairo. The twentieth anniversary edition of the document states the following about reproductive rights:

> Reproductive rights embrace certain human rights that are already recognized in national laws, international human rights documents and other consensus documents. These rights rest on the recognition of the basic right of all couples and individuals to decide freely and responsibly the number, spacing, and timing of their children and to have the information and means to do so, and the right to attain the highest standard of sexual and reproductive health. It also includes their right to make decisions concerning reproduction free of discrimination, coercion, and violence, as expressed in human rights documents.[9]

Reproductive rights inherently assume an active, rational, intentional, and responsible agent that would be able to take certain actions "freely." These actions to be undertaken by such an agent can be assumed then to be "responsible" actions, as implied by the statement granting an individual the reproductive right to "decide to freely and responsibly." Reproductive rights are invoked to advocate on behalf of those for whom a certain type of agency is understood as compromised or altogether lacking. The lack of agency is often evidenced in too many children, unplanned pregnancies, and difficulties managing responsibilities associated with raising children. This is in contrast to the assumed responsible and freely deciding rational agent who has two children within a two-parent, employed, preferably middle-class family. By the reproductive rights framework relying on this sort of an agent as its subject, the definition and use of reproductive rights further entrenches and reinforces problematic understandings of the relationship between race, class, fertility control, and law and the connections between rationality, intention, and responsibility. Relying on reproductive rights as a way to advocate for the underprivileged and marginalized in society further strengthens and roots these communities in the margins and can facilitate the means for more policing and governance.

Saidiya Hartman asks us to consider the ways that certain notions about freedom and humanity, and the correctives to slavery, may have served to further entrench subjection.[10] She highlights "the ways that the recognition of humanity and individuality acted to tether, bind and oppress."[11] It is in this vein that Hartman's book "examines the forms of violence and domination enabled by the recognition of humanity, licensed by the invocation of rights and justified on the grounds of liberty and freedom."[12] Furthermore, she investigates

> the role of rights in facilitating relations of domination, the new forms of bondage enabled by proprietorial notions of the self, and the pedagogical and legislative efforts aimed at transforming the formerly enslaved into rational, acquisitive, and responsible individuals. From this vantage point, emancipation appears less the grand event of liberation than a point of transition between nodes of servitude and racial subjection.[13]

Though she is specifically speaking about the experiences in the United States, her provocations are informative in thinking and analyzing the situation in Brazil. The ending of slavery "liberated" a population of black and brown marked bodies into a societal context built and reliant on their subordination, an anti-black society with no place for them.

Similarly, I interrogate assumptions about the power of the discourses of sexual and reproductive rights, individual choice, sexual freedom, anti-racism, and genocidal accusations against the government to necessarily alleviate the experiences of an over-reliance on sterilization and the loss of the power over one's body as a woman. This essay demonstrates the ways that legislative regulation has not improved women's control over their bodies in Brazil, but rather intensified the control of black and brown women's bodies by medical personnel, the state and men.

In this chapter then, I am demonstrating the implicit effects of the invocation of rights rhetoric specific to sexual and reproductive rights that seemingly provide more options and freedom of choice in women's control of their

50 *U. Felicia Edu*

reproductive and sexual lives. I link these effects to what is then implied and assumed in terms of individuality and responsibility of women that fails to consider the social marginalization that makes the exercise and realization of certain rights impossible for particular population groups, more specifically, black and poor women. I map out the way that a denial of a tubal ligation for a poor black woman can facilitate the marginalization/marginalizing of herself and her children into *marginais*, bodies marked for premature death through state violence. I am positing that this then facilitates and even encourages a certain type of governing and policing of her body, which comes to be racialized, even if spoken of only in terms of class. The notions and ideas of black women as always already sexually available, hypersexual, and uncontrollable further construct black women as irresponsible, irrational, and in need of discipline. These constructions of black womanhood, sexuality, and motherhood, along with socially marginalized realities, such as precarious living conditions and poor to no access to quality health care, including contraceptives, are read as problems of blackness and gender. I demonstrate how this structural racism, sexism, and violence become the basis for the creation and distribution of discourses, authority, and policies about black women's bodies and their reproductive products, often serving to further marginalize.

I am asking that we consider the ways that reproductive rights shape ideas about the self and thus the way these population groups are imagined and legislated about—what discourses are created and circulate about these poor, black and brown women, and their lack of responsibility, rationality, and their willingness/ability to participate in the consumption driven sense of Brazilian society. It is my intention that we can begin to see how the notions of freedom and individuality make women who have an unplanned pregnancy culpable for their inability to prevent pregnancy, even when using a contraceptive method and when their intention was to have fewer or none at all.

Vignette 1: Paula

We sat outside as the crowded one-room abode, rented by Paula and her partner, offered no privacy for our interview. Paula is a dark brown, tall, curvy, Catholic woman with a deep soothing voice. She wore a fitted dress, showing off a body that hardly resembled one belonging to a woman who had recently given birth, let alone 4 times. She sat across from me and took the microphone I offered and we began. Two of her children wanted to come and be with their mother. She told them to go back inside. She is 27, and has been with the same partner, who is also the father of her children, since 15 years of age. She has four living children out of five pregnancies. She only wanted two and would have tied her tubes after her second child, but could not because of her young age.

She told me that she had never worked as anything and her husband was unemployed. Nonetheless, she had classified herself and her family as *classe C*, C class or middle class. According to the *Fundação Getulio Vargas*[14] (FGV), *Instituto Brasileiro de Pesquisa Econômica Aplicada*[15] (Ipea) and *Instituto Brasileiro de Geografia e Estatística*[16] (IBGE), class C has a monthly income of

Negras *and Reproductive Rights in Brazil* 51

between 1,064 *reais* and 4,591 *reais*.[17] She had not specified their monthly income. I had not asked her to elaborate on this point. She had gotten pregnant at 16 with her first daughter and had her in 2002. Two years later in 2004, she had her son. Paula had dreamt of having only two children, a boy and a girl. But, as she said, she had realized her dream, plus an extra two. It would have been six had she not miscarried twins. In 2004, eight months after having her son, she found out that she was five months pregnant.

> I found out like this. I was having a fever. I had taken an, an *antipironha*. After, I went to the emergency room. I didn't know I was pregnant; if I had known I wouldn't have gone. So I lost my pregnancy. It was two children. It was twins in my stomach.[18]

If she could have been sterilized after her second child she would have.

> I dreamed a lot, playing with dolls and calling the doll my daughter (laughter) ... (responding to my question of how many children she had wanted) I wanted two.... A girl came first, which is Isabella, who is 10 years old. After came the boy. But, there. If in the case that I could have, since then. I would have cut [tied my tubes] to not have more. I would have cut since then. But I couldn't because of my age.[19]

Unable to secure a tubal ligation, she had become pregnant a third time. She'd given birth to Isaura and tried different methods for preventing a future pregnancy. Paula described the criteria she tried to meet in order to get a tubal ligation:

> After Isaura, I did lots of exams because they said that there were lots of exams. Lies. They said that to tie/estrangular, you had to do exams ... transvaginal exam, ultrasound. They ask for exams to see if the person had heart problems ... high blood pressure or diabetes. They ask all this. I told them I didn't have heart problems and I wasn't diabetic. Nonetheless, they still asked for the exams and I did them all.[20]

Despite her efforts to demonstrate that she met the criteria that would make her eligible for a tubal ligation, the distance between her residence and the location of the surgery proved to be 60 kilometers too much.

> So the day they were supposed to do the surgery, it was to be done in Dias d'Avila, understood? And I live in Salvador so I didn't have a way to get there, no one to take me because at that time there was no ambulance. So I stayed without doing it. That was 2007; I was 22.[21]

Her attempts at contraceptive use were in vain.

> After Isaura was born, I went and I put the IUD three times. It didn't stay. Because they say that the IUD avoids, right, so that we won't have another

52   *U. Felicia Edu*

> child with it. I put the one for 10 years. I put it the first time. It came out of place. I put it the second time, it came out of place. I put it in the third time. I didn't put it again. I continued taking injections.[22] I stayed swollen and the doctor suspended [the injections].[23]

Contrary to popular narratives and discourses of poor, un- and under-educated women lacking knowledge, willpower, discipline and motivation to seek out contraception to protect themselves against unwanted/unplanned pregnancies and children, Paula attempted to make use of the contraceptive methods available to her. Three times she attempted the IUD, which was rejected by her body, meaning that the IUD provided by SUS was not a viable method for her to use against pregnancy. She tried the hormonal injections, which made her body swell to a point that her doctor suspended the prescription. Paula did not discontinue the hormonal injections because her body became esthetically unpleasing, a common criticism leveled at poor women, but rather at her doctor's orders based on a concern for her health. She also tried to use the pill, but her living conditions made storing away from children and easily accessing it at a regular time each day very difficult, nullifying its protective possibilities. She then tried to take the hormonal injections again, which caused her blood pressure to rise. Again her doctor suspended her use of the hormonal injections. As nothing was working, and in an attempt to stave off another pregnancy, she began using a medicine for its non-indicated uses, but stopped. A month later, she was pregnant with her most recent son.

Her son was four months old when I interviewed her. He had taken to his fair father in complexion and was a chubby, alert, and well-mannered baby. He looked healthy and thriving. He had yet to see a pediatrician because doctors were on strike. His mother, Paula, had been three times to three different places to try to get her tubes tied, each refusing her. She explained,

> They said I have to wait so I'm waiting because if I had the money, I won't lie, I would pay 700 reais and do it.... They said no because at the moment, SUS is not doing the surgeries. Because I don't have health care.... They have a goal, I don't know how many people per month, so I have to wait. So they told me to wait and come back in January.[24]

This goal she refers to was later explained to me by others as a quota that hospitals had; they were not to surpass that number of sterilizations per month. She informed the medical personnel of her need for a contraceptive method that did not have hormones or at least had a low dosage of hormones. She had been told to make an appointment, but could not because the doctors were on strike. An acquaintance had suggested that she go see the politician and doctor Mauricio Trinidade so that he could help her resolve her issue. But even he was not attending to the tubal ligation needs of the community. Even if he were, it would have been in Santo Amaro de Purificão. The ambulance would take her there, but she would have had no way of getting home. "We don't have means for another child. Truthfully, we don't have means for this last baby, but..."[25]

Paula is poor and black, which, in Brazil, more often than not go hand-in-hand in ways that serve to naturalize the relationship between poverty and blackness. Her poverty may not immediately mark this story as extraordinary, but she deviates from the standard case, which depicts poor women in particular as over(e)productive due to their ignorance of available methods or reluctance to try and/or adhere to a contraceptive regimen and "responsible fertility expectations." Paula differs from this depiction of the poor Brazilian mother. She demonstrates this in her rationalized desire to only have two children, her attempts to actively stop her fertility, her willingness and persistence in trying methods that reduce the chances of failure due to human error (IUD and tri-monthly injections) and her persistence in trying to secure a tubal ligation. She was able to advocate for herself with medical personnel in terms of needing a low dosage hormonal contraceptive, but even this was thwarted due to a lack of funding sufficient to provide this sort of contraceptive option for those reliant on SUS. In one sense, her poverty and blackness make it difficult to secure effective and appropriate contraceptives. But I am arguing against the seeming naturalization of poverty, and particularly blackness, as deterrents to having the "proper" number of children. There is more at work that we should be thinking about based on the ways that Paula, as black and poor, does not fit the general image of black women/mothers and their relationship to contraceptives.

Black Reproduction, Labor, and Genocide

I would later interview a famous and controversial doctor in Brazil. When I asked him about mass sterilizations of black women in Brazil being claimed to be part of a genocidal plan, he responded:

> Don't go for this path (genocidal plan for sterilizations) because you're going to come to a wall. There is no logic in that. We want more blacks, we want more of that labor pool. Whoever wants labor in Bahia, it has to be black (laughter). There's nowhere to run.[26]

This doctor was explaining to me why the notion that the Brazilian government and/or public health and medical personnel were carrying out a genocide against the black population through sterilizations was absurd. For him, especially in Bahia state, the need for manual labor, often poorly compensated, disallows the logic of a genocide of the black population. In other words, the black population provides the pool from which cheap labor can be drawn, thus making genocide a futile endeavor. These labor-intensive jobs are often hard to distinguish from those jobs performed by enslaved Africans in the past. This difficulty of distinguishing the past work of enslaved Africans from the current manual labor positions seemingly reserved for the black population in Brazil, as expressed by the doctor's comment, naturalizes the role of black people in Brazil and their permanence in poverty. The predominance of black people working those jobs is explained by a lack of education, lack of ambition and/or lack of capacity to do more intellectually taxing jobs, which serves to mask the systematic structure

54 *U. Felicia Edu*

that ensures that black people remain eligible only for labor-intensive, low-wage jobs. It should come as no surprise the correlation between the predominance of black women in the labor-intensive position of domestic maids and their poor health outcomes.

> According to a study conducted by AMNB (Brazilian Black Women's Network), black women are champions in the performance of housework without labor rights guaranteed and mortality rates by maternal death as a result of complications during pregnancy, childbirth and the postpartum period.[27]

Much like during slavery when black women served as domestic maids, without guarantee of any rights, today one of the few positions most readily open to black women remains that of the domestic maid. Black women in these positions are usually underpaid, often have wages withheld with no recourse to recoup unpaid wages, and are subject to varying types of abuse at the hands of their employers. Race is tied to class in such a way as to inhibit the social mobility of blacks through social capital, status, educational levels, and occupation, while particular labor must be performed by the black body. This is significant in a context where access to contraceptives and the ability to realize one's ideal family size can facilitate certain navigations of the social order and one's positioning within it.

The doctor quoted above makes a link between blackness and labor, and not class and labor, which is often the manner in which inequalities and differences are discussed. And though often discussed as a problem of class and highly disparate wealth distribution, the doctor's discussion in terms of race verbalizes the seemingly invisible (ignored) historical legacy and societal structuring that has created a system in which blacks are always already understood as abnormal, deviant, criminal, and occupants of the lowest rungs of society. While the doctor used the logic of needing black bodies to replenish the labor pool necessary to do work, as a way to deny the feasibility of a genocide against the black population, the tension inherent in this situation must be further examined. When black women lead in terms of maternal mortality, which is avoidable by reducing the number of pregnancies a woman has, especially unwanted pregnancies, and have poorer access to quality health insurance, effective contraception and a tubal ligation when she wants, genocide it may not be but it is certainly troubling in a way reminiscent of treatment of slave women in the United States.[28]

In "Killing the Black Body," Roberts describes a moment when a pregnant slave is to be whipped. In order to "save"/"preserve" the safety of the "new product"—her baby—a ditch is dug into which the pregnant woman lies to protect the unborn from the beating that she nonetheless must receive. The contradiction, the seeming care and attention to the unborn cargo inside a poorly nourished and overworked body that wasn't worthy of being considered for some other form of punishment seems to parallel a Brazilian government that continues to ignore, marginalize, and criminalize the very population upon which it depends for manual, unskilled, and often unpaid labor. One reading of

Negras *and Reproductive Rights in Brazil* 55

the doctor's comment would read the poor implementation and funding of the national family planning program and monthly quotas, which restrained doctors' ability to confidently provide tubal ligations and have the costs recovered, as a careless, if not intentional, way to ensure that the national labor pool was never depleted.

Another reading would view it as the unexpected and unforeseen results of a plan to provide women with more options to exercise their reproductive and sexual rights. But this reading is exactly what I would like to trouble. I am arguing against framing these instances—no access to effective contraception or denied tubal ligation—as exceptions. These instances should be seen as part and parcel of the system, working just as it was envisioned and designed to function. This is a system that makes use of language and ideas such as reproductive and sexual rights, freedom, choice, and humanity to further perpetuate violence and dominance over certain parts of the population. This is not to insinuate that women are not also having their reproductive rights violated in the more obvious way of being sterilized without their consent or serving as the targets of anti-poverty campaigns that function through the distribution of contraceptives, because surely they are. These two work in tandem, one logic that views black "excessive" reproduction as vital to stocking the labor pool with black bodies, and another logic that sees black procreation, generally, as a problem.

Vignette 2: Maria

I jumped off the bus, greeted by the sound of the ocean crashing into the huge rocks some feet behind the houses blocking the view of the beach. I walked 5–10 minutes along a street lined with food and clothing markets until I had reached her house. I called her on my phone and she unlocked the door from inside her apartment. I made my way up the stairs and walked into an expansive living room with a shower of sunlight pouring in from the home's street facing window. I had heard this woman's story in abbreviated form. Her story particularly intrigued me as the first to offer a counter-narrative to that of widespread sterilization and governmental anti-black genocidal plans through sterilization. As she would put it later in the interview,

> So, what folks say, that it is an easy thing, that they are tying tubes like (pause). I don't know. I believe that for the, for the cities, for the, for the interior, it should happen, because by the form too, there are a lot of people that have a lot of children. There are 20 and 25 year old girls that already have 5, 6. So, in these places, truly, you have people that ask the doctor "look, I want that (pause) tie my tubes" because when they are in their 30s, 40s, they would have given birth to 12, 16. But its not that the government is "hey, go tie tubes, tie tubes, right. Sterilize the women". It's not really like that.[29]

Maria, the lady of the house, is a light brown complexioned, stylish, married mother of four. She is a stay-at-home mom, while her foreign-born husband

56 U. Felicia Edu

works outside the home. The decision to be a stay-at-home mom was not because she couldn't find work, but rather because she and her husband felt it the best option for childcare for their young daughters. Unlike Paula, Maria did not consider herself and her family middle class ("No, don't put middle class, please ... Poverty. We're considered. I'm not rich! I'm not rich."), despite the fact that they lived in a nicer part of the city, had a car, and were able to consume considerably well, especially considering the number of children they had.

Her sister was there helping her out as Maria had injured her foot, making her a lot less mobile. Her youngest daughter, crawling, was soon taken into another room while Maria's next daughter in age sat quietly watching Kirikou. Maria had had her first two children with two different men before she had met her current husband. Her husband is the father of the last two children. When I asked how many children Maria had wanted, she said two. The first two had not been planned, her third child was the only one she had planned for. She blamed a lack of sexual education and open discussion for her first pregnancy. The second one she described as something that just happened. As she explained her planned pregnancy:

> And seven years later, I was pregnant again. But it was by choice. And already in this third one, I really wanted to tie my tubes because I didn't want more, isn't it. This third child was one. It was discussed a lot between myself and my, my partner, that we wanted, he didn't have any child. And, and it allowed a maturing that we were going to stay together, we like each other, and, I wanted to have this child.... When I had my second child, I was that I didn't want more. Right? So when I met my partner, that we stayed together and that we resolved that we were going to stay together, it was with him that I had the baby that, eh, that I got pregnant and lost it right? A miscarriage. And from there, we decided, after that pregnancy that no, no, we'll go along, that we would have the girl. That we would have her. But in this third one, I was real clear that it would be my last one, that we didn't, I didn't want and he also didn't want because my son was already 15.[30]

This third child and Maria's desire to tie her tubes had also been discussed extensively with her doctor.

> So it came [the pregnancy] and the whole pregnancy, I was always telling the doctor that I was having this consciousness that I didn't want more, that I wanted to do the tubal ligation, that I didn't want to have more children.[31]

Maria's doctor, also a professor at UFBA (the Federal University of Bahia) asked that Maria bring her partner to the doctor's office so that he could also confirm. Legally, Maria still needed her partner's authorization to be able to perform the procedure. Her partner went and gave his verbal consent. The agreement she had with the doctor had been:

Negras and Reproductive Rights in Brazil   57

if the baby was born normally, a normal birth, that we would do it [the tubal ligation] later, by way of the belly button, that is done. And because I have a tendency to not have passage; so if it was a caesarian birth, a caesarian, that she would do the tubal ligation.[32]

Had it been a normal birth, it would have been at Maria's house and they would have paid. As it was a caesarian, she gave birth at the hospital at UFBA, a public hospital, and the state paid. If Maria had gone to a private hospital, with this same doctor, it would have been more expensive and not paid by the state.

Maria impressed upon me how intent she was to get her tubes tied after this third child and how much she had made this clear with her doctor, throughout the nine months of prenatal care—right up until the last time she saw her doctor before getting anesthesia for the caesarian birth.

And at the time of the exam, when she, she was going, she sent me to go for surgery, I spoke with her, "Mrs. is not going to forget my tubal ligation." She, "ok." She "go speak with your husband, say bye, right, tell that you are going into the operating room." Ok. And I went for my surgery.[33]

When Maria returned to her doctor for her one-month review, and asked about her tubal ligation, the doctor had "forgotten." Later in the meeting, the doctor said that Maria had also needed to have a signed document by her husband confirming that he agreed with the tubal ligation. And this paper also would have required authentication by a judge. Maria alludes to what she thinks may have made the difference in her doctor's decision to not perform the sterilization; the fact that she had gone to a public hospital to deliver and not her doctor's private practice. The doctor drew on a stipulation in the law to explain not providing Maria with the tubal ligation they had agreed upon. Maria believes that this extra stipulation would itself have been "forgotten" if she instead had gone to a private hospital to deliver.

Maria managed to get a tubal ligation after her next birth: "But it [the birth] was in a private hospital, with a private doctor. It wasn't public. (pause) I think that that had to have facilitated also ... that it happened [the tubal ligation] because it was private."[34] Her new doctor had also somewhat alluded to the fact that Maria should have gone to a different hospital, a private one, so that she could have been able to tie her tubes. Maria's first meeting with her new doctor had been a tearful one in which she had expressed her desires, again, to tie her tubes after the birth of the fourth child.

When I did with this doctor on the first day, I was like—including that I cried sometimes with her, [imitating a voice that is crying], "but I didn't want to be pregnant again. I don't even know." She, "no, it's ok. Now, I'm going to d-do the tubal ligation because, shoot, you already have three." She, "don't worry because I'm not going to forget."[35]

Her new doctor seemed to feel for her given that she already had three children. Perhaps the doctor's ability to see the excessiveness of three children was

58   U. Felicia Edu

facilitated by the fact that the birth was to take place in a private hospital with a patient who had private insurance to help pay the bill. It should be stated that despite tubal ligations considered part of what enables a woman to exercise her reproductive rights, not all insurance companies cover tubal ligations. Luckily, hers was one that covered tubal ligations.

This flexibility in manipulating the law throws into question the validity of these claims by doctors of fear of sterilizing women so as not to be sued afterwards when a woman regrets her decision. The law makes it clear what criteria women must meet to be able to get a tubal ligation. The policies and governing of SUS further constrict the implementation of the law and access of women to tubal ligation. Doctors' ability to exercise their own scrutiny in discerning who to provide with a tubal ligation further compounds the scenario for women. Maria was finally able to get her tubal ligation. But only after getting pregnant again, her third unplanned pregnancy, fourth pregnancy in total. She had gone to a private hospital where her friend also happened to work as an anesthesiologist. Her private insurance freed her from dependence on SUS. Though she had had to have another child to have her tubal ligation, she was more fortunate than some of her friends who still could not get tubal ligations.

When I asked why, if she really did not want another child and after realizing that her doctor had not indeed sterilized her, Maria did not use other forms of contraceptives, the issue of expense never came up.

> No, I didn't try (in reference to IUD). I didn't try. Real-really like this, I didn't, or I was using the condom right? Or when I was going to use the pill, I didn't didn't accept, so I stayed with the condom and sometimes nothing.[36]

It was merely that they (contraceptives) didn't work for her. As she explained, she lacked discipline. Sometimes she and her partner went on the impulse and had intercourse without a condom. When Maria took the pills, she had stomach problems. Other middle class women that may have verbalized not wanting more children but were hesitant to get their tubes tied, opted for other contraceptive methods, usually a method that they paid for themselves. It seems that with contraceptives and sterilizations there are always at least two types: the cheap and/ or free, ineffective/less effective easily accessible version vs. the more expensive, highly effective, less easily accessible version. The latter version tends to be most available outside SUS, thus, the user usually pays.

Black women in Brazil, around the late 1980s, took the lead in pursuing and addressing the issue of high rates of sterilizations of women, particularly poor, and black and brown women. Other women's groups and black movement groups joined in. A campaign was launched against the mass sterilizations of women, accusing the government of a genocidal plan against black Brazilians. This resulted in official inquiries that were coordinated by the government, in the early 1990s, to investigate the practice of rampant sterilizations and make changes to the law. Sterilization ceased to be illegal and the law outlined criteria for sterilization, including for example the age restrictions and minimum number of living children.

Emilia Sanabria discusses in her work the way that the packaging of sex hormones in contraceptives serves to differentiate between two forms of citizenship, two types of "configured users," those who can make an individual choice and those who need their fertility strictly controlled.[37] SUS, *Sistema Único de Saúde*, is the state-funded public health service in Brazil, which emphasizes inclusion and universalism, as imagined in the rhetoric of health as a fundamental human right. While the public sector homogenizes, standardizes, and massifies the population it serves, the private sector personalizes and emphasizes individual choice. Sanabria points out how the latter is based on notions of personal autonomy, individual choice, and self-enhancement, while the former is framed in terms of the individual moral responsibility to the collective.

Sanabria draws on Brazilian anthropologist Roberto DaMatta to highlight the central tension upon which Brazilian modernity operates, between the formal embrace of the principles of equality and individualism and a tacit hierarchical mode or relationality. In other words, the social reality in Brazil is marked by a separation between those that are mere citizens, subject to the law, versus those that deem themselves special, deserving of personalized treatment and exempt from the law. James Holston points to the way that Brazilian citizenship actually serves to "manage social differences by legalizing them in ways that legitimate and reproduce inequality."[38]

Thus those that can pay, pay for the best and most effective types of contraceptives, while those that cannot pay, rely on SUS to provide poorer quality and less effective contraceptives that often distort women's bodies. Those with money have the choice of going to a beachside, sanitary, and private abortion clinic, while those that can't afford, rely on their devices to abort and pray for a kind doctor or just life if their abortion is botched, as abortion is illegal in Brazil. Similarly, those with money can pay their doctor or a private doctor to sterilize them. Those without money either take their chances going to the interior of their state, hope for a stroke of luck during election time, wait for a spot once SUS is less packed, or do not sterilize and run the risk of another unplanned pregnancy. Even though one has managed to ascend to the middle class, this does not always translate to the ability to buy a sterilization, as Maria's case illustrated. Black women are also more likely to give birth vaginally, further reducing the possibility of negotiating a tubal ligation at birth.[39] As discussed before, the terms used to discuss inequality are those of public vs. private sector and citizenship. What is unspoken but implicit is that the public sector refers largely to the poor and black. The hierarchical mode or relationality is one in which those that are mere citizens and subject to the law, are the poor and black.

Alaerte Martins points out that despite the reluctance and difficulty in collecting and analyzing data by race in Brazil, the data that is available illustrates that black women in Brazil live in some of the worst conditions, both in terms of life and health, and they have the worst levels of income and education.[40] Anna Pagano, citing Martins, points out that epidemiological data shows that blacks experience higher rates of maternal and infant mortality, in comparison to whites.[41] Emanuelle Goes and Enilda Nascimento point out that the barriers created by racial and gendered inequalities and perpetuated through institutional

60 *U. Felicia Edu*

racism impede and make it difficult for black women, who also represent the poorest segments of the population, to utilize and access health services, as compared with white women's experiences.[42] Furthermore, their analysis points to the lack of healthcare coverage that black women suffer, making them more reliable on SUS for their healthcare coverage.[43]

Sonia Beatriz dos Santos has remarked, in a field note in her dissertation, upon the way that black women's experiences of treatment by health professionals during their pregnancies revealed mistreatment, violence, and an understanding of such women by the health professionals as "dirty, polluted" and "promiscuous" women.[44] Black women felt that their condition of pregnancy was viewed as "something shameful and immoral" by the health professionals.[45] Black women expressed being perceived as "inappropriate, unprepared and irresponsible to experience motherhood" in ways that dos Santos summarized as the notion that motherhood "almost automatically becomes incompatible with black women because they are considered 'naturally' immoral, like prostitutes."[46] Restated elsewhere in her dissertation, dos Santos calls our attention to the "process of dehumanization in which black women's sexual and reproductive health has been treated and portrayed as abnormal, threatening to the moral order, and in need of regulation, and in many cases, of eradication through invasive medical interventions."[47]

Besides the structural violence meted out on black women by Brazilian culture and society, Black men are also not as interested in creating families with black women. Their own endeavors to climb the social ladder through marriage and reproduction with lighter complexioned women serves to reinforce the negative stereotypes of black women as producers of marginals and threats to national and international security. As such, an informant lamented: "Black women learned to live with solidão (loneliness). Not because we want to or like it but because it is the reality. Black men often don't want to create families with us."[48] When a woman does decide to choose to end her reproductive capacities without a partner, the process becomes even further complicated. She may be denied because she has no partner to give consent, as required by the law and/or will be forced into a process to somehow prove that she is single.

Though feminists and other activists have worked to improve the orientation of services, increase contraceptive options, improve the quality of reproductive and sexual health, and make more accessible options for quality contraceptives for women, the adoption of rights rhetoric and the legal correctives have failed to translate on the ground for particular populations of women. This is not to say that the law should not have been implemented but rather to caution our quickness to adopt and repeat the human rights rhetoric and laws particularly because of the ways that they differentially apply to black people in different contexts. We must pay attention to the simultaneous and seemingly opposed strategies in place; on one hand, black women are seen as responsible for ove(re)producing and reproducing poorly and at the margins, and thus in need of a paternalistic control from above; on the other hand, black women are necessary reproducers of a kind of labor pool and a particular kind of consuming class that allows and facilitates the continuance and perpetuation of dominance of a certain class of people.

Negras *and Reproductive Rights in Brazil* 61

We cannot afford to focus only on the economic aspect of the issue or think of it in terms of citizenship in Brazil or only speak about it in terms of rights, sexual freedom, and individual choice, to which blacks were never meant to be included. To do so is to continue to elide the way that race and racism function in shaping and impacting the ways in which women live as women, mothers, sexual beings, and citizens in very meaningful ways. Paying attention to race allows us to see the ways that things have in fact remained relatively the same, albeit shifting in some ways the mechanisms by which they work. We must pay attention to race, racism, and the role it plays in the process of social and physical reproduction, those moments at which the anatomo-political and bio-political axes intersect. Paying attention to this process makes more apparent the ways that notions of citizenship, humanity imbued with rights and individuality, and a reliance on the law to resolve issues of abuse and oppression, have served to further entrench hierarchies, distinctions between humans and delineate groups for life and groups for something not quite life.[49]

Notes

1 Ugo Edu, Fieldnotes, Salvador, Brazil, April 2012.
2 DHS, *Pesquisa Nacional Sobre Demografia E Saúde* (Rio de Janeiro: BEMFAM, IGBE, [1996]).
3 Ibid.
4 Andre Caetano, "Fertility Transition and the Diffusion of Female Sterilization in Northeastern Brazil: The Roles of Medicine and Politics," (2001).
5 Family Health International (FHI), "Research Project Examines Adolescent Pregnancy, Sterilization in Brazil," http://www.fhi360.org/research-project-examines-adolescent-pregnancy-sterilization-brazil-july-1998 (accessed August 7, 2014).
6 José Alberto Magno Carvalho and Laura Rodríguez Wong, "Demographic and Socio-Economic Implications of Rapid Fertility Decline in Brazil. A Window of Opportunity," in *Reproductive Change in India and Brazil*, eds. George Martine, Monica Das Gupta and Lincoln C. Chen (Delhi: Oxford University Press, 1998); Population Reference Bureau, *2009 World Population Data Sheet* (2009).
7 Center of Research and Assistance in Human Reproduction.
8 Ibid.
9 International Conference on Population and Development (ICPD), Programme of Action, 2013 Conference Report, Paragraph 7.3, www.unfpa.org/resources/icpd-beyond-2014-international-conference-human-rights.
10 Saidiya Hartman, *Scenes of Subjection: Terror, Slavery, and Self-Making in Nineteenth-Century America* (New York: Oxford University Press, 1997), 5.
11 Ibid., 5.
12 Ibid., 6.
13 Ibid., 6.
14 Getulio Vargas Foundation.
15 Brazilian Institute of Applied Economics Research.
16 Brazilian Institute of Geography and Statistics.
17 Brazilian currency. Depending on the exchange rate, could be the equivalent of a range between $532 and $2,295.50 USD a month.
18 Paula (pseudonym), interviewed by Ugo Edu, May 18, 2012, Interview W7, transcript.

62   *U. Felicia Edu*

19 Ibid. She used the word *cortar*, which means to cut, which is how I have translated it here. Based on the context of our conversation though, Paula didn't mean a literal cut but rather used this term to refer to the procedure to sterilize her/tie her tubes, a cutting of the tube so as to disrupt the pathway for the egg and sperm to meet.
20 Ibid.
21 Ibid.
22 Injections like this refer to hormonal injections taken every three months to avoid pregnancy.
23 Paula (pseudonym), interviewed by Ugo Edu, May 18, 2012, Interview W7, transcript.
24 Ibid.
25 Ibid.
26 Dr. Magalhães (pseudonym), Interviewed by Ugo Edu, June 12, 2012, Interview D1, transcript.
27 Emanuelle Goes, "AMNB vai denunciar situação da mulher negra na OEA." *População Negra e Saúde* (blog). October 23, 2012. http://populacaonegraesaude.blogspot.com/2012/10/amnb-vai-denunciar-situacao-da-mulher.html. Translated by Ugo Edu.
28 Dorothy Roberts, *Killing the Black Body: Race, Reproduction, and the Meaning of Liberty* (New York: Vintage Books, 1997).
29 Maria (pseudonym), Interviewed by Ugo Edu, April 12, 2012, Interview W6, transcript.
30 Ibid.
31 Ibid.
32 Ibid.
33 Ibid.
34 Ibid.
35 Ibid.
36 Ibid.
37 Emilia Sanabria, "From Sub-to Super-Citizenship: Sex Hormones and the Body Politic in Brazil," *Ethnos* 75, no. 4 (2010), 377–401.
38 James Holston, *Insurgent Citizenship: Disjunctions of Democracy and Modernity in Brazil* (Princeton: Princeton University Press, 2008).
39 Emanuelle F. Goes and Enilda R. Nascimento, "Mulheres Negras E Brancas: As Desigualdades no Acesso E Utilização De Serviços De Saúde no Estado Da Bahia," in *Saúde Da População Negra*, eds. Jurema Werneck, Luís Eduardo Batista and Fernanda Lopes (Petrópolis, RJ: DP et Alii, 2012), 255. It is worth noting that caesarian births are considered a more modern way of giving birth than naturally. Some women are left to give birth naturally as a form of humiliation and marginalization, putting aside the problem with over-medicalizing births.
40 Alaerte Leandro Martins, "Mortalidade Materna De Mulheres Negras no Brasil," *Cadernos De Saúde Pública* 22, no. 11 (2006), 2473–2479.
41 Anna Pagano, "Afro-Brazilian Religions and Ethnic Identity Politics in the Brazilian Public Health Arena," *Health, Culture and Society* 3, no. 1 (2012), 2.
42 Goes and Nascimento, *Mulheres Negras E Brancas: As Desigualdades no Acesso E Utilização De Serviços De Saúde no Estado Da Bahia*, 255.
43 Ibid.
44 Sonia Beatriz dos Santos, "Brazilian Black Women's NGOs and their Struggles in the Area of Sexual and Reproductive Health: Experiences, Resistance, and Politics" (PhD Diss, The University of Texas, Austin), 1–481.
45 Ibid.
46 Ibid.
47 Ibid.
48 From a personal communication with an informant, Salvador, Brazil, 2011.
49 Emilia Sanabria, "From Sub- to Super-Citizenship: Sex Hormones and the Body Politic in Brazil," *Ethnos* 75, no. 4 (2010), 377–401.

References

Caetano, Andre. "Fertility Transition and the Diffusion of Female Sterilization in Northeastern Brazil: The Roles of Medicine and Politics." In *25th General Population Conference of the International Union for the Scientific Study of Population. Salvador, Brasil.* 2001.

Carvalho, José Alberto Magno and Laura Rodríguez Wong. "Demographic and Socio-Economic Implications of Rapid Fertility Decline in Brazil. A Window of Opportunity." In *Reproductive Change in India and Brazil*, edited by George Martine, Monica Das Gupta and Lincoln C. Chen. Delhi: Oxford University Press, 1998.

DHS. *Pesquisa Nacional Sobre Demografia E Saúde*. Rio de Janeiro: BEMFAM, IGBE, 1996.

dos Santos, Sonia Beatriz. "Brazilian Black Women's NGOs and their Struggles in the Area of Sexual and Reproductive Health: Experiences, Resistance, and Politics." PhD Diss, The University of Texas, Austin, 2008.

Family Health International (FHI). "Research Project Examines Adolescent Pregnancy, Sterilization in Brazil." accessed August 7, 2014, www.fhi360.org/research-project-examines-adolescent-pregnancy-sterilization-brazil-july-1998.

Goes, Emanuelle F. and Enilda R. Nascimento. "Mulheres Negras E Brancas: As Desigualdades no Acesso E Utilização De Serviços De Saúde no Estado Da Bahia." In *Saúde Da População Negra*, edited by Jurema Werneck, Luís Eduardo Batista and Fernanda Lopes, 255. Petrópolis, RJ: DP et Alii, 2012.

Hartman, Saidiya. *Scenes of Subjection: Terror, Slavery, and Self-Making in Nineteenth-Century America*. Oxford: Oxford University Press, 1997.

Holston, James. *Insurgent Citizenship: Disjunctions of Democracy and Modernity in Brazil*. Princeton: Princeton University Press, 2008.

Martins, Alaerte Leandro. "Mortalidade Materna De Mulheres Negras no Brasil." *Cadernos De Saúde Pública* 22, no. 11 (2006): 2473–2479.

Pagano, Anna. "Afro-Brazilian Religions and Ethnic Identity Politics in the Brazilian Public Health Arena." *Health, Culture and Society* 3, no. 1 (2012): 2.

Population Reference Bureau. *2009 World Population Data Sheet*, 2009.

Roberts, Dorothy. *Killing the Black Body: Race, Reproduction, and the Meaning of Liberty*. New York: Vintage Books, 1997.

Sanabria, Emilia. "From Sub-to Super-Citizenship: Sex Hormones and the Body Politic in Brazil." *Ethnos* 75, no. 4 (2010): 377–401.

4 Human Rights and Physical Capital

Panacea to Sustainable Development in Africa

Jonathan Ali Ogwuche

Introduction

All societies have ethical standards—norms and beliefs addressing what is right or wrong, permissible or not permissible. These moral standards are established by people and vary over time and among societies. They are, therefore, social constructs, made by people and for people. Many of these rights respect the origin of what we today call civil and political rights. Today's understanding of human rights came with the birth of the United Nations. These rights are enshrined in the Universal Declaration on Human Rights, and two International covenants (the International Covenant on Civil and Political Rights and the International Covenant on Social, Economic and Cultural Rights), and UN Conventions. Human rights are basic standards aimed at securing dignity and equality for all. International human rights laws constitute the most universally accepted standards for such treatment.

Human rights became a focus of international law long before environmental concerns did. While the United Nations Charter of 1945 marked the beginning of modern international human rights law, the Stakeholders' Declaration of 1972 is generally seen as the starting point of the modern international framework for environmental issues.[1] This is evident as "the environment is not an abstraction but represents the living space, the quality of life and the very health of human beings, including generations unborn."[2] Forty-two years ago, the United Nations Conference on the Human Environment was held in Stockholm, where the international community declared that

> Man has the fundamental right to freedom/equity and adequate conditions of life, in an environment of a quality that permits a life of dignity and well-being, and he bears a solemn responsibility to protect and improve the environment for present and future generations.[3]

This grand statement has provided the basis for subsequent elaboration of a human right to environmental quality.[4]

In 1992, the Earth Summit broadened its focus on the human environment, in order to elaborate the need for integration between development and the environment. This Rio Declaration proclaims in principle that, "human beings are at the center of concerns for sustainable development" and that "they are entitled to a healthy and productive life in harmony with nature."[5] Inherent in the Rio Declaration was the notion that development is more than just a factor of economic growth, but must also include the right to effective access to physical capital (environmental infrastructure and social services). Measuring development should also include social indicators such as life expectancy, literacy, and access to physical capital services.[6]

Among the human rights treaties, only the 1981 African Charter on Human Rights and People's Rights proclaim environmental rights in broadly qualitative terms. The case for a right to environment comes in the form of claims to a decent or viable environment, that is, to a substantive environmental right which involves the promotion of a certain level of environmental quality. Environmental rights would give environmental quality comparable status to the other economic and social rights, and would recognize the vital character of the environment as a basic condition of life, indispensable to the promotion of human dignity and welfare, and to the fulfillment of other human rights.[7] Article 24 of the African Charter provides that "all peoples shall have the right to a clean, healthful, and safe environment favorable to their development."[8] This article defines the right to environment in terms of human needs, rather than for its own sake. To further buttress this, Article 11 of the African Charter on Human and People's Rights, held in Banjul in 1991, proclaims that "everyone shall have the right to live in a healthy environment and to have access to basic public services" (physical capital).[9]

A more sophisticated understanding of the relations between human rights and the environment begins with an appreciation of the basic environmental function on which human life depends. The livelihoods of the people are determined predominantly by the environmental context in which they live and the constraints and opportunities the environment presents. This context also determines the livelihood assets accessible to people.[10] Of the five assets, physical capital is identified as a public, rather than private investment, and includes water supply and sanitation, roads, electricity, health and educational institutions.[11] The United Kingdom Department for International Development considers physical capital as a provider of environmental services for improvement in the quality of life.[12]

As a society, we must understand that everything and anything that influences our environment directly influences our human conditions, and so a violation of our environment is a violation of our human rights. This, therefore, calls for a clear understanding of the nexus between human rights and physical capital, and to develop the necessary mechanisms and laws to guarantee socially and environmentally sustainable development.

Physical Capital in Pre-Colonial, Colonial, and Post-Colonial Africa

Brett Frischmann popularized the Economic Theory of Infrastructure and Commons Rights in 2005 with the argument that certain important resources

66   J. Ali Ogwuche

should be seen as a right and used equitably for the benefits of all members of a society.[13] African Nationalists' philosophy of social welfare was dominant in the early stage of political independence of African states because of endogenous attempts to promote sustainable development.[14] According to Akinwale, different models of the philosophy include Obafemi Awolowo's democratic socialism in Nigeria, Kenneth Kaunda's humanism in Zambia, Kwame Nkrumah's conscientism in Ghana and Leopold Senghor's negritude in Senegal.[14] Unfortunately, the military dictators who overthrew civilian governments after a few years of political independence displaced the nationalists' philosophy that could have engendered development of physical capital in Africa. Public resistance to acute shortage of physical capital associated with decades of dictatorship contributed to the adoption of neoliberal reforms after successful transition from dictatorship to democracy in the 1980s.[15]

Efforts geared toward the provision of physical capital in Africa had been quite impressive, but the efforts nose-dived since the advent of imperialism on its triplets, namely, slave trade, colonialism, and post-colonialism. Nkrumah recognized neo-colonialism as the last stage of imperialism.[16] The experience with slave trade and colonialism in Nigeria, for instance, cannot be forgotten. According to Afigbo, following the abolition of the slave trade, the Nigerian kingdoms were colonized, and this overshadowed the distinctive artifacts of the skilled artisans and ironworkers among the Nok that provided useful tools for traditional physical capital.[17] Some of the earliest carvings of the Nok were taken to museums in Australia and European countries such as Britain, France, and Germany. It is evident that the artistic prowess of the Nok is still relevant to the contemporary society especially in terms of its contribution to tourism.

Subsequently, traditional physical capital was modernized in the context of colonialism. While trans-Atlantic trade routes were followed by railways and tarred roads, indigenous education was complemented with a proliferation of schools from pre-primary institutions to higher educational institutions. Also, colonialism resulted in the establishment of new institutions such as the armed forces, public service, hospitals, and the energy sector. The major physical capital established during the colonial era included electricity, tarred roads, railways, ports, pipe borne water, health center, communication networks, and schools. However, these forms of physical capital served the few elites who lived in cities where the facilities and services could only be accessed. The crop of African leaders who succeeded the colonial masters, who attempted to maintain and extend the inherited colonial physical capital, failed due to official negligence and mismanagement of resources. This can be aligned with the African Peer Review Mechanism (APRM), which was established in 2003 as a development framework for the monitoring of agreed norms of political, economic, and corporate governance in Africa.[18] Historically, the role of private investment in physical capital in Africa has been limited, particularly due to the weak enabling environment that underpins physical capital development. The enabling environment encompasses the policy framework, regulations that include tariff setting and procurement, and sound public institutions for the management of physical capital systems.[19]

Industrialization is a critical engine of economic growth and development. That Africa remains the poorest region of the world, where 34 of the 50 Least Developed Countries are located, and in which poverty is on the increase, is a reflection of its low level of physical capital development.[20] Inadequate and unreliable physical capital services are common in the majority of communities in Africa. Most households do not have access to safe drinking water, electricity, access roads, etc. These services support quality of life and form the basis of a healthy and robust economy.

Investment in physical capital is critical to the promotion and sustenance of industrial development in Africa. The continent cannot harness its comparative advantage of using natural resources as the cornerstone of industrial development, converting comparative advantages into competitiveness, without adequate and efficient physical capital.[21] It is therefore critical to address these deficiencies in order to unlock Africa's productive potential and maximize physical capital's impact on economic growth, environmental improvement, and human development. To achieve this requires investment in physical capital development.

Physical capital development is critical for economic growth and poverty reduction. In Africa, physical capital can potentially contribute as much as 2 percent to Gross Domestic Product (GDP), with particular positive effects in East and Central Africa.[22] In other parts of the developing world, notably in China, massive investments in physical capital established the backbone for other economic activities, such as manufacturing, which in turn fueled economic growth. A similar path lies open for African countries. Increased access to physical capital services such as roads, electricity, water, and sanitation, among others, can entail direct social benefits such as health and education, thereby helping to achieve sustainable economic, industrial, and social development.

Physical Capital as Human Right Concern

Physical capital is crucial to development, and the human right to physical capital is fundamental to life and health.[23] Access and adequacy of physical capital, such as water, are preconditions for the realization of all other human rights.[24]

Under international human right laws, physical capital is indirectly protected as a human right. In the 1948 Universal Declaration of Human Rights, the 1986 International Covenant on Economic, Social and Cultural Rights (ICESC), and the 1966 International Covenant on Civil and Political Rights, physical capital is not explicitly mentioned as a human right. It is however implied through other human, economic and socio-cultural rights, such as the right to life, right to an adequate standard of living, and the right to health.[25]

To fully effectuate a human right to life requires the recognition and support of the fundamental conditions necessary to support life. The Human Rights Committee has interpreted the rights to life to require a state to take positive measures to support "appropriate means of subsistence."[26] Physical capital is, no doubt, an essential component of achieving the means of subsistence, as it is necessary to produce food, shelter, mobility, and other elements necessary for human survival.

68   *J. Ali Ogwuche*

The ICESC, the instrument under which the United Nations Economic and Social Council (ECOSOC) operates, recognizes several other rights that may encompass the right to physical capital, such as the rights to adequate housing and food; both are fundamental components of the right to an adequate standard of living.[27]

The right to develop, which requires "equality of opportunity for all is their access to basic resources..." may also provide a basis for the right to physical capital.[28] A right to physical capital based on the right to develop would require that access to affordable physical capital should not place a disproportionate economic or physical burden upon any particular segment of the society.

Other ICESC rights have also provided a basis for the recognition of a right to physical capital. For instance, physical capital is essential for securing livelihoods (right to gain a living by work) and enjoy certain cultural practices.[29] Provision of physical capital, such as water, satisfies human basic need as well as safeguarding the ecosystem.[30] It was not until 2002 that the United Nations, through the UN Committee on Economic, Social and Cultural Rights, officially adopted water as a human right, by the adoption of various General Comments relevant to the environment and sustainable development; notably General Comment No. 15 that "the human right to water entitles everyone to sufficient, safe, acceptance, physically accessible and affordable water for personal and domestic uses."[31]

People living in poverty are inevitably more affected by the ever-increasing competition for physical capital. For instance, WEHAB Working Group notes that in the poorest countries, one in five children dies before the age of five mainly from water-related infectious diseases arising from insufficient water availability in both quantity and quality.[32] Drinking water access and quality continue to be a fundamental problem, since some three billion people are expected to suffer water shortages in the year 2025; many of the world's current conflicts are caused or exacerbated by the lack of or insufficiency of physical capital.[33] For example, the Darfur war in Sudan began when drought and desertification forced Arab nomads to move to the Southern Darfur region, where they had to compete with African farmers for water.

Deficiency in physical capital can hamper economic activities and weaken human development efforts. Poor physical capital quality has been found to undermine productivity among manufacturing firms in Africa, especially in low-income countries in central Africa.[34] Moreover, the continuing deterioration of physical capital is exacerbating existing poverty and discrimination. Agreeing with this, Kelly[35] laments the provision of physical capital for the African population in ways that enhances and nurtures the earth's natural resources and ecosystems, while supporting our survival, as the challenge of our times.[36] Realizing the human right to physical capital in a sustainable manner must, therefore, be considered a vital component of poverty reduction policies and the panacea to sustainable development in Africa.

Scope of Human Right to Physical Capital

The right to physical capital is both a human right in itself and a basic requirement for the implementation of other rights, including health.[37] In the view of International Covenant on Economic, Social and Cultural Rights (ICESCR), the right to physical capital has three dimensions—quantity, quality and accessibility.[38] The quantity must be at a minimum, sufficient to meet basic needs, in terms of utility. The quality must be safe, and for some services such as water, free from contamination. It must have physical accessibility, which must be within reach of the users. Additionally, economic accessibility or affordability must be ensured. However, the Commission on Human Rights warns that the adequacy of drinking water should be interpreted in a manner consistent with human dignity, and not in a narrow way, by mere reference to volumetric quantities and technologies, or by viewing water primarily as an economic good.[39] The right to physical capital is directly related to the right to the highest attainable standard of health.[38] On the right to health, the ICESCR notes that safe and portable drinking water, as an underlying determinant of health, has to be made available in sufficient quantity within the State through functioning public health and healthcare facilities, goods and services, as well as programs.[40]

At the regional level, standards have been developed to govern the right of access to physical capital, especially drinking water, which is complimentary to those developed by the United Nations system. Latin American states have endorsed a universal right to have access to basic public services (physical capital).[41] In Africa, the African Commission on Human Right and Peoples Rights has held that failure by a government to provide basic services (physical capital) constitute a violation of the right to health.[42] In Europe, there is a body of jurisprudence, which in effect applies a right to clean water, though it was not explicitly mentioned in the European Convention for the Protection of Human Rights and Fundamental Freedoms. However, the European Court of Human Rights already has the substantial body of precedents, which in effect apply for a right to clean water.[43]

Theoretical Discussions on the Nexus between Human Rights and the Environment

In 2011, the United Nations has come up with two theoretical discussions on the nexus between human rights and the environment, with special emphasis on physical capital. First, in an attempt to discover the nature of the relationship between human rights and the environment, the United Nations identified three major approaches to explaining this.[44] The first approach postulates that the environment is a precondition to the enjoyment of human rights. This approach underscores the fact that life and human dignity are only possible where people have access to an environment with basic facilities (physical capital).

The second approach submits that human rights are tools to address environmental issues, both procedurally and substantively. This approach emphasizes the possibility of using human rights to achieve adequate levels of environmental

70   J. Ali Ogwuche

protection. From a procedural perspective, rights, such as access to physical capital, are central to securing governance structures with respect to environmental issues. From a substantive perspective, this approach underscores the environmental dimensions of certain protected rights.

The third approach proposes the integration of human rights and the environment under the concept of sustainable development. Accordingly, this approach underscores that societal objectives must be treated in integrated manner, and the integration of economic, environmental, and social issues to achieve sustainable development. These three approaches have influenced global vision, policymaking, and development of jurisprudent relating to human rights and the environment, and the debate over the recognition of a new human right to a healthy environment with physical capital.

The second theoretical discussion is on the right to a healthy environment. The survival and development of humanity and the enjoyment of human rights are dependent on a healthy and safe environment with basic physical capital. This is in line with Article 11 of the UNDHR that recognizes the right to the highest attainable standard of living and mental health and education. People must have access to the underlying building blocks of good health, such as adequate physical capital, which includes housing, safe, and potable water, sanitation, and a healthy environment. Article 11 also guarantees the right to an adequate standard of living including housing and continuous improvement of living standards. The right to adequate housing encompasses more than the provision of basic shelter. This means that housing or shelter must fulfill certain basic criteria such as security of tenure, availability of utilities and other social services, affordability, habitability and accessibility.

Access to water is necessary for life and thus the fulfillment of all other rights. Although it is not explicitly mentioned in the text of Article 11, it is considered a fundamental aspect of the right to an adequate standard of living. However, human rights entitle everyone to safe, sufficient, acceptable, affordable, and physically accessible water for personal and domestic uses. The water provided has to be of good quality, free from elements that might harm a person's health, and a minimum quantity of approximately 50–100 liters per person per day.[45]

The aim of the right to education is to realize the full development of the human personality and sense of dignity. The right to education also includes the right of equal access to education and equal enjoyment of educational facilities, which should be available, accessible, culturally and ethically acceptable. Brett Frischmann's theory of infrastructure (physical capital) explains the importance of public accessibility to physical capital.[46] Frischmann argues that public access to physical capital would generate values for a society.[47]

As environmental awareness grows owing to increased scientific evidence and ethical thinking, there is increasing constitutional recognition of environmental rights and responsibilities globally.[48] This also reflects the growing awareness of the importance of environmental values and greater recognition that life of dignity on the planet is only possible in a healthy environment with access to adequate physical capital.

Human Right and Physical Capital in the Context of Sustainable Development

Sustainable Human Development (SHD) is the development that places people at the center of all development activities.[49] The central purpose of SHD is to create an enabling environment in which all human beings live secure and creative lives. SHD is directed toward the promotion of human dignity and the realization of all human rights—economic, social, cultural, and political. This calls for the integration of a complex array of environmental, social and economic issues within the umbrella of sustainable development. This is in line with the integration of human rights and the environment in the context of sustainable development, as these linkages become increasingly established in international law.

The intersection between the environment and economy was explored in depth in the 1992 Earth Summit in Brazil and led to the recognition of sustainable development as the key concept capable of integrating environment and development. In his Grotius Lecture in 2009, Achim Steiner, Executive Director of the UN Environmental Programme, elaborated on the term "green economy" to describe an "economic system that recognizes the properties of healthy ecosystems as the backbone of economic and social well-being and as a precondition for poverty reduction."[50] The theme of green economy, according to him, involves elaborating on the growing recognition of a fundamental link between ecosystem services and human rights.

A connection between the environment and human rights was expressed in 1989, where a fundamental duty to preserve the ecosystem was recognized and the right to live in dignity in a viable global environment.[51] In 1990, the United Nations General Assembly (UNGA) observed that environmental protection is indivisible from the achievement of full employment of human rights by all.[52] Sustainable development entails not only economic growth, but an emphasis on structural change as well. Viewing development in purely economic terms ignores many other factors that influence the lives of people in developing nations. These other social and political factors of economic growth have become an ingrained part of how we now define sustainable development.

In 2002, a joint expert seminar was convened by the UN Commission on Human Rights and United Nations Environment Program, to assess progress in promoting and protecting human rights in relation to environmental questions since the 1992 Rio Declaration. Walls Topfer, Executive Director, UNEP, addressing the 57th session of the Commission on Human Rights declared that:

> Human rights cannot be secured in a degraded or polluted environment. The fundamental human right is threatened by pollution or degradation, environmental condition clearly help to determine the extent to which people enjoy the basic rights to life, health.[53]

With regard to substantive rights, it is noted that the link between human rights and environmental protection should be affirmed as an essential achievement of

72   J. Ali Ogwuche

sustainable development; and a growing recognition of a right to secure, healthy and ecologically sound environment.[54] These can be justified in two ways: worldwide, 13 million deaths (23 percent of all deaths) could be prevented each year by making our environment healthier, and better environmental management could prevent 42 percent of deaths from malaria, 41 percent of deaths from lower respiratory infections in developing countries (with 20 percent in developed countries); and 94 percent from diarrheal diseases.[55]

Poverty is a multidimensional concept, and seen as a deprivation of human rights. In the urban context, it is translated largely in terms of lack of access to adequate basic physical capital.[56] This gives credence to what D. Mitlin says that given a fixed income, to be poor in income terms in a high-density settlement with no infrastructure and services, which results in a worse development outcome than to be poor in a settlement with appropriate physical capital and service levels.[57] In other words, it makes no sense pursuing a policy that will raise the economic condition of the urban area or to focus on direct benefits for the poor when the wider environment in which the poor seek to secure livelihoods remains hostile. Therefore, any strategy that will enhance economic, as well as the environmental conditions, of any area should be pursued. That strategy is the use of physical capital, which not only promotes sustainable economic and social conditions, but also enhances environmental development, management, and sustainability. This is in line with the World Bank's Mission Statement: to fight poverty with passion and professionalism for lasting results; to help people help themselves and their environment by providing physical capital.[58]

An explicit recognition of the right to a healthy environment is thus central to the attainment of sustainable development. Sustainable development requires environmental protection, development, and management. Environmental degradation leads directly and indirectly to violation of human rights. Most, if not all, of the strategies to achieve the Millennium Development Goals (MDGs) operate within the context of physical capital, as well as within a human rights framework. Therefore the MDGs physical capital and human rights commitments are complementary and mutually reinforcing.

Human Right to Physical Capital: State Obligations

In line with Frischmann's theory of physical capital, the state is generally responsible for the provision of physical capital through diverse revenue sources including state resources and tax from citizens and organizations. In addition, classical social contract theorists argue that the state must guarantee law and order, human dignity, and social welfare.

Recognizing the rights to physical capital as a human right imposes three obligations by the State. The World Health Organization (WHO) recognizes the obligations as to respect, protect, and fulfill.[59] The obligation to respect prohibits actions that underpin the right, including such activities as pollution (for water), from state owned facilities.[60] The obligation to protect the right to physical capital requires that states implement permitting procedures or other regulatory

Panacea to Sustainable Development in Africa   73

systems to control private sector behavior that might interfere with the right to physical capital. In addition, the obligation to fulfill the right to physical capital includes a responsibility to facilitate "enjoyment of the right and promotion of the right through education measures."[61]

Utilizing human rights protections changes the terms of discourse from one of charity to one of entitlement with corresponding State obligations.[62] It therefore means that categorizing a right to physical capital as a human right means that:

- Physical capital is a legal entitlement, rather than a commodity or service provided on a charitable basis.
- Achieving basic and improved levels of access should be accelerated.
- The least served are better targeted and therefore inequalities decreased.
- Communities and vulnerable groups will be empowered to take part in decision-making processes through their needs assessment, and participation during the implementation of physical capital projects.

The means and mechanisms available in the United Nations human rights system will be used to monitor the progress of states' parties in realizing the right to physical capital and hold governments accountable.[63]

Constitutional Rights on the Environment (Physical Capital): The African Experience

A constitution is a fundamental expression of a State's core values and principles. Today, a vast number of countries incorporate provisions related to environmental issues into their national constitutions. The human right to a healthy, safe, and sustainable environment is referenced in numerous national constitutions and regional conventions, as well as recognized by the UN human rights bodies. Most States use various constitutional rights to protect the environment and human rights. The right to life, a fundamental right, has been extended to include the right to a healthy environment. The trend toward constitutional recognition of the right to a healthy environment began with the 1972 declaration of the United Nation's Conference on the human environment, popularly known as the Stockholm Declaration. The Stockholm Declaration provided a strong impetus for environmental protection by the international community. Also, the International Covenant on Economic, Social and Cultural Rights requires States to formally recognize the rights within their national legislation, and to provide laws and regulations to fulfill these essential human rights. Since its adoption, more than 100 states have made explicit references to environmental rights and responsibilities in their national constitutions. Since then, the number of national constitutions that incorporate environmental rights and responsibilities has increased significantly. For instance, in Nigeria, the only relevant rights are those contained under the social objectives, and states that "in furtherance of the social order, the sanctity of the human person shall be recognized and human dignity

74 J. Ali Ogwuche

shall be maintained and enhanced."[64] The state shall direct its policy toward ensuring that:

- All citizens, without discrimination on any group whatsoever, have the opportunity for securing adequate means of livelihoods as well as adequate opportunity to secure suitable employment.
- Conditions of work are just and humane, and that there are adequate facilities for leisure and social, religious and cultural life, and
- There are adequate medical and health facilities for all persons.

The only environmental objective states that the State shall protect and improve the environment and safeguard the water, air, land, forest, and wildlife of Nigeria. Besides this, there is no single provision on environmental rights (and duties) in the constitution. In addition, the provision in the constitution presupposes that the government of Nigeria should always take necessary precautions to protect the rights of the people in all policies formulated to exploit natural and human resources of the State.

Since the publication of General Comment 15, the number of States recognizing the human right to physical capital, especially water, has doubled. Most African countries have enshrined the right to water within their national constitutions or have framed the right explicitly or implicitly within national legislation. For example, South Africa's constitution, adopted in 1996, has been praised as the model social rights constitution. Section 27.1(a) confirms that everyone has the right to access sufficient food and water. Section 3 of the Water Services Act 108 of 1997 contains the right of access to basic water supply and sanitation. Similarly, the Constitution of the Federal Republic of Ethiopia, 1994, provides in Article 90 that policies shall aim to provide all Ethiopians access to health and education, clean water, housing, food and social security. Article 92 states that the government shall endeavor to ensure all Ethiopians live in a clean and healthy environment and that people have the right to full consultation and to the expression of their views in the planning and implementation of environmental policies and projects that affect them directly. More recently, in Morocco, Water Law, Law No. 10–95, 1995, states that the development of water resources must allow for the availability of water in sufficient quantity and quality for the benefit of all users.

Further states' positions to obligations to the right to water can be viewed on the information portal on the human rights to water and sanitation.[65] However, being part of State Constitutions and Policies, these sections are sufficient and, therefore, cannot be made a ground for a justifiable right to the environment. Even though there is increasing constitutional recognition of environmental rights and responsibilities globally, indicating a growing awareness of the importance of environmental values and greater acceptance of a right to a healthy environment, there is such a gap in the area of an environmental component of physical capital. Physical capital is only being implied to exist in the provisions for "adequate water," "adequate means of livelihoods," and "adequate facilities."[66]

Obstacles to Improved Access and Human Rights to Physical Capital

A number of obstacles have been identified as being impediments to improved access and human right to physical capital. The Joint United Nations Environment Programme (UNEP) and the Office of the High Commissioner for Human Rights (OHCHR) identify lack of political will on the part of the government to see physical capital as one of its basic responsibilities that they owe the citizens of their countries.[67] Other obstacles include lack of planning, unequal distribution of services, and privatization.[68] According to the definition of physical capital as a human right, governments are responsible for ensuring that everyone has access to physical capital. This means that human rights cannot be sold or withheld even when people cannot afford to pay. This right has been violated in a number of countries, especially Nigeria, where, for instance, in prepaid water meters, electricity meters, and toll fares for roads are used. This means that when people cannot afford to pay, they are denied these services, and like water, they are forced to use contaminated water, which results in an increase in water-borne diseases.

The World Health Organization (WHO) has observed that 1.1 billion people do not have access to an improved water supply that should be able to provide each person with 20 or more liters of safe water each day.[69] However, the target of the 7th MDG goal of ensuring environmental sustainability is to halve the proportion of people without access to physical capital and social services by the year 2015. The United Nations reports that to reduce this, four things must happen:[70]

- Governments and countries need to recognize that environmental infrastructure and social services (physical capital) must be accessible and affordable to all, including those who are too poor to pay.
- Governments and countries need to develop national strategies that will improve environmental infrastructure and social services (physical capital), as well as reduce poverty.
- International aid must double.
- A global action plan needs to be developed to emphasize the priority of providing adequate infrastructure and social services to all.

Financing Physical Capital Development in Africa: The Role of African Diasporas

For so many years, African countries have featured physical capital as one of the main focal areas in their national development plans. In 2002, NEPAD adopted a short-term action plan on physical capital to promote regional integration by bridging the physical capital gap. In addition, heads of State and governments of African countries endorsed a number of priority physical capital projects and appointed champions for their development at the African Union Assembly in 2011 in Ethiopia. The G8 also established the Infrastructure Consortium for

76   J. Ali Ogwuche

Africa (ICA) at the G8 Gleneagles Summit in 2005 to act as a platform for increasing financing commitments by G8 countries and some key development finance institutions for Africa's physical capital.

The World Bank also undertook a major study called the African Infrastructure Country Diagnostic (AICD), aimed at expanding knowledge on the state of Africa's infrastructure. The AICD, funded by France, Germany, United Kingdom, the European Union, and others, aimed to stimulate public actors and development partners in their efforts to support Africa's physical capital by identifying the needs and key policy issues.

An important aspect in physical capital is the need for and benefits from a regional approach. Economies of scale from regional physical capital can reduce costs of construction and services compared to those that are developed and used on a country-by-country basis.[71] In particular, regional physical capital is suitable from Africa's geographical perspective as it increases trade, improves security, saves money, strengthens natural resources management, addresses the needs of landlocked countries, and builds on national and regional comparative advantages.[72]

The AICD estimates that US$93 billion per year is required to develop African physical capital. Major investments in building, maintenance and the operation of infrastructure assets are required to reverse the current infrastructure backlog. Africa's current spending is US$45 billion; there is thus a financing gap of US$48 billion.[73] The primary source of physical capital financing in African countries remains domestic. In many low-income countries, physical capital development has been confined to public finance sources only, which has left physical capital needs largely unaddressed.[74] It is therefore imperative to diversify sources of financing for physical capital development in Africa.

Among the recommended solutions is the leveraging of the diaspora.[75] The diaspora is a generic term used to denote people of African descent residing outside Africa.[76] Diaspora should be seen as a potential resource rather than as a concern; a potential human and social capital that can make a significant contribution to the development of physical capital of the home countries of origin. African diaspora constitute one of Africa's greatest offshore assets because of the potential of its contribution to the provision of physical capital. To buttress this, Mr Chike Nwoffiah, founder of the Silicon Valley African Film Festival, said that the destiny of the continental African is intricately interwoven with the destiny of the diaspora African.[77] The African Union has been encouraging the diaspora to play a key role in the development of the continent. In 2007, the African Union partnered with the World Bank to launch the African Diaspora Program (ADP), with the sole purpose of supporting the African Union in its diaspora global program and projects. To this end, members of the diaspora, governments, multilateral institutions, and private entities should think creatively about how to further leverage the resources that diaspora Africans have to offer. A variety of innovative funding mechanisms can channel investment to basic public physical capital projects and social services. Africans in diaspora can either use a range of financing instruments and mechanisms such as investment bonds, blended grants, guarantees, or export credit agency instruments or support country efforts to leverage private investments in physical capital provision.[78]

Summary and Conclusion

One of the biggest obstacles to achieving sustainable development in Africa is a lack of investment in physical capital. According to Richard Cambridge, Manager of the African Diaspora Program at the World Bank, Africa requires $96 billion in investment annually if it is to grow its economy by 5 percent a year, and concludes that much of the remainder could potentially originate from diasporas.[79] The financing gap for Africa's physical capital, need to be filled by Africans in diaspora. To achieve this requires the right framework conditions, including macroeconomic stability, good governance, and a strong enabling environment.

Notes

1 SANDS, *Principles of International Environmental Law*, 2003: 292.
2 ICJ Reports, "Legacy of the Threat or Use of Nuclear Weapons," *Advisory Opinion*, 1996: 241–242.
3 Principle 3 of the Declaration of the United Nations Conference on the Human Environment, UN Document A/Con/48/14/Rev.1, 1973.
4 L. B. Sohn, "The Stockholm Declaration on the Human Environment," *Harvard International Law Journal*, 14, 1973: 423.
5 Principle 1 of the Declaration of the United Nations Conference on the Human Environment, UN Document A/Con/48/14/Rev.1, 1993.
6 Amartya Sen, *Development as Freedom*, 1999.
7 C. Boyle, "Human Rights or Environmental Rights?" Paper presented at Fordham University Law School, 2007.
8 Article 24 of the African Charter on Human and Peoples Rights.
9 Article 11 of the African Charter on Human and Peoples Rights.
10 C. Moser, "The Asset Vulnerability Framework: Reassuring Urban Poverty Reduction Strategies," *World Development* 26 (1998): 1–19; and C. Rakodi "A Livelihoods Approach: Conceptual Issues and Definitions," in *Urban Livelihoods: A People-Centred Approach to Reducing Poverty*, eds. Rakodi and Lioyd-Jones (London: Earthscan Publications Ltd, 2002).
11 C. Rakodi, "A Livelihoods Approach: Conceptual Issues and Definitions."
12 DFID *Achieving Sustainability: Poverty Elimination and the Environment* (London, 2000).
13 B. M. Frischmann, "An Economic Theory of Infrastructure and Commons Right," *Minnesota Law Review*, 89 (2005): 917–1030.
14 A. A. Akinwale, "The Menace of Inadequate Infrastructure in Nigeria," *African Journal of Science, Technology, Innovation and Development* 2 (2010): 207–228.
15 E. E. Okafor, "Public Bureaucracy and Development in Nigeria: A Critical Overview of Impediments to Public Service Delivery," *CODESRIA*, Bulletin 3 and 4 (2005): 67–69.
16 K. Nkrumah, *Neo-Colonialism: The Last Stage of Imperialism* (Panaf Books, 1965).
17 A. Afigbo, "African and the Abolition of Slave Trade," (Keynote note address delivered at the international conference, organized by the Omohundro institute of early America history and culture, Elmina, Ghana, 2007).
18 R. Herbert and S. Gruzd, *The African Peer Review Mechanism: Lessons From the Pioneers.* (International Monetary Fund Regional Economic Outlook, 2010)
19 OECD, "Mapping the Support for Africa's Infrastructure Investment," (Being a report presented at the Joint DAC-Trade committee working party meeting Paris, 2012).
20 OECD, *Promoting Pro-Poor Growth: Policy Guidelines for Donors* (Paris, 2006).
21 African Union Conference of Ministers, "Action Plan for the Accelerated Industrial Development of Africa," (First extraordinary session September 24–27, 2007).
22 OECD, *Africa Infrastructure Diagnostics* (Paris, 2010).

78 J. Ali Ogwuche

23 Commission on Human Rights Resolution, "Report on the Fifty Eight Session" (Economic and social records supplement No. 3, 2002).

24 A. E. Boyle and M. R. Anderson, *Human Rights Approaches to Environmental Protection* (Oxford: Clarendon, 1996): and HRH the Prince of Orange, *No Water No Future: A Water Focus for Johannesburg* (2002).

25 UNCSD, *Fifth Session at 22* (UN Document E/CN.17.1997/9, 1997): and General Comment No. 15 *Right to Water* (Committee on Economic, Social and Cultural Rights, 29th Session, Agenda Item 3, UN Document E/C.12/2002/11, 2002); Asian Development Bank, "Water for All," available at www.adb.org/water/. Accessed January 12, 2014.

26 UN, "Document No. CCPR/C/Rev. 1" (UN Committee on Human Rights, 1989).

27 General Comment No. 15 *Right to Water* (Committee on Economic, Social and Cultural Rights, 29th Session, Agenda Item 3, UN Document E/C.12/2002/11, 2002).

28 Right to Water, "An Introduction to the Right to Water," available at www.right towater.org.uk. (2003), accessed January 23, 2014.

29 UNDP, *Integrating Human Rights into Sustainable Development* (New York: UN Publications, 1998).

30 General Comment No. 15, *Right to Water*.

31 UN, "Protection of the Quality and Supply of Freshwater Resources."

32 General Comment No. 15, *Right to Water*.

33 WEHAB, Working Group *A Framework for Action on Water and Sanitation* (2002).

34 WHO, *The Global Water Supply and Sanitation Assessment*, available at www.int/ docstore/ (Geneva, 2000), accessed January 30, 2014.

35 Kelly "China in Africa: Curing the Resource Curse with Infrastructure and Modernization" *SP Law and Policy*, 12, no. 3 (2012): 35–41.

36 IMF, *Regional Economic Outlook* (Paris, 2010).

37 Kelly, "China in Africa: Curing the Resource Curse with Infrastructure and Modernization," *SP Law and Policy* 12 no. 3 (2012): 35–41.

38 See Commission on the Promotion of Human Rights, 2002.

39 See SDWF, *Safe Water*, available at www.safewater.org; and *The Right to Water* (UN Sheet No. 35).

40 See the Commission on Human Rights Resolution No. e/cn.4/2002/58.

41 The protocol of San Salvador signed in 1988 and entered into force in 1999.

42 See Article 11.1 of ICESCR.

43 See Article 3 and 1 respectively of the Universal Declaration of Human Rights.

44 See Article 16 of the African Commission on Human and People's Rights against Zaire (Communication 25/89, 47/90, 56/91, and 100/93), cited by the Office of the High Commission for Human Rights, 2002.

45 Office of the High Commission for Human Rights, "Human Rights, Poverty Reduction and Sustainable Development, Health, Food and Water," A background paper for the World Summit on Sustainable Development, Johannesburg, August 26–September 4, 2002.

46 United Nations High Commission for Human Rights, *Analytical Study on the Relationship Between Human Rights and the Environment* (Report of the United Nations High Commission for Human Rights, Human Rights Council, 19th Session, December 16, 2011).

47 Monash University, *Human Rights Translated* (Castan Centre for Human Rights, 2008).

48 A. A. Akinwale, "The Menace of Inadequate Infrastructure in Nigeria."

49 B. M. Frischmann, "An Economic Theory of Infrastructure and Commons' Right," in *Minnesota Law Review* 89 (2005): 917–1030; and B. M. Frischmann, "Infrastructure Commons in Economic Perspective" in *First Monday* (online), 12, no. 6, June 4, 2007.

50 United Nations High Commission for Human Rights, *Analytical Study on the Relationship Between Human Rights and the Environment*.

51 Office of the High Commission for Human Rights, "Human Rights, Poverty Reduction and Sustainable Development, Health, Food and Water."

Panacea to Sustainable Development in Africa   79

52 United Nations General Assembly (UNGA), "Need to Ensure a Healthy Environment for the Well-Being of Individuals," (UNGA Resolutions 45/94).
53 World Health Organization (WHO), "Questions and Answers on Health and Human Rights," available at www.who.int/hhr/en/new3787/10msk.pdf, 2000, accessed February 2, 2014.
54 Jonathan Ogwuche, "Assessment of Physical Capital as a Sustainable Livelihoods Approach to Poverty Reduction in Otukpo Urban Area, Nigeria," (PhD diss., Enugu State University of Science and Technology, Enugu, Nigeria, 2005).
55 D. Mitlin, "The Urban Context and the Poor," in *Urban Livelihoods: A People-Centred Approach to Reducing Poverty*, eds. Rakodi and Lioyd-Jones (London: Earthscan Publications, 2003).
56 World Bank, "Making Sustainable Commitments: An Environmental Strategy for the World Bank," (Washington, D.C., 2001).
57 World Health Organization (WHO), "Water for Health Enshrined as a Human Right," (Geneva, 2002).
58 General Comment No. 15, *Right to Water*.
59 Ibid.
60 Julia Hausermann, "Rights and Humanity: A Human Rights Approach to Development," Presentation at the inaugural WaterAid Lecture (London: City University, 1999).
61 Ibid.
62 P. Ruchi, "Rights and Humanity, from Communities' Hands to MNG's Booths," (A Case Study from India on right to water, 2003).
63 See Chapter 2, Section 17 (2a-h) of the Constitution of the Federal Republic of Nigeria, 1999.
64 Constitution of the Federal Republic of Nigeria.
65 Sida, "Realising the Human Right to Water and Sanitation," (SIDA Reference Paper, 2013).
66 Water Law in Morocco, No. 10–95, 1995.
67 "Rio+20: Joint Report OHCHR and UNEP, Human Rights and the Environment," United Nations Conference on Sustainable Development (Rio de Janeiro, Brazil, 2012).
68 D. Mitlin, "The Urban Context and the Poor," in *Urban Livelihoods: A People-Centred Approach to Reducing Poverty*, eds. Rakodi and Lioyd-Jones (London: Earthscan Publications, 2003); Jonathan Ogwuche, "Assessment of Physical Capital."
69 WHO, "The Global Water Supply and Sanitation Assessment," Available at www.int/docstore/ (Geneva, 2000), accessed January 30, 2014.
70 UN, *The Millennium Development Goals* (New York, 2007).
71 IMF, *Regional Economic Outlook* (Paris, 2010).
72 Ibid.
73 OECD, *Africa Infrastructure Diagnostics* (Paris, 2010).
74 Ibid.
75 Ibid.; Almaz Negash, *What Is the Role of the African Diaspora in Ensuring the Renaissance of the Continent?* (Sunnyvale, CA: African Diaspora Network, 2012).
76 John Oucho, "African Diaspora and Remittance Flows: Leveraging Poverty?" (Paper prepared for the African migration yearbook, 2008).
77 Ibid.
78 Almaz Negash, *What Is the Role of the African Diaspora*.
79 OECD, "Mapping the Support for Africa's Infrastructure Investment," A report presented at the Joint DAC-Trade Committee Working Party Meeting (Paris, 2012).

References

African Commission on Human and People's Rights against Zaire. Communication 25/89, 47/90, 56/91, and 100/93. Office of the High Commission for Human Rights, 2002.
African Union Conference of Ministers. "Action Plan for the Accelerated Industrial Development of Africa." First Extraordinary Session. September 24–27, 2007.

80   J. Ali Ogwuche

Afigbo, A. "Africa and the Abolition of Slave Trade." Keynote address delivered at the International Conference, organized by the Omohundro Institute of Early America History and Culture. Elmina, Ghana, 2007.

Akinwale, A. A. "The Menace of Inadequate Infrastructure in Nigeria." *African Journal of Science, Technology, Innovation and Development*, 2, no. 3 (2010): 207–228.

Asian Development Bank. "Water for All." 2004. Available at www.Adb.org/water/

Boyle, A. "Human Rights or Environmental Rights? A Reassessment." Paper Presented at Fordham University Law School, 2007. Available at: www.law.ed.ac.uk/file_down load/publications/0_1221_humanrightsorenvironmentalrightsareasses.pdf

Boyle, A. E. and Anderson, M. R. *Human Rights Approaches to Environmental Protection*. Oxford: Clarendon, 1996.

Brixiova, Z., Mutambatsere, E., Ambert, C., and Etienne, D. "Closing Africa's Infrastructure Gap: Innovative Financing and Risks." *African Economic Brief*, 2, no. 1 (2011).

Commission on Human Rights Resolution. "Report on the Fifty Eight Session." Economic and Social Records Supplement No. 3, 2002.

Development Support Monitor. "Rural Infrastructure in Africa: Unlocking the African Moment." *Development Support Monitor Paper Series*, No. 1, 2012.

DFID. *Achieving Sustainability: Poverty Elimination and the Environment*. London, 2000.

Dovelyn, R. and Newland, K. *A Handbook for Policy Makers and Practitioners in Home and Host Countries*. No date.

Frishchmann, B. M. "An Economic Theory of Infrastructure and Commons Night." *Minnesota Law Review*, 89 (2005): 917–1030.

Frischmann, B. M. "Infrastructure Commons in Economic Perspective." First Monday (online) 12(6), June 4, 2007.

General Comment No. 15. UN Committee on Economic, Social and Cultural Rights, 29th Session, Agenda Item 3, UN Document E/C.12/2002/11 Right to Water. 2002.

Hausermann, J. "Rights and Humanity: A Human Rights Approach to Development." Presentation at the Inaugural Water Aid Lecture. London: City University, 1999.

Herbert, R. and Gruzd, S. *The African Peer Review Mechanism: Lessons From the Pioneers*. International Monetary Fund Regional Economic Outlook, 2010.

HRH the Prince of Orange. *No Water No Future: A Water Focus for Johannesburg*. 2002.

ICJ Reports, "Legacy of the Threat or Use of Nuclear Weapons," *Advisory Opinion* (1996): 241–242.

IMF. *Regional Economic Outlook*. Paris, 2010.

International Covenant on Economic, Social and Cultural Rights (ICESCR).

Kelley. "China in Africa: Curing the Resource Curse with Infrastructure and Modernization." *SP Law and Policy*, 12, no. 3 (2012): 35–41.

Mitlin, D. "The Urban Context and the Poor." In *Urban Livelihoods: A People-Centred Approach to Reducing Poverty*, eds. Rakodi and Lioyd-Jones. London: Earthscan Publications, 2003.

Monash University. *Human Rights Translated*. Castan Centre for Human Rights, 2008.

Moser, C. "The Asset Vulnerability Framework: Reassuring Urban Poverty Reduction Strategies." *World Development*, 26, no. 1 (1998), 1–19.

Negash, Almaz. *What Is the Role of the African Diaspora in Ensuring the Renaissance of the Continent?* Sunnyvale, CA: African Diaspora Network, 2012.

Nkrumah, K. *Neo-Colonialism: The Last Stage of Imperialism*. Panaf Books, 1965.

OECD. *Promoting Pro-Poor Growth: Policy Guidelines for Donors*. Paris, 2006.

OECD. *Africa Infrastructure Country Diagnostics*. Paris, 2010.

OECD. "Mapping the Support for Africa's Infrastructure Investment." A report presented at the Joint DAC-Trade committee working party meeting. Paris, 2012.

Panacea to Sustainable Development in Africa 81

Ogwuche, Jonathan, "Assessment of Physical Capital as a Sustainable Livelihoods Approach to Poverty Reduction in Otukpo Urban Area, Nigeria." PhD diss., Enugu State University of Science and Technology, Enugu, Nigeria, 2005.

Okafor, E. E "Public Bureaucracy and Development in Nigeria: A Critical Overview of Impediments to Public Service Delivery" in *CODESRIA Bulletin 3 and 4* (2005): 67–69.

Oucho, John. "African Diaspora and Remittance Flows: Leveraging Poverty?" *African Migration Yearbook*. 2008.

Rakodi, C. "A Livelihoods Approach: Conceptual Issues and Definitions." In *Urban Livelihoods: A People-Centered Approach to Reducing Poverty*, eds. C. Rakodi and Lloyd-Jones. London: Earthscan Publication Ltd, 2002.

Right to Water. *An Introduction to the Right to Water*. 2003. Available www.Righttowater.Org.Uk. Accessed January 23, 2014.

Ruchi, P. *Rights and Humanity, from Communities' Hands to MNG's Booths*. A Case Study from India on right to water, 2003.

Sands, Philippe. *Principles of International Environmental Law*. Cambridge University Press, 2003.

Sen, Amartya. *Development as Freedom*. London: Oxford University Press, 1999.

Sohn, Louis. "The Stockholm Declaration on the Human Environment." *The Harvard International Law Journal*, 14, no. 3 (1973): 451–454.

UN Document No. CCPR/C/Rev1, UN Committee on Human Rights. 1989.

UN. Document A/Con/48/14/Rev.1, The Declaration of the United Nations Conference on the Human Environment, 1973.

UN. "Protection of the Quality and supply of Freshwater Resources: Application of Integrated Approaches to the Development, Management and Use of Water Resources." *Agenda 21*, Chapter 18, New York: United Nations Publications, 1992.

UN. Human Rights and Transnational Corporations and Other Business Enterprises, UN HRC Res. 17/4. 2011.

United Nations General Assembly. *Need to Ensure a Healthy Environment for the Well-Being of Individuals*. UNGA Resolutions 45/94.

United Nations High Commission for Human Rights. *Analytical Study on the Relationship between Human Rights and the Environment*. 19th Session, December 16, 2011.

UNCSD. *Fifth Session at 22*. UN Document E/CN.17.1997/9. 1997.

UNDP. *Integrating Human Rights into Sustainable Development*. New York: UN Publications, 1998.

UNGA. Need to Ensure a Healthy Environment for the Well-Being of Individuals. UNGA Resolution 45/94. 1990.

United Nations. The Millennium Development Goals. New York: United Nations, 2007.

WEHAB Working Group. *A Framework for Action on Water and Sanitation*. 2002.

WHO. *The Global Water Supply and Sanitation Assessment*. Available at www.int/docstore/ (Geneva, 2000) Accessed January 30, 2014.

World Bank. *Making Sustainable Commitments: An Environmental Strategy for the World Bank*. Washington D.C., 2001.

World Health Organization (WHO). *Water for Health Enshrined as a Human Right*. Geneva, 2002.

World Health Organization (WHO). *Questions and Answers on Health and Human Rights*. 2000. Accessed February 2, 2014. Available at www.who.int/hhr/en/new3787/10msk.pdf.

Part II
Race, Racism, and Discrimination

5 Yearning for Whiteness

Racial Identification Among the Coloureds of Antigua, 1660s–1860s

Nsaka Sesepkekiu

Perhaps the most significant occurrence, which had the greatest impact on the shaping of the modern Anglo-Caribbean, was the more than two centuries of African enslavement. As a result of slavery, the region's historical recollection has been divided into four great periods including the pre-slavery societies, slave-societies, also termed plantation societies, the post-slavery societies, and then post-independence societies; independence is often recalled as the penultimate expression of black emancipation in the region, as regional historians have found it difficult to separate slavery from colonialism. Slavery was a political, legal, economic, and social system, which transformed the overwhelming number of incoming Africans into what some historical anthropologists have termed the "New World Negro."[1] At emancipation in 1834, while the majority of regionally born and resident whites still affectionately referred to European kingdoms as their home, for the overwhelming majority of non-whites the new world was their final destination with many having only vague memories of an increasingly estranged culture and people in a remote land. The racism and legal disadvantages which underpinned the slave societies in all territories, lasting centuries, had created a myriad of African descended people whose identities were, and remain, difficult to determine and catalog, while those of the white population remained fixed and attached to ideas of racial and sometimes ethnic purity, religion and wealth. Under the imperial system that operated until the end of slavery, each colony was permitted to have its own local assembly, which passed laws to benefit their planter classes. As a result, there were significant differences in the laws governing race, identity, personhood and rights from one colony to another. In the older Leeward Island colonies, with the exception of Barbados where the "one-drop rule" was codified into law, the ability to gain rights was directly linked to a genetic movement away from Africaness.[2] The emergent group of mixed race individuals, legally divided into slaves and Free Coloureds, often represented an in-between group who, though disadvantaged when compared to the dominant white populations, were granted greater rights, which re-affirmed an improvement by virtue of having some white blood.

The "Free Coloureds," like all "freed" people, strove to gain the legal privileges of personhood, subjecthood, and citizenship, which required them to relinquish their African and black identities and erase any trace or mention of an African identity if they were to have any chance at social mobility or even mere

86   N. Sesepkekiu

acceptance as a "free" person. After emancipation, there was an even greater effort by all non-white groups to cease being Africans, which had long been established as a disadvantageous identity, and begin the process of transformation into Creoles or Negroes.[3] For one section of Coloureds however, the aim was to attain the status of White as emancipation removed the last legal barriers to them attaining the long desired status. In the decades that followed emancipation the members of this group undertook a project, which would eventually lead to a mass exodus, and a later dying off, of its members as they yearned for whiteness.

Many historians have found it an extremely difficult task to categorize people's identities especially when there are a significant number of factors, which may affect such categorizing. The use of the term African during the seventeenth century through to the modern period, except as understood by modern Pan-Africanists, would normally be understood in the Anglophone Caribbean as a designate for those born or coming from Africa. Indeed the notion of being part of an African Diaspora is often rejected by many contemporary regional inhabitants who favor the use of the all-encompassing terms "black" or "West Indian." This is in part because many acknowledge or believe that they have a mixed ancestry, while others have continued to reject Africa as a land and place with which they have no real connection to, other than through genetics and history. Indeed by the mid-1700s the creole slaves of the Leeward Islands, those born and raised in the Americas, had begun to separate themselves by using the term African as a term for those coming from Africa, while using the term "Negro" inter-changeably with that of "Creole" to refer to themselves. The situation was further compounded by the fact that while whites often pejoratively used the term "Negro" to refer to those who called themselves "Coloured," some blacks also termed some mixed race persons "White" while calling others "Black"; often to designate which Coloureds had shown some affinity to the black slave population's causes.

Discussing coloured freedmen in the pre-emancipation British West Indies, Arnold A. Sio correctly highlighted the problem of lack of historical sources to construct a complete history of the entire group, which was sub-divided into a number of cultural, economic, and political spaces.[4] This lack of sources for the non-elite Coloureds has led to historians often using the terms Coloured, Brown and middle-class interchangeably.[5] This pattern reflected not only the contents of available sources, but also the interpretation and understanding of the peculiar economic, socio-political, and cultural history where class and skin color were inextricably linked until the mid-twentieth century.[6] There was also the problem of the intersection of slave status and racial status as there was a significant number of mixed race slaves, as well as a significant number of freed blacks. Censuses for Antigua used a simple three-tier division of the society, which has led to a contemporary oversimplification of then notions of identity among the population.[7]

The arrival in and subsequent colonization of the Americas by Europeans resulted in the creation of new cultures to which many have applied the term "Creole" as a noun as well as a descriptive reference for persons of any race

Racial Identification in Antigua, 1660s–1860s   87

born in New World of Old World genetic heritage, whether or not they were culturally or genetically mixed. By the mid-eighteenth century, the colonists of the Leeward Islands used the term to designate the numerically superior, regionally born Africans, and their descendants, whether they were mixed and unmixed.[8] The New World white populations were able to maintain European identities despite their creolization, while Africans born and raised in the Americas were categorized as a distinct group with a distinct culture though the culture had remained identifiably and indistinguishably African.[9] Etymologically rooted in the Ibero-Romance "negro" meaning black, the term "Negro" was adopted by English and later British colonists to refer to non-Europeans of various hues throughout the globe.[10] However, in the British West Indies (BWI) the term quickly became synonymous with the African populations born or brought to the region. By the mid-1700s, as plantation societies were consolidated, the Anglo-Europeans applied the term exclusively to those born to African parents and grandparents in the Americas to confer a superior social status on those who had been born and raised in the Americas and those drawn directly from Africa. During the same period, the terms "Creole" and "Negro" began to be used interchangeably in some Anglophone Caribbean territories as terms of reference for all regionally born non-whites who had an African ancestry to differentiate them from those arriving from Africa.[11] In most cases, the local Whites and Coloureds of all classes used the term "Negro" to distinguish the darker creole non-whites from lighter creole non-whites; the term "Negro" being used exclusively to refer to those with "pronounced African features" while the term "Coloured" was used to designate persons having a mixed ancestry or affluence.

Both "Negro" and "Coloured" have fallen into disuse in North Atlantic academic discourses largely owing to the impact and influence of the civil rights movements and the African-American demands for re-assessments of the usage of the terms, which they declared derogatory.[12] However, this changed attitude on the use of the abovementioned terms has had very little influence on the writing of Anglo-Caribbean history within the region as the region's socioracial and historical-linguistic dynamics were and remain markedly different from those of the North Atlantic.[13] Consequently, many Caribbean historians have continued to use both terms owing to their historical value. In his work on Barbados' free coloured population entitled *The Unappropriated People*, J.S. Handler used the term "Coloured" to refer to all persons of mixed ancestry.[14] Handler used the term interchangeably with "Freeman" which he used to refer to both free "Negroes" and "Free Coloureds" during slavery. Handler opted to use the term "Negro" throughout his work where it appeared in direct quotations from his source materials but also in other places when being used "in [socio-historical] context which makes it clear the term being used to refer to non-whites in general."[15] Handler correctly posited that the terms' usages and understandings differ in the West Indian-British and US academics and consequently authors of Caribbean history can use the terms within their appropriate historical setting.[16] The latter observation was made by Thome and Kimball when they visited Antigua in the late 1830s and pointed out that Antigua's racial terms must be understood in their own social spaces and to use them interchangeably "in accordance with the usage in the United States would have occasioned endless confusion in the narrative."[17] Writing about Jamaica's coloured population, Gad Heuman also used the term "Coloured" to refer to persons of mixed ancestry and like Handler adopted the term "Freeman" to refer to all free non-whites during the slave era in Jamaica because, as he stated, they were treated the same under the law.[18] However in Antigua the law made a legal distinction between "Free Coloureds" and "Free Negroes" and granted them different rights and freedoms with the greatest restrictions being placed on the unmixed freed men.[19] This factor affected marriage patterns among the freed non-whites as well as their allegiances, somatic norm image and possible group identities before and after emancipation. Other terms such as "black," "ex-slave" and "laboring population" or "laboring classes," which were generally used during the period to refer to the darker non-whites, while useful at times, are often too wide in their meaning and during the historical period under discussion included poor Coloureds.

Historians studying Antigua have continued to use both "Negro" and "Coloured," because in some cases they remain the most appropriate and unambiguous terms of reference for discussing some non-whites in the territory prior to the twentieth century. D. Hall in his *Five of the Leewards* used both terms in a number of places throughout his work. Hall used "Negro" as a reference term for the darker segment of the non-white population, which made up the bulk of the so-called "laboring population."[20] His use of the term demonstrated an acknowledgment of its historical usage, while implicitly acknowledging its limitations as the group to which he was referring also contained many persons of mixed ancestry. D.B. Gaspar also used the term "Negro" throughout his work to refer to the unmixed non-whites of African ancestry while the term "Coloured" was reserved for those of mixed European-African ancestry. Unlike many BWI territories, Antigua had a comparatively low rate of miscegenation in the pre-emancipation period and though there were distinctions within the groups based on ancestry these were generally unimportant, largely because, unlike Jamaica, there was no means of changing one's racial category except from "Negro" to "Coloured."[21]

M. Lazarus-Black stated, "not surprisingly Antiguans never developed a large brown middle-class or complex vocabulary of colors that was then used to legally distinguish the rights of persons of different hues" as was the case of other territories like Jamaica.[22] Lazarus-Black also pointed to the difficulty in removing the abovementioned terms from the island's historical writings and argued for their continued use where appropriate to the historical narrative because "colour categories were and remain 'real' and 'realised' for West Indians and students of their history and historically, they have marked social and legal possibility on the body."[23] The historical-anthropologist Susan Lowes has argued that past terms used for categorizing Antiguans must be used in their historical setting, because to do otherwise is to lose the original meanings of their users. Accordingly, she stated that many modern terms and their usages including "brown," "black" and "afro" created categories that were "fraught with difficulties" and in many cases proved to be inaccurate and imprecise.[24] One

Racial Identification in Antigua, 1660s–1860s 89

example of this is the term "Creole," which is often used by authors of Caribbean history to refer to anyone born in the New World. The historian Gad Heuman in his *Between Black and White* used the term to refer to persons born in the New World whether African or European descended or of pure or mixed ancestry.[25] While this categorization may be useful for Jamaica, which is doubtful, in the case of Antigua it is not only inappropriate but also misleading as the term "Creole" began to be used exclusively for the non-white population as early as 1702, and by the discussion period it was being used by colonists as a reference term for the darker section of the non-white population.[26]

During the slave era legal distinctions and differential rights and freedoms between "Free Negroes" and "Free Coloureds" helped to create a noticeable and determined cadre of free Coloureds whose main aim appeared to have been escape from their African ancestry through biological mixing and acculturation. Susan Lowes has pointed out that, unlike those in Jamaica, the Coloureds of Antigua tended to highlight their white ancestry as well as choosing marriage partners whose culture was definitively English or English creole and had openly rejected the art, philosophy, and culture of Africa.[27] The members of this group included a number of landed and slave-owning men and women who did not acknowledge kinship with other persons of mixed ancestry except those who were wealthy, educated, and looked closest to white.[28] After emancipation, with the law no longer able to determine the qualifications for coloured group membership, the aforementioned Coloureds became the voice of the "Coloured Community" and limited its membership to only a select few who met the aforementioned criteria. The vast majority of the mixed race cast-offs, uneducated and without wealth, were inevitably lumped with the blacks and became part of the "laboring population" while the wealthier Coloureds co-opted the title of "Coloured" for themselves.[29] Church-based histories and reports have encouraged and supported the idea that the entire coloured population were all members of the middle-class. This was especially the case in the Anglican and Methodist churches, whose coloured members were chiefly drawn from the well-to-do and better-educated Coloureds.

The use of the term "Negro" during the discussion period was complex as many whites and mixed race persons used it pejoratively to refer to darker complexioned non-whites alluding to their pronounced African features, while in other cases it was used to differentiate creolized blacks from those who had maintained a strong African cultural heritage as well as those arriving from Africa.[30] The term was also used in legislation and consequently designated certain categories of persons within their definitions, including the term "Free Negroes" which was used exclusively to refer to non-whites who had no-evident European ancestry or proof of such ancestry.[31] Perhaps more importantly enslaved Africans and African-descended persons were legally and socially termed and stigmatized "slaves" and consequently the "Free Negro" became a position to which slaves could aspire. The latter term thus became a socio-political identifier, which separated the free and therefore superior blacks from the enslaved blacks. The term "Negro" thus became part of Antigua's black population's socio-political and socio-economic lexicon, which largely explains its

90   N. Sesepkekiu

continued usage in the post-emancipation period by those wishing to cast themselves as fully creolized and distance themselves from their African past including their slave heritage.[32] In the post-emancipation period both Whites and upper-class Coloureds used the term interchangeably with "ex-slave," "freedman," "laborer," "laboring classes" and "blacks" to refer exclusively to the darker section of the non-white population as well as poorer Coloureds and those of questionable or distant coloured ancestry, whether they had been ex-slaves or ex-freed men.

In the larger territories, such as Jamaica, the coloured population was significantly varied in its phenotype and creole culture, and consequently that group was split into a number of identifiable sub-groups based on the abovementioned differences.[33] In Antigua, the coloured population was more phenotypically and culturally homogenous, in part owing to the territory's small size which facilitated greater communication and familiar and familial kinship ties.[34] During the era of slavery, the laws of Antigua recognized "Coloured" as a separate group of non-white "freed men" with European ancestry.[35] They were granted greater privileges than their darker counterparts including the right to vote once they had met the franchise qualification.[36] The Coloureds were socially divided into a number of groups based on their distance from their black or white ancestor and consequently the term "brown," which suggested an in-betweenness, became synonymous with them.[37] Prior to emancipation the Coloureds were divided into three main groups; the enslaved and poor, the "aspiring Coloureds," and the "accepted Coloureds."[38] After emancipation this three strata division was replaced by a new three strata hierarchy composed of the "working Coloureds," the "aspiring Coloureds" and the "accepted Coloureds."[39] It was the "aspiring Coloureds" along with a few from the latter who formed the "Coloured Community" in post-emancipation Antigua, which sought to exclude all but the rich, phenotypically white, and educated Coloureds from their membership in their attempt to gain greater political and social participation in the institutions dominated by the island's white colonial elite.[40]

While phenotype was a significant variable, which determined group membership within the "Coloured Community," class was an equally important variable, which allowed some darker-skinned Coloureds to gain membership, though informally, in the community.[41] A number of "aspiring Coloureds" had been significant property owners before emancipation, while others gained their lands through inheritance and purchase after emancipation. Raised within the elite colonial social circles and having been granted the same rights as many of the territory's affluent whites, a small number of "accepted Coloureds" opted to live their dual identities in the realm that brought them the most benefit and opt out of making alliances with the "aspiring Coloureds" with whom they generally had had no shared experiences, expectations or goals. Their cultural outlook and lack of challenge to the white elites with whom they felt themselves in partnership meant that a significant number of them have disappeared from the historical records, because they melded so well into the white colonial gentry. One of the more prominent of the "accepted Coloureds" of the discussion period was John Athill, the son of John Athill Snr. once the Speaker of the Assembly, whom

Racial Identification in Antigua, 1660s–1860s 91

many Coloureds accused of not supporting the causes of the "Coloured Community" and attempting to "emulate" his white counterparts.[42] Athill's case demonstrated some of the divisions among the Coloureds in Antigua and dispels the myth of a single and unified coloured group although the available historical sources often directs historians to focus on the aspiring Coloureds.

In Antigua, as in the rest of the empire, Britishness and subjecthood were inextricably linked to whiteness and British ancestry. The 1351 statute *De natis ultra mare* mandated that in order for hereditary subjecthood to be transferred the mother of the child had to be married to the English father,[43] which posed many problems for mixed persons in Antigua whose fathers were papist, not a subject of the realm or were not married to the mother.[44] An early Assembly act which prohibited sexual relations and marriages between the enslaved and freemen, implicitly meaning white men, further complicated the position of the offspring of such unions.[45] The Establishment's unwillingness to solemnize inter-racial unions and the Assembly's refusal to recognize dissenter marriages prior to emancipation limited the possibility of the passage of subjecthood through marriage, which left many *freed people*, coloured and black, in legal limbo with reference to their official status.[46] Despite this, by the early nineteenth century a small number of Coloureds were officially recognized as subjects, but these were members of powerful planter families such as the Athills and the Gilberts whose economic and political position in the society permitted them to be considered subjects with the same "rights" as those granted to the colony's unmixed British-descended population. Subjecthood was important for a number of reasons including gaining the ability to buy, sell, will, or inherit property, which in laws of the period could only be transferred from one subject to another.[47] Subjecthood was also a prerequisite for men who desired to become eligible to participate in the colony's elections and governance. Antigua's legislators appear to have been always mindful of the implications of granting subjecthood too freely and successfully limited and openly denied its conferral, along with its accompanying benefits, to the overwhelming majority of the island's population, both enslaved and free, until emancipation.

During the discussion period, the subject and the citizen were not considered to be the same. Indeed, a number of early modern English jurists even questioned the notion that all subjects could be citizens; citizenship was bound up with political freedom and access to the franchise, and therefore, had to be limited to a select group.[48] As a result of the abovementioned criteria "Britishness" and sometimes "Englishness" became the determining criteria for citizenship eligibility in some British colonies despite the voluntary participation of the Welsh, Scots and Irish in the colonial project.[49] Beginning as an English empire, the idea of Britishness became invariably linked with Anglo-Saxonism as the main prerequisite for political participation in governing the colonies.[50]

Religion was also a very important factor in determining one's eligibility to become a citizen despite the British government's guarantee that all its subjects would be allowed free practice of their Christian religions. Established as an English Colony, Antigua reflected the Protestantism of its founders and made laws to ensure that "papists" and other non-Establishment subjects did not gain

92   N. Sesepkekiu

citizenship. The later acts of union put a strain on Antigua's system especially when Scots and Irishmen began moving to the island in significant numbers during the 1700s. In response, the Assembly passed an act, which made it easier for Protestant aliens to gain subjecthood with the possibility of their children gaining citizenship once qualified, while openly prohibiting the entrance of "distinguished Papist," including English Catholics, who were all expelled from the territory in 1702.[51] The assembly also prohibited aliens, Jews and papists from holding of any high office including assemblyman or becoming freeholders.[52] In the middle of the century a new act renewed the strengthened clauses of 1702 by making it more difficult for Catholics and other non-conformists to participate in governance or hold public office.[53] As a result of these requirements, many aspiring Coloureds attempted to become full members of the Anglican Church, but most were rejected as this was seen as the planter's church. Consequently the overwhelming majority of Free Coloureds became members of the Methodist church, which granted them English credibility and some respectability among the laboring populations. The aspiring Coloureds then began a program to restrict black membership into what had become their church in order to maintain a non-black character as they could not yet declare a white character.

The concept of a "freeman" was also important to determining eligibility for citizenship. Discussing eligibility for citizenship, one English commentator explained that "freemen" should be "men of property, or persons able to live of themselves; and those who cannot subsist in this independence … [are] servants."[54] From its establishment Antigua's Assembly restricted the franchise and eligibility for high posts, elected and appointed, to Protestant freemen who were landed English subjects. As the slave society increased in numbers and miscegenation and manumission became more frequent the laws of Antigua recognized "Free Negroes" and "Free Coloureds" as separate categories of free people within the territory. Until 1834, all free non-whites were considered *freed men* who, owing to their slave ancestry, were not inalienably entitled to the same "rights" as the colony's free men.[55] Consequently, while many Coloureds, in part owing to their white heritage, were allowed to become freeholders with voting rights, this was incremental and granted only to those who had been sufficiently acculturated into the colonial gentry. The subject status of Free Negroes was deliberately left ambiguous until emancipation, which enabled the Assembly to legally prohibit them from ever becoming citizens by limiting the amount of land they could legally own. Moreover, all landless free non-whites were ordered to bind themselves to white families and work for them without pay until they were able to purchase their own land.[56] As a consequence, of the aforementioned legislation Antigua had very few validated subjects and even fewer citizens at emancipation. The overwhelming majority of the island's citizens were members of the small group of about 20 powerful families who owned the island's estates augmented by a few affluent Coloureds whose culture and allegiance seemed to cast them more with the white elites than their non-white brethren.

The evidence given to the Select Committee on the Commercial State of the West Indies largely reflected the sentiments of the anti-slavery segment of Antiguan free society. Henry Loving, a Free Coloured slave owner and editor of the *Weekly Register*, supported immediate emancipation.[57] Like Coloureds throughout the region, Loving may have opposed slavery largely because he understood that as long as it existed all Coloureds would continue to be equated with an assumed slave ancestry, no matter how distant, which would continue to disadvantage them in their struggles for greater socio-political acceptance and power.[58] The Free Coloureds periodically highlighted the plight of the enslaved as a means of promoting their own advancement but never lost sight of the place the majority of blacks were to occupy in a free society.[59] Loving's support for emancipation may have also had a more personal dimension, as he was an aspiring Coloured whose mother had been a slave, while he too had been a slave for the first nine years of his life; emancipation could eliminate the status hierarchy and close the social divide between Free Coloureds and Freed Coloureds.

In the five-year period following emancipation the Antiguan sugar industry had been hit by two severe droughts and a hurricane, and another soon arrived, allowing no time for recovery.[60] The disaster was devastating to the economy, as the damaged properties were out of commission for several months, during which production was considerably curtailed.[61] As a direct result, there was an exodus of planters with some selling off of lands in small plots, which encouraged greater land ownership among non-whites. Hitherto most of the failed or abandoned plantations were bought up by other planters or the Assembly, but owing to the poverty caused by the previous years of crisis, the planters were impotent to check the growth of a non-white land-owning class. A considerable portion of the land that became available was purchased by the aspiring Coloureds.[62] A greater amount of land was purchased by the already enfranchised Coloureds who were members of the colonial gentry and whose families had been slave and estate owners, and therefore did not challenge or meaningfully impact on the existent politico-economic hierarchy.[63] The pattern of land purchases by the affluent and accepted Coloureds also helps to explain why, despite their loss of the land monopoly and significant coloured land ownership, the number of electors failed to increase and the plantocracy maintained its political dominance and control for the rest of the period.

Although after August 1, 1834, race could no longer be a legal basis for discrimination within Antiguan society, the inextricable link between class, race, and color made the race-based legal restrictions easier to maintain without inciting reproach from the home government. This enabled the Assembly to frame and pass a series of laws designed to prevent a swamping of planter privileges by the non-white population. The pre-emancipation qualifications for the franchise were effective in restricting non-white and non-plantation interests' access to power especially during the first four years of freedom.[64] Indeed, very few persons, even among whites, were enfranchised, and in some districts the larger planters stood unopposed owing to their control of almost all the land in their voting district. In 1833, Governor MacGregor suggested that changes should be made to Antigua's laws to allow an expansion of the franchise in anticipation of the changes emancipation would bring.[65] The Assembly continually shelved the issue and muted all discussions raised on it for three years following the governor's suggestion. The situation came to a head in 1836, when a number of prominent Coloureds pressured MacGregor into action. He subsequently made enquiries into the reasons why more Coloureds had not been granted the franchise despite being qualified under the existent law.[66] A crisis ensued between the governor and Assembly, which had been brewing since his public insistence that food be provided for the laboring classes in the aftermath of the 1835 hurricane, which had embarrassed the Assemblymen into granting the requested aid.[67] The Assembly resisted all attempts by the governor to suggest amendments to the laws governing the franchise, which prompted MacGregor to suspend the body.[68] The governor found himself in a public conflict with the Assemblymen and when the Assembly was reconvened MacGregor was faced with political exile. The governor's queries and proposals had threatened to expose the planters' political and legal meanderings and possibly break their monopoly on voting and Assembly membership and consequently they were vehemently resisted. The crisis dragged on for months before the governor gave up the question, which was then almost immediately quieted except for the complaints and lamentations of the disenfranchised affluent Coloureds. Throughout the crisis, the governor received correspondences of support from the Coloured community in whose interests he seemed to be fighting. They also sent a number of unsuccessful petitions to the Assembly, the Council and the Colonial Office on his behalf. The Assembly could not reasonably and sensibly shift its position.

In late 1837, the issue was raised once again by the new governor Sir William Colebrooke who queried whether there was any existent legislation which prevented the legal registration of persons who had qualified for the franchise.[69] The governor had remained in doubt despite being assured that no such restrictive laws were in operation and qualifications were based on those established by an act of 1705.[70] The Leeward Island Assembly elections of 1837 soon demonstrated the exclusivity of the franchise with a total 323 electors and four districts having no polls.[71] In the aftermath of the elections, Colebrooke again raised the question.[72] In April 1838, Colebrooke was petitioned by a group of Coloured businessmen calling themselves the "Committee of Freeholders of Antigua" who claimed that there was a deliberate program of disenfranchisement carried on by the Assembly.[73] The Assembly responded by threatening to halt all government business and sent a letter of complaint to the governor over his handling of the issue and what they termed his "high-handed rulership."[74] Though silenced on the issue the governor remained convinced of the Assembly and Council's deliberate legal meanderings designed to limit non-white and non-plantation interests' participation in local elections.[75] Unfortunately, faced with a unified and determined Assembly the governor was impotent to effect the necessary changes in the registration of electors and it was left to individual persons to seek those entitlements.[76]

The continued clamoring and lobbying of the Coloured Community pushed the Assembly into making changes to the existent laws, but it was not the changes the Coloureds had worked for. In 1842, the Assembly passed a new act that significantly increased the property qualifications for the franchise.[77] The assembly raised the qualifying income and tax rate so high that all wealthy planters and estate managers qualified for the franchise. There was also a

Racial Identification in Antigua, 1660s–1860s 95

re-organization of the voting districts, which placed most of the island's registered voters in six voting districts including St. John's, Falmouth and English Harbor. The changes inaugurated by the act made it extremely difficult for all but the richest members of Antiguan society to become qualified as either candidates or voters, and dashed many of the affluent Coloured's hopes of gaining a significant voice in local politics. While there was no voters schedule showing the relative number of voters from each class or racial group, it is certain that only the most affluent Coloureds qualified to vote as the Coloured Community continued to argue for electoral reform after the passage of the 1842 act. The majority of the Coloured Community remained disenfranchised, while those who did qualify were resident in St. John, Falmouth and English Harbor, which reduced their ability to impact on the composition of the Assembly for the rest of the discussion period. However, by 1840 there was at least one coloured member of the Assembly. This might have been insignificant except for the fact that both coloured liberation and slave emancipation had occurred within a decade of his election to the Assembly. Additionally, it marked a new era of non-white participation in Antiguan politics and although there were no evident policy shifts within the Assembly, it was now faced with the prospect of more coloured members in the future and even a black member one day.

Prior to emancipation, the well-educated aspiring Coloured's incessant protests for equality became a major source of annoyance to the planter-class who saw them as attempting to rise above their natural station. However, after emancipation the categorization was extended to include some members of the formerly enslaved population who, according to one contemporary, had become pompous to the point of arguing with "their superiors" as if "they were learned councils in law."[78] However, contrary to this panicked characterization, the education of the black population produced persons who had learnt little beyond the ideas of subservience contained in their Christian education, which convinced most ex-slaves of the certainty that their subordinate position in the society was necessary for their progress in free society and part of a divine plan. On the other hand, the former affluent free coloured population became even more emboldened to challenge the colonial elite for a share of power.[79] The differing outcomes owed as much to the different starting points of both groups at emancipation, as well as the social realities of racism, shadism, classism, and ideas of belonging and privilege within the colony during the discussion period.

Prior to emancipation, education in the British West Indies was generally only available to the white population with most planters preferring private English tutors as they believed it would help in maintaining the "pure" accents of the home country.[80] A small number of slaves were sometimes taught to read by their masters, while an even smaller number were given education alongside whites at the same institutions.[81] However, the missionaries undertook the majority of the informal education carried on among the enslaved.[82] The Moravians are generally claimed to have been the first to have undertaken this task among Antigua's enslaved. Coming from German and Danish speaking areas of Europe, many settled permanently on the island and ministered among the slaves and freed blacks in an effort to convert them to Christianity. The Methodists, who arrived

96 *N. Sesepkekiu*

on the invitation of Nathaniel Gilbert, began missionary work among the slaves soon after arriving and claimed some 6,000 members by 1793.[83] The various missionaries did have some differences in their teachings, but the essence of what they taught was the same owing in part to a perceived limiting intelligence of the African-descended Negroes.[84]

Antigua's affair with "popular" education began with coloured Ann Hart Gilbert's school at English Harbor in 1809, which was quickly followed by others established by her brother-in-law and sister, Charles and Elizabeth Thwaites, also coloured, and the Moravian James Light. By the mid-1820s, the Church Missionary Society, under the influence of a cousin to the Gilberts named William Dawes, a colored man, was funding sixteen "schools" with 204 students, some of which took both free and enslaved children.[85] The more affluent Coloureds opened a number of their own schools, which reportedly catered exclusively to their group in an attempt to separate themselves from the darker population. However, monetary demands for school maintenance and teachers' wages permitted some affluent dark-skinned Coloureds to gain admission into the institutions. Coloured girls were thought more vulnerable owing to their perceived superior beauty over the blacks and their feminine fragility owing to their white blood. Owing to prevailing shadism, coloured girls often refused to work on plantations except as servants and as a result, many opted for what contemporary observers euphemistically labelled "concubinage."[86] In an effort to reform this group Ann Hart Gilbert, herself a Coloured, with the aid of the English Harbour Circle and the Methodists established the Female Refuge Society located at English Harbour and the Distressed Female Friend's Society at St. John's, to educate them and make them respectable wives for coloured gentlemen.[87] The students were admonished not to seek spouses from among the black laboring classes owing to their "brute mannerism" and "offensive beliefs" and prevent "miscegenation" between the brown and black "races" and classes.[88]

The school system was heavily influenced by the politics of class, race, and color nepotism and the aspiring Coloureds were fortunate to have had the support of many missionary and charitable groups. Indeed, while they were also involved in the churches they were not the sycophantic beadles characteristic of the black ministers.[89] A significant number were comparatively well educated and held positions of influence within the churches and their auxiliary institutions. From these pulpits, they were able to direct the churches' resources toward the development of their group including establishing and maintaining exclusive schools, as well as securing teaching positions for group members at church-administered schools. Consequently, coloured females were recruited as teachers at higher rates than blacks, partly because many were members of the middle-class families whose politico-economic networks and control of influential positions within the missionary churches gave them the ability to manipulate and influence teacher recruitment. Additionally, missionaries preferred to employ coloured females partly because they thought them more Christian and cultured than the blacks. One Moravian missionary explained the preference for coloured teachers lay in the perceived "debasing and stupefying influence of the ignorance, sloth and depravity of various kinds, too generally prevailing in Negro

Racial Identification in Antigua, 1660s–1860s 97

families" but if trained from young it "might be possible" to wrest the Negroes from their nature.[90]

The majority of graduates of Ann Hart Gilbert's schools, which had been established at St. John's and English Harbour prior to emancipation, were able to secure teaching posts because the schools' major benefactors included the coloured-dominated Christian Missionary Society, the English Harbour Circle, and the Methodist Church.[91] The majority of pre-emancipation schools catered almost exclusively to Free Coloureds, which helped to cement their position in post-emancipation Antigua as the more educated of the non-white population. A considerable number of blacks were also hired as teachers during the period, but the vast majority of these seemed to have been females who had gained their qualifications after emancipation and were generally hired as teacher's assistants rather than teachers. Locally sourced teachers' wages were comparable to those of the plantation laborers, but the prestige offered by the positions allowed teaching to be viewed more prestigiously. The overwhelming majority of affluent coloured men were not interested in the prospect of low remunerative occupations with very little prestige among their group and no obvious political value.[92] Despite coloured dominance, the increased demand for teachers provided a few social mobility options for some members of the "Negro" population. Despite the apparent social mobility away from plantation labor, the post-emancipation education system was not intended as a harbinger of social change and equality for either teacher or student.

Coloured progress in post-emancipation Antigua was partly a product of their strong group networks, as well as a system that was re-organized to facilitate and ensure their success.[93] In 1840, the Mico Charity declared an official policy of educating Antigua's coloured population "for all the pursuits of civilized life including commerce, or learned professions" to prepare them to "take their legitimate rank among the great family of man."[94] James Miller, a coloured man who was also the local agent for the Mico Training School and one of the authors of the above-written policy statement, was described by Br. J. Morrish as his being the most qualified individual on the island even when compared to Europeans.[95] He was a teacher as well as an administrator who consistently lobbied for greater coloured education and advancement. Miller also organized special classes for coloureds girls who wanted to qualify as teachers after which he frequently used influence to get them teaching jobs in the Mico Charity schools, as well as those of the Wesleyans and Moravians.[96] Members of the coloured community joined in this effort by giving financial support while others volunteered their time and skills, including individuals such as Sarah Brown, who taught sewing and dress making to lower middle-class coloured girls and boys until her death in 1835.[97] The coloured community was smaller and more tightly knit than the black community and this closeness was re-enforced by their perpetual in-betweenness that compelled them to band together for the elevation of the group. It might also be argued that because a significant number of them were comparatively well educated and formed what can be described as a middle-class they were more receptive to such ideas of unity and material and political progress which tends to be present in such classes. Their fight was not the same as the "Negroes," whom

98   N. Sesepkekiu

many of them continued to openly despise, but their progress was still part of the greater non-white challenge to white domination.[98]

It was said of the churches in Antigua that the whites were Anglicans, browns were Methodists, and blacks were Moravians. Up to the end of the discussion period, no non-whites had been ordained as priests, nor were there any non-white appointments to administrative posts within the Establishment. During the same period, a significant number of blacks and Coloureds were appointed ministers, sextons, and lower level administrators for both Moravians and Methodists. This situation may have been in part due to the greater bureaucracy and formalized structure within the Establishment, which made appointments more difficult than in dissenter churches. However, evidence given before a Royal Commission of Enquiry in 1897 indicated that the Establishment had continued an established policy of dissuading non-whites from entering the church as ordained priests. The Moravians and Methodists, as missionary stations, could more easily ordain someone to be a preacher and have it confirmed later by their headquarters, and consequently there was greater hope for progress within the missions and very little prospect within the Establishment.

For both the Methodists and Moravians the recruitment and appointment of black neophytes to supervisory positions made ex-slave conversion and compliance an easier task. The appointees were members of their congregants' communities and many had experienced the difficulties and disadvantages of poverty, racism, and slavery. Many in the black community saw their occupation as very prestigious, which encouraged others to follow, if not in their occupational steps, their behavior and practices. The Methodists also practiced a restrictive racial policy toward their non-white appointees, especially those who had become more qualified than their white counterparts and had applied for supervisory posts over them. The Methodists circumvented the problem of appearing discriminatory by posting qualified Coloureds to head new missions in other parts of the British West Indies and Africa.

In the early 1830s, just prior to emancipation, Antigua's affluent Coloureds had been one of the most politically disadvantaged and underrepresented in the region relative to their demographic size and wealth. Indeed, while the majority of Antigua's affluent Coloureds were fighting for voting privileges, St. Christopher (St. Kitts) had already had three coloured assemblymen prior to emancipation.[99] The passage of Antigua's emancipation act theoretically prohibited the use of racial categories as a means of denying "rights" and privileges to any group within the territory, though it was not until 1860 that it was codified.[100] This initiated a push by the affluent Coloureds to redefine themselves as a single group based on class, culture, and phenotypic characteristics as a means of increasing and improving their cultural criteria for privilege. As part of their program of group reinvention, the more affluent Coloureds began to recruit members through sponsorship programs, which provided school places, special mentoring, arranged marriages, and job opportunities for those Coloureds whose phenotypes exhibited the traits that demonstrated evidence of what Edward Long called "amended blood."[101] While class remained an important variable, color and shade were equally important entrance requirements for the membership in a

Racial Identification in Antigua, 1660s–1860s 99

group, whose then and aspiring positions were largely predicated on the inherent pigmentocratic nature of Antiguan society. As a direct consequence of the adoption of the aforementioned policies of classism, racism, and shadism some persons who had hitherto been legally categorized as "Coloured" were thenceforth relegated to the position of "blacks" and "Negroes" by the affluent Coloureds, although many still clung to their mixed heritage and refused to accept the labels. This rejected group re-emerged in the early twentieth century as the territory's coloured population after the large-scale flight of the island's recognized coloured community.

As a part of their program, the affluent coloureds limited their search for marriage partners to members of their new group and affluent whites. However, the group's numbers diminished significantly during the latter part of the nineteenth century owing to large-scale migration of coloured men, which limited prospective spouses available to remaining female members who preferred "racial" exclusivity to mixing with the black population.[102] During the discussion period, Antigua's coloured population remade itself into a smaller more clearly identifiable and exclusive community based on selected racial characteristics and wealth, which helped to make them more powerful during the first decade of freedom but also sowed the seeds of their eventual demise during the following century.

Recurrent economic crisis in the sugar industry led to a significant migration of white males to other colonies while the imposition of crown colony rule prompted a flight of significant numbers of well-to-do coloured men from the island in the late 1860s. According to S. Lowes, the overwhelming majority of the remaining female members of the coloured community refused to marry downward in terms of class and race. As a result, by the end of the century the female portion of the coloured community was, "a host of elderly never married women of modest means, without political or economic power, and socially isolated from those below and those above."[103] The initial successes gained by the women of the coloured community were comparatively more significant than those of their male counterparts when one considers the goals of each sex. Being members of the same group, their destinies were inextricably linked, and as the men fell and then left in great numbers it signaled the beginning of the fall of the exclusivist coloured women of Antigua.

Prior to August 1, 1834, the coloured community's discriminatory practices toward both free and enslaved blacks was seen by the blacks as confirmation of their support for slavery and black subjugation. In the post-emancipation period, the continued lack of Coloured interest or support for issues affecting black Antiguans further polarized both groups of non-whites into opposing camps, while both were attempting to effectively challenge an increasingly united white plantocracy. The lack of competent and effectual black leadership had left this task available to their lighter brethren for whom whiteness and its accompanying privileges was the ultimate aim. Hilary Beckles' characterized the British West Indian coloured populations as being in perpetual ambivalence vis-a-vis both slaves and planters and further described those of Barbados as "firmly proplanter."[104] This overly simplistic categorization failed to consider the variations within the political and economic environment of the various territories, within

100   N. Sesepkekiu

which each coloured group operated, as well as the changed aims of each group after emancipation. Antigua's aspiring Coloureds were decidedly publicly neutral as it offered the safest position amidst the reality of planter power and the uncertainty of black reaction. Far from being neutral, they favored and consistently sought alliances with the white population who continuously spurned their overtures. Their veneer of neutrality was also an attempt to mask their ambitions for a coloured-only progressive movement. They had drawn their lines of segregation and placed the blacks on the other side of the social divide.[105]

By contrast, in both Barbados and Dominica, the Coloureds were able to rally the black population behind them through well-orchestrated public acts and orations of racial solidarity. In societies in which there was what F. Fanon termed an epidermalization of inferiority in blackness and a concurrent elevation of whiteness, the Coloureds inevitably took the positions of guidance and leadership over the non-white group.[106] Sincere or not, in a great act of politicking the Coloured leadership publicly declared its intention to struggle for the expansion of the franchise to all non-white Barbadians.[107] It was a testament to Barbados' coloured community that MacGregor, having been continually thwarted in Antigua, was able to achieve much more in Barbados where he was able to appoint a significant number of aspiring Coloureds to a variety of high ranking civil and vestry positions between 1838–1839.[108] Whereas in other territories, Coloureds of all classes took up the causes of the blacks and propelled themselves by their action, leaving the blacks in a lulled ignorant contentment, Antigua's affluent Coloureds wore their disdain publicly to the ultimate detriment of their group's potential for greater progress. The few affluent Coloureds who argued the "Negro's" cause, such as Henry Loving, were a tolerated oddity among their group. It would not be until the early twentieth century that the island's not-so-affluent Coloureds took up the mantle of leadership and thereby charted a new course in the struggle for workers' rights.[109]

By the mid-1860s, Antigua's coloured community had gained much of the desired dream of attaining whiteness as understood in the colonial zeitgeist of the period. The population was distinct and had become part of the planter-class, their children were thoroughly English in speech, manners, dress and religion, and owing to their selective breeding, use of astringents and the impacts of the tropic sun on the white population, they had become phenotypically white. However, political power remained in the hands of the "true white" elites who were apt to remind the upstarts of the slave heritage, which was easy in such a small territory and where churches recorded racial ancestries. The passage of the Encumbered Estates Act signaled the beginning of the end of coloured political and economic ascendency within the territory. The act allowed British firms to replace the white planters as the economic brokers of the colony. The act was reflective of a deeper problem in the colony, the end of "king sugar." This fall of the traditional English Protestant planter class meant that the assembly would be filled by papists and non-whites, a condition that neither the British government nor the local white population were willing to accept. The Assemblymen, therefore, agreed to allow the adoption of the crown colony system in order to save the colony from what seemed an imminent takeover by undesirables.

Racial Identification in Antigua, 1660s–1860s 101

In response, there was a large exodus of affluent Coloureds to Canada, which was then seeking migrants. By the end of the 1870s, the overwhelming majority of the members the island's coloured community had left the island, leaving behind only a few hundred pseudo-affluent Coloureds who maintained their aloofness to the end. In his assessment of the decline of the Coloureds in Antigua, the Antiguan Historian Tim Hector poignantly stated that,

> Antigua and Barbuda is the only place in the world where a relatively prosperous Colored Class ... preferred to eliminate itself, chose to become extinct, when it numbered thousands, rather than align itself with Blacks here. They preferred to migrate to Canada. They preferred to remain childless. Colored spinsters were numerous. They preferred to in-breed. They preferred any and all of these courses rather than marry or mate reproductively with a black person, off whom they made their living. Not even the venal mulattoes of Haiti were so self-destructive in their race hatred.... A whole class of persons, the second largest class of persons, after Blacks, in Antigua and Barbuda, disappeared almost entirely due to what can only be termed hatred for Blacks.[110]

Discussing the impact of the flight of the coloured men in the 1860s, Susan Lowes stated that,

> by the 1860's entire branches of each [coloured] family had disappeared. Those members who remained were from the less prominent branches, were less wealthy and held far fewer appointed and elected positions.... Thus if family members had stayed and had children, and if those children in turn had stayed and had children their numbers would have increased geometrically. Yet the opposite was the case.[111]

Having attained their white status, the former Free Coloureds of Antigua refused to relinquish the hard-earned status and carried it with them to their graves. Their yearning to be white paid dividends for the majority of their members, but ultimately sowed the seeds of their self-destruction.

Notes

1 See F.S. Herskovits, ed., *The New World Negro: Selected Papers in Afro-American Studies* (Bloomington: Indiana University Press, 1966).
2 F.J. Davis, *Who is Black?: One Nation's Definition* (Philadelphia: Pennsylvania State University Press, 2001), 180–184.
3 D.V. Nicholson, *Africans to Antiguans: The Slavery Experience* (St. John's: Museum of Antigua and Barbuda, 2003).
4 Arnold A. Sio, "Marginality and Free Colored Identity in Caribbean Slave Society" in G. Heuman and J. Walvin, eds., *The Slavery Reader* (New York: Routledge, 2003), 668–670.
5 S. Lowes, "The Peculiar Class: The Formation, Collapse and Reformation of the Middle-Class in Antigua, West Indies, 1834–1940" (PhD diss. Columbia University, 1994), 14; D. Hall, *Five of the Leewards, 1834–1870* (St. Lawrence, Barbados: Caribbean University Press, 1971), 151.

102 *N. Sesepkekiu*

6 P. Henry, *Peripheral Capitalism and Underdevelopment in Antigua* (New Brunswick, NJ: Transaction Books, 1985), 184–186.

7 R.M. Martin, *History of the Colonies of the British Empire in the West Indies, South America, North America, Asia, Austral-Asia, Africa and Europe* (London: W.H. Allen, 1843), 81.

8 C. Allen, "Creole: The Problem of Definition," in V.A. Shepherd and G.L. Richards, eds., *Questioning Creole: Creolisation Discourses in Caribbean Culture* (Kingston: Ian Randle Publishers, 2002), 23; S.X. Goudie, *Creole America: The West Indies and the Formation of Literature and Culture in the New Republic* (Philadelphia: University of Pennsylvania Press, 2006), 7–10.

9 K. Braithwaite, *The Development of Creole Society in Jamaica* (Oxford: Clarendon Press, 1971), xv; K. Braithwaite, *Contradictory Omens: Cultural Diversity and Integration in the Caribbean* (Kingston: Savacou Publications, 1974), 11.

10 W.E. Moore, *American Negro Slavery and Abolition: A Sociological Study* (New York: Arno Press, 1980), 1–2; J.D. Forbes, *Black Africans and Native Americans: The Language of Race and the Evolution of Red-Black Peoples* (New York: Blackwell, 1988), 83–87.

11 R.B. Wells, *The Population of the British Colonies in America before 1776: A Survey of Census Data* (Princeton: Princeton University Press, 1975), 39.

12 B. Jacobs, *Race Manners: Navigating the Minefield Between Black and White in an Age of Fear* (New York: Arcade Publishing, 2006), 147; L.H. Fuchs, *American: Race, Ethnicity and the Civic Culture* (Middletown, CT: Wesleyan University Press, 1990), 182–183.

13 See B.W. Higman, *Slave Populations of the British Caribbean, 1807–1834* (Baltimore: Johns Hopkins University Press, 1984), 19–21.

14 J.S. Handler, *The Unappropriated People: Freedmen in the Slave Society of Barbados* (Baltimore: Johns Hopkins University Press, 1974), 5.

15 Ibid., 6, 68.

16 Ibid., 5.

17 J.A. Thome and J.H. Kimball, *Emancipation in the West Indies: A Six Months Tour in Antigua, Barbados and Jamaica in the Year 1837* (New York: Published by the American Anti-Slavery Society, 1839), xiv.

18 G. Heuman, *Between Black and White: Race, Politics and the Free Coloreds in Jamaica, 1792–1865* (Westport, CT: Greenwood Press, 1981), xix.

19 Clauses XXII–XXVI of *An Act for the better government of Slaves and Free Negroes* (June 28, 1702); CO 9/6 Assembly Minutes, January 4, 1728; E.V. Goveia, *Slave Society in the British Leeward Islands at the End of the Eighteenth Century* (Westport, CT: Greenwood Press, 1980), 218.

20 D. Hall, *Five of the Leewards, 1834–1870* (St. Lawrence, Barbados: Caribbean University Press, 1971), 34, 58, 153, 153–154, 163, 173, 180.

21 S. Lowes, "The Peculiar Class," 13–14; J.S. Handler, *The Unappropriated People*, 68–69; B. Edwards, *The History, Civil and Commercial, of the British Colonies in the West Indies*, Vol. 2 (London: Printed for John Stockdale, 1794), 217; See also E. Long, *The History of Jamaica*, Vol. II (London: Printed for T. Lownders, 1774) Book II, 320–321, 332; see also *Recopilacion de leyes de los reinos de las Indias, mandadas imprimir y publicar por la Magestad católica del rey don Carlos II. neustro señor* (Madrid: Boix, 1841), 10.

22 M. Lazarus-Black, *Legitimate Acts and Illegal Encounters: Law and Society in Antigua and Barbuda* (Washington, DC: Smithsonian Institute, 1994), 99.

23 Ibid., xxiii.

24 S. Lowes, "They Couldn't Mash Ants: The Decline of the White and Non-White Elites in Antigua, West Indies, 1834–1900," in K.F. Olwig, ed., *Small Islands, Large Questions: Society, Culture and Resistance in the Post-Emancipation Caribbean* (London: Frank Cass, 1995), 3.

25 G. Heuman, *Between Black and White: Race, Politics and the Free Coloreds in Jamaica, 1792–1865* (Westport, CT: Greenwood Press, 1981).

Racial Identification in Antigua, 1660s–1860s   103

26 Clause XIV of *An Act for further encouraging the settlement of this Island catego-rized the islands population as being composed of English, Scots, Irish and Cariole (Creole) subjects*; Mrs. Lanaghan, *Antigua and the Antiguans: A Full Account of the Colony and its Inhabitants From the Time of the Caribs to Present*, Vol. 1 (London: Saunders and Ottley, 1844), footnotes on pages 188 and 200.

27 S. Lowes, "Time and Motion in the Formation of the Middle Class in Antigua 1834–1944," Paper presented to the American Anthropological Association, Chicago, November 1987.

28 V.L. Oliver, *The History of Antigua*, Vol. 1 (London: Mitchell and Hughes, 1894), clii and Vol. 3, 305–318, 355–390.

29 Mrs. Lanaghan, *Antigua and the Antiguans*, Vol. 1, 92, 164–167, 180–182, 200; J.A. Thome and J.H. Kimball, *Emancipation in the West Indies*, 37–38.

30 N.I. Painter, *Creating Black Americans: African American History and Its Meaning, 1619 to the Present* (New York: Oxford University Press, 2006), 54.

31 Clauses XXII–XXVI of *An Act for the better government of Slaves and Free Negroes* (Antigua, June 28, 1702).

32 Mrs. Lanaghan, *Antigua and the Antiguans*, Vol. 1, 47–48, 50, 147.

33 J.D. Forbes, *Black Africans and Native Americans: The Language of Race and the Evolution of Red-Black Peoples* (New York: Blackwell, 1988), 233.

34 *Select Committee on Extinction of Slavery in British Dominions, Report, Minutes of Evidence, Appendix, Index* (1831–1832). P.P. (721) Vol. XX.1, 159.

35 Clause II of *An Act for establishing a Registry of Slaves in the Island of Antigua* (Antigua, March 18, 1817).

36 CO 9/6 Assembly Minutes (Antigua), January 4, 1728

37 S. Lowes, "The Peculiar Class," 13; Mrs. Flannigan, *Antigua and the Antiguans*, Vol. 1, 165.

38 D. Hall, *Five of the Leewards, 1834–1870*, 153.

39 Mrs. Lanaghan, *Antigua and the Antiguans*, Vol. 2, 170, 182; J. Sturge, and T. Harvey, *The West Indies in 1837: Being the journal of a visit to Antigua, Montserrat, Dominica, St. Lucia, Barbados, and Jamaica; Undertaken for the purpose of ascertaining the actual condition of the Negro population of those islands* (London: Hamilton, Adams and Company, 1838), 9.

40 Arnold A. Sio has questioned the traditional perspective that the free coloureds in pre-emancipation societies "emulated" the white elite. Citing the lack of sources on the poorer non-whites, Sio argued that it was incorrect to use the images of the well-to-do coloureds as representative of the entire group. It is telling from Sio's work that there is some agreement that the affluent free coloureds did seek to "emulate" the white colonial elite in an attempt to gain greater privileges and freedoms as those granted to those considered to be their racial and cultural superiors [A.A. Sio, "Marginality and Free Colored Identity" 668–670.]. Antigua's post-emancipation "coloured community" reportedly mimicked all the cultural norms of the white elites while disassociating themselves from the poorer and darker members of the society and their "racial group." Mrs. Lanaghan explained that "the smart people (affluent coloreds) I have been describing imitate in everything their fairer brethren, they are ironically termed black buckras" [Mrs. Lanaghan, *Antigua and the Antiguans*, Vol. 2, 121, footnote]. The reported actions of Antigua's post-emancipation "coloured community" has led historians of Antigua to consistently cast them as "emulators" of the elite whites. D. Hall, using the term "aspiring coloureds" to identify the aforementioned group, stated that when "a black or colored man did in some measure succeed he tended to identify himself with whites rather than people of his own colour" [D. Hall, *Five of the Leewards, 1834–1870*, 151.]. Moreover B. Dyde noted that "most [Coloureds] wanted nothing better than to be accepted by the whites as partners in a system ordered in such a way as to keep the black population just where it was" [B. Dyde, *A History of Antigua: The Unsuspected Isle* (London: Macmillan Education Ltd., 2000), 187.]. Perhaps more importantly many contemporary

104 *N. Sesepkekiu*

observers, both white and coloured, described the behavior of the elite coloureds as a form of mimicry of the culture of the group into which they were seeking access [See for example CO 7/37 MacGregor to Stanley, November 2, 1833].

41 See for example C.O. 7/44 Light to Glenelg, November 18, 1836.

42 D. Hall, *Five of the Leewards, 1834–1870*, 151–152.

43 Re-affirmed by Act of 4 Geo. III c. 21, sec 1(1731).

44 See Clauses II–V of *An Act for establishing a Register's Office, and the several Fees that belong thereunto* (Antigua, April 13th 1668); Clauses II–XI of *An Act for establishing and confirming of Inhabitants of this island in their Title to their Lands* (Antigua, January 9, 1676); Clause XIII of *An Act for the better Regulation and Settlement of the Register's Office* (Antigua, November 3, 1698); S.F.C. Milson, *Historical Foundations of the Common Law*, 2nd ed. (Toronto: Butterworths, 1981), 124–134; K. Kim, *Aliens in Medieval Law: The Origins of Modern Citizenship* (Cambridge: Cambridge University Press, 2000), 110; R. Burn, *Ecclesiastical Law* (London: S. Sweet, V. & R. Stevens & G.S. Norton, 1842), 158–159.

45 D.B. Gaspar, *Bondsmen and Rebels: A Study of Master-Slave Relations in Antigua* (Durham, NC: Duke University Press, 1993), 167.

46 *An Act for compelling the reputed Fathers of illegitimate White Children to make Competent Provision for them; and secure and indemnify the Parishes of this Island from being chargeable with them* (Antigua, Act No. 439 of 1786).

47 Clauses II–XII of *An Act for establishing and confirming of Inhabitants of this island in their Title to their Lands* (Antigua, January 9, 1676); Clause XIX of *An Act for the better regulation and Settlement of the Register's Office* (Antigua, November 3, 1698).

48 D. Heater, *A Brief History of Citizenship* (Edinburgh: Edinburgh University Press, 2004), 59, 67.

49 D. Judd, *Empire: The British Imperial Experience from 1765 to the Present* (London: HarperCollins, 1996), 3.

50 P.B. Rich, *Race and Empire in British Politics* (Cambridge: Cambridge University Press, 1986), 13–14; C. Bridge and K. Fedorowich, eds., *British World: Diaspora, Culture and Identity* (London: Frank Cass Press, 2003), 3.

51 Clause X of *An Act for further encouraging the settlement of this Island* (Antigua, June 28, 1702); *An Act for confirming Foreigners inhabiting in this Island, in their Estates, to them and their Heirs forever* (Antigua, Act No. 60 of 1681); Clauses III–XIV of *An Act for further encouraging the settlement of this Island* (Antigua, June 28, 1702); *An Act to Prevent Papist and reputed Papist from settling in any of His Majesty's Caribbee Leeward Islands in America* (Act No. 22 of 1701).

52 See for example *An Act against Jews ingrossing Commodities imported in the Leeward Islands and trading with Slaves belonging to the Same* (Antigua, August 31, 1694); *An Act to repeale a certain Act against the Jews* (Antigua, December 10, 1701; Act 30 of 1702).

53 *An Act to prevent the Increase of Papist and Nonjurers in this Island, and for better governing those who are already settled here* (Antigua, Act No. 148 of 1715).

54 H.T. Dickinson, *Liberty and Property: Political Ideology in Eighteenth-Century Britain* (London: Mathuen, 1979), 89.

55 See B.C. Howard, *Report of the decision of the Supreme Court of the United States, and the Opinions of the Judges thereof in the case of Dred Scott versus John F.A. Sandford* (Washington D.C.: Cornelius Wendell, 1857), 84–85; G. Crabb, *A History of English Law* (London: Baldwin and Cradock, 1829), 8; for a discussion on Barbados see J.S. Handler, *The Unappropriated People*, 70.].

56 Clause XXII of *An Act for the Better Government of Slaves and Free Negroes*.

57 Claimant No. 661b in *Return on Sums Awarded by Commission of Slave Compensation 1837–38*, 82–86.

58 A.O. Thompson, *The Haunting Past: Politics, Economics and Race in Caribbean Life* (London: M.E. Sharpe, 1997), 225–227.

Racial Identification in Antigua, 1660s–1860s   105

59 D. Hall, *Five of the Leewards, 1834–1870*, 153.
60 *Periodical Accounts* (Vol. IV), p. 445; WMMS/WIC-A 1833–1845 Bates to General Secretary, August 14, 1837.
61 CO 7/47 Colebrooke to Glenelg, June 13, 1837.
62 See CO/Indentures 1834–1839.
63 V.L. Oliver, *The History of Antigua*, Vol. 1, 355–380.
64 CO 7/51 Colebrooke to Glenelg, August 17, 1838.
65 ROE 373 Circular Memorandum, June 13, 1833.
66 CO 7/43 MacGregor to Glenelg, July 4, 1836.
67 CO 7/43 *Antigua Herald and Gazette*, August 13, 1836; CO 7/43 *Weekly Register*, August 9, 1836.
68 CO 7/43 *Antigua Herald and Gazette*, August 13, 1836.
69 CO 7/48 Colebrooke to Council (Antigua), October 10, 1837.
70 CO 7/48 McCleod to Colebrooke, October 6, 1837.
71 CO 7/48 Colebrooke to Glenelg, December 21, 1837.
72 CO 7/50 Colebrooke to Glenelg, January 20, 1838.
73 CO 7/50 Colebrooke to Glenelg, April 3, 1838.
74 *Select Committee Report on the Colonies* (1840). P.P. Vol. XXXIV, 513.
75 CO 7/52 Colebrooke to Glenelg, August 17, 1838.
76 C.O. 28/172 Colebrooke to Grey (Enclosure 16), March 27, 1850.
77 *Reports to Secretary of State on Past and Present State of H.M. Colonial Possessions, 1863* (1864: Part I and II), 6.
78 *Periodical Accounts* (Vol. XVII), 337.
79 D.U. Farquhar, *Missions and Society in the Leeward Islands, 1810–1850: An Ecclesiastical and Social History* (Newton, MA: Mt. Prospect Press, 1999), 148.
80 H. Coleridge, *Six Months in the West Indies* (London: L.J. Murray, 1825), 241.
81 D.B. Gaspar, *Bondsmen and Rebels: A Study of Master-Slave Relations in Antigua*, 44; I. Berlin and P.D. Morgan, eds., *Cultivation and Culture: Labor and the Shaping of Slave Life in the Americas* (Charlottesville: University of Virginia Press, 1993), 19; O.M. Blouet, "Slavery and Freedom in the British West Indies, 1823–1833; The Role of Education," *History of Education Quarterly* (Special Issue on the History of Literacy), Vol. 30, No. 4 (Winter, 1990), 603.
82 *Report of the Select Committee on the Extinction of Slavery Throughout the British Dominions: Report, Minutes of Evidence, Appendix and Index*. P.P. Vol. XX.1 No. 721, 583.
83 J. Latimer, "An Historical and Comparative Study of the Foundations of Education in British, Spanish and French West Indies" (PhD Thesis, University of London, 1952), 21–22.
84 H. Fergus, *A History of Education in the British Leeward Islands, 1838–1945* (Mona: University of the West Indies Press, 2003), 21.
85 D.U. Farquhar, *Missions and Society in the Leeward Islands, 1810–1850*, 104.
86 W.A. Green, *British Slave Emancipation: The Sugar Colonies and the Great Experiment* (Oxford: Oxford University Press, 1991), 20; J. Sharpe, *Ghosts of Slavery: A Literary Archaeology of Black Women's Lives* (Minneapolis: University of Minnesota Press, 2003), 60–63.
87 CMS Dawes to the Secretaries of Church Missionary Society, May 11, 1825.
88 S. Lowes, "The Peculiar Class," 413–414; P. Henry, *Peripheral Capitalism and Underdevelopment in Antigua* (New Brunswick: Transaction Books, 1985), 66.
89 WMMS/WIC-A 1833–1845 Beecham to Cox, November 29, 1844.
90 *Periodical Accounts* (Vol. XVII), 358–350.
91 Rev. L. Tyerman, *The life and times of the Rev. John Wesley, M.A., founder of the Methodists* (New York: Harper and Brothers Publishers, 1872), 298–299; S. Méndez Méndez and G.A. Cueto, *Notable Caribbeans and Caribbean Americans: A Biographical Dictionary*, 198–199.
92 RH-MC/SR Out Letters: Mico Institution and School of Industry, May 4, 1836.

106   *N. Sesepkekiu*

93 D.U. Farquhar, *Missions and Society in the Leeward Islands, 1810–1850*, 29–30.
94 RH-MC/SR Secretaries to Trustees 1840.
95 *Periodical Accounts relating to the missions of the Church of the United Brethren established among the heathen* (Vol. XIV), 393.
96 Ibid., 107.
97 Ibid., 75–76.
98 RH-MC/SR Out Letters, May 4, 1836.
99 E.L. Cox, *Free Colored in the Slave Societies of St. Kitts and Grenada, 1763–1833* (Knoxville: University of Tennessee Press, 1984), 108.
100 Clause LVI of An Act for the Further Amendment of the Law and the Better Advancement of Justice (Antigua, October 26, 1860).
101 E. Long, *The History of Jamaica*, Vol. II (London: Printed for T. Lownders, 1774) Book II, 332.
102 Tim Hector, "The Black Condition, Here and Now" in *The Outlet* (Antigua), February 8, 2002.
103 S. Lowes, "They Couldn't Mash Ants," 44.
104 H. Beckles, "On the Backs of Blacks: The Barbados Free-Coloreds, Pursuit of Civil Rights and the 1816 Slave Rebellion" quoted in M.J. Newton, *The Children of Africa in the Colonies: Free People of Colour in Barbados in the Age of Emancipation* (Baton Rouge: Louisiana State University Press, 2008), 70.
105 R.E. Crist, "Changing Cultural Landscapes in Antigua, BWI," *American Journal of Economics and Sociology*, Vol. 13, No. 3 (April, 1954), 231.
106 F. Fanon, *Black Skin, White Mask* (New York: Groves Press, 2008), xi.
107 *The Liberal* (Barbados), December 1, 1838.
108 M.J. Newton, *The Children of Africa in the Colonies: Free People of Colour in Barbados in the Age of Emancipation*, 185–187.
109 G. Richards, "Race, Labor and Politics in Jamaica and St. Kitts, 1909–1940" in V.A. Shepherd, ed., *Working Slavery, Pricing Freedom: Perspectives from the Caribbean, Africa and the African Diaspora* (Kingston: Ian Randle Publishers, 2002), 502–520.
110 Tim Hector, "The Black Condition, Here and Now."
111 S. Lowes, "They Couldn't Mash Ants," 43.

References

Allen, C. "Creole Then and Now: The Problem of Definition," in *Caribbean Quarterly* Vol. 44 (March–June, 1998), 33–49.
Berlin, I. and P.D. Morgan, eds. *Cultivation and Culture: Labor and the Shaping of Slave Life in the Americas*. Charlottesville: University of Virginia Press, 1993.
Blouet, O.M. "Slavery and Freedom in the British West Indies, 1823–1833: The Role of Education," *History of Education Quarterly* (Special Issue on the History of Literacy), 30, No. 4 (Winter, 1990), 625–643.
Braithwaite, K. *The Development of Creole Society in Jamaica*. Oxford: Clarendon Press, 1971.
Braithwaite, K. *Contradictory Omens: Cultural Diversity and Integration in the Caribbean*. Kingston: Savacou Publications, 1974.
Bridge, C. and K. Fedorowich, eds. *British World: Diaspora, Culture and Identity*. London: Frank Cass Press, 2003.
Burn, R. *Ecclesiastical Law*. London: S. Sweet, V. & R. Stevens & G.S. Norton, 1842.
Coleridge, H. *Six Months in the West Indies*. London: L.J. Murray, 1825.
Cox, E.L. *Free Colored in the Slave Societies of St. Kitts and Grenada, 1763–1833*. Knoxville: University of Tennessee Press, 1984.
Crabb, G. *A History of English Law*. London: Baldwin and Cradock, 1829.

Crist, R.E. "Changing Cultural Landscapes in Antigua, BWI," *American Journal of Economics and Sociology*, 13, No. 3 (April, 1954): 225–232.

Davis, F.J. *Who is Black?: One Nation's Definition*. State College, PA: Pennsylvania State University Press, 2001.

Dickinson, H.T. *Liberty and Property: Political Ideology in Eighteenth-Century Britain*. London: Mathuen, 1979.

Dyde, B. *A History of Antigua: The Unsuspected Isle*. London: Macmillan Education Ltd., 2000.

Edwards, B. *The History, Civil and Commercial, of the British Colonies in the West Indies*, Vol. 2. London: Printed for John Stockdale, 1794.

Fanon, F. *Black Skin, White Mask*. New York: Groves Press, 2008.

Farquhar, D.U. *Missions and Society in the Leeward Islands, 1810–1850: An Ecclesiastical and Social History*. Newton, MA: Mt. Prospect Press, 1999.

Fergus, H. *A History of Education in the British Leeward Islands, 1838–1945*. Mona: University of the West Indies Press, 2003.

Forbes, J.D. *Black Africans and Native Americans: The Language of Race and the Evolution of Red-Black Peoples*. New York: Blackwell, 1988.

Fuchs, L.H. *American: Race, Ethnicity and the Civic Culture*. Middletown, CT: Wesleyan University Press, 1990.

Gaspar, D.B. *Bondsmen and Rebels: A Study of Master-Slave Relations in Antigua*. Durham, NC: Duke University Press, 1993.

Goudie, S.X. *Creole America: The West Indies and the Formation of Literature and Culture in the New Republic*. Philadelphia: University of Pennsylvania Press, 2006.

Goveia, E.V. *Slave Society in the British Leeward Islands at the End of the Eighteenth Century*. Westport, CT: Greenwood Press, 1980.

Green, W.A. *British Slave Emancipation: The Sugar Colonies and the Great Experiment*. Oxford: Oxford University Press, 1991.

Hall, D. *Five of the Leewards, 1834–1870*. St. Lawrence, Barbados: Caribbean University Press, 1971.

Handler, J.S. *The Unappropriated People: Freedmen in the Slave Society of Barbados*. Baltimore: Johns Hopkins University Press, 1974.

Heater, D. *A Brief History of Citizenship*. Edinburgh: Edinburgh University Press, 2004.

Henry, P. *Peripheral Capitalism and Underdevelopment in Antigua*. New Brunswick, NJ: Transaction Books, 1985.

Herskovits, F.S. ed. *The New World Negro: Selected Papers in Afro-American Studies*. Bloomington: Indiana University Press, 1966.

Heuman, G. *Between Black and White: Race, Politics and the Free Coloreds in Jamaica, 1792–1865*. Westport, CT: Greenwood Press, 1981.

Heuman, G. and J. Walvin, eds. *The Slavery Reader*. New York: Routledge, 2003.

Higman, B.W. *Slave Populations of the British Caribbean, 1807–1834*. Baltimore: Johns Hopkins University Press, 1984.

Howard, B.C. *Report of the decision of the Supreme Court of the United States, and the Opinions of the Judges thereof in the case of Dred Scott versus John F.A. Sandford*. Washington DC: Cornelius Wendell, 1857.

Jacobs, B. *Race Manners: Navigating the Minefield Between Black and White in an Age of Fear*. New York: Arcade Publishing, 2006.

Judd, D. *Empire: The British Imperial Experience from 1765 to the Present*. London: HarperCollins Publishers, 1996.

Kim, K. *Aliens in Medieval Law: The Origins of Modern Citizenship*. Cambridge: Cambridge University Press, 2000.

108   N. Sesepkekiu

Latimer, J. "An Historical and Comparative Study of the Foundations of Education in British, Spanish and French West Indies." PhD diss., University of London, 1952.

Lazarus-Black, M. *Legitimate Acts and Illegal Encounters: Law and Society in Antigua and Barbuda*. Washington DC: Smithsonian Institute, 1994.

Long, E. *The History of Jamaica*, 2 Vols. London: Printed for T. Lownders, 1774.

Lowes, S. "The Peculiar Class: The Formation, Collapse and Reformation of the Middle-Class in Antigua, West Indies, 1834–1940." PhD diss., Columbia University, 1994.

Lowes, S. "Time and Motion in the Formation of the 'Middle Class' in Antigua 1834–1940," Paper presented to the American Anthropological Association, Chicago, November 1987.

Martin, R.M. *History of the Colonies of the British Empire in the West Indies, South America, North America, Asia, Austral-Asia, Africa and Europe*. London: W.H. Allen, 1843.

Méndez, S. and G.A. Cueto. *Notable Caribbeans and Caribbean Americans: A Biographical Dictionary*. Westport, CT: Greenwood Press, 2001.

Milson, S.F.C. *Historical Foundations of the Common Law*, 2nd edn., Toronto: Butterworths, 1981.

Moore, W.E. *American Negro Slavery and Abolition: A Sociological Study*. New York: Arno Press, 1980.

Mrs. Lanaghan, *Antigua and the Antiguans: A Full Account of the Colony and its Inhabitants From the Time of the Caribs to Present*, Vol. 1. London: Saunders and Ottley, 1844.

Newton, M.J. *The Children of Africa in the Colonies: Free People of Colour in Barbados in the Age of Emancipation*. Baton Rouge: Louisiana State University Press, 2008.

Nicholson, D.V. *Africans to Antiguans: The Slavery Experience*. St. John's: Museum of Antigua and Barbuda, 2003.

Oliver, V.L. *The History of Antigua*, Vol. 3. London: Mitchell and Hughes, 1894.

Olwig, K.F. ed. *Small Islands, Large Questions: Society, Culture and Resistance in the Post-Emancipation Caribbean*. London: Frank Cass, 1995.

Painter, N.I. *Creating Black Americans: African American History and Its Meaning, 1619 to the Present*. New York: Oxford University Press, 2006.

Recopilacion de leyes de los reinos de las Indias, mandadasimprimir y publicarpor la Magestadcatólicadelrey don Carlos II. neustroseñor. Madrid: Boix, 1841.

Rich, P.B. *Race and Empire in British Politics*. Cambridge: Cambridge University Press, 1986.

Sharpe, J. *Ghosts of Slavery: A Literary Archaeology of Black Women's Lives*. Minneapolis: University of Minnesota Press, 2003.

Shepherd, V.A. ed. *Working Slavery, Pricing Freedom: Perspectives from the Caribbean, Africa and the African Diaspora*. Kingston: Ian Randle Publishers, 2002.

Sturge, J. and T. Harvey. *The West Indies in 1837: Being the journal of a visit to Antigua, Montserrat, Dominica, St. Lucia, Barbados, and Jamaica; Undertaken for the purpose of ascertaining the actual condition of the Negro population of those islands*. London: Hamilton, Adams and Company, 1838.

Thome, J.A., and J.H. Kimball. *Emancipation in the West Indies: A Six Months Tour in Antigua, Barbados and Jamaica in the Year 1837*. New York: Published by the American Anti-Slavery Society, 1839.

Thompson, A.O. *The Haunting Past: Politics, Economics and Race in Caribbean Life*. London: M.E. Sharpe, 1997.

Tyerman, Rev. L. *The Life and Times of the Rev. John Wesley, M.A., founder of the Methodists*. New York: Harper and Brothers Publishers, 1872.

Wells, R.B. *The Population of the British Colonies in America before 1776: A Survey of Census Data*. Princeton: Princeton University Press, 1975.

6 *The African Drum, Bantu World* and South Africa–United States Transnational Linkages, 1949–1954

Derek Charles Catsam

Transnational Inklings

The period from 1949 to 1954 marks the true break point in the histories of race relations in both South Africa and the United States. In South Africa, the National Party was able to rise to power and quickly consolidate its rule through the rapid implementation of apartheid laws. The legal system would be the key factor in the United States as well, as individuals, groups, and the NAACP and its Legal Defense Fund used the court system to attack "separate but equal." By 1955, the futures in both countries appeared to be taking dramatically different shape, although no outcome was inevitable.

It was also during this time-period that activists and interested observers in each country began paying more attention to what was going on in the other. Black Americans and their white allies in the fight against Jim Crow took notice of the onset of apartheid and especially of the Defiance Campaign. Black South Africans continued their interest in American and especially black American popular culture. True transnational engagement would still be for the future, but the first step was this wave of increased transnational interest.

In the early 1950s, Americans interested in human rights were beginning to look beyond America's borders. The American athlete, entertainer, lawyer, and activist Paul Robeson had become a preeminent spokesman for a human-rights driven international vision. But Robeson, like many human rights activists, was too tainted by his attraction to Communism even for organizations like the NAACP, which roundly condemned his ties to the Soviet Union and to Communist organizations in the United States.[1] Robeson's dilemma was also one that fractured the civil rights struggle that was emerging in the United States. On the one hand, those on the left, including Communists and socialists, were among its most vocal and able potential allies. On the other, the increasingly shrill tenor of anti-Communism that was becoming dominant in the United States meant that mainstream civil rights organizations were forced to make a Hobson's choice—either shun these potential allies (or at least keep them hidden) or else run the risk of being tainted with Communism and thus being rendered ineffective. Anti-Communism therefore counted among its victims a more ardent internationalist campaign against white supremacy.

Nonetheless, when the National Party rose to power black Americans took notice and condemned the deluge of legislation creating the apartheid state.

110   D. C. Catsam

Early on, the NAACP condemned World Bank loans to South Africa and called for greater internationalism in the fight against colonialism. But the organization ultimately became more inward-looking, focusing on America's domestic problems rather than on global issues.[2] The NAACP's withdrawal thus represents a road not taken for the country's largest civil rights organization and as a result for a more international struggle against white supremacy.

The Defiance Campaign marked the first large-scale American engagement with South African affairs. Walter Sisulu, the secretary general of the African National Congress (ANC) and one of the vital members of the generation that had forced the ANC to take a more aggressive approach to the country's racial and political crisis, put out a call for international support of the Defiance Campaign. Robeson, W. E. B. DuBois, and others responded through their work on the Council on African Affairs (CAA), though that organization had been weakened as a result of Robeson's and DuBois' battering at the hands of the anti-Communists. The CAA had been engaged in South African affairs since the mid-1940s when its advocacy for South Africans included campaigning for famine relief, supporting the African Mineworkers Union Strikes of 1946, and lobbying to the United Nations about that country's precarious political situation. The CAA did what it could in response to the Defiance Campaign, raising money and holding rallies, but in the words of historian Penny von Eschen, "these efforts took place on the sidelines, for domestic anti-Communism had cast a pall on the burgeoning post-war urban civil rights movement," especially for those organizations with demonstrable or plausible ties to communists.[3] The grim irony is that the CAA had managed to strengthen ties with the ANC in ways that might have indicated a blossoming of relations in the years to come. CAA leaders had engaged in correspondence with a range of ANC figures, including Sisulu, Z. K. Matthews, Oliver Tambo, and R. T. Bokwe. Sisulu in particular cherished his ties with the Americans.[4] The CAA represents the ultimate example of roads not taken due to the crude and imprecise bludgeoning weapon that was anticommunism.

Another organization also responded to Sisulu's call for greater international engagement. Americans for South African Resistance (AFSAR), which emerged to support the ANC's Defiance Campaign, tried to thread the leftist needle. Organized by radicals and liberals who were "wary of the Communist Party for its Soviet ties" the organization nonetheless believed firmly in "direct action based on anticolonial convictions."[5] AFSAR had ties to the Congress of Racial Equality, the Fellowship of Reconciliation, and the Socialist Party and, along with the CAA, it organized meetings and demonstrations supporting the ANC and raised money for the South African cause. In the words of historian Brenda Gayle Plummer, "a roster of persons associated with [AFSCAR] cross-indexes the civil rights, civil liberties, and social welfare movements."[6] Among these names are Roger Baldwin, Dorothy Day, Clarence Senior, Bayard Rustin, James Farmer, Canada Lee, and Adam Clayton Powell, as well as the founders, Reverend Donald Harrington of Community Church, George Houser, a Methodist minister and Fellowship of Reconciliation stalwart, and Reverend Charles Y.

South Africa–United States Linkages, 1949–1954   111

Trigg of Harlem's Salem Methodist Church, all of whom themselves had fingers in other human rights pies.

The American Committee on Africa (ACOA) was a third organization that forged transnational ties with South Africans and grew out of AFSAR. Formed in 1953 by AFSAR co-founder George Houser ACOA would become the preeminent organization linking Americans with African struggles.[7] ACOA was formed in part as a response to the Defiance Campaign, which Houser had supported throughout the previous year. Houser refused to work with the CAA, because the ACOA was explicitly anticommunist. In Houser's words,

> The Communists will tend to make the most of the South African conflict, not because of basic concern for the South African people, but because they may be able to use the situation to bolster their own partisan position in the international power struggle.[8]

Houser was neither the first nor would he be the last committed American advocate for human rights and racial justice who would question the motives of the Communists when they sought common cause with racial struggles in the United States and abroad. But, it is certainly hard to imagine that W. E. B. DuBois and Paul Robeson of the CAA were anything other than committed to the cause of racial equality. DuBois, the quintessential advocate of the Pan-Africanist ideal, abandoned Communism for precisely the reasons that Houser identifies—he felt that race was at best a secondary consideration for the Communists.[9] And there is a further irony in Houser's stance, in South Africa the ANC and Communists had forged what would prove to be a successful and long-standing alliance, albeit one forged only after the Communists subsumed their class-based demands and interpretation to the non-racial anti-apartheid vision of the ANC.

Events in South Africa in the 1940s and 1950s, "barely made a ripple beyond the small Africanist community in the United States," according to Donald Culverson, who has written extensively about American anti-apartheid campaigns. He argues that "growing but largely invisible economic, political, ideological, and strategic relationships between the United States and South Africa effectively kept antiapartheid protest from entering the policy-making process."[10] The American engagement with the Defiance Campaign hardly represented a tipping point or even made any real impact but it did reveal early stages of transnational engagement between the anti-apartheid and Jim Crow worlds.

Not all engagement was at the organizational level, however. While many African Americans may not have done much to tip the scales of justice in South Africa, many were paying a great deal of attention. Part of the transnational endeavor involved simple intellectual engagement. On both sides of the Atlantic, engaged persons, black and white, were committed to getting to understand what was going on across the ocean and to pushing for some kind of action, even if that action was yet unarticulated.

112   D. C. Catsam

The African Drum and Cultural Connections

South Africans too followed events in the United States, though without the organizational infrastructure that occurred among American blacks. The emergence of *The African Drum* magazine in 1951 (the title was later shortened to *Drum*) proved to be a central moment in transnational awareness as *Drum*'s editors and writers consistently looked across the Atlantic, particularly at cultural trends. Former test cricket player, journalist, and broadcaster Robert Crisp founded the magazine, which struggled until its takeover soon after by Jim Bailey, a former R.A.F. pilot and son of South African business magnate and financier Sir Abe Bailey. The first of the magazine's many successful editors was Anthony Sampson, a future Nelson Mandela biographer, and he and his stable of writers and photographers helped provide a "record of naivete, optimism, frustration, defiance, courage, dancing, drink, jazz, gangsters, exile and death."[11]

In May, 1951 *The African Drum* revealed an interest in American questions, revealing a Pan African vision by including stories about Walter White of the NAACP predicting "that racial discrimination in all forms would be abolished in the Southern States within the next ten years," and another about a lawsuit in which the boxer Joe Louis found himself embroiled and including them in a news roundup section called "Drum African News."[12] In September 1951, the magazine began compiling a roundup of "Negro Notes From U.S.A." which included various cultural, sporting, historical, and other brief stories about the experiences of American blacks.[13]

As the months progressed the magazine took on more overtly political topics. Although *Drum* was never first and foremost a political magazine, its very emergence on the scene in South Africa represented something of a political moment inasmuch as it gave black South Africans a true voice and allowed them to work as equals with whites. Peter Magubane who began work at *Drum* as a driver and messenger in 1955, and eventually worked in the photographic department, later noted,

> *Drum* was a different home; it did not have apartheid. There was no discrimination in the offices of *Drum* magazine. It was only when you left *Drum* and entered the world outside the main door that you knew you were in apartheid-land. But while you were inside *Drum* magazine, everyone there was a family.[14]

Before long, prominent American writers began appearing in the pages of *Drum*. In August 1952, for example, the black American writer John Henrik Clarke published a short story to much fanfare.[15] In the same month, a reader, J. Morgan, from Cape Town, had a letter published in the magazine. "I would like more articles on American Negro life," he wrote. He also called for "more facts about the different tribes of Africa. More pages devoted to music. Also," he proclaimed, "I think there are far too many pictures."[16] In the months and years to come he got almost all that he asked for, save for that last request, as photography would always be central to *Drum*'s work.

Drum merged the serious with the frivolous. Z. K. Matthews, the head of the department of Law at the Native College at Fort Hare and the ANC's Cape President, had just returned from a trip to the United States when *Drum* interviewed him in its April 1954 issue. Although he talked a great deal about South African issues, he also made some astute observations about the situation in the United States. He noted that Americans were "very sympathetic" to the plight of Africans in South Africa, emphasizing in particular the involvement of "organisations such as Churches, Universities, Trade Unions, Clubs, etc." though he also observed that "the government is much more careful and cautious." He had traveled to the United States in 1935 and noticed "a great change," as back in the 1930s "the Negroes didn't seem all that interested in African problems. They said they were Americans, not Africans, and seemed anxious to forget their African backgrounds."[17] In his recent trip he saw a great deal of interest in African Nationalism, some of it quite ardent.

When asked "are the American Negroes really becoming integrated with the whites?" Matthews presented an optimistic view:

Yes, more and more. Even some of the states that have recently been opposing the opening of primary and secondary schools to Negroes, have opened their universities to Negroes. They are finding that they cannot afford "separate but equal" institutions even if it were possible. In Texas four years ago they built a university for Negroes only which cost 12 million dollars. Now they find they cannot afford to keep it Negro, they are admitting whites too.

There was the case of the Negro student who complained of unequal facilities in a separate law school created for the one man, with professors and lecturers. But even then he complained that he didn't have fellow-students—so they had to admit him to a white university![18]

Matthews' interview, which clearly seems to be referencing the 1950 *Sweatt* case, appeared in South Africa in the month before the *Brown* decision and in the West African edition in the month that followed *Brown*.

Nonetheless, *Drum* continued to be more interested in fashion than in politics and American fashion in particular drew the magazine's coverage. An article on models segues, "from the Orient and its slant-eyed beauties we move to America—and world renowned 'cheesecake!'"[19] Fashion, trends, and stories of true love continued to dominate the coverage of the United States. In November 1954, the magazine featured "Glamour on Wheels! Latest in travel dress for American ladies!"[20] The reality for the bulk of black "ladies" in both the United States and South Africa was that daily travel was anything but glamorous. In the end, in the words of Shaun Johnson, a historian of the black press in South Africa, in the 1950s *Drum* retained "an element of thorough investigative reporting documenting black grievances" and "nurtur[ed] some of South Africa's finest writers," but it also "encapsulated the essence of 'gee whiz' journalism."[21]

114   *D. C. Catsam*

The Bantu World Looks at African America

If *Drum* took a breezy look at questions of culture, and sometimes the political implications of culture, *The Bantu World* increasingly emphasized racial politics in the period from 1949 to 1954 albeit from a decidedly non-radical perspective. In 1932, during the worldwide economic depression, a white entrepreneur named BC Paver established Bantu Press (Pty) Ltd. Less concerned with the publishing industry than with the profit motive, Paver initially tried to satiate the growing African middle-class demand for European goods, a market he thought that the white business world had left untapped. When he could not get those interests to take him seriously Paver realized, in a stroke that one historian has identified as "a crucial turning-point in black press history," that only by involving himself in publishing, and therefore advertising, could he prove the efficacy of black purchasing power in segregated South Africa, a purchasing power not coincidentally increasing in conjunction with rising African literacy rates.[22] He also wanted to "provide the Native people with a platform for fair comment and presentation of their needs and aspirations."[23]

Paver enjoined a range of white liberals, most notably J. D. Rheinholt-Jones, who was then head of the South African Institute of Race Relations, to invest in his new company, which also co-opted, purchased, or otherwise steamrolled a range of local black periodicals. But by the end of 1932 more than half of the shareholders were Africans. The establishment of *The Bantu World*, which published as a weekly newspaper from April 1932, marked a vital moment in South African publishing. Modeled after the flourishing British broadsheets, most notably the *Daily Mirror*, *The Bantu World* "spearheaded the shift from a local to a mass black press, as well as a redefinition of the role and strategy of that press."[24]

The editors of *The Bantu World* had to walk a tightrope between the interests of its readers and of its increasingly corporate overseers, especially as Paver's influence waned and that of the Argus Printing and Publishing Company, which would be the majority shareholder of Bantu Press (Pty) Ltd from 1933 to 1952, increased. The Argus company was in turn controlled by the mining industry. In the process of gaining control, Argus bought out most of the other shareholders, including the Africans. Nonetheless, the targeted African readers, who hardly needed a newspaper to tell them that conditions for blacks in South Africa were woeful and not improving, would have rejected an editorial attempt to manipulate their opinions too clearly in favor of those of white corporate interests. The dilemma was that of what one observer has called a "captive African commercial press." By 1954, the number of African newspapers was down to seven, all of them with white ownership, and *Bantu World*, which was based and had most of its circulation in the Witwatersrand, accounted for a quarter of the country's black newspaper circulation. The newspaper served as a crucial "arbiter of taste in urban African politics and culture."[25]

The Bantu World (which would become *The World* in 1955) therefore could often seem conservative, but it most accurately reflected the problematic place of liberalism within South Africa and especially when articulated by black South

South Africa–United States Linkages, 1949–1954 115

Africans. The editorial stance throughout this period then rejected the excesses of apartheid, urged progress for Africans (and often by Africans), eschewed radicalism and especially Communism, but also subtly supported the Programme of Action and Defiance Campaign (or at least opposed the arrest of its leaders, including Nelson Mandela, Walter Sisulu, and other prominent figures) and embraced the more temperate aspects of the emerging Congress Movement. In some ways, one can suggestively draw links between this approach to challenging white supremacy and that of Booker T. Washington and his followers, as opposed to W. E. B. DuBois, in the United States. Indeed, R. V. Selope Thema, who served as the first editor of *The Bantu World* from 1932 to 1952, explicitly embraced Washington as a role model.[26]

The overwhelming majority of stories—more than 80 percent according to one analysis—in *The Bantu World* were devoted to either black issues or issues related to race.[27] With very few exceptions, when the newspaper covered the United States it did so through the lens of race relations and civil rights. At least within this context *The Bantu World* and its writers and editors would have fit comfortably within the ambit of those who fit the (admittedly gendered) common American term "race men." On rare occasions the newspaper would look at American politics—and for a while in the 1950s the Korean War earned front page coverage—but generally speaking African American culture and the politics of civil rights (however obliquely the latter might have been covered—the editors clearly trusted their readers to be able to draw the connections) provided the bulk of *The Bantu World*'s coverage of America. Thus when the paper covered the "Tense Battle" for the Port of Pusan the article emphasized how "among the American forces trying desperately to hold back the Communist advance in the central sector is the Negro regiment known as the Blockhousers."[28]

Much like *Drum, Bantu World* paid more than passing attention to American, particularly black American, culture. The newspaper had a sports section, with a significant proportion of the coverage going to local boxing and football. But perhaps surprisingly for those who have long concluded that "blacks don't play rugby," that football received significant coverage, with the Witwatersrand's many African and Coloured teams receiving special focus (and with clear if somewhat discrete pride showing whenever "native" teams conquered white sides). Local boxers had colorful nicknames like "One Round," "Joltin' Joe," and "King Kong" and their triumphs blared across headlines.

Occasionally, however, American sports would creep into the overwhelmingly locally focused sports coverage. On several occasions in 1950 and 1951, the paper published small articles on basketball, once explaining the game's rules, which indicates a certain level of the American sport's penetration into the fringes of the South African sporting scene. Oddly the rules call for a nine-on-nine game that seems more akin to the six-on-six version of basketball still played by high school girls in rural parts of the United States than to the five-on-five version of the game that prevailed in the United States by the 1940s.[29] On one occasion a story trumpeted the popularity of the game in Natal's schools in a story about a September 1950 tournament—including black and white teams and coaches—that likely played by rules similar to those published a few months

116　*D. C. Catsam*

earlier, as some of the games ended with scores of 8–4 and 4–2.[30] There was a similar display of "American Basketball in Johannesburg" where "big matches were played" in which the scoring proficiency was considerably more impressive, with the first quarter ending 12–8 (and the final score going curiously unannounced).[31]

The political tightrope that the editors had to walk occasionally appeared even in the sports and cultural coverage of the paper. On the one hand the paper celebrated the success of black American boxers, allowing subtext to be as important as text, such as a pair of stories recounting when a pair of "American Negro[es] from Paris" (which itself may be a fascinating story) won fights. Aaron Wilson "knocked out Jack London, former British heavyweight champion" in the first round with a punch that would have "knocked out any man," and in the other "Star" contest Babe Bay outpointed Canadian Roy Wouters in a 10-round middleweight fight.[32]

To be sure, these are modest examples spread over a few months, and while it seems unlikely, may simply have represented slow news weeks when the editors needed to fill sports pages. But even then, the paper chose sports in which black Americans had succeeded or else a sport, basketball, that in whatever bastardized version was gaining some level of support within South Africa.

More telling, and indicative of the globalization of consumer society in the 1940s and 1950s, American sports figures were appearing in *Bantu World* advertisements for Coca Cola by 1953. For years, the paper had advertised the products of American-based companies, which likely represented the connections between the United Kingdom and South Africa as much as direct transnational economic transfers between the United States and South Africa. Boston Shoes, Pepsi Cola, Kodak's Brownie camera, Pepsodent and Colgate toothpastes, Ponds "Vanishing Cream," Vicks VapoRub, and Gillette razor blades all advertised in *Bantu World*, many of them regularly.[33] But in the Coca Cola ads popular black American athletes served as the spokespeople for Coca Cola in South Africa.

Among the featured sports stars in the ads of the company based in segregated Atlanta, Georgia were: Sugar Ray Robinson, "retired undefeated Middleweight and Welterweight Boxing Champion ... One of the greatest fighters in the history of the sport"; Sweetwater Clifton, pioneering black player in the National Basketball Association, and an "outstanding Negro sportsman ... famous for his clever control when handling the ball"; Ted Rhodes, "the well known American Negro professional golfer" whose "swing is rated to be the finest in golf today!"; and one ad featured two track stars, Alice Coachman and the legendary Jesse Owens, "outstanding American Negro athletes" who "have represented the U.S.A. in the Olympic Games." Owens "has been called the greatest runner in America since 1900."[34] It does not seem over deterministic to assert that the confluence of American products, black American athletes, an ad-revenue hungry newspaper, and a black audience clearly interested in black accomplishments beyond the increasingly restrictive confines of apartheid was no coincidence.

Black entertainers too provided fodder for the readers of *Bantu World*, and in the South African winter of 1953, there was another circumstance where South African and American paths crossed in what was decidedly not coincidental. In

South Africa–United States Linkages, 1949–1954   117

July 1950, a number of black American actors, most prominent among them Canada Lee, a former boxing championship contender turned actor, and Charles McCrae, arrived in South Africa to begin production on the film version of Alan Paton's *Cry the Beloved Country*. McCrae had played a part in a musical called "Lost in the Stars," which had depicted a version of Paton's bestseller.[35] Recognizing the potential conflicts attendant with American actors playing South African figures, director Zoltan Korda explained:

> Despite advice I received to the contrary, I made every effort to make a thorough search in South Africa for capable actors who would be able to take the lead in the film. I went to many cities of the Union. Though I met a number of impressive aspirants I was not able to get persons of sufficient standard to act in such an important film. I did not desire to reduce the literary value of the novel by taking actors who would not please the world but I have insisted from the beginning that if in South Africa suitable men were not available then I would have to import well-known actors from other countries.[36]

As it was,

> many Africans were thrilled to learn Negroes were in the city and at every street corner of Johannesburg groups were talking and discussing the presence of their brothers from America. Many expressed a keen desire to see them, let alone talk to them.

In response, Korda was pleased to announce that once filming was done "an announcement will be made through the 'Bantu World'" that would explain arrangements for the South African public to "meet the Negro actors before they return to the States."[37]

Occasionally the evocations of American popular culture revealed *The Bantu World*'s inner political tensions. In late 1950 and early 1951 Paul Robeson, the outspoken American performing star and former star athlete, earned *Bantu World*'s attention. The American had enjoyed accomplishments of the sort that ordinarily would have earned him nearly fawning coverage. But his political radicalism—and his willingness to associate with Communists and speak out against the Cold War's deleterious effects on domestic politics, especially though not solely on blacks—meant that he crossed the invisible but very real line that the *Bantu World*'s editors had laid down as fervent anti-Communists.

Thus when Josh White, a black American singer, testified before the ardently anti-Communist House Un-American Activities Committee and spoke critically of Robeson, *Bantu World*'s coverage was sympathetic to White. White had claimed that Robeson's assertions that African Americans should not fight for the United States against Cold War enemies were "both wrong and an insult," and he claimed that Robeson had been "played for a sucker by the Communist Party," which used issues like lynching and Jim Crow "for their own purposes." He claimed, "when the communists and their kind talk about democracy and equality

118   *D. C. Catsam*

they are using double talk. They use those good words to cover up bad intentions but for simple folk it takes time to catch on." White followed testimony by baseball legend Jackie Robinson who had similarly denounced Robeson.[38] Just a few months later Sugar Ray Robinson too singled out Robeson for scorn, and he told reporters in New York, "if the things the Communists say were true, I would never be in the position I am today." Robinson was responding to comments he had made when he was in Paris, where he defended America: "In our grand democracy we have yet to reach a full perfection, but I know that the United States has made it possible for a Negro with ability, whether in business, science, statesmanship, or sports to achieve the top."[39] This last assertion reflected that Robinson had been successful despite American racism but hardly provided a template for the vast majority of black Americans in the era between World War II and *Brown v. Board*. When Robinson spoke, black American soldiers were fighting and dying in Korea under still-segregated conditions.

Bantu World also wrote fairly regularly about literature, poetry, journalism, and other writing connected not only to the African experience, but also to the culture and history of the black American experience. Black American writing featured regularly in Dr. R. H. W. Shepherd's regular "Literature and Life" column, in which he would draw larger historical and political context from prominent writers. He wrote about the National Baptist Publishing House, founded by a former slave that produced voluminous writings, including publications for Sunday schools; He paid particular attention to poetry, including that of Phillis Wheatley and Paul Lawrence Dunbar. He explored the significance of the poets of the Harlem Renaissance who "set forth the poetry of protest, rebellion and despair."[40]

Shepherd even praised the timelessness of W. E. B. DuBois's *The Souls of Black Folk*, which "will last as long as American literature endures."[41] But perhaps in keeping with the beliefs of longtime editor Selope Thema, Shepherd was especially fulsome in his praise of Booker T. Washington, and though he is clear-eyed and fair about the great DuBois-Washington divide, Shepherd at least validates Thema's stands through the sort of context that the typical reader of *Bantu World* would understand.[42]

And yet wherever the editors fit on the political spectrum, and however their tempered approach to radical politics, some of the clearest indications of where the *Bantu World*'s South African "race men" stood came in the simple fact that a large percentage of the coverage of African American life came in the form of reportage about civil rights issues and accomplishments. Oftentimes carrying subtitles or titles like "Negro Progress and Achievement," or "News From America"—which almost universally meant news from black America, these pieces, short and long, celebrated achievements. Sometimes they celebrated classes of people—the growing numbers of black students in American colleges and universities, the growing numbers of successful black businessmen, the increasing role of African laborers, including those entering unions, and the increasing number of African American professionals.[43]

In the last few months of 1950 *Bantu World* published a series of articles, carrying the title "Negro Progress and Achievement," from George S. Schuyler, the prominent conservative black author, journalist, and social commentator whose political views in some ways aligned with those of the publishers and editors of *The Bantu World*. Schuyler provided a misplaced triumphal view of African American achievement that rejected both radical politics and especially Communism. Schuyler's was a rose-colored view that was not especially popular among the bulk of African Americans, but his writings still represented an attempt to show more of the black American experience to a black South African audience clearly interested in news of black achievement away from South Africa.[44]

Bantu World celebrated successful and prominent black American individuals on a regular basis. Ralph Bunche was celebrated for going from being the grandson of a slave to becoming the first black person to win the Nobel Peace Prize.[45] A regular columnist told readers how "Two phrases—'first' and 'only Negro'— ring with familiar rhythm through the biography of 75-year-old Mary McCleod Bethune. Hers is a real success story."[46] Quentin Wright, director of the South Africa Institute of Race Relations wrote about meeting Bunche, but also Dr. Channing Tobias, Director of the Phelps-Stokes Fund in New York.[47] Others who received favorable coverage thousands of miles from their bases of operation included Edith Sampson, an alternate delegate for the United States to the United Nations and Charles Mahoney, a black lawyer who represented the US at that same body.[48] Lois Lippman was a Bostonian who moved to Washington, DC to become the personal secretary to one of President Eisenhower's special assistants.[49] "News From America" regularly featured blurbs about local, state, regional, and national black success stories. It is perhaps telling that the volume of these stories continued to grow through 1954.[50]

Furthermore, *Bantu World* often looked to the United States and the question of race there in order to shed light on the same questions in South Africa. Comparing Jim Crow in the South and apartheid in South Africa the editors noticed "a thousand and one glaring instances of the violation" of racial separation in South Africa, leading them to believe that "the authorities would do well to begin immediately removing these inequalities which are incompatible with principles of a fair and unselfish apartheid."[51] In other words, taking apartheid on its own, purest terms, officials were failing. It would seem that the editors were even endorsing a form of separate but equal. Instead, they were addressing the absurdity and expense of this form of separation in a subtle but unmistakable manner. The editorial focused on segregated transportation—railways rather than buses, though many of the same issues inhered. Returning to the "fair and unselfish" apartheid they seemed to advocate, the editors noted:

> As in America, the doctrine will be found very expensive. More and better benches with "Non-Europeans Only" on them will have to be provided. More first and second class accommodation for non-Europeans will have to be provided. Not only at railway stations, but in every area of public life the present inequalities will have to be remodeled into equalities. To be more just, the Africans whose ratio is to the Europeans four to one, should have quantitatively superior facilities to those of the European minority.[52]

120   *D. C. Catsam*

The editors recognized that "apartheid along these lines is bound to be beset with formidable difficulties." But they had a ready solution: "treat white, black, brown, yellow, and coloured members of the South African community as one society."[53] This editorial represents a relatively rare occasion of the paper overtly calling for the end of apartheid.

The paper's readers similarly looked to the United States and recognized that the countries shared a worrisome trend. One reader, J. S. Motsielea of Krugersdorp observed:

> Under the cloak of suppressing Communism, the present-day government is grimly set upon a course of ruthless oppression in willfully and totally disregarding the freedoms one normally associates with democratic institutions the world over.[54]

The author believed that South Africa's particular form of ardent anti-Communism, which was inextricably bound with racial policies, was "Swartism," and that it was "typified … by the naming and banning of persons" and could "hardly be distinguished from McCarthyism."[55]

The editors looked to the United States to draw lessons—positive and negative—from boycotts. Even as the Congress Movement engaged in the Defiance Campaign and implemented the Programme of Action, the *Bantu World* looked to the example of James Weldon Johnson who had cautioned against reliance on boycott movements without the backing "by real power and through organization." The editors believed that "the struggle of the American Negro can teach the African many valuable lessons," but they drew conservative lessons as well as radical ones from what they saw across the Atlantic.[56]

This conservative tendency (within the range of anti-segregationist politics) celebrated calls for integrationism, noting that the first role of American blacks was "to become an American and to do all he can to obliterate any line of demarcation between him and his white fellow countrymen."[57] To this end these South Africans looked to the NAACP, and in the wake of the *Brown* decision, praised the organization "which since its inception put up a relentless but dignified fight against anything that stood in the way of 'the advancement of the coloured people' in America" and celebrated the fact that the lawyers winning cases against Jim Crow "were all Negroes."[58] Beyond the NAACP, the editors believed that the ANC should look to "the Negro Americans, 'our brethren 'neath the western skies,' [who] have a great deal to teach us," emphasizing the success of black American businesses, insurance companies, and banks "handling globular amounts of money."[59]

The papers also wanted to make clear to black South Africans, "don't be anti-white." The editors called for upliftment, but invoked Booker T. Washington's words, "I shall allow no man to drag me so low as to hate him." They concluded, "No matter how low we may be dragged, at no level should we feel that the evil thing called hate may be regarded as a virtue."[60] The *Bantu World* approach very much reflected the mainstream of the American struggle for civil rights perhaps even more than it did that of black, coloured, and Indian South Africans.

The Bantu World **Goes to America**

Not all of the observation of the United States took place from the editor's offices in Langlaagte. One of the most significant forms of engagement that the *Bantu World* sustained with America, and especially black America, was through its correspondents' trips to the United States and the reportage they sent back to readers in the townships and the cities.

In August 1954, Reverend Bertram Moloi went to the United States for several weeks to serve as a delegate at a series of events, including the Second Assembly of the World Council of Churches at Northwestern University in Evansville, Illinois, just outside of Chicago, and the Pan-Anglican conference in Minneapolis, Minnesota.[61] Moloi's observations, sent in three articles called "Lessons I Learned At Evanston," were predominantly connected to his spiritual mission. And yet, he knew that his readers would be interested in matters of race, and he did not disappoint.

One of the highlights of his experience in Chicago came when the Chicago Symphony Orchestra played for the delegates. "The soloist," Moloi noted, "was a Negro, Miss Price, who also sang a few Negro spirituals." Thousands "listened to this great Negro singer who received wonderful applause."[62] Moloi found it "surprising to note that ... 'the big speakers' at the Assembly [of the World Council of Churches] were nearly all Non-Europeans" from all across the world. Particularly noteworthy was Dr. Benjamin Mays, the President of Morehouse College who was also a member of the National Baptist Convention, whose speech was "the Church amidst ethnic and racial tensions." On the whole, the experience clearly proved valuable to Moloi, and he emphasized how the Assembly concluded that "racial discrimination cannot be based on Scripture," a takeaway that would clearly resonate with his readers.[63]

On April 1, 1953, the *Bantu World* announced the appointment of a new editor, Jacob Meaniselwa Nhlapo, a respected academic who had been the first African from the Free State to receive his BA degree from the University of South Africa. He embarked on a teaching career during which he earned a number of certificates as well as his PhD from McKinley-Roosevelt Extension College in Chicago. Nhlapo was familiar to readers of the *Bantu World* as a result of his dispatches, "Letter From the States," or "Letter From U.S.A." written between August 1952 to January 1953, during which time he traversed thousands of miles and made myriad stops with particular emphasis on colleges and universities ranging from elite research universities to prominent historically black colleges and universities to liberal arts colleges and state universities.[64]

Nhlapo was effusive about his experiences in America and he visited dozens of schools, oftentimes with the political activist and academic Z. K. Matthews, his colleague and friend. He noted how in Harlem the "Negro people look so much like the Africans in Johannesburg or Bloemfontein that it seems every African in South Africa has his or her double in this wonderful Negro city." He hoped to make "a good study of Harlem so as to bring Africans in South Africa inspiration."[65] Indeed, this seemed to be his larger mission—to explore, observe, and understand American higher education, particularly as it related to black

122 D. C. Catsam

Americans. Further, he took as many opportunities as he could "to speak to the Negroes about Africa and to endeavor to build a bridge between them and the Africans."[66] Nhlopa was

> highly intrigued to find the Negro so much like his African brother in colour and many other respects. The African can, however, learn many things from the Negro, and the Negro is by no means above learning much from the African.[67]

Nhlapo seemed to take particular pleasure in experiencing the great Negro colleges in the country, including Morehouse, Spelman, Howard, Fisk, Tuskegee, Dillard, Hampton Institute, Wilberforce, Lincoln, and others. He enjoyed meeting the students and faculty, sitting in on lectures and classes and delivering his own in which he shared African histories, cultures, and languages.

These sorts of interactions reveal that the connections between black South Africans and their American counterparts were episodic but real. As the years passed the transnational networks would expand significantly and become more deeply, overtly political. *Drum* and *Bantu World* played a vital role in the emerging post-war transnational American-South African movements against white supremacy.

Notes

1 William Minter, Gail Hovey, and Charles Cobb, Jr., eds., *No Easy Victories: African Liberation and American Activists over a Half Century, 1950–2000* (Trenton, NJ: Africa World Press, 2008) 15–16.
2 Minter, *et al.*, *No Easy Victories*, 16.
3 Penny Von Eschen, *Race Against Empire: Black Americans and Anticolonialism, 1937–1957* (Ithaca: Cornell University Press, 1997), 137.
4 Von Eschen, *Race Against Empire*, 137–138.
5 Minter, *et al.*, *No Easy Victories*, 16.
6 Brenda Gayle Plummer, *Rising Wind: Black Americans and U. S. Foreign Affairs, 1935–1960* (Chapel Hill: University of North Carolina Press, 1996), 232.
7 On ACOA and Houser's engagement with the region more generally see George Houser, *No One Can Stop the Rain: Glimpses of Africa's Liberation Struggle* (New York: The Pilgrim Press, 1989).
8 Quoted in von Eschen, *Race Against Empire*, p. 143.
9 On DuBois, Communism, Pan Africanism, and race in the 1940s and early 1950s see Eric Porter, *The Problem of the Future World: W. E. B. DuBois and the Race Concept at Midcentury* (Durham: Duke University Press, 2010).
10 Donald R. Culverson, "From Cold War to Global Interdependence: The Political Economy of African American Antiapartheid Activism, 1968–1988," in Brenda Gayle Plummer, ed., *Window on Freedom: Race, Civil Rights, and Foreign Affairs 1945–1988.* (Chapel Hill: University of North Carolina Press, 2003), 222.
11 Mike Nicol, *Good-looking Corpse: World of DRUM—Jazz and Gangsters, Hope and Defiance in the Townships of South Africa* (London: Secker & Warburg, 1991).
12 *The African Drum*, May, 1951, 21 (White) and 24 (Louis). I want to thank my one-time graduate assistant Mr. David Seng for his help in going through the 1950s run of *Drum* magazine.
13 *The African Drum*, October, 1951, 10.

South Africa–United States Linkages, 1949–1954   123

14 Quoted in "A Brief History of 'Drum'," South African History Online, www.sahistory.org.za/brief-history-drum (Accessed on September 16, 2011).

15 John Henrik Clarke, "The Boy Who Painted Christ Black," *Drum*, August 1952. *Drum* also published international editions geared especially toward the rest of sub-Saharan Africa. This story appeared simultaneously in the September international edition.

16 "More About Negroes," J. Morgan, letter to the editor, *Drum*, August 1952/International issue September 1952, 20.

17 "Drum Interviews Prof. Matthews," *Drum* April 1954/June 1954 West African edition, 25.

18 Ibid., 25.

19 "In America!" *Drum*, October 1954, 55.

20 "Glamour on Wheels!" *Drum*, November 1954, 69–71.

21 Shaun Johnson, "An Historical Overview of the Black Press," in Keyan Tomaselli and P. Eric Louw, *The Alternative Press in South Africa* (Bellville: Anthropos, 1991), 23.

22 Johnson, "An Historical Overview of the Black Press," 20–21; see also T. Couzens, "A Short History of 'The World' and Other Black Newspapers 1832–1960," (PhD Dissertation, University of the Witwatersrand, 1982), 29.

23 See Les Switzer, "*Bantu World* and the Origins of a Captive African Commercial Press," in Switzer, ed., *South Africa's Alternative Press: Voices of Protest and Resistance, 1880–1960* (Cambridge: Cambridge University Press, 1997), 189. This chapter represents an expansion of Switzer's article, "Bantu World and the Origins of a Captive Commercial Press in South Africa," *Journal of Southern African Studies*, Vol. 14, No. 3 (April 1988), 351–370.

24 Johnson, "An Historical Overview of the Black Press," 21–22. See also Switzer, "*Bantu World* and the Origins of a Captive African Commercial Press," 189–190.

25 See Switzer, "*Bantu World* and the Origins of a Captive African Commercial Press," 190.

26 See ibid., 193.

27 See ibid., 197–199.

28 *The Bantu World*, August 5, 1950.

29 *Bantu World*, July 29, 1950. (All references are to the version published in the Witwatersrand and distributed across South Africa unless otherwise indicated—*The Bantu World* did have other editions, including one for West Africa and one for Swaziland.)

30 *Bantu World*, September 30, 1950.

31 *Bantu World*, March 17, 1951.

32 *Bantu World*, December 10, 1949.

33 See, for example, *Bantu World* issues from April 15, July 22, July 29, August 5, and Sept. 30, 1950.

34 These ads appeared regularly from 1953, but see, for example, *Bantu World* issues from February 28, March 28, April 11, April 25, July 4, and August 29, 1953.

35 *Bantu World*, July 29, 1950.

36 *Bantu World*, August 5, 1950.

37 Ibid.

38 *Bantu World*, September 9, 1950.

39 *Bantu World*, January 13, 1951.

40 See, for example, *Bantu World*, August 26 and September 9, 1950.

41 *Bantu World*, August 26, 1950.

42 *Bantu World*, May 19, 1951.

43 See, for example, *Bantu World*, February 4 and August 12, 1950; February 9, 1952.

44 *Bantu World*, October 21, October 28, and November 4, 1950.

45 *Bantu World*, September 30, 1950. See also March 8, 1952 issue.

46 *Bantu World*, October 7, 1950.

124 D. C. Catsam

47 *Bantu World*, March 8, 1952.
48 *Bantu World*, October 21, 1950 and September 25, 1954.
49 *Bantu World*, October 30, 1954.
50 See, for example, *Bantu World*, November 7, 1953; July 3, July 31, August 7, August 28, September 11, September 25, and October 30 1954.
51 *Bantu World*, June 20, 1953.
52 Ibid.
53 Ibid.
54 *Bantu World*, September 14, 1953.
55 Ibid.
56 *Bantu World*, March 8, 1954.
57 *Bantu World*, April 10, 1954.
58 *Bantu World*, May 29, 1954. See also June 5, 1954.
59 *Bantu World*, November 27, 1954.
60 *Bantu World*, July 17, 1954.
61 *Bantu World*, October 23, 1954.
62 *Bantu World*, October 30, 1954.
63 *Bantu World*, November 13, 1954.
64 See *Bantu World*, August 16, 30, September 13, November 1, 22, 29, December 13, 1952, January 3, 10, 17, February 21, April 11, 1953.
65 *Bantu World*, August 16, 1952.
66 *Bantu World*, August 30, 1952.
67 *Bantu World*, September 13, 1952.

References

Couzens, T. "A Short History of 'The World' and Other Black Newspapers 1832–1960," PhD Dissertation, University of the Witwatersrand, 1982.

Culverson, Donald R. "From Cold War to Global Interdependence: The Political Economy of African American Antiapartheid Activism, 1968–1988," in Brenda Gayle Plummer, ed., *Window on Freedom: Race, Civil Rights, and Foreign Affairs 1945–1988*. Chapel Hill: University of North Carolina Press, 2003.

Houser, George. *No One Can Stop the Rain: Glimpses of Africa's Liberation Struggle*. New York: The Pilgrim Press, 1989.

Johnson, Shawn. "An Historical Overview of the Black Press," in Keyan Tomaselli and P. Eric Louw, *The Alternative Press in South Africa*, Anthropos: Bellville, 1991.

Minter, William; Hovey, Gail; and Cobb, Jr., Charles, eds. *No Easy Victories: African Liberation and American activists over a Half Century, 1950–2000*. Trenton, NJ: Africa World Press, 2008.

Nicol, Mike. *Good-looking Corpse: World of DRUM—Jazz and Gangsters, Hope and Defiance in the Townships of South Africa*. London: Secker & Warburg, 1991.

Plummer, Brenda Gayle. *Rising Wind: Black Americans and U. S. Foreign Affairs, 1935–1960*. Chapel Hill: University of North Carolina Press, 1996.

Plummer, Brenda Gayle, ed. *Window on Freedom: Race, Civil Rights, and Foreign Affairs 1945–1988*. Chapel Hill: University of North Carolina Press, 2003.

Porter, Eric. *The Problem of the Future World: W. E. B. DuBois and the Race Concept at Midcentury*. Durham: Duke University Press, 2010.

South African History Online. "A Brief History of 'Drum'," www.sahistory.org.za/brief-history-drum (Accessed on September 16, 2011).

Switzer, Les., "Bantu World and the Origins of a Captive Commercial Press in South Africa," *Journal of Southern African Studies*, Vol. 14, No. 3 (April 1988).

Switzer, Les, ed. *South Africa's Alternative Press: Voices of Protest and Resistance, 1880–1960*, Cambridge: Cambridge University Press, 1997.

Switzer, Les. "*Bantu World* and the Origins of a Captive African Commercial Press," in Switzer, ed., *South Africa's Alternative Press: Voices of Protest and Resistance, 1880–1960*. Cambridge: Cambridge University Press, 1997.

Tomaselli, Keyan and Louw, P. Eric. *The Alternative Press in South Africa*. Bellville: Anthropos, 1991.

Von Eschen, Penny. *Race Against Empire: Black Americans and Anticolonialism, 1937–1957*. Ithaca: Cornell University Press, 1997.

7 Organized Labor and the Struggle for Black and Working-Class Citizenship in Cienfuegos, Cuba, 1899–1902

Bonnie A. Lucero

"Our negroes are mostly uneducated laborers," Bartolomé Masó, a prominent Cuban patriot assured American military officials in the first year of the United States occupation of the island (1899–1902). Cuban patriots emerging from the battlefield confronted widespread anxieties among the wealthiest residents in Cuba that the empowerment of men of African descent within the Cuban Army would translate into the disintegration of the racial order in post-war society. These men "gravely predict[ed] Cuba's future as a second Hayti or Liberia—a negro republic," an idea Masó characterized as "manifestly absurd." Dismissing racial arguments against Cuban sovereignty, he claimed, "our negroes will work as before in the cane-fields, and I see no reason to anticipate trouble from them."[1]

Over the course of 30 years of struggle for independence against Spain, the war effort had become entwined with struggles of people of African descent and workers for social justice. These rather radical aspects of the revolution assumed new political significance with the inauguration of the military occupation. As Americans strayed from their initial commitment to free Cuba from Spanish tyranny to the alleged pacification of the island, the future birth of the Cuban republic became contingent on the ability of Cuban political leaders to demonstrate their ability to self-govern. The linchpin of capacity to self-govern was social order, which required the abandonment of revolutionary commitments to social justice.

Even though 12 years had passed since the final abolition of slavery in 1886, planters and merchants still relied heavily upon black labor to plant, harvest, and transport their sugar. They had increasingly employed imported Spanish laborers over the last quarter of the nineteenth century, but formerly enslaved men and women remained a vital source of labor in the most important economic sector in central Cuba, the sugar industry.[2] Many families remained on the plantations on which they were born or had lived most of their lives, and continued to work for the same *hacendados* after they achieved freedom, while others established themselves as *colonos*, independent cultivators of sugar, who were usually bound to the large mills who bought and processed their raw cane.[3] Black labor was vital to the expansion of railroad lines. At the ports, black men also provided the labor to load the sugar onto steamers destined for the United States and elsewhere since at least the 1880s.[4]

The war transformed labor conditions in two main ways. First, the Cuban and Spanish armies both prohibited work on sugar estates and persecuted laborers who remained on the estates.[5] The persecution of laborers by both Spanish and Cuban armies discouraged workers from returning to the estates after the war, while reducing the amount of work available in the ports. Second, the participation of large numbers of rural dwellers in the Cuban army empowered these countrymen to expect more from their society. This was especially the case for black men like Quintín Bandera and Claudio Sarría who had ascended in the ranks of the Cuban army.[6] As a result, veterans were more reluctant simply to return to the lowest paying jobs in sugar and related sectors, and they may have been more inclined toward collective action to demand better working conditions. These competing aspirations and anxieties of veterans of African descent and wealthy sugar barons ensured that the rise of organized labor in the city of Cienfuegos during the American military occupation was a contentious, even violent process.

Indeed, the struggle to define the parameters of power for laborers was inseparable from the debates and conflicts over the racial order in post-war Cuban society. Port workers, most of whom were black, eschewed racial characterizations, demanding a living wage based on their status as honorable men and heads of household. At the same time, merchants and planters turned to disparaging assessments of the moral character of the laborers and sometimes employed overtly racial arguments to promote an increasingly repressive agenda against labor. These commercial elites argued that a free and independent Cuba would be synonymous with chaos, ruin, and racial disorder, and during the first years of the military occupation, some elite planters even upheld American annexation as the key to prosperity and order.

The seemingly indefinite duration of American rule fostered great uncertainty about Cuba's future sovereignty, thereby exacerbating the political implications of these struggles. Cuban patriots-turned-political elites feared that the successful organization of a black and mixed-race work force would delay the withdrawal of American forces from Cuba because it appeared to be a threat to the racial order. Moreover, they learned early on in their tense confrontations with American military officials that support for a broadly defined citizenship would condemn them as unfit to self-govern. In their zeal to secure the transition from an occupied territory to an independent republic, Cuban patriots transformed themselves from compatriots of the laborers into one of their staunchest enemies.

The intensity of these struggles between laborers and commercial elites with their allies in local government reveal that these were more than just battles over wages and conditions. The constant renegotiation of relations between urban labor and local commercial elites during the first several years after the war marked one heretofore understudied part of a broader struggle over the definition of the boundaries of citizenship in the emerging republic.[7] By defending the dignity of their work as a value that entitled them to certain rights and quality of life, workers put forth a powerful argument for inclusion in the emerging nation. Yet, the perpetual attacks against organized labor by the wealthiest men of the island signaled a strong rejection of the expansive citizenship workers proposed.

128   B. A. Lucero

Even Cuban authorities hesitated to accept the inclusion of these black and racially ambiguous workers. These meta-struggles over the boundaries of Cuban citizenship and the political future of the island crippled the labor movement during the early years of the republic, eventually silencing one of the loudest voices against the consolidation of a white Cuban republic.

The Rise of Organized Labor after the War

The redistribution of the Cuban population during the war fostered a significant influx of men and women into the largest cities. The population of Cienfuegos, the island's fourth largest urban center, increased by 18,164 inhabitants between 1887 and 1899.[8] Of the 59,128 people residing in the municipality of Cienfuegos in 1899, 30,038 lived in the city of Cienfuegos. The increase in the urban population catalyzed a disproportionate rise in the urban working class. In cities like Cienfuegos, gainful employment slumped well below the provincial average, suggesting greater than normal unemployment among urban populations. Only 38 percent of the population over 10 years of age in Cienfuegos city had gainful employment in 1899, where gainful employment was defined as the reliance on a profession, trade or branch of work to support oneself. The city of Santa Clara found only 37 percent of its population gainfully employed in a province averaging over 40 percent.[9] Fierce competition for the few available urban jobs contributed to the persistence of low wages, while one American official reported that "the slave idea" still prevailed among certain plantation owners.[10]

Compounding the scarcity of gainful employment were the exorbitant prices of urban subsistence. Housing, even in the smallest tenement room cost 12 pesos silver in Cienfuegos, a significant portion of a worker's monthly wages.[11] Food prices, estimated at 30 *centenes* per capita per day, strained the finances of poor and working-class families. The destruction of domestic food crops during the war forced Cubans to import much of their food from the United States.[12] Most working-class families could not afford to buy meat because of the exorbitant prices due in part to the destruction of herds during the war. Even when conditions had improved marked by 1902, an American observer noted that "the man who tries to support a family on a workingman's wages in Habana, Cienfuegos or any of the larger cities of Cuba has a rather difficult problem before him."[13] The high price of necessities in the cities likely contributed to high rates of petty crime, including petty theft, robbery and cattle thieving.[14]

Responding to these unique labor conditions after the war, numerous associations of workers—some with roots in the late colonial period—emerged with renewed vigor in the first months of the military occupation. Between 1899 and 1900, diverse groups of laborers organized to represent their interests and fight for their economic survival. The result was an explosion of unions during the first year of American rule. By early 1900, police records identify at least 26 officially registered organizations explicitly labeled as unions (gremios) in Cienfuegos. Among the unions were diverse trades, skilled and unskilled workers from cow-milkers and tobacco workers to bakers and day laborers. Several other clubs also reflected collective action among workers, including the *Círculo de Trabajadores* (Workers'

Black Citizenship in Cuba, 1899–1902 129

Club), at the same time as numerous other organizations based on nationality, ethnicity, and common interest afforded a semblance of safety networks for the poor and working classes to barter and pool resources.[15]

At the core of the organized labor movement in Cienfuegos were the workers of the Port. As early as the 1870s, black workers in Cienfuegos had developed organizations to represent the interests of dockworkers.[16] By the 1880s, black stevedores actively negotiated with business interests in the municipal courts.[17] Over the course of three decades, a humble association of laborers, the Gremio Unión de Estibadores (Stevedore Union), emerged as one of the most powerful organizations of collective action in American-occupied Cuba. By the turn of the century, stevedores, alongside lightermen and longshoremen, confronted the wealthiest merchants and planters of the city to demand better working conditions, more control over hiring practices, and higher rates of compensation. By confronting the commercial elite directly, the stevedores violated prevailing expectations of racial etiquette and challenged elite pretensions to perpetuate the colonial social hierarchy that they had fought so many years to dismantle.

Port workers performed a variety of different jobs and were essential in keeping the shipment of goods in and out of Cienfuegos. Lightermen operated lighters, boats that transported the goods between the ships anchored in the Port and the docks. Longshoremen loaded and unloaded cargo from the littoral, while stevedores loaded and unloaded cargo on the docks located on the southernmost frontier of the city bordering the historically black neighborhood of Marsillán. Most aspects of port work involved heavy manual labor and required tremendous physical strength, agility, and endurance as working hours tended to be long. Work was generally dangerous, inconsistent, and poorly remunerated, making the livelihoods of many laborers precarious. The port workers' unions aimed to defend the interests of workers, secure higher wages, and provide safer labor conditions amidst the punishing conditions of port work. These goals seemed to be very attractive to laborers. In 1899, over 100 workers had joined the stevedore union. By 1901, the union boasted a membership of at least 250, illustrating that a substantial proportion of the total union member had joined after the war of independence.[18]

In contrast to the other urban unions, the stevedore union was composed of a large proportion of men of African descent. Although it included men of diverse places of origin, including a few European (mainly Spanish) immigrants, the vast majority of union members were men of African descent. Roughly one in five men who joined the stevedore union between January 1899 and May 1902 were confirmed veterans of the Cuban army, many of African ancestry. The number was likely substantially higher, but numerous union members had patronymics too common to ascertain for certain whether they participated in the revolution.[19] In 1904, the first year for which racial statistics are available, only 5 of the 35 men who joined the union were classified as white.[20] The 30 other men joining that year identified themselves as black or mulatto. Surviving photographs of stevedores from the early twentieth century suggest that some members may have had Chinese ancestry as well, though their racial labels privileged their African descent. Black men also composed the leadership of the stevedore union. Indeed, the president of

130   B. A. Lucero

the union for the majority of the military occupation was Romualdo Amezquita, a politically well-connected mulatto man.[21]

Many of the union members of the union came from several of the largest plantations in the area, on which they or their parents had been enslaved. Of those workers who joined during the military occupation, five held the patronymic Sarría, indicating former slave status on the Soledad sugar plantation once owned by one of the most prominent slave-owning families of the region. Another man with the last name of Pombert is likely to have toiled as a slave on the Hormiguero estate, owned by the Ponvert family. Yet another member, Teodoro Terry, probably worked on the Caracas estate owned by the Terry family. Other patronymics among the union members, including Acea, Tartabull, Abreus, and Quesada suggest that formerly enslaved men and their descendants were represented strongly in the stevedore union.[22] At least one of these men donned the "ethnic" label of Congo, indicating African birth.[23] This coveted union job offered the possibility of upward mobility for former enslaved people who sought a certain level of economic stability.

The union explicitly listed a variety of African societies and associations of color of Cienfuegos with whom it maintained official relations.[24] Among the associations of color recognized by the union were the prestigious *Sociedad Minerva*, and the *Institución Antonio Maceo*. The union also sustained relations with the African societies including *Divina Caridad, Santa Bárbara, and San Cayetano*, and *Cabildo Congo*, though the latter was not listed officially, perhaps due to the explicit ethnic affiliation in the name.[25] Membership in the union sometimes coincided with leadership in societies of color. Francisco Garmendia served as vice president of the *Cabildo Congo* in 1902 at the same time as he occupied the position of *cabeza de cuadrilla* in the stevedore union and union member Juan de Dios Torres held key leadership positions in the same association and a parallel ethnic association called *Sociedad de Instrucción y Recreo de Africanos Nación de Portugués San Teresa de Meditando*.[26] These overlapping memberships suggest important overlaps between the labor unions' class-based aims and the racial and ethnic collaboration among the societies of color.

Although the main objective of the union was to represent the interests of workers, there is evidence of a certain commitment to racial justice, individually and collectively. Local court records indicate that Daniel Rufalé, alias "Machete," became involved in a brawl with the owner of a local café in 1894 to protest the prohibitively high price he charged blacks for coffee.[27] The union as a whole supported the progressive racial agendas of other associations across the island, and even internationally.[28] For example, the union sent a delegation to Havana in support of a strike by tobacco workers seeking higher wages and the de-segregation of the schools for children at the tobacco factories. Stevedores agreed to support the tobacco workers to help promote the "learning of all Cuban children without distinction of color."[29] Although racial activism was not central to the union mission, the deliberate decisions to maintain direct ties with black associations and to sustain individual and collective ties to racial protest suggest an attempt to harness the moment of political transition to foster a more inclusive citizenship and socially just society.

Black Citizenship in Cuba, 1899–1902 131

The Dilemma of Class Solidarity in a Black Union under American Rule

The racial composition of the union presented unique challenges for the workers. The mobilization of black workers confirmed the worst fears of planters and merchants, seemingly substantiating speculation that the war had destroyed the racial order upon which the island's wealth rested. Sensationalist depictions of the labor union fit comfortably within an already-existing framework of racial conflict, characterized by constant rumors of black rebellion and the specter of "Negro rule." Class-based confrontations between the large, organized and militant black union and the white commercial elite assumed racial significance, emerged as a threat to order, and swiftly became another reason for the necessity of prolonging American tutelage.

The ephemeral nature of port work only exacerbated certain negative perceptions of stevedores among the local elite. Because of the large number of workers and the limited work available, Cienfuegos stevedores often went weeks without being assigned to a job. Some men responded to the scarcity of work by seeking alternative forms of employment, whether licit or not. Petty theft, some violence, and participation in the sex industry were familiar to at least a portion of stevedores.[30] After all, port workers frequented the historically-black portside neighborhood of Marsillán, housing dozens of cafés, bars, illicit gambling houses as well as the city's informal red light district, as they awaited the shape-up, took a meal, attended union meetings or gathered after work. Violence occasionally erupted among stevedores as well, sometimes due to the harsh and physical nature of the work.[31]

Union leaders recognized that the violence and vice in which some workers participated potentially subjected the union to harmful racial stereotypes and contributed to the elite image of the union dishonorable, illegitimate and *uncivilized*. Attempting to bolster the reputation of the union as a respectable institution on par with white associations, they eschewed race-based characterizations. Instead, they emphasized a culture of respectability, based in part on an appropriation of middle-class values perceived to be the underpinnings of patriotic claims to political power.[32]

At the heart of projecting the union as a respectable and honorable institution was the emphasis on the dignity and prestige of the working-class family. To uphold the image of working-class men as respectable, honorable breadwinners, union leaders enacted a strict code of conduct among its members. The union leadership demanded that its members engage in "proper" behavior, etiquette, and order at work and in public. This meant using polite language, avoiding profanity and violence, and remaining calm so as to preserve "moral order." The high value union leaders placed on orderly behavior was evident in the vigilant surveillance, maintenance of an internal justice system, and strict discipline maintained by the union.[33] Union leaders argued that these restrictions were necessary to protect the prestige of the association.[34] Yet, the implication of this code of conduct was that the union was trying to counter racialized assumptions linking working-class black men to violence, vagrancy, vice, and crime.

132   B. A. Lucero

In addition to enforcing behavior deemed respectable among the union members, one of the most salient features of union strategy was the evasion of racial language in confrontations with capitalists. In the series of major strikes in 1899 and 1900, workers avoided pitching their struggle in terms of race, even though this was clearly a significant factor in the way elites handled union demands. Instead, they made modest demands, justified in terms of the necessity of fulfilling accepted roles for men as breadwinners.

Even as workers attempted to dodge the racial bullet, race became central to negotiations between capital and labor under American rule. In the strike of April 1899, for example, the commercial elite disparaged modest union gains as harmful to their interests, unreasonable, and even excessive, while American military officials sought to use force to crush the union. The way commercial elites and military officials described the workers suggests that one of the main reasons they found union demands so excessive was that they came from those of supposedly inferior social status of the union members.

The words of American Walter B. Barker, Captain of the Port of Cienfuegos, provide a glimpse into the American allies of prominent commercial elites viewed the port workers. Although he served as an arbiter between the two sides of the conflict, Barker unabashedly advocated in favor of the propertied classes during the strike, characterizing the workers as "a rabble element acting in the guise of a labor union," and a "low, disorderly element," as well as claiming their were "unjust." Barker recommended "drastic action" to suppress the strikers and threatened to detain workers and even "shoot 'em on the spot," in the event of disorder.[35] Although hostility toward striking laborers was certainly to be expected, the threat of extralegal violence against the strikers was strangely reminiscent of post-Reconstruction scare tactics aimed at preventing blacks from voting in states such as Barker's home of Mississippi. His disparaging descriptions and threats of violence reflected an increasing willingness among military authorities across the island to use violence to control poor and working-class Cubans, a level of repression that would likely be "acceptable" only if levied against a racial other.

The April strike marked a turning point in that this was one of the last times workers secured a substantial victory over capital. Workers secured a 50-cent increase in their wages, and double time on holidays.[36] Nevertheless, the gains achieved by the union were marred by the ominous precedent Barker had set with his demands for military action and his own threat of violence. In subsequent labor disputes, American military officials played an increasingly significant role in subsequent conflicts with laborers. Moreover, the specter of social disorder became a recurring motive in the ways planters and merchants wrote about the union. Nowhere is this more evident than in the next major labor conflict, the strike of February 1900.

Racialization of Organized Labor in the Strike of February 1900

In February 1900, dockworkers struck work for the seventh time within one year. While the union demanded higher wages and better working conditions for

Black Citizenship in Cuba, 1899–1902 133

the workers, planters and merchants rejected these demands as excessive, merchant and planters sought to derail it by the most effective means they had at their disposal. The specter of racial unrest provided that tool. Just as the Spanish had characterized the insurgents as black to delegitimize them among wealthy sympathizers, planters and merchants sometimes resorted to similar racial arguments to undermine the demands of stevedores.

Labor leaders articulated their claims unapologetically while emphasizing their desire to foster agreement and cooperation with employers. On February 5, 1900, Antonio Gómez Sosa, president of the Lightermen's union submitted a new tariff schedule to employers, all the while assuring them of his desire "to harmonize your interests with ours."[37] Although Gómez Sosa expressed his willingness to compromise, merchants focused on what they perceived as a unilateral action by a subordinate group against their interests. In his response to the lightermen, merchant Nicolás Castaño wrote to military authorities complaining that the strikers had failed to consult with the employers before changing the tariffs, implying that business interests were the only ones with the authority to change the terms of work. "Neither can we, nor should we consent to impositions of any kind, and much the less to tolerate that what belongs to us be governed and regulated by whom for the same is unauthorized nor has any right to," he wrote angrily.[38] Considering themselves "at the mercy of the Laborers associations," two dozen merchants and businessmen of Cienfuegos, joined Castaño in protest, petitioning General Wood to dissolve the labor unions.[39] Defending economic stratification, Castaño and his allies articulated a vision of Cuban society that centered on the social and economic subordination of the working classes.

No one more than Edwin F. Atkins bristled before the labor demands. As the owner of Soledad, one of the largest sugar mills in the island, he had thousands of dollars at stake in each shipment of his sugar. Strikes such as the one in February threatened to paralyze his business. Atkins insisted that conceding to the demands of workers would only serve to legitimize their authority. He cited the tumultuous history of organized labor in Cienfuegos, growing more powerful each day since the beginning of American military rule. "This is the seventh strike within a year," Atkins complained. In 1898, wages for lightermen were fixed at $2.50–$3.50, and the captains of the lighters received $3.50–$5.25, Spanish gold, per round trip from landing to ship anchored in bay and return.[40] "Wages having been fixed in previous settlements, the merchants feel they cannot submit to further demands, without serious consequences, and there are possibilities of matters taking a critical turn."[41] With ever-increasing demands for higher wages, the unions jeopardized the high profit margins of the property owners.

Similar to the way Barker depicted laborers during the April 1899 strike, Atkins attributed the increase in the demands of laborers in 1900 to agitators, thereby delegitimizing the claims of the workers. The label of agitator often referred to men, often veterans leading movements intended to provoke radical political or social change. In American-occupied Cuba, political and social radicalism were often interchangeable concepts aimed at undermining the legitimacy of demands among veterans for immediate and absolute independence and racial inclusion.

134   B. A. Lucero

Unlike most commercial elites of Cuban and Spanish extraction, Atkins dared to speak of race directly and explicitly, not fearing its potential ramifications for his patriotism. Days after the strike began, he wrote frantically to General Wood claiming that the black workers were the real perpetrators of the disorder, while the Spanish workers only stopped work out of fear of retaliation:

> Careful inquiry satisfied me that the lightermen who are Spaniards are satisfied as a class with present wages, and would go to work did they not fear to disobey the orders of the union, which seems to be dominated by certain Cubans.[42]

The Spaniards "were afraid of the negroes and Cubans who, they said, would kill them if they disobeyed orders or refused to join their association," he wrote.[43]

Although Atkins tended toward the extreme, military officials like Barker agreed with his assessment. He concurred that the strike was yet another example of agitators inciting the lower classes and judged that the demands lacked merit: "their claims [are] not founded on justice but an imposition on merchants and apparently the work of a few agitators for no other purpose than to keep themselves in prominence."[44] He also claimed that most "reasonable" workers wanted to return to work, but fear for their safety. This attempt to undermine the strike by enflaming existing differences among the workers paralleled earlier strategies among property owners to secure American military protection of their estates by claiming that Spaniards were unsafe from violent attack.[45]

Labor Militancy and Unfitness for Self-Government

A prominent advocate for American annexation of Cuba, Atkins vehemently protested against what he saw as the failures of civil authorities to defend propertied interests. Claiming that the civil authorities were not acting with sufficient force against the strikers, he demanded the presence in Cienfuegos of the commanding general of the province, General Wilson: "The civil authority is timid and unable to cope with the situation." Atkins characterized the strike as an emergency, and urged military authorities to use US troops to quell the strike.[46] By calling for military intervention in civil affairs to end the strike, Atkins bolstered his claim that Cubans needed American tutelage.

Civil authorities assured the military government that they could handle the strike. Mayor José Antonio Frías ordered the police to prevent the strikers from marauding around the port, but this only exacerbated the anxieties among commercial elites like Atkins.[47] He alleged that leading government employees and the chief of police sympathized with the strikers, tapping into existing fears among military officials in Cienfuegos that Cuban civil authorities, especially the historically multiracial and veteran-centered police force collaborated with disorderly elements. He argued that the Cuban authorities had no interest in upsetting the strikers because they were trying to ensure their re-election the following year.[48] According to Atkins, the civil authorities were as much of a

Black Citizenship in Cuba, 1899–1902 135

problem as the strikers, a not-so-subtle argument for military action to suppress the strike. James H. Wilson, Commanding General of Matanzas and Santa Clara eventually threatened military action when Barker informed him that the strike interfered with the shipment of government goods.

Civil authorities at the municipal and provincial level appealed to military authorities to refrain from sending in troops. Dozens of letters and telegrams from mayor Frías, José Miguel Gómez, the Civil Governor of Santa Clara Province, José de Jesús Monteagudo, the Chief of the Rural Guard and Commanding General Wilson to General Wood and the Adjutant General repeatedly confirmed that there was never any threat to order.[49] The threat of military intervention "seemed to alarm the alcalde," Frías most of all, and with good reason.[50] During his first year in office, Cienfuegos had been marred by seemingly endless conflicts between Americans and Cubans, earning him the reputation as incompetent and revolutionary among commercial elites and American military officials.

Seeking to defend his own authority and political positions, not to mention Cuban autonomy over civil affairs, the mayor assured military authorities that he and his men could maintain order *without* US military interference. He again pledged to protect strike-breakers, promised the competence of the police and described the strikers as entirely "pacific."[51] Finally, the strike ended when a commission of Frías, Barker, two laborers, and two merchants agreed in late February to deny the request for higher wages in favor of payment in American currency rather than Spanish gold.[52]

The port workers of Cienfuegos had returned to work, and business resumed its usual rhythm, but profound changes were underway. Civil authorities effectively repelled military suppression of the workers, but police served decidedly in the favor of the commercial elite. Civil authorities relied on the support of the workers to renew their claims to power in the coming June elections, likely making them more reluctant to crush the strike by force. On the other hand, they simultaneously relied on a tenuous and often contentious relationship with American military authorities for their political power. Appeasing military officials meant responding to the demands of the commercial elite, and defending the interests of the wealthiest residents of the region. This entailed controlling labor unions and severing potential links between the apparatus of repression and the alleged disorderly element.

Even though Frías in many respects failed the workers by caving to American and commercial interests, Wood deemed his actions insufficient demonstrations of loyalty to the military government and another indication of his incompetence. He forced Frías and Gómez Sosa both to resign from their government posts, appointing Leopoldo Figueroa, a conservative Cuban veteran, as interim mayor.[53] Though a Cuban veteran, Figueroa seemed to have learned from Frías important lessons in how to interact with the military government. He quickly became one of the staunchest collaborators with American military officials, securing their support to such a degree that they engineered his fraudulent election in June 1900.

136 B. A. Lucero

Breaking the Union in the Era of the Platt Amendment

The eruption of an island-wide series of strikes in early 1901 catalyzed an important re-adjustment in the relationships between workers and merchants. While port workers demanded higher wages and a shorter work day and other workers such as railroad workers and lumbermen struck in solidarity, commercial elites vowed to "take a stand" against the laborers whose "demands are increasing day by day, and are being carried beyond all reason."[54] Although they continued to complain to military officials, merchants and planters such as Atkins began to change their strategies to fight the union in early 1901.

In Cienfuegos, threat of a strike in February 1901 prompted some planters to begin to act independently of the military government to subdue labor. Their timing was unmistakable. Shifting political circumstances, including the submission of the Platt Amendment to the Cuban Constitutional Convention in early March 1901, rendered appeals to the military government less effective than in previous years. The possible outcomes were limited to two: the convention could accept the amendment and with it a conditional American-supervised sovereignty, or they could reject it which would likely delay, perhaps indefinitely, the withdrawal of American forces. In either event, planters benefited because they trusted that Americans would suppress labor in case the occupation as extended, and if the Convention accepted the Platt Amendment, Cuban authorities would be subject to American surveillance, likely forcing greater conservatism on their part. Moreover, planters confided to a greater degree in the conservative leadership of US-backed Figueroa, and doubted the possibility of civil support for the union.

The competitive nature of employment in dock work afforded employers an exorbitant degree of influence over the livelihoods of individual laborers especially during the hiring process.[55] Commercial elites, with Atkins at the forefront, sought to bypass the union leadership in order to exploit the fierce competition among workers for the limited jobs available. He devised a plan to deal directly with individual laborers: "I have a special rate with one of the best men in Cienfuegos, who for a long time has loaded all my vessels and steamers." Atkins claimed that the main benefit in employing his stevedores was that he had more control over them:

> the ship gets the benefit of the rate as I make nothing out of it, but it is an advantage that our chartered steamers employ our man, as I have control over him and he reports to me once or twice a day.[56]

Control over laborers, better than a commission on the work they performed, ensured that his products would be loaded onto ships, thereby guaranteeing his continued profits from sugar.

This strategy was not altogether new for merchants and property owners in Cienfuegos. They had employed strikebreakers in previous conflicts with the port workers' unions, a method made much easier by the steady stream of foreign workers, so long as they were white, imported to the island throughout the period of American occupation.[57] In 1899, Atkins exploited his personal relationship with a former slave and president of the lightermen's union by bribing him to convince his comrades to return to work.[58] In January 1900, shippers tried bypass the union by employing "white and desirable" immigrants to load and unload freight, driving down the prices of labor, even though the union possessed "recognized right" to perform such work.[59] When union leaders disputed this action, Judge Advocate Edgar S. Dudley cited the convention that unionized dockworkers would handle freight on the docks but noted that no law protected this custom. The absence of any law protecting the sole right of union laborers to perform the loading and unloading work provided shippers an opportunity to undermine union interests without direct military force.

Employer manipulation of the shape up may have had earlier roots, but it emerged as a central feature of relations between labor and capital following the announcement of the Platt Amendment. By early 1902, American military officials noted that "some employers have refused to abide by this rule of the gremio" requiring their delegates to mediate labor contracts.[60] By guaranteeing work to certain stevedores who were willing to cooperate with him, Atkins and other employers undermined the solidarity binding laborers to the union. When Atkins began to co-opt certain labor leaders, this system became problematic and led to extreme inequality in the distribution of work.

Stevedores in Cienfuegos confronted the challenges of preferential hiring practices amidst a series of negotiations between port workers and commercial elites in the Port of Havana, whereby they agreed on the tariff rates for the handling of over 50 items. These changes were consolidated in military orders 71, 72, and 76, measures designed to prevent future strikes prevent pilfering, and reduce the cost of labor.[61] The imposition of Military Order #59 (MO 59) in February 1902 applied Havana tariffs to Cienfuegos and allowed employers to specify the number of men they wanted to hire for each job.

In some ways, the application of a fixed tariff in Havana and Cienfuegos was a testament to the strength of the union in securing tangible gains for workers during the first years of the occupation. Shippers and consignees frequently complained about the "exorbitant" cost of labor in Cuba, criticizing the low productivity of the men and the necessity of employing a full gang of men selected by a union officer, regardless of the amount of work to be completed. According to one official from the United States Department of Labor,

> the Cuban stevedore will prefer a job and a system of payment by which he can work three or four days a month for $15 and be in enforced idleness the rest of the time than one by which he can earn $50 a month and have continuous employment.[62]

These disparaging attitudes toward Cuban workers formed the backdrop of the fixed tariff orders.

Indeed, despite its indication of union success, MO 59 also limited the agency of the union in defending the interests of the workers by limiting the possibility of strikes. Some workers equated this action with the establishment of a trust and

138   B. A. Lucero

a monopoly that would "take away our daily bread, which we have earned with so much fatigue."[63] In Cienfuegos, about one third of unionized workers were "idle or working part time," though the numbers were likely much higher for occupations of sporadic and seasonal nature like dock work.[64] Without control over hiring, the union could not guarantee the equitable distribution of employment to the men.

The crippling effects of MO 59 emerged most clearly in the failed attempts of Cienfuegos stevedores to change the unfavorable terms in early 1902. In March, they attempted to increase the tariff for unloading cattle above the rate specified in MO 71, and mandate that all workers loading or unloading must be members of the union. This met with stiff resistance from ship owners, who wrote to Leonard Wood, requesting that he reverse this raise. One man argued that "if they are required to conform to this note of the stevedores' union the union will feel at liberty to issue other notes and restrictions whenever they deem advisable."[65] Another ship owner claimed that "the distressed condition of this country does not allow the granting of those new demands," appealing to the military governor to "watch for the prosperity of the Island and prevent the conflicts which may very soon arise in consequence of the announced strike of the stevedores."[66] While Wood quickly dismissed stevedores' claims to higher tariffs for cattle discharging, the debate over control of hiring was much more protracted and contentious.

Union officials appealed to military authorities to help enforce union control over hiring. Florentino Pascual, a representative of the union, claimed that employers flouted the authority and rights of the union, "themselves imposing in an arbitrary matter the said personnel."[67] The president of the Havana stevedore union, Benigno Suárez wrote in support of Pascual's petition claiming the delegate control over hiring was customary in the capital.[68] Even former Cienfuegos mayor Gonzalo García Vieta came to the defense of the workers, writing to Hugh L. Scott that the workers "have suffered the impositions of the contractors without making a strike, willing as they are not to make trouble and expecting justice from Gen. Wood or you."[69] Wood's failure to support the requests of the union set in motion a process of internal struggle within the stevedore union. Inequalities in access to work combined with the precarious economic situation of many working-class families combined to exacerbate existing cleavages within the union, whether political, personal, or professional. Union leaders recognized the favoritism of employers in hiring certain stevedores, but certain workers, especially those who benefited from the new arrangements, sought to preserve the status quo.

The problem of how to determine employment plagued stevedores in Cienfuegos, causing conflict among union members. Most union meetings after MO 59 were consumed with arguments over hiring procedures.[70] While one faction of the union sought to preserve existing hiring arrangements, an opposing group argued that the imposition of Havana's tariffs would be best. One union member, Federico Ramírez, summed up the argument in favor of allowing the Delegates to name the workers so as "to avoid the vengeance of the Contractors on those who know how to reclaim their rights against the foreigners who oppose a law by the government and the union."[71] Ramírez identified a potent source of tension among the workers—that some members were more militant and more

Black Citizenship in Cuba, 1899–1902 139

committed to the union cause than were others. Perhaps he also alluded to a difference in the perception of militancy: whereas black labor militancy was rapidly criminalized and chastised by white contractors and merchants, white labor was typically viewed as more rational and reasonable.[72] This very observation, however, proved so divisive that numerous union members walked out of the meeting. Clearly, the issue of hiring divided union members who found favor with employers and those who feared that discrimination would prevent them from earning their rightful share of the work.[73]

By late 1902, fragmentation within the union reached the breaking point. Rumors that a group of former union members had broken away to form a separate labor organization reached the meeting hall.[74] Although the new union, *Gremio Mutuo*, was not established officially until 1904,[75] leaders of *Gremio Unión* (the original union) feared that the establishment of a new union could destroy the position of the workers after the union had worked so hard toward the "emancipation of the Stevedores of this Port."[76] Indeed, the debate over hiring practices proved sufficient to undermine the solidarity among one of the most powerful labor organizations of the island, shifting the power firmly in favor of employers.

The next time workers in Cienfuegos attempted collective action, prominent Cuban patriots cemented the recent victories of these businessmen with swift government repression. The workers had struck work in solidarity with Havana tobacco workers following the slaying of strikers by police and rural guardsmen on "Bloody Monday," November 24, 1902.[77] Observers in Cienfuegos complained that workers blocked streets and gathered menacingly at the wharves, alluding to the centrality of the predominantly black dockworkers in labor activism in that port city.[78] Workers in the nearby sugar zones of Cruces and Lajas allegedly forced laborers to abandon their jobs and destroyed sugar estates belonging to Americans and one owned by vice-president, Luis Estévez Romero. The alleged threat to order was made that much more pressing due to the perception that many of these workers were black. In fact, the Círculo de Obreros of Cruces actually held its meetings at the house of the Centro Africano.[79] The eruption of violence within historically-peaceful local labor movement (war years aside) signaled the frustration of workers to achieve what they saw as a dignified place in the Republic.

Provincial and national political elites quickly and violently reiterated the place they envisioned for workers in the Cuban republic. President Tomás Estrada Palma ordered Provincial Governor José Miguel Gómez, already under pressure from the Círculo de Hacendados de Cienfuegos, to repress the demonstrators and restore order.[80] Rural guardsmen at the behest of Gómez captured and assassinated labor leaders on December 7. In the face of internal fragmentation, mounting victories for employers, and violent state repression against unions, port workers scrabbled to regain their local footing by collaborating with other labor organizations. Yet, the blow dealt by the military government and reinforced by the administrations of Estrada Palma and Gómez cemented the greatest fears of black veterans and workers across Cuba: the Republic that they had helped bring to life fell short on the promises of social justice.

140   *B. A. Lucero*

Conclusions: The Demise of the Union and the Consolidation of "Urban Order"

"At the close of the revolution in 1898 the blacks as a whole dropped into their accustomed place and resumed their industries. Some remained in the field until the final disbandment in the spring of 1899."[81] This assertion appeared in a November 1906 edition of *The Herald*, shortly after the onset of the second American intervention. To a certain degree, this statement rightly points out the overwhelming continuities in the social structure before and after the war of independence. Reading this article, Americans might have assumed that blacks willingly returned to the low-paying jobs in cane cutting, manual and day labor. More accurately, however, it shows how successful American and Cuban authorities were in stamping out alternative visions of the emerging republic, particularly those proposing a more expansive vision of citizenship.

Yet, this assertion does not take into account the long years of struggle, the occasional victories, and the perseverance through defeat that powered the organized labor movement after the revolution. In 1899, the stevedore union of Cienfuegos flouted the expectations of wealthy planters, American military officials, and even some prominent Cuban patriots by refusing to assume positions of servitude vis-à-vis commercial elites. The stevedore union presented a potent challenge to the relationship between capital and labor with its militant demands for higher wages and better working conditions. Simultaneously, the union challenged the urban order in Cienfuegos by denying commercial elites absolute control over the urban spaces straddling the port and bordering the city center.

The racial background of many of the stevedores presented unique problems for the union. Fortified by the influx of numerous Cuban veterans and displaced rural people in the months after the war, the union had a diverse and multi-racial membership, but was composed primarily of men of African descent.[82] From the perspective of merchants and planters, the stevedore union was more than an association of workers. It was a union of blacks, Cuban veterans, and most feared of all, black veterans. The organization of a large number of black men and veterans fit comfortably into an already-existing framework of an allegedly impending race war, an idea based upon anxieties among wealthy property owners that an armed black population with military experience would overthrow white rule on the island. Confrontations between the union and the commercial elite took on racial undertones, as property owners like Atkins delegitimized labor demands based on racial arguments. Stevedores, however, avoided references to race almost completely. Cienfuegos' stevedores eschewed racial language to embrace the multi-racial character of the union membership, an alliance that would lend the union great credibility and strength, as Alejandro de la Fuente rightly notes.[83] Yet, the language of class, specifically the idea of being a respectable working-class man, provided black stevedores a way to dispel racialized imaginings of union activities, even if they were port-paralyzing strikes. In 1899, and to a certain extent in 1900, the union was able to secure various gains for workers, in the face of fierce petitioning from merchants and planters to disband the unions by force.

Black Citizenship in Cuba, 1899–1902 141

The shifting tides of Cuban politics, beginning in 1901, contributed to the gradual dismantling of the united front once boasted by the stevedore union, marking the close of an epoch in Cienfuegos. The stevedores were one of the last strongholds of black authority in the urban center, in the vital portside neighborhood of Marsillán. With internal dissension consuming the union, commercial elites were able again to consolidate their control over the port and commerce. Although the men of African descent still composed the majority of port workers, the authority of organized labor had been severely compromised, forcing black workers to search for alternative avenues of social justice in an increasingly white republic.

In 1902, Victor S. Clark, an official of the US Department of Labor ironically asserted that "Cuba is one of the most democratic countries in the world. Nowhere else does the least-considered member of a community aspire with more serene confidence to social equality with its most exalted personage." Yet, behind this patronizing observation, Clark revealed the disparities between worker claims to equality and the dominant practice of citizenship in the emerging Cuban republic: The worker, he claimed "frequently confounds ideals with realities, and as his ideal of himself is usually an exalted one, this does not incline him to diffidence or humility."[84] While MO 59 curbed union power and fomented fragmentation among workers, and their former compatriots under government order violently repressed their demonstrations, stevedores had not simply "dropped into their accustomed place" to accept the second-class citizenship implied in the stillbirth of the Cuban republic; they had struggled with limited success and much difficulty to secure dignity for workers regardless of race in a supposedly colorblind society.

Notes

1 George Clarke Musgrave, *Under Three Flags in Cuba: A Personal Account of the Cuban Insurrection and Spanish-American War* (Boston: Little, Brown and Company, 1899), 163.
2 Edwin F. Atkins to Brooks, January 30, 1899, Volume II.19, Massachusetts Historical Society, Atkins Family Papers (Hereafter cited as MHS/EFA).
3 "Spanish Treaty Claims Commission: Edwin F. Atkins against the United States," February 4, 1899, Box.II.4, MHS/EFA; Rebecca J. Scott, *Slave Emancipation in Cuba: The Transition to Free Labor, 1860–1899* (Pittsburgh: University of Pittsburgh Press, 1986), 240.
4 Damian Yzarzagaza and Esteban García versus Manuel Soriano, "Acta de Conciliación," September 18, 1889, File 18, Provincial Historical Archive of Cienfuegos, Juzgado Municipal de Cienfuegos (Hereafter cited as APHC/JMC).
5 "Edwin F. Atkins, Petition before the Spanish Treaty Claims Commission," December, 1905, Box.II.4, folio 54 MHS/EFA; Edwin F. Atkins to Honorable Edward F. Uhl, December 9, 1895, Volume II.39, MHS/EFA; Edwin Farnsworth Atkins, *Sixty Years in Cuba, Reminiscences of Edwin F. Atkins* (Cambridge: Private print at the Riverside Press, 1926), 228, 191; "Edwin F. Atkins to Consulate of the United States, Cienfuegos," January 20, 1897, Volume II.39, folio 121, MHS/EFA; Peter M. Beal to United States Consul, Cienfuegos, January 21, 1897, Papers of the United States Consul at Cienfuegos, Microfilm Reel #6, Walter Royal Davis Library, University of North Carolina at Chapel Hill (Hereafter cited as WRD/UNC/USCC).

142   B. A. Lucero

6 Orlando García Martínez, "La Brigada de Cienfuegos," 182–183; Edwin Farnsworth Atkins, *Sixty Years in Cuba* (Cambridge: Riverside Press, 1926), 323–324; Edwin F. Atkins to James H. Wilson, October 5, 1899, Box 2, James H. Wilson Papers, Manuscript Division, Library of Congress, Washington, D.C. (Hereafter cited as, LOC/MD/JHW).

7 The excellent work Rebecca Scott does consider issues of citizenship with regard to rural workers in the vicinity of Cienfuegos, and Joan Casanovas examined urban labor during the late colonial period, but the in-depth study of urban labor in the provincial city of Cienfuegos is rare. Rebecca J. Scott, "Race, Labor, and Citizenship in Cuba: A View from the Sugar District of Cienfuegos, 1886–1909," The Hispanic American Historical Review 78:4 (1998): 687–728; Joan Casanova, *Bread or Bullets: Urban Labor and Spanish Colonialism in Cuba, 1850–1898* (Pittsburgh: University of Pittsburgh Press, 1998).

8 United States War Department, Cuban Census Office, *Report on the Census of Cuba, 1899* (Washington, D.C.: Government Printing Office, 1900), 180.

9 Ibid., 156.

10 Fred S. Foltz to Adjutant General, February 3, 1900, Box 83, File 664, United States National Archives, Military Government of Cuba Records, Record Group 140, Entry 3 (Hereafter cited as USNA/MGC/RG 140/ E 3).

11 Victor S. Clark, "Labor Conditions in Cuba," *Bulletin of the Department of Labor* 41 (July 1902): 744–748.

12 D. Dudley, "Report on Inspection of Cienfuegos," December 18, 1898, Box 5, File 95 ½, United States National Archives, Records of the United State Army Overseas, Record Group 395, Entry 1446 (Hereafter cited as USNA/RUSA/RG 395/E 1466).

13 Clark, "Labor Conditions in Cuba," 744.

14 Cienfuegos City Council Minutes, Cienfuegos, January 26, 1898, April 13, 1899, APHC/AC; Isidro Tomás Suárez, "Testimony before Spanish Claims Committee, Case 293," February 26, 1904, Box 142, Part 3, Folder 2, United States National Archives, Spanish Claims Commission, Record Group 76, Entry 352 (Hereafter cited as USNA/SCC/RG 76/E 352); J.H. Hysell, "Report Regarding jail at Cienfuegos," May 22–26, 1899, Box 8, File 4074, USNA/RUSA/ RG 395/E 1331.

15 Civil Government of the Province of Santa Clara, Section of Public Order and Police, "Relación de las sociedades existentes en esta Provincia," April 1900, Box 36, No File, USNA/RUSA/RG 395/E 1331.

16 Assorted papers of the societies of instruction and recreation Club de Obreros de Cruces, Provincial Historical Archive of Cienfuegos, Registro de Asociaciones (Hereafter cited as APHC/RA); Collector of Customs, Cienfuegos, "Telegram," January 18, 1900, Box 61, File 504, Hereafter cited as, USNA/MGC/RG 140/E 3.

17 Damian Yzarzagaza and Esteban García versus Manuel Soriano, "Acta de Conciliación," September 18, 1889, File 18, APHC/JMC.

18 Major A. H. Bowman "Reports on Recent Strike at Cienfuegos," March 9, 1900, Box 31, File 1378, USNA/RUSA/RG 395/E 1331.

19 Gremio Mutuo de Estibadores de Cienfuegos, Lista de Socios, 1902, APHC/MP; Carlos Roloff, *Indice alfabético y defunciones del Ejército Libertador de Cuba, guerra de independencia, iniciada el 24 de febrero de 1895 y terminada oficialmente* (Havana: Imprenta de Rambla y Bouza, 1901).

20 Gremio Mutuo de Estibadores de Cienfuegos, "Libro de Identificación del Gremio Mutuo de Estibadores de Cienfuegos," 1904, Archivo Provincial Histórico de Cienfuegos, Fondo Movimiento Portuario (Hereafter cited as, APHC/MP). Only four workers identified as white joined the union in 1904.

21 Enrique Collazo, *Los sucesos de Cienfuegos* (Havana: Imprenta C. Martínez y Compañía, 1905), 33; Gremio Mutuo de Estibadores de Cienfuegos, Book of Meeting Minutes, November 28, 1902, APHC/MP. Cámara de Representantes, *Memoria de los trabajos realizados durante la primera legislatura ordinaria* (Havana: Imprenta de Rambla y Bouza, 1917), 15, 49–53.

Black Citizenship in Cuba, 1899–1902 143

22 Luis J. Bustamante, *Diccionario Biográfico Cienfueguero* (Cienfuegos: n.p., 1931), 177; Rebecca J. Scott, *Degrees of Freedom: Louisiana and Cuba After Slavery* (Cambridge, MA: Harvard University Press, 1998), 22. The Terry family owned numerous sugar plantations in south-central Cuba. Nine members with the last name Sarría appear on the member roster, four of whom joined in 1904. The slaves of the Sarría estate were numerous, and by the 1880s made up a substantial part of the workforce of one of the largest sugar central in Cuba: Soledad owned by Bostonian Edwin F. Atkins. At least four members held the last name Quesada, suggesting a connection with the Cienfuegos plantation Santa Rosalía, owned by José Quesada, and eventually becoming part of the Constancia estate. The Tartabulls were also represented in the union, connecting it to the old Caridad plantation owned by José Tartabull. At least one former slave with the last name Pombert, appears on the membership roster, showing the connection with the last of the three largest plantations in Cienfuegos: the Hormiguero estates, owned by Elias Ponvert.

23 Gremio Mutuo de Estibadores de Cienfuegos, Lista de Socios, 1902, APHC/MP.

24 Gremio Union de Estibadores de Cienfuegos: Lista de Socios, 1902, f. 170–171, APHC/MP.

25 Assorted papers of the societies of instruction and recreation Divina Caridad, Santa Bárbara, and San Cayetano, APHC/RA.

26 Cabildo Real Congo San Antonio de Paduá, Society Documents, 1902, APHC/RA; Sociedad de Instrucción y Recreo de Africanos Nación de Portugués San Teresa de Meditando, Society Documents, 1902, APHC/RA; Gremio Mutuo de Estibadores de Cienfuegos, Book of Meeting Minutes, March 14, 1907, APHC/MP

27 Manuel Fernández versus Daniel Rufalé and Manuel Casanova, January 2, 1894, Juicios de Falta, File 1307, APHC/JMC.

28 The Union supported the Strike of Typographers in the United States in December 1905, for example. Gremio Mútuo de Estibadores de Cienfuegos, Book of Meeting Minutes, December 13, 1905, APHC/MP. The union was also invited to participate in the American Federation of Labor in Detroit in July 1905. Gremio Mútuo de Estibadores de Cienfuegos, Book of Meeting Minutes, July 19, 1905, APHC/MP.

29 Gremio Mútuo de Estibadores de Cienfuegos, Book of Meeting Minutes, November 24, 1902, APHC/MP.

30 Parda Pía Nodal versus Magín Torres, January 4, 1896–January 29, 1896, File 1348, Archivo Provincial Histórico de Cienfuegos, Juzgado Municipal de Cienfuegos, Juicios de Falta (Hereafter cited as, APC/JMC/JF); "El moreno Magín Torres versus el idem Don Máximo Cuesta," February 10, 1894–February 13, 1894, APC/JMC/JF.

31 Gremio Mútuo de Estibadores de Cienfuegos, Book of Meeting Minutes, September 10, 1902, APHC/MP.

32 Walter B. Barker to Louis V. Caziarc, "Relative to the Strike of Laborers at the Government Dock, and the Statement of Same," April 7, 1899, Box 6, File 2905, USNA/RUSA/RG 395/E 1466.

33 Gremio Mútuo de Estibadores de Cienfuegos, Book of Meeting Minutes, September 27, 1902, January 21, 1905, APHC/MP.

34 Gremio Mútuo de Estibadores de Cienfuegos, Book of Meeting Minutes, 1902–1907, APHC/MP.

35 Walter B. Barker to Louis V. Caziarc, "Relative to the Strike of Laborers at the Government Dock, and the Statement of Same," April 7, 1899, Box 6, File 2905, USNA/RUSA/RG 395/E 1466.

36 Major A. H. Bowman "Reports on Recent Strike at Cienfuegos," March 9, 1900, Box 31, File 1378, USNA/RUSA/RG 395/E 1331.

37 Lightermen's Union, "New Tariffs," February 5, 1900, in Major A. H. Bowman, "Reports on Recent Strike at Cienfuegos," March 9, 1900, Box 31, File 1378, USNA/RUSA/RG 395/E 1331.

38 Lightermen's Union, "New Tariffs," February 5, 1900, in Major A. H. Bowman, "Reports on Recent Strike at Cienfuegos," March 9, 1900, Box 31, File 1378, USNA/

144   *B. A. Lucero*

RUSA/RG 395/E 1331; Castaño, Cacicedo, Huike, Terry and 20 others to General Leonard Wood, February 21, 1900, Box 61, File 504, USNA/MGC/RG 140/E 3.

39 Ibid.

40 The rate of wages varying according to the size of the lighter and distance.

41 Edwin F. Atkins to General Leonard Wood, February 21, 1900, Box 61, File 504, USNA/MGC/RG 140/E 3.

42 Ibid.

43 Atkins, *Sixty Years in Cuba*, 315.

44 Walter B. Barker to Adjutant General, February 21, 1900, Box 31, File 944, USNA/RUSA/RG 395/E 1331.

45 Merchants, "Ask for American Soldiers to Preserve Better Order," January 27, 1899, Box 3, File 323, USNA/RUSA/RG 395/E 1466.

46 Ibid.

47 Major A. H. Bowman "Reports on Recent Strike at Cienfuegos," March 9, 1900, Box 31, File 1378, USNA/RUSA/RG 395/E 1331.

48 Ibid.

49 José Miguel Gómez to General Leonard Wood, March 1, 1900, Box 61, File 504, USNA/MGC/RG 140/E 3; General Wilson to Adjutant General, February 23, 1900, Box 61, File 504, USNA/MGC/RG 140/E 3; General Wilson to Adjutant General to General, March 1, 1900, Box 61, File 504, USNA/MGC/RG 140/E 3; José de Jesús Monteagudo to General Wilson," February 28, 1900 USNA, Box 31, File 1128, USNA/RUSA/RG 395/E 1331.

50 Atkins, *Sixty Years in Cuba*, 316.

51 José Antonio Frías, "Telegram Acknowledging Receipt of Two Messages," February 24, 1900, Box 61, File 504, USNA/MGC/RG 140/E 3; Mayor Frías to General Leonard Wood, February 21, 1900, Box 61, File 504, USNA/MGC/RG 140/E 3; Mayor Frías to General Leonard Wood, February 24, 1900, Box 61, File 504, USNA/MGC/RG 140/E 3; Mayor Frías to Adjutant General, February 23, 1900, Box 61, File 504, USNA/MGC/RG 140/E 3.

52 Edwin F. Atkins to General Leonard Wood, February 28, 1900, Volume II.20, MHS/EFA; Mayor Frías to General Leonard Wood, February 28, 1900, Box 61, File 504, USNA/MGC/RG 140/E 3.

53 Atkins, *Sixty Years in Cuba*, 316; José Miguel Gómez, "Telegram Advising That Doctor Frías Delivered Office to Leopoldo Figueroa," March 2, 1900, Box 55, File 347, USNA/MGC/RG 140/ E 3.

54 Gerardo A. Cárdenas to Lieutenant Colonel, 2nd [U.S.] Infantry, February 12, 1901, Box 122, File 18, USNA/MGC/RG 140E 3; "La Situación," *El Popular*, January 3, 1901, Box 122, File 18, USNA/MGC/RG 140/E 3; Edwin F. Atkins to General Leonard Wood, "Telegram," February 7, 1901, Box 122, File 18, USNA/MGC/RG 140/ E 3; Walter B. Barker, "Enclosing Names of Leaders of the Riot at Santa Clara," March 20, 1901, Box 122, File 18, USNA/MGC/RG 140/E 3; Major Hatfield, "States that Captain Arteaga of the Rural Guard was Ordered to Ciego to Carry Out Instructions," April 5, 1901, Box 122, File 18, USNA/MGC/RG 140/E 3; Commanding officer, Mackenzie Barracks, "Reports Strike Conditions at Santa Cruz," March 18, 1901, Box 122, File 18, USNA/MGC/RG 140E 3; Edwin F. Atkins to O. H. Stilling, February 4, 1901, Volume II.22, MHS/EFA.

55 Anna Green, "The Work Process," in *Dock Workers*, II, ed. Sam Davies, Colin J. Davis, David e Vries, Lex Heerma van Voss, Lidewij Hesselink and Klaus Weinhauer (Burlington, VT: Ashgate, 2000), 562.

56 Edwin F. Atkins to E.P. Searle, April 7, 1901, Volume II.23, MHS/EFA.

57 Alejandro de la Fuente, "Two Dangers, One Solution: Immigration, Race, and Labor in Cuba, 1900–1930," *International Labor and Working-Class History* 51:1 (1997): 39.

58 Frederick Cooper, Thomas C. Holt, and Rebecca Jarvis Scott, *Beyond Slavery: Explorations of Race, Labor, and Citizenship in Postemancipation Societies* (Chapel Hill: University of North Carolina Press, 2000), 93; Atkins, *Sixty Years in Cuba*, 314.

Black Citizenship in Cuba, 1899–1902 145

59 G.D. Meikeljohn and L.S. Gage, "Letter from Assistant Secretary of War Enclosing One from the Secretary of the Treasury, Both in Relation to the Entry of Chinese in Cuba," January 17, 1899, Box 1, File 486, USNA/MGC/RG 140/ E 3; Colonel Tasker H. Bliss, "Enclosing a Telegram in which he Acknowledges Receipt of Copies of U.S. Immigration Laws which are to be Applied to the Island of Cuba" April 27, 1899, Box 11, File 2772, USNA/MGC/RG 140/E 3; Collector of Customs, "Telegram: States Spanish American Iron Company and The Cuba Company Request Authority To Import 620 Laborers, Porto Ricans, White, Able-bodied, Selected," July 17, 1901, Box 185, File 2837, USNA/MGC/RG 140/E 3; Collector of Customs, Cienfuegos, "Telegram," January 18, 1900, Box 61, File 504, USNA/MGC/RG 140/E 3.

60 James Dudley, "2nd Endorsement," April 28, 1902, Box 228, No File, USNA/MGC/RG 140/E 3.

61 Tasker Bliss to Adjutant General, June 24, 1901, Box 188, File 3003, USNA/MGC/RG 140/E 3; José Rivero Muñiz, *El movimiento obrero durante la primera intervención: Apuntes para la historia del proletariado en Cuba* (Las Villas: Universidad Central de las Villas, 1961), 177.

62 Clark, "Labor Conditions in Cuba," 732.

63 "General Wood, alerta," *El Estibador*, June 24, 1901, Box 188, File 3003, USNA/MGC/RG 140/E 3.

64 Clark, "Labor Conditions in Cuba," 775.

65 Asmus Leonard, "States There Has Arisen a Question at Cienfuegos Respecting the Stevedores' Tariff for Discharging Cattle," March 27, 1902, Box 228, File 101, USNA.MGC/RG 140/E 3.

66 Manuel Roy, *et al.* to Military Governor of Cuba, [n.d.], Box 228, No File, USNA/MGC/RG 40/ E 3.

67 Florentino Pascual to Military Governor of Cuba, April 16, 1902, Box 228, No File, USNA/MGC/RG 140/E 3.

68 Benigno Suárez to Military Governor of Cuba, April 14, 1902, Box 228, No File, USNA/MGC/RG 140/ E 3.

69 Gonzalo García Vieta to Hugh L. Scott, April 9, 1902, Box 228, No File, USNA/MGC/RG 140/E 3.

70 Military order #59 stated:

> *Havana, February 28, 1902.* In view of the mutual agreement entered into on February 22, 1902, in the office of the Captain of the Port of Cienfuegos, by the representatives of the shipping interests, labor unions and contractors of said port, in the absence of the Adjutant General of the Department, accepting the tariffs and conditions now in force in the Port of Havana, the Military Governor of Cuba directs that Orders Nos. 71 and 76, series 1901, these Headquarters, as well as all duly authorized tariffs and agreements this date in force in the Port of Havana be made applicable likewise to the port of Cienfuegos and binding upon all parties concerned. In all cases where labor is hired the employer shall be judge of the number of men to be employed.

71 Gremio Mútuo de Estibadores de Cienfuegos, Book of Meeting Minutes, April 5, 1902, APHC/MP.

72 Edwin F. Atkins to General Leonard Wood, February 21, 1900, Volume II. 29, MHS/EFA.

73 Gremio Mútuo de Estibadores de Cienfuegos, Book of Meeting Minutes, April 5, 1902, APHC/MP.

74 Gremio Mútuo de Estibadores de Cienfuegos, Book of Meeting Minutes, October 20, 1902, APHC/MP.

75 Gremio Mútuo de Estibadores de Cienfuegos, Memoria del Gremio Mútuo de Estibadores del Puerto Cienfuegos, 1904–1948, APHC/MP.

146 *B. A. Lucero*

76 Ibid. In Havana, the stevedore union underwent a similar split in January 1901. American military officials guessed that this spilt resulted from "some internal cause of dissatisfaction," and this was "purely a personal one," as both unions demanded the same wage. Collector of Customs of Cuba to Adjutant General, January 2, 1901, Box 122, File 18, USNA/MGC/RG 140E 3.

77 Pedro Luis Padrón, *¿Qué república era aquella?* (Havana: Editorial de Ciencias Sociales, 1986), 26; Lillian Guerra, *The Myth of José Martí: Conflicting Nationalisms in Early Twentieth-Century Cuba* (Chapel Hill: University of North Carolina Press, 2005), 138–146.

78 "Despacho," *La Lucha*, November 27, 1902.

79 Assorted papers of the Centro Africano, APHC/RA.

80 Herbert G. Squiers to Tomás Estrada Palma, November 27, 1902, quoted in Padrón, *¿Qué Republica*, 29; José de la O García to Alcalde Municipal de _____, November 1902, quoted in John Dumoulin, "El primer desarrollo del movimiento obrero y la formación del proletariado en el sector azucarero. Cruces 1886–1902," *Islas* 48 (1974): 23–24.

81 "Cubans, Ugly, Plot Against Liberals," *The Herald*, November 16, 1906, Volume II.64, MHS/EFA.

82 Clark, "Labor Conditions in Cuba," 687.

83 De la Fuente, "Two Dangers…," 32.

84 Clark, "Labor Conditions in Cuba," 780.

References

Archives and Libraries

Massachusetts Historical Society (MHS)
Atkins Family Papers (EFA)
Provincial Historical Archive of Cienfuegos (APHC)
Juzgado Municipal de Cienfuegos (JMC)
Fondo Movimiento Portuario (MP)
Registro de Asociaciones (RA)
Walter Royal Davis Library, University of North Carolina at Chapel Hill (WRD/UNC)
United States Consul at Cienfuegos (USCC)
Library of Congress, Manuscript Division (LOC/MD)
James H. Wilson Papers (JHW).
United States National Archives (USNA)
Records of the United State Army Overseas, Record Group 395 (RUSA/RG 395)
Military Government of Cuba Records, Record Group 140 (MGC/RG 140)
Spanish Claims Commission, Record Group 76 (SCC/RG 76/E 352)

Published Primary Sources

Bustamante, Luis J. *Diccionario Biográfico Cienfueguero*. Cienfuegos: n.p., 1931.

Cámara de Representantes, *Memoria de los trabajos realizados durante la primera legislatura ordinaria*. Havana: Imprenta de Rambla y Bouza, 1917.

Clark, Victor S. "Labor Conditions in Cuba," *Bulletin of the Department of Labor* 41 (July 1902): 663–793.

Collazo, Enrique. *Los sucesos de Cienfuegos*. Havana: Imprenta C. Martínez y Compañía, 1905.

Musgrave, George Clarke. *Under Three Flags in Cuba: A Personal Account of the Cuban Insurrection and Spanish-American War*. Boston: Little, Brown and Company, 1899.

Roloff, Carlos. *Índice alfabético y defunciones del Ejército Libertador de Cuba, guerra de independencia, iniciada el 24 de febrero de 1895 y terminada oficialmente.* Havana: Imprenta de Rambla y Bouza, 1901.

United States War Department, Cuban Census Office, *Report on the Census of Cuba, 1899.* Washington, D.C.: Government Printing Office, 1900.

Secondary Sources

Atkins, Edwin Farnsworth. *Sixty Years in Cuba, Reminiscences of Edwin F. Atkins.* Cambridge, MA: Private print at the Riverside Press, 1926.

Casanova, Joan. *Bread Or Bullets: Urban Labor and Spanish Colonialism in Cuba, 1850–1898.* Pittsburgh: University of Pittsburgh Press, 1998.

Cooper, Frederick, Thomas C. Holt, and Rebecca Jarvis Scott. *Beyond Slavery: Explorations of Race, Labor, and Citizenship in Postemancipation Societies.* Chapel Hill: University of North Carolina Press, 2000.

De la Fuente, Alejandro. "Two Dangers, One Solution: Immigration, Race, and Labor in Cuba, 1900–1930," *International Labor and Working-Class History* 51:1 (1997): 30–49.

Dumoulin, John. "El primer desarrollo del movimiento obrero y la formación del proletariado en el sector azucarero. Cruces 1886–1902," *Islas* 48 (1974): 3–66.

García Martínez, Orlando. "La Brigada de Cienfuegos: un análisis social de su formación." In *Espacios, silencios y los sentidos de la libertad. Cuba entre 1878 y 1912,* edited by Fernando Martínez Heredia, Rebecca J. Scott y Orlando F. García Martínez, 163–192. Havana: Ediciones Unión, 2001.

Green, Anna. "The Work Process," in *Dock Workers,* 2 volumes, II: 560–579, edited by Sam Davies, Colin J. Davis, David e Vries, Lex Heerma van Voss, Lidewij Hesselink and Klaus Weinhauer. Burlington, VT: Ashgate, 2000.

Guerra, Lillian. *The Myth of José Martí: Conflicting Nationalisms in Early Twentieth-Century Cuba.* Chapel Hill: University of North Carolina Press, 2005.

Muñiz, José Rivero. *El movimiento obrero durante la primera intervención: Apuntes para la historia del proletariado en Cuba.* Las Villas: Universidad Central de las Villas, 1961.

Padrón, Pedro Luis. *¿Qué república era aquella?* Havana: Editorial de Ciencias Sociales, 1986.

Scott, Rebecca J. *Slave Emancipation in Cuba: The Transition to Free Labor, 1860–1899.* Pittsburgh: University of Pittsburgh Press, 1986.

Scott, Rebecca J. "Race, Labor, and Citizenship in Cuba: A View from the Sugar District of Cienfuegos, 1886–1909," The Hispanic American Historical Review 78:4 (1998): 687–728.

Scott, Rebecca J. *Degrees of Freedom: Louisiana and Cuba After Slavery.* Cambridge, MA: Harvard University Press, 1998.

Part III

Discrimination and Resistance

8 State Violence, Radical Protest and the Black/African Female Body

Kanyinsola O. Obayan

What have we, women, done to warrant our being taxed? We women are like trees which bear fruit. You should tell us the reason why women who bear seeds should be counted.[1]

Introduction

In the epigraph above, Eniyidia of Mbiopongo, one of the participants of the Women's War of 1929, extends the problematic of the war beyond the colonial imposition of taxes to the realm of femininity and sexuality. Although most of the literature written on the Women's War of 1929 primarily focuses upon it as a major instance of anti-colonial resistance in Nigeria, the impact of the war far exceeds its conventional interpretations as it can be used as praxis to understand global dialectics of gender, activism, and the body politic. The Women's War was more than just a struggle against colonial taxation; instead, it was a struggle against the structural erasure of indigenous femininity and its practices within the colonial project.

Situating the women of 1929 within the proposed colonial narrative of absence provides a rubric through which the quote above can be fully conceptualized. By referring to women's reproductive capabilities, Eniyidia of Mbiopongo centers the female body within this narrative, and in doing so, offers a novel way of understanding the historic moment. Considering the ways in which the women organized and protested against the colonial regime using bodily undress, or nakedness, it would seem that the body emerges as both rationalization and justification for the women of 1929. Interestingly enough, the colonial administration did not hold the same bodily preoccupations as the women and were seemingly preoccupied with the taxes.

The successful implementation of taxation was the rationale behind the widespread inquiries and investigation about the Women's War of 1929. As a result, the primary objective of the colonialists was to investigate why the women opposed the tax. This reason is articulated by women involved in the conflict: "How are we women to pay tax? Where can we get the means from to pay it? That was our grievance, and we made the demonstration to make you feel that we were aggrieved."[2] Underlying these women's responses is the unwavering notion that taxing and counting women was fundamentally wrong. Nevertheless,

152   K. O. Obayan

it is clear that the colonial administrators either failed to understand the women's rationale or simply deemed it as insignificant, because they simply proceeded to punish the women for their "misconduct" and did not attempt to remedy the situation.

Another instance of this ideological clash between the colonial administration and the women is present in the labeling of the incident. The colonial powers labeled the incident as a riot and referred to it as such in their archives, while the women labeled it *Ogu Umunwaanyi*, or Women's War. How is it that the colonial authorities were so completely and consistently wrong about the women's positionality regarding the war? In this chapter, I argue that there is an inherent incompatibility between the British colonial system of thought at the time and the indigenous Igbo and Ibibio systems of thought that motivated the Women's War. As a result, we must read the Women's War as a clash between different epistemological conceptualizations of the female body and its political materiality. The word "body" here not only refers to the corporeal body, but it also refers to its attendant existential and cultural state of being. Thus, when the Igbo and Ibibio women of 1929 resisted using the indigenous practice of naked protest, they were purposely disarticulating the grammar of coloniality by imposing the problematic of the "obscene" female body onto the colonial regime, while asserting their right to the control of indigenous femininity and its practices.

The Women's War of 1929: Historical Background

The Women's War (*Ogu Umunwaanyi*) of 1929 was a resistance movement led by Igbo and Ibibio women in the small southeastern Nigerian village of Oloko against the unfair taxation of the British colonial government.[3] The British colonial government first introduced taxation to southeastern Nigeria by counting and taxing Igbo men in 1925.[4] Administrators worried, however, about the native tax previous assessors' calculation of the tax rates so they ordered for a reassessment of taxes in 1929. By this time, the economic situation had also changed; palm oil prices had fallen and the taxes, set at 1925 levels, become burdensome to all, especially women.[5] Besides, women in Oloko village had already begun holding meetings in the form of their traditional *mikiri* concerning the possibilities of tax reassessment.[6] Thus, when Mark Emeruwa, the agent of the Oloko Warrant Chief, Okugo, entered the compound of Nwanyeruwa and told her to count her goats and sheep on November 23, 1929, Nwanyeruwa refused and demanded to know if Emeruwa's mother had ever been counted.[7] Provoked by Nwanyeruwa's comments, he proceeded to choke her and Nwanyeruwa seized his throat in an attempt to save her life. When news of the incident and its implication got out, the women were prepared and quickly mobilized themselves to action. They utilized pre-established market networks to quickly spread the message to neighboring villages. The women began to push back at Emeruwa's compound with singing, dancing, and shouting to protest Nwanyeruwa's attack and colonial taxation.[8] This persisted until dawn when Emeruwa eventually came out of his compound and admitted that Okugo had ordered the counting. Afterwards, the women demanded Emeruwa lead them to Okugo's compound.

The women then marched to the compound of Okugo and sang, danced and shouted until he had them forcibly removed.[9] As a result of the forceful removal, several women were injured and wounded. By this time, word of the women's initial protest and attack had reached neighboring villages and women began to arrive in Oloko from surrounding areas to join the protest.

On November 26, the women marched *en masse* to Okugo's compound and demanded he step down from his office by asking for his chieftaincy cap; in response, Okugo fled to the Native Court building. After which, the women in the affected Native Court areas began the traditional process of "sitting on a man," where they camped out in the compounds of the warrant chiefs, burned Native Court builds, and exposed their naked body publicly.[10] The traditional practice of "sitting on a man" is a legitimate form of social protest employed by Igbo women that drew upon cultural notions of female ritual power to check the individual or collective excess of male power.[11]

Eventually, the protest ended when the British district officer came and conducted investigations.[12] After which, he tossed Okugo's chieftaincy cap to the women and had him arrested. The women interpreted these incidents as signs of success and other women began organizing and rebelling against the Native Authorities.[13] These rebellions were not as successful and became increasingly violent as colonial administrators called large numbers of soldiers and police officers in to repress them. These instances between the women and the troops killed over 50 women and wounded another 50. It is important to note that no men were killed or even seriously injured. After a month of struggle, general order was restored although mild infractions persisted until 1930.

The Women's War of 1929 was a significant historical moment because it was not only an anti-colonial movement but it was also predominantly female-orchestrated. Despite the colonial government's attempt to rewrite the war's revolutionary ethos under the title of riot, the Women's War of 1929 was a radical attempt to critique and to some extent, disarticulate the colonial project. Inevitably, the war was not simply a protest against colonial taxation policies, but it was a direct attack against the excesses and injustice of the colonial state apparatus. Caroline Ifeka-Moller has posited that the Women's War was a specific response to the disruptions of traditional socio-political customs.[14] Since the incursion of British coloniality into the region, women had lost significant amounts of power originally vested in them by religious tradition. The joint forces of education and Christianity had managed to reconstruct indigenous practices of femininity into Western narratives of gender. For instance, the marketplace was traditionally seen as a feminine space because women were the primary administrators of the space and had to perform certain traditional rites to maintain the general welfare of the marketplace. However, with the introduction of colonialism, men began to enter into trading and disrupted traditional notions of the marketplace.[15] Unsurprisingly enough, the majority of these men were Christianized. This along with the colonial government's introduction of Western-devised structures, such as the Warrant Chief System and taxation, were seen as direct attacks on the indigenous ways of life, particularly in regard to the women, whom the colonial government specifically excluded from its processes.[16]

154   K. O. Obayan

Additionally, of all the provinces in which the British colonial government introduced the system of indirect rule, the southeastern region proved to be the most difficult because its socio-political structures were not similar to the other regions. With both the Yoruba in the southwest and the Hausa in the North, there were pre-existing structures with similar powers, such as the Yoruba obas and the northern emirs.[17] However, decentralized Igbo institutions appeared chaotic to the British, who were used to the supposed order of the North.[18] As a result, the British colonial government sought to instill "order" through the installation of the Warrant Chief System that replaced traditional titled men with male warrant chiefs.[19]

The Warrant Chief System combined different and sometimes conflicting villages under the rule of an artificial "chief," who "usurped the traditional position of the popular assembly, settled cases on his own authority, prosecuted those who attempted to seek justice though the traditional methods and acquired the power to commandeer the age-grades to do his own private biddings."[20] This practice was a radical departure from preexisting Igbo political traditions. Initially, the British attempted to take this difference into consideration and consulted with village elders. However, the consultative structure became ineffective as the warrant chiefs began the corrupt practices of promoting each other and filling posts amongst themselves. The warrant chiefs were culprits of autocratic and violent excesses against their own communities, which further delegitimized colonial powers in the eyes of the Igbo people.

The colonial apparatus reified and exacerbated indigenous patriarchal systems primarily by its introduction of Western notions of gender and the subsequent attempt by Christianized natives to gender indigenous religion, which was a base of socio-political power mainly attributed to women. In doing this, the colonial system and its Victorian morality imposed a system of double patriarchy on African women, because there was already an indigenous patriarchal system, although they were kept in check by the general reverence of women's ritual power.

With the introduction of taxation against women, the Igbo women used it as an opportunity to counter and redress the wide-scale wrongs of the colonial government and their representatives. The women generally perceived the foreign structures as a direct threat to their traditional livelihoods so it was extremely crucial that they drew upon traditional practices of femininity to assert their agency. Why is it that the women of 1929 resorted to the use of naked protest to oppose colonial forces? Investigating nuances of nakedness and corporeality within Western and indigenous African discourses can help to inform our understanding of the Women's War as well as improve our methodological and theoretical analyses of gender, feminism, and coloniality within Africa. Therefore, I begin my discussion on naked protest with an analysis of Western and pre-colonial African bodily discourses with emphasis on the female body.

Western Body Discourses

Despite claims to rationality and bodylessness, modern Western thought has always been predicated on the imagination and conception of the embodied "Other."[21] Western social theory's bodily preoccupation is rooted in the notion

Protest and the Black/African Female Body   155

"that difference and hierarchy in society are biologically determined."[22] As scholars like Achille Mbembe have argued, colonial power was been predicated on masculinized, sexualized notions of the body and specifically, the phallus.[23] Consequently, colonialism has always been overly preoccupied with gendered and sexualized interpretations of the body. Individuals who were powerful in Western societies, particularly men, established their authority by emphasizing their biological superiority (phallus in the case of Mbembe), or bloodline while those who were not powerful became feminized and regarded as biologically inferior. As a result, biology was instrumental in framing Western hegemonic paradigms of race, gender, and class. The physical body was in turn conceptualized within Manichean, Cartesian discourses of mind/body, where the rational mind was glorified over the sensual flesh. Within this binary, the body and its vices were debased and relegated to lower societal others, "women, primitives, Jews, Africans and the poor," while the mind and its virtues were attributed to men, Europeans and the wealthy.[24] Thus, the Western conception of the female body as other became a pervasive element of Western institutions and justified the creation of normative gender roles.

Under this Western binary, men and women were naturally constructed as oppositional positionalities, and these categories were used to justify their inclusion and exclusion in general society. It is also within this space that the female body emerges as the embodied other, devoid of rationality and rife with carnality. The negative perceptions of the female body manifest in the iconic image of the exposed female body. The undressed female body has been portrayed as inherently evil due to its consistent association with unbridled sexuality and sensuality that pollutes and corrupts all things male.[25] This feminine archetype is based upon Judeo-Christian creation stories, where the first woman, Eve, desecrated the Garden of the Eden by eating from the forbidden fruit of knowledge, and thus cast mankind into sin. Consequently, the female body, and its attendant femininity, became perpetually associated with evil in Western historical reality and had to be controlled accordingly.

Although there have been various methods used to delimit the femininity of Western women since creation, I focus upon two important historical hallmarks in the development of modern Western thought: classical Greco-Roman art and nineteenth-century Victorianism. Greco-Roman art was extremely important in controlling the female body because it attempted to glorify the nude female form.[26] Its devotion to the celebration of human physical beauty sought to depict the purity and innocence of the human body—an image rooted in man's original state before the Fall of Man. Originally, the Greeks only glorified the nude male form in sculpture, requiring women to be fully clothed until the fourth century BC. However, with the nude Venus, the Greeks endeavored to introduce the physical beauty of the female form to traditional Western society. Despite the Greeks' attempt to elevate the meaning of Western femininity beyond primitive eroticism, they could not escape the inscribed sexuality of the female body, and as Kenneth Clark has stated, "no proper female nude lacks an erotic message, whatever its degree or method of idealization; and one element governing the way this message is carried is the visible relation of the nude body to its absent, invisible

156   K. O. Obayan

clothing."[27] In other words, the Eros of nudity is intrinsically linked to clothing because the lack of clothing within Western culture almost always suggests an inescapable problematic. Additionally, Greco-Roman art fails to transcend the erotic of the female body because its inherent desire to idealize female form is predicated upon the masculine gaze and its perceptions of beauty and femininity, which then only functions to reinforce male libidinal economies.[28]

Similar to Greco-Roman art's inscription of the conventional feminine corporeality, nineteenth-century Victorianism also managed to constrict the female body. Extreme conservatism and morality were pervasive aspects of the Victorian era. The society was marked by distinct definitions of gender roles; a man's place was in the public sphere because he possessed the masculine qualities of rationality, aggression, and independence, while a woman's place was in the private sphere because she possessed feminine qualities of irrationality, passivity, and submission.[29] According to Susan Kent, "women were so exclusively identified by their sexual functions that nineteenth-century society came to regard them as 'the Sex.'"[30] The expectations of women in Victorian society were primarily purported by women themselves. With the rise of the Cult of Domesticity in the era, women were expected to embody four principal virtues: piety, purity, domesticity, and submissiveness. There were strict definitions of acceptable fashion and behavior. In such a context, nakedness and indecency was not only deplorable but also unimaginable. These notions of gender and womanhood were in turn already firmly embedded within Western imaginaries before the advent of colonialism. Thus, when the nineteenth-century colonialists encountered the unclothed natives, they instantly deemed them as primitive and animalistic especially in regards to the unclothed female body.[31]

The iconic image of the "naked native" was central to the colonial enterprise, because it gave the colonialists room to justify their violent actions under the guise of benevolence and enabled them to mutually constitute whiteness as the epitome of culture and civilization. Thus, the image of the naked native became emblematic of colonial primitiveness, savagery, and inferiority, and indicative of the absence of civilization. Due to the construction of whiteness in relation to blackness, white bodies were vested in the delineating differences between the races because "whiteness carried it with particular privileges from which those with brown or black skin were excluded," which meant black bodies were constitutively raced, gendered and sexed through the discursive practices of science, literature, and art.[32] The widely disseminated images of naked black women with long, dangling breasts were used to represent the unbridled sexuality, degraded femininity and black savagery, which was nothing like the pure femininity of white womanhood.[33] Black women and/or blackness came to be viewed as closer to animals, thus positioning them "as a site for male endeavor and bravery"—"desirable and repulsive, available and untouchable, productive and reproductive, beautiful and black."[34] Moreover, the colonial preoccupation with the naked savage's body (evidenced by various photographs and drawings from the era) symbolized in many ways a need for "control over the body observed, a panoptical maneuver that signaled colonial possession, colonial knowledge, and desire."[35] Thus, the naked state of the native suggests their need to be controlled and dominated.

Protest and the Black/African Female Body 157

This notion of control and domination was inherently mediated through the organizing principle of patriarchy.[36] Specifically in regards to southeastern Nigeria, the British saw "the most extreme, the most intractable characteristics of femininity such as the climate in which they lived; their purported savagery and lack of culture; the discrete and scattered nature of their social and political organization," which "found its most unsettling expression in habits of undress practiced by many Igbo women."[37] These attributes thus required the British to bring order and stability into the messy and uncivilized world of the Igbo, primarily through a Western patriarchal refashioning of gender. Contrarily, the state of undress in Nigeria is not unique to the colonial period but it is fundamentally linked to traditional discourses of the body as a natural human conduit to the supernatural and metaphysical realms of the cosmos.

African Body: Nakedness, Ritual, and Religion

Departing radically from Western Cartesian modes of thought, notions of nakedness in Africa are fluid and varied, shifting meanings constantly within temporal and spatial cultural imaginations.[38] These notions are based upon a pre-existing world sense that utilizes multi-dimensional cyclical ways of perceiving the universe. According to Achille Mbembe, the chronos of African existence is "neither a linear time or a simple sequence but an interlocking of presents, pasts, and futures that retain their depths of other presents, pasts, and futures, each age bearing, altering, and maintain the previous ones."[39] African religious scholar John S. Mbiti also states that, "in many places, circles are used as symbols of the continuity of the universe. They are the symbols of eternity, of unendingness, of continuity."[40] These principles of synchronicity and circularity actively manifest themselves within indigenous African cosmology with its belief in the continuity of life after death; subsequently, African religious beliefs permeated every aspect of life since it was responsible for maintaining balance between the natural and supernatural dimensions of the universe, thus making it virtually inseparable from culture, and cultural practices.[41]

Pre-colonial Nigerian cultures articulate this reality through their multivalent conceptualization of dress and undress. As a result, Western attempts to impose a singular meaning to dress and undress upon this paradigm were completely outside the framework of the traditional imaginary. Contrary to colonial historiography and its iconic imagery of "naked" natives, clothing was existent in pre-colonial Nigeria, as some cultures such as the Yoruba had developed methods to process, dye, and sew cloth centuries before the colonial conquest.[42] Generally, possession of cloth was a marker of social status because it was not easily accessible to all.[43] Those who were wealthy, such as royal families, traditional chiefs, elders and merchants, mainly wore it to distinguish themselves from the lesser masses. Therefore, nakedness was not the constant state of pre-colonial Nigerian peoples and additionally, instances where people were naked did not readily translate into Western preconceptions of undress.[44]

Definitions of dress and undress were instead read within specific socio-cultural moments, and varied widely depending upon who was undressed, why

158   *K. O. Obayan*

they were undressed, and how they undressed.[45] General society was the primary mediator and interpreter of these moments, and thus determined community standards of acceptability. The standards of undress, or nakedness, were largely determined by how its manifestation either contradicted or reinforced notions of community culture.[46] Within both Yoruba and Igbo cultures, nakedness in the public marketplace is deemed unacceptable because it is considered deviant or anti-societal structure.[47] According to Okediji, being caught naked in public is a fear of Yoruba adults, because it is a state commonly associated with incurable madness or witchcraft confession; "whatever is publicly seen naked has lost is value and significance and has become cheapened or worthless."[48] Thus, nakedness, in this instance, indicates permanent social damage.

The notion of social damage is further explicated through Igbo interpretations of nudity in the marketplace that also translates this form of nakedness into lunacy or preliminary to witchcraft confession, and regards it as a refusal to be human.[49] In this context, the shedding of clothes represents the shedding of humanity because the madman "removes the garment of civil behavior and shrugs away the tightly woven web of Igbo social relations," which is antithetical to "their understanding of how personhood is communally constructed."[50] Underlying these interpretations of the madman's nakedness are not just simply notions of loss and privation but there are more profound meanings of dispossession and deprivation—a stripping or discarding of something one is supposed to have. This interpretation signifies a position of degradation and shame due to the madman being placed outside of humanity and considered permanently liminal.[51]

Nonetheless, semiotics of clothing still remains complex within pre-colonial cultural contexts. For the Igbo, being naked, *oto*, or semi-naked is required for certain ritual ceremonies—"initiation, healing rituals, and parts of funerals" because it suggests "signs of openness, incompleteness, and the creative ambiguity of body boundaries within ritual contexts."[52] Often times, particular deities necessitate their diviners to strip down to a loincloth to display openness to the spirits. On the other hand, regular people such as individuals preparing to take traditional chieftaincy titles may be required to be naked in order to demarcate their positionality in the spiritual realm as "other" as well as prepare them "for re-clothing in new and socially significant garments" during the ritual performance.[53] Additionally, young performers in cultural dance troupes may also be semi-naked and very rarely fully naked, but even then, they are usually clothed in paint and jewelry. In these instances, ritual activity functions as a form of social skin that clothes participants since their acts of nakedness are considered communal and suggestive of "a desire to join with others," and never descend completely into an anarchical form of self-expression.[54] Among the Yoruba people, being naked is not inherently required during ritual activities. In contrast, cloth seems to hold a symbolic value in Yoruba religion and is commonly used in reference to specific orisas—*aso funfun*, white cloth, *aso dudu*, black cloth, and *aso pupa*, red cloth. Generally within the context of traditional society, there are certain instances where public nakedness is acceptable such as with infants and to some extent, women. The public nakedness of women is often dependent on context; for instance, being totally or partially naked was common for a

Protest and the Black/African Female Body 159

majority of women and was not seen as unacceptable, but this was dependent on the manner in which these women were naked. If the women were protesting and demonstrating an injustice, their nakedness was seen as taboo and highly dangerous especially in regard to older, post-menopausal women. However, under normal circumstances for the Yoruba, if for any reason the rest of the body is naked, the genital area must at least be covered, because they are believed to contain essence or vital force.[55]

Present within most African cultures is the belief that power or essence exists in all living things; consequently, human beings are owners of this power and it is said to be "concentrated in certain body parts, specifically the eyes, mouth, hands and fingers, breasts, anus and genitals."[56] Amongst these body parts, the genitals are considered most potent because they are related to sexuality and reproduction, especially the female genitals. There is a prevalent belief in African culture that reproduction is necessary to the sustenance and maintenance of natural life. Women, being the conduits of this necessary life process, are therefore revered as the mothers of the earth. As a result, motherhood in African society is considered a position of power and most African women regard bearing children as a vital expression of their femininity. Furthermore, the position of mother strengthens a woman's status in the community, providing her with standing in the wives' association and giving her influence in her husband's family. Conversely, a woman who is unable to reproduce is often castigated and reproached within society because she is not deemed a "complete or true" woman. Prominent motifs of the importance of motherhood are visibly seen in Igbo and Ibibio cosmology. Specifically within Igbo religion, one of the most important functions of women in ritual and religion is to make ritual sacrifice and offerings to the female deities of human fertility to ensure individual and community fertility.[57] These ideologies are representative of the complexity of indigenous African perceptions toward women and have informed the gendering of societal, cultural, and political processes.

The Role of Women in Pre-Colonial Nigeria

Traditionally, women occupied extensive wide-ranging roles in pre-colonial Nigerian society and were seen as pillars of their communities. This is because pre-colonial (traditional) communities did not articulate gender roles within a compartmentalized dualistic space of domination and subordination that frames the man as being in direct opposition to the woman. Instead, gender roles within these societies were complementary and strongly rooted in traditional African notions of community, cooperation, and collectivism. Within traditional Igbo societies, political power was decentralized and accessible to all members of the community because "status was largely achieved, not ascribed."[58] This existing structure enabled women in these societies to obtain power and status in ways that Western women could not. As Glo Chukukere has stated, "in Nigeria, women enjoy constitutional rights that are still denied Western women.... Nigerian women have historically held substantial economic powers, whether through agriculture, petty-trading, or wholesale business enterprises" and even

160   *K. O. Obayan*

in the face of sexist patriarchal marginalization, Nigerian women have asserted their rights and mobilized themselves in opposition to oppressive traditional structures.[59] Despite this stated reality, entrenched patriarchal systems were, in fact, existent in pre-colonial Nigeria, although these systems do not always function within the boundaries of Western notions of gender oppression. To show that women were, in fact, significant players in pre-colonial society this section explores the role of women in pre-colonial Igbo and Ibibio society.

Pre-colonial Igbo and Ibibio society was community-based and community-driven, which meant that societal relationships were informed by what the community needed. At any given time, a woman could occupy multiple roles as mother, sister, daughter, and wife; these positions were opaque in nature because the intersection of these identities could bestow women with different responsibilities and opportunities within society. For instance, the institution of motherhood was a highly valued and powerful position within society and anything that promoted good motherhood was generally accepted.[60] To obtain and maintain the status of mother, women usually got married and became wives. Within polygamous marriages, wives were afforded relative amounts of autonomy based on seniority; the senior wife is usually absolved from the more menial tasks like cooking. These examples display the flexibility of what a woman's work and place was.

Notwithstanding, pre-colonial society was in fact patriarchal and conferred status and property upon women based on ties to their lineage group. Among the Ibibios, the social structure is constructed on a patrilineal system, where descent is traced through the male line only to a common known ancestor.[61] Therefore, "children born into the marriage succeed to offices and property only in the patrilineage, though complementary filiation. One does not have to contest for offices or rights to property in one's mother's lineage."[62] Although Igbo society is generally regarded as a patrilineal, however, the patriliny performed in Igboland is different from those in Ibibioland because the Igbo society utilized a system of double descent.[63] The system of double descent appropriated individuals to both their mother's matriline and father's patriline. This system enabled individuals to inherit property and wealth through their mother and father regardless of their sex. Similarly, in both Igbo and Ibibio societies, there was a dual sex system that had parallel gender institutions such as "kingship institution, age grades, secret societies and titles societies," which allowed both male and female interest groups to handle their own community affairs.[64] Women, therefore, had no men representing their political and economic interests, and were relatively autonomous in the community. The double descent and dual system ensured that women were not relegated to the background in the community.

Due to the parallel sex institutions, women were active in politics because they had to advocate and represent their interests within society. Within Igbo Society, the central female political figure in the community was the *Omu*, or queen, whose position as figurehead was parallel to the king. Her position was not derived from her relationship to King; "she [was] neither the wife of the king or the daughter of a king without a male."[65] Instead, she was an elderly post-menopausal woman, who was admired for her wealth, intellect, and character in

Protest and the Black/African Female Body   161

society. The *Omu* administers the female aspects of the community so she was responsible for the community market and other women's activities. In order to assist the *Omu*, there were two separate women's associations composed of women in the community. These associations are the *Otu Umuada*, consisting of women indigenes of the village, and *Otu Inyemdi*, consisting of women married into the village. Women in these groups held regular meetings, or *mikiri*, to discuss community issues.

Like the Igbo, Ibibio women's involvement in parallel sex institutions allowed them to organize pressure methods in projecting the interest of women as daughters, wives, mothers, farmers, traders, and members of the community.[66] Oftentimes, societal notions of gender were suspended for certain titled women in powerful secret cults particularly for older women because they were considered mothers of all. *Iban Isong* or women of the land was the women's traditional government that served as an umbrella organization for other women's association in Ibibioland.[67] As an umbrella organization, *Iban Isong* was extremely powerful and could impose sanctions against any community member that spoke rudely about any woman's reproductive organs. In certain cases, offenders could be subjected to death. Overall, women were revered in their political positions because they were believed to control the ritual bases that affirmed political rule.

Along with their political obligations, these same structures also administered the women's involvement in the community economy. As young girls, women were socialized to hold occupations in order to increase family finances. Although the man was expected to provide for the family, the existence of polygamous marriages made this unfeasible. Therefore, women had to be financially independent so that they could provide for their children. In Ibibioland, women were active laborers in their communities; they do the principal part of the farm work, much of the fishing, often undertake the smoking, and always the marketing of the "catch," together with the making and selling of the great water jars and other native pottery."[68]

Among the Igbo people, however, women dominated the market despite the fact that subsistence farming was the main form of economic activity for all members of the community.[69] As a result, the administration of the market was one of the *Omu*'s main roles since trade and commerce was primarily associated with Igbo women in traditional society. The *Omu* and her cabinet not only oversaw daily market operations but they also set the prices of commodities and determined the rules of operation. Through trading and selling farming surpluses, women were able to achieve economic independence from their husbands, which gave them agency in traditional societies. These structures remained relatively unchallenged until the advent of British colonialism in the nineteenth century.

Colonial Disruption of Traditional Women's Roles

The British incursion into modern-day Nigeria was a pre-meditated and inherently violent process that actively ruptured indigenous societal structures and

162   *K. O. Obayan*

transformed them to suit colonial imaginaries. Prior to colonialism, the British government had been mainly limited to the trading of slaves and agricultural commodities.[70] Full-blown colonialism was facilitated by the abolition of the transatlantic slave trade in 1807. The trade in palm oil, peanuts, and cocoa were already profitable ventures for them and the expansion of trade into the rich Nigerian hinterlands seemed even more promising. With the abolition act of 1807 and the subsequent decision to establish a naval patrol to enforce the act, the British had an excuse to justify their presence in the area. They strategically began to intervene in local affairs and manipulate competing indigenous groups to increase their influence. After much strategic intervention and large-scale violence, the British succeeded in annexing Lagos in 1851 and established a colony in 1861. Primarily, they limited themselves to the Lagos Colony; however, missionaries and traders started to request political assistance from the British. By the late 1880s, the British had declared a protectorate over the central and eastern coast of Nigeria, and had given a governing charter to the Royal Niger Company in Lokoja, who used extensive "force and violence of military to dominate commerce and establish political control."[71]

Although it is apparent that the colonial apparatus utilized violent force to establish and legitimate its authority. The colonialists also employed other mechanisms such as Western education, Christianity and the system of indirect rule to achieve their purposes of civilizing and colonizing natives, which were also equally violent and destructive.[72] These institutions were central to the colonial narrative because they redefined societal structures and reshaped social relationships, especially those existing between men and women.

During the colonial period, the institutions of Christianity and Western education were intrinsically linked and played a critical role in Westernizing indigenes. Although there were various missionary groups in Africa at the time, the three main ones in Nigeria were the Anglican Church Missionary Society (CMS), the Wesleyan Methodist Missionary Society, and the Foreign Mission Board of the Southern Baptist Convention of the United States. Of these three, the CMS was initially the most prominent. Christianity first arrived in modern-day Nigeria amongst the Yoruba in the 1840s.[73] Afterwards, the newly converted Yoruba played a significant role in spreading the gospel to other parts of Nigeria. One of the most prominent amongst these converts was the Yoruba missionary Samuel Ajayi Crowther, who led a CMS mission to spread Christianity in Igboland.[74] The Christian missionaries sought to change African societies because their traditional practices such as polygamy were seen as backwards and primitive.[75] In order to do this, the missionaries with the backing of the colonial government used education as a tool to socialize and Christianize the masses. As a result, the Wesleyan mission established the first school in 1842.

Missionary education was extremely deliberate in its attempt to inculcate Western societal notions, especially about gender roles. As a result, there was an inherent gender bias in the education system and the missionaries utilized sex-differentiated curricula: "boys had at least two hours of class preparation every day while the girls were learning to sew and embroider."[76] This training prepared boys to be employed in the colonial apparatus as "clerks, catechists,

Protest and the Black/African Female Body   163

pastors, missionaries, and diplomats," while the women were prepared to be virtuous Christian wives and mothers.[77] Thus, Christianity and education only helped to reinforce the inherent male bias of Western society and transpose those biases culturally onto traditional African mindsets.

Central to this objective of coloniality was the rational authority of colonial socio-political bureaucratic structures such as the indirect rule system that reconstructed traditional socio-political structures. After several years of informal colonial rule, the British finally consolidated and named the country Nigeria in 1914.[78] Upon this achievement, they began implementing the colonial policy of indirect rule. Indirect rule was a system that utilized indigenous rulers to govern the colonial territory. The rationale of the system was based on the British belief that indigenous people had intimate knowledge of cultural practices. As a result, the British initiated the Native Authority System, an autocratic system that invested traditional chiefs with excessive powers. The Native Authority System also began to administer the judiciary system, which primarily was a community affair. Normally, in traditional society, there was no sole authority that dictated community affairs; instead, there were many associations of men and women that represented community interests and checked political power. In addition to the divestment of power from the community, the native authority system alienated women from traditional state structures and stripped them of power.

The colonial government's anti-women policies were only furthered with the introduction of taxation in colonial Nigeria. Although the main goal of taxation was to financially source local native authorities, Falola has stated that "colonial taxation was a demonstration of colonial power and domination."[79] It was simply an indication to British authorities of their imperial conquest. In 1906, the British government started taxing local populations in northern Nigeria with the help of locally appointed emirs, who were given instructions on "how to exercise power, collect revenues, and spend revenues."[80] While the northerners were resistant to taxation, large-scale resistance did not appear until taxation was introduced in southern Nigeria. Immediately after its introduction in 1916, people protested against its occurrences. These protests proved to be relatively effective because the British postponed extending taxation into southeastern Nigeria for a couple of years. Eventually, in 1927, taxation began in the southeastern region and was met with minor protests, but it was not until 1929 that a major resistance was led.

Some Conclusions

According to Caroline Ifeka-Moller, the women's bodily responses such as nakedness and making obscene gestures were important to the resistance movement because underlying the facts of taxation and coloniality was the subsumed narrative of marginalization and decreased autonomy.[81] To put it in her words, women were upset because they were becoming "as men."[82] This notion of de-feminization was central to why the women resisted as they did. In others words, understanding the women's use of naked protest is essential to fully conceptualize the revolutionary ethos of the women warriors in 1929. Notably, the Women's War was not the only instance when women used nakedness to challenge state power.

164   *K. O. Obayan*

Even before the historical moment of the Women's War in 1929, there was an earlier manifestation in 1925 called the Nwaobioala, where older Igbo women dancers were stripping younger women in the marketplace in order to display the morality of their bodies, and seizing the property of Christian women and unspecified men.[83] Traditionally, younger women's bodies went uncovered so that older women in the community easily observed their chastity such as signs of pregnancy. The colonial period changed this practice, as younger women were the main beneficiaries of colonial socialization, i.e., clothing. Thus, the Nwaobioala of 1925 shows a rejection of colonial (Western) mores and customs through the discarding of younger women's clothing. Comparably, the Abeokuta Women's Revolt of the late 1940s used genital cursing to protest against the unfair taxation of local market women by the Alake of Abeokuta, a Sole Native Authority ruler of the colonial government.[84] When colonial authorities were sent to quell the disturbance, "the women brandished their menstruation cloth causing the police to take to their heels."[85] It is a popular belief that "if a man is struck by a women's menstrual cloth he will have bad fortune for the rest of his days."[86] Consequently, both of these incidents show a natural tendency for African women to use their bodies to militate against oppositional forces.

This use of bodily agency by African women is connected to indigenous roles of femininity such as motherhood that were generally seen as exceptionally powerful. Traditional culture held women as the physical and metaphysical mothers of the land and people. Within cultural paradigms, these powers were known and feared by all. According to Bastian, the cultural phenomena of genital cursing among Igbo women occurs in several stages, "moving from a verbal suggestion (Do you want to see where you come from?), to an expressive movement (untying the waistcloth in a public and ceremonious gesture), to the actual removal of lower garments and display of the genitals."[87] This inherently suggests that there is a deliberateness and calculation to which women resist bodily. It is never impulsive or reckless but it is a decisive motion to expose: but what exactly? Okediji indicates that exposure of genitalia suggests a desire to express truth or to reveal what is hidden.[88] Thus, it seems that the women's use of the naked suggests an intention to expose the truth about violent colonial attempts to re-fashion indigenous bodies within the narrative of Western body politics. Consequentially, the women of 1929 were not simply behaving "obscenely"; instead, they were calculatedly forcing the imperial powers to confront the inherent problematic of naked uncivilized African bodies within their compartmentalized framework: these women were using their bodies as revolutionary mechanisms.

Notes

1 Aba Commission of Inquiry, *Notes of Evidence Taken by the Commission of Inquiry Appointed to Inquire into the Disturbances in the Calabar and Owerri Provinces, December 1929* (London: Waterlow & Sons, 1930), 79.
2 Toyin Falola and Adam Paddock, *The Women's War of 1929: A History of Anti-colonial Resistance in Eastern Nigeria* (Durham, NC: Carolina Academic, 2011), 275.

Protest and the Black/African Female Body 165

3 Falola and Paddock, *Women's War of 1929*, 15.
4 Ibid.; Judith Van Allen, "'Sitting on a Man': Colonialism and the Lost Political Institutions of Igbo Women." *Canadian Journal of African Studies* 6.2 (1972), 173.
5 Van Allen, "'Sitting on a Man,'" 173.
6 Ibid.; Falola and Paddock, *Women's War of 1929*, 16
7 Van Allen, "'Sitting on a Man,'" 173.
8 Falola and Paddock, *Women's War of 1929*, 25.
9 Ibid.
10 Van Allen, "'Sitting on a Man,'" 174.
11 Ibid.
12 Falola and Paddock, *Women's War of 1929*, 27.
13 Van Allen, "'Sitting on a Man,'" 174.
14 Caroline Ifeka-Moller, "Female Militancy and Colonial Revolt: The Women's War of 1929, Eastern Nigeria," *Perceiving Women*, ed. Shirley Ardener (New York: Wiley, 1975), 127.
15 Misty L. Bastian, Marc Matera and Susan Kingsley Kent, *The Women's War of 1929: Gender and Violence in Colonial Nigeria* (Basingstoke: Palgrave Macmillan, 2012), 127.
16 Oyèrónké Oyěwùmí, *The Invention of Women: Making an African Sense of Western Gender Discourses* (Minneapolis: University of Minnesota, 1997), 123.
17 Toyin Falola, *Colonialism and Violence in Nigeria* (Bloomington: Indiana University Press, 2009), 86.
18 Bastian *et al.*, *The Women's War of 1929*, 45.
19 Victoria Oluomachukwu Ibewuike, "African Women and Religious Change: A Study of the Western Igbo of Nigeria: With a Special Focus on Asaba Town" (PhD diss., Uppsala, 2006).
20 Falola, *Colonialism and Violence in Nigeria*, 80.
21 Oyěwùmí, *Invention of Women*, 1.
22 Ibid.
23 Mbembé, *On the Postcolony*, 13.
24 Oyěwùmí, *Invention of Women*, 3.
25 Judith Hoch-Smith, "Radical Yoruba Female Sexuality," In *Women in Ritual and Symbolic Roles*, ed. Judith Hoch-Smith (New York: Plenum, 1978), 246.
26 Anne Hollander, "Fashion in Nudity," *The Georgia Review* 30.3 (1976), 7.
27 Ibid.
28 Adeline Marie Masquelier, "Dirt, Undress, and Difference," Introduction, *Dirt, Undress, and Difference: Critical Perspectives on the Body's Surface* (Bloomington: Indiana University Press, 2005), xvii.
29 Susan Kingsley Kent, *Sex and Suffrage in Britain, 1860–1914* (Princeton, NJ: Princeton University Press, 1987), 24.
30 Kent, *Sex and Suffrage in Britain*, 32.
31 Masquelier, Introduction, xxiv.
32 Catherine Hall, "Of Gender and Empire: Reflections on the Nineteenth Century," in *Gender and Empire*, ed. Phillipa Levine (Oxford: Oxford University Press, 2004), 49; Phillipa Levine, "States of Undress: Nakedness and the Colonial Imagination," *Victorian Studies* 50.2 (2008), 212.
33 Jennifer L. Morgan, "'Some Could Suckle over their Shoulder': Male Travelers, Female Bodies, and the Gendering of Racial Ideology, 1500–1770," *The William and Mary Quarterly* 54.1 (1997), 169.
34 Levine, "States of Undress," 200; Morgan, "Some Could Suckle over their Shoulder," 170.
35 Levine, "States of Undress," 207.
36 Kathleen Wilson, "Empire, Gender, and Modernity in the Eighteenth Century," in *Gender and Empire*, ed. Phillipa Levine (Oxford: Oxford University Press, 2004), 25.

166   K. O. Obayan

37 Bastian *et al.*, *The Women's War of 1929*, 45 and 54.
38 Ibid.
39 Mbembé, *On the Postcolony*, 16.
40 John S. Mbiti, *Introduction to African Religion*, 2nd edn., (Oxford: Heinemann, 1991), 37.
41 Oyeronke Olajubu, *Women in the Yoruba Religious Sphere* (Albany: State University of New York Press, 2003), 2.
42 Akinbileje Thessy Yemisi and Joe Igbaro, "Proverbial Illustrations of Yoruba Traditional Clothings: A Socio-Cultural Analysis," *The African Symposium* 10.2 (2010), 2.
43 Misty L Bastian, "The Naked and the Nude: Historically Multiple Meanings of Oto (Undress) in Southeastern Nigeria," in *Dirt, Undress, and Difference: Critical Perspectives on the Body's Surface*, ed. Adeline Marie Masquelier (Bloomington: Indiana University Press, 2005); Moyo Okediji, "The Naked Truth: Nude Figures in Yoruba Art," *Journal of Black Studies* 22.1 (1991), 34.
44 Masquelier, Introduction, 2.
45 Bastian, *Naked and the Nude*, 4.
46 Ibid.
47 Ibid.; Okediji, *The Naked Truth*, 8.
48 Ibid.
49 Bastian, *Naked and the Nude*, 4.
50 Ibid.
51 Ibid., 6.
52 Ibid., 5–6.
53 Ibid., 6.
54 Ibid.
55 Okediji, *The Naked Truth*, 9; Phillips Stevens, "Women's Aggressive Use of Genital Power in Africa," *Transcultural Psychiatry* 43.4 (2006), 3.
56 Stevens, "Women's Aggressive Use of Genital Power in Africa," 3.
57 Agbasiere, *Women in Igbo Life and Thought*, 97.
58 Van Allen, " 'Sitting on a Man,' " 168.
59 Glo Chukukere, "An Appraisal of Feminism in the Socio-Political Development of Nigeria," in *Sisterhood, Feminism and Power: From Africa to the Diaspora*, ed. Obioma Nnaemeka (Trenton, NJ: Africa World Press, 1998), 135.
60 Ibid., 30; Oyěwùmí, *Invention of Women*, 75.
61 J.O. Charles, "Marriage and Lineage Segmentation in Ibibioland," *Anthropological* 38.1 (1996), 82.
62 Ibid.
63 Ibewuike, *African Women and Religious Change*, 49.
64 Ibid., 51.
65 Ibid., 62.
66 Felicia Abaraonye, "Gender Relations in Ibibio Traditional Organizations," *Dialectical Anthropology* 22 (1997), 206.
67 Ibid., 210.
68 Talbot, *Woman's Mysteries of a Primitive People*, 112.
69 Agbasiere, *Women in Igbo Life and Thought*, 37.
70 Falola, *Colonialism and Violence in Nigeria*, 1.
71 Ibid., 7.
72 Frantz Fanon, *The Wretched of The Earth* (New York: Grove Press, 1963), 8.
73 Ibewuike, *African Women and Religious Change*, 137.
74 Ibid., 136.
75 Ibid., 137.
76 Ibid., 131.
77 Ibid., 135.
78 Ibewuike, *African Women and Religious Change*, 156.
79 Falola, *Colonialism and Violence in Nigeria*, 79.

80 Ibid., 84.
81 Ifeka-Moller, "Female Militancy and Colonial Revolt," 135.
82 Ibid.; Misty L. Bastian, "Dancing Women and Colonial Men: The Nwaobiala of 1925," in *"Wicked" Women and the Reconfiguration of Gender in Africa*, eds. Dorothy Louise Hodgson and Sheryl McCurdy (Portsmouth, NH: Heinemann, 2001).
83 Bastian, "Dancing Women and Colonial Men," 109.
84 Judith Byfield, "Taxation, Women and the Colonial State: Egba Women's Revolt," *Meridians* 3, no. 2 (2003), 250.
85 Prince, "The Yoruba Image of the Witch," 798.
86 Ibid.
87 Bastian, *Naked and the Nude*, 13.
88 Okediji, *The Naked Truth*, 37.

References

Aba Commission of Inquiry. *Notes of Evidence Taken by the Commission of Inquiry Appointed to Inquire into the Disturbances in the Calabar and Owerri Provinces, December 1929*. London: Waterlow & Sons, 1930.

Abaraonye, Felicia. "Gender Relations in Ibibio Traditional Organizations," *Dialectical Anthropology* 22 (1997): 205–222.

Adedokun, Kemi. *Underneath the Baobab Tree: An Examination of Nigerian Feminism through the Lens of the Amina Lawal Case*. Thesis. Dartmouth College, 2012. Web. May 11, 2013.

Afigbo, A.E. "Revolution and Reaction in Eastern Nigeria: 1900–1929 (The Background to the Women's Riot of 1929)," *Journal of the Historical Society of Nigeria* 3, no. 3 (1966): 539–557.

Agbasiere, Joseph Thérèse. *Women in Igbo Life and Thought*. London: Routledge, 2000.

Bastian, Misty L. "Dancing Women and Colonial Men: The Nwaobiala of 1925." In *"Wicked" Women and the Reconfiguration of Gender in Africa*. Eds. Dorothy Louise Hodgson and Sheryl McCurdy. 109–129. Portsmouth, NH: Heinemann, 2001.

Bastian, Misty L. "The Naked and the Nude: Historically Multiple Meanings of Oto (Undress) in Southeastern Nigeria." In *Dirt, Undress, and Difference: Critical Perspectives on the Body's Surface*. Ed. Adeline Masquelier. 1–27. Bloomington: Indiana University Press, 2005.

Bastian, Misty L., Marc Matera and Susan Kingsley Kent. *The Women's War of 1929: Gender and Violence in Colonial Nigeria*. Basingstoke: Palgrave Macmillan, 2012.

Buckley, Thomas C.T., and Alma Gottlieb. "A Critical Appraisal of Theories of Menstrual Symbolism." Introduction. *Blood Magic: The Anthropology of Menstruation*. Berkeley: University of California Press, 1988.

Byfield, Judith. "Taxation, Women and the Colonial State: Egba Women's Revolt." *Meridians* 3, no. 2 (2003): 250–277. *JSTOR*. 2003. Web. January 28, 2013.

Charles, J.O. "Marriage and Lineage Segmentation in Ibibioland," *Anthropological* 38, no. 1 (1996): 81–92.

Chukukere Glo. "An Appraisal of Feminism in the Socio-Political Development of Nigeria," in Obioma Nnaemeka, ed. *Sisterhood, Feminism and Power: From Africa to the Diaspora*. 133–148. Trenton, NJ: Africa World Press, 1998.

Falola, Toyin. *Colonialism and Violence in Nigeria*. Bloomington: Indiana University Press, 2009.

Falola, Toyin, and Adam Paddock. *The Women's War of 1929: A History of Anti-colonial Resistance in Eastern Nigeria*. Durham, NC: Carolina Academic, 2011.

168   *K. O. Obayan*

Hall, Catherine. "Of Gender and Empire: Reflections on the Nineteenth Century," in *Gender and Empire*, ed. Phillipa Levine. 46–76. Oxford: Oxford University Press, 2004.

Hoch-Smith, Judith, and Anita Spring. Introduction. *Women in Ritual and Symbolic Roles*. New York: Plenum, 1978.

Hoch-Smith, Judith. "Radical Yoruba Female Sexuality." In *Women in Ritual and Symbolic Roles*. Eds. Judith Hoch-Smith and Anita Spring. 245–267. New York: Plenum, 1978.

Hollander, Anne. "Fashion in Nudity." *The Georgia Review* 30, no. 3 (1976): 642–702. *JSTOR*. Web. November 4, 2013.

Ibewuike, Victoria Oluomachukwu. *African Women and Religious Change: A Study of the Western Igbo of Nigeria: With a Special Focus on Asaba Town*. Uppsala: Victoria O. Ibewuike, 2006.

Ifeka-Moller, Caroline. "Female Militancy and Colonial Revolt: The Women's War of 1929, Eastern Nigeria." In *Perceiving Women*. Ed. Shirley Ardener. 127–157. New York: Wiley, 1975.

Kent, Susan Kingsley. *Sex and Suffrage in Britain, 1860–1914*. Princeton, NJ: Princeton University Press, 1987.

Leith-Ross, Sylvia. *African Women: A Study of the Ibo of Nigeria*. New York: Praeger, 1939.

Levine, Phillipa. "States of Undress: Nakedness and the Colonial Imagination." *Victorian Studies* 50, no. 2 (2008): 189–219.

Masquelier, Adeline Marie. "Dirt, Undress, and Difference." Introduction. *Dirt, Undress, and Difference: Critical Perspectives on the Body's Surface*. Bloomington: Indiana University Press, 2005.

Mbembé, J. -A. *On the Postcolony*. Berkeley: University of California Press, 2001.

Morgan, Jennifer L. "'Some Could Suckle over their Shoulder': Male Travelers, Female Bodies, and the Gendering of Racial Ideology, 1500–1770." *The William and Mary Quarterly* 54, no. 1 (1997): 167–192.

Morgan, Jennifer L. Laboring *Women: Reproduction and Gender in New World Slavery*. Philadelphia: University of Pennsylvania Press, 2004.

Offiong, Daniel A. *Witchcraft, Sorcery, Magic and Social Order: Among the Ibibio of Nigeria*. New Haven: Fourth Dimension Publishing, 1991.

Okediji, Moyo. "The Naked Truth: Nude Figures in Yoruba Art." *Journal of Black Studies* 22, no. 1 (1991): 30–44. *JSTOR*. Web. October 30, 2013.

Olajubu, Oyeronke. *Women in the Yoruba Religious Sphere*. Albany: State University of New York Press, 2003.

Oyěwùmí, Oyèrónkẹ́. *The Invention of Women: Making an African Sense of Western Gender Discourses*. Minneapolis: University of Minnesota, 1997.

Prince, R. "The Yoruba Image of the Witch." *The British Journal of Psychiatry* 107, no. 449 (1961): 795–805.

Stevens, Phillips. "Women's Aggressive Use of Genital Power in Africa." *Transcultural Psychiatry* 43, no. 4 (2006): 592–599.

Talbot, D. Amaury. *Woman's Mysteries of a Primitive People, the Ibibios of Southern Nigeria*. London: Cassell and Company, 1915.

Umeora, O.U.J, and V.E Egwuatu. "Menstruation in Rural Igbo Women of South East Nigeria: Attitudes, Beliefs and Practices." *African Journal of Reproductive Health* 12 no. 1 (2008): 109–115. *JSTOR*. Web. November 8, 2013.

Van Allen, Judith. "'Sitting on a Man': Colonialism and the Lost Political Institutions of Igbo Women." *Canadian Journal of African Studies* 6, no. 2 (1972): 165–181. *JSTOR*. Web. October 26, 2013.

Yemisi, Akinbileje Thessy and Igbaro Joe. "Proverbial Illustrations of Yoruba Traditional Clothings: A Socio-Cultural Analysis." *The African Symposium* 10, no. 2 (2010): 46–59. *Google Scholar*. Web. October 6, 2013.

Wilson, Kathleen. "Empire, Gender, and Modernity in the Eighteenth Century," in *Gender and Empire*, ed. Phillipa Levine. Oxford: Oxford University Press, 2004.

9 Revolution at the Crossroads

Re-Framing the Haitian Revolution from the Heights of Platons[1]

Michael Becker

In *Silencing the Past*, Michel-Rolph Trouillot contended that the Haitian Revolution was "unthinkable" not just because it militated against the interests of planters, but because it could not be "conceive[d] within the range of possible alternatives, that which perverts all answers because it defies the terms under which the questions are posed."[2] He argued that this epistemological block continued into the contemporary historical scholarship, which had not yet "broken the iron bonds of the philosophical milieu in which it was born ... a continuous Western discourse on slavery, race, and colonization."[3] The recent resurgence of scholarly interest in the Haitian Revolution has taken Trouillot's frustrations to heart; it has become increasingly difficult to write Atlantic history without giving the Haitian Revolution its due.[4]

In bringing the revolution back into view, scholars have elaborated a vision organized around the revolutionary army and its leaders—most often Toussaint L'Ouverture, but also increasingly Jean-Jacques Dessalines. In narrating the history of the revolution first through the rise of the army and then its battles, historians are able to present a fairly linear narrative, relatively easy to track in the archive. Revolutions, though, do not lend themselves to this sort of straightforward narration. They rarely have one definite beginning, rather bubbling forth in a variety of places at once. Yet, while figures like Georges Biassou, Makandal, Boukman Dutty, and Sans Souci make guest appearances in anecdotes and footnotes, spiritual leaders, maroons, smaller insurgent groups, or really even the mass of enslaved people not enlisted in the revolutionary army are not understood as motive forces of the revolution.

It may help to think the Haitian Revolution in Anthony Bogues's terms, as a "Legba Revolution," occurring at the crossroads of the Atlantic world and of colonial modernity, and depending on the syncretism of political ideas across traditions.[5] Within vodou, Legba is the guardian of the crossroads, the source of divine creative power, and the initial procreative whole.[6] To signal Legba as symbol of the revolution indicates its critical place within Caribbean history and, indeed, the struggle for Black freedom in the modern world. However, to call on Legba is also to call on his function as "guardian of the sacred gateway, of the *Grand Chemin*, the great road leading from the mortal to the divine world."[7] The concept of a Legba Revolution invokes ancestors and the often covert struggles waged by enslaved people in the Americas. Their traditions of resistance—freedom dreams,

Re-Framing the Haitian Revolution   171

but also strategized resistance—made the Haitian Revolution possible. Enslaved people not only harbored hopes, desires, and visions of a more free world, but had also engaged in conscious struggles at micro and macro levels in order to bring those visions into being. Thus, their successors drew on both their rich and vibrant political visions and their deep practical experiences waging political struggle under brutal and violent domination.

Enslaved people crossed the Atlantic with few material possessions, but they came with detailed memories of their homes and a set of cultural, political, and intellectual traditions. These would serve as an important foundation for the ways of life and resistance that they created in the Americas. As Vincent Brown has contended, the political life of enslaved people cannot be understood simply as a "typical battle between partisans," but as "a struggle to construct a social being that connected the past and the present" and "an attempt to withstand the encroachment of oblivion and to make social meaning from the threat on anomie."[8] Spiritual practice, drawing on African religious practices or the melding of African, Christian, and indigenous Caribbean practices into the new religion known as vodou, served as an important place for working through terror and trauma, for seeking spiritual solace in a context of great distress and pain, both physical and psychic, and a space of community that provided dignity and humanity for people that were often denied both, as well as a material space for organizing resistance.[9] Provision grounds, small plots of land where enslaved people grew food for subsistence, could serve to preserve African foodways and medicinal practices, as well as an economic toehold for enslaved people who sold the resulting produce in markets. Sometimes, over many years, an enslaved person could even earn enough to buy their freedom.[10] Further, markets themselves served as an important social space for the transfer of news and the creation of community among enslaved people living on different plantations.[11] Marronage, running away from bondage to find a space of relative freedom, either for a few days or for years at a time, was one of the significant and consistent forms of resistance, serving to establish and maintain ties around the region and even the colony.[12] Enslaved people struggled to create a social world that valued their lives, freedom, and dignity, in the midst of a system predicated on their dehumanization and devaluation.

Were scholars more attentive to this deeper history and the variety of emergent political forms, the Haitian Revolution might not seem as singular an event within the Atlantic context, but rather a moment when a set of rather common dynamics in other colonial Caribbean contexts had an opening, due to metropolitan distractions, to unfold into an unusual sequence of events which shook the foundations of colonial power. I hope, through grounding my analysis in a specific place and moment—a revolt around the southern port city of Les Cayes, just at the moment when enslaved people across the colony began to take up arms en masse—to defamiliarize the narrative of the revolution and compel readers to see it through fresh eyes.

I focus here for several reasons. First, these events are unique in that they represent the first explicit demand for the complete abolition of slavery in Saint Domingue. They also serve as an example of a particularly large maroon

172   M. Becker

community (10,000–12,000 people) and a militant example of enslaved people's self-activity in the south—contrary to prevailing scholarly wisdom that the stories of revolution in the south are those of free people of color. Second, the sources are particularly rich. In addition to the usual government documents and military reports, the contents of four mailbags, seized by a British privateer from a French merchant vessel, have been preserved in the High Court of the Admiralty Papers in the British National Archives. These letters span the crucial months of November 1792 to January 1793 and allow an unusual degree of insight and precision. Third, studying Platons—one of the earliest episodes of the revolution in the south—allows some insight into the ways in which enslaved people mobilized and built political power in this moment and provides a glimpse at routes untaken which might have arrived at different ends.

The Revolt at Platons

The southern province, isolated from the mainland by high mountains and rough currents around the cape, was settled late in the colonial process.[13] It was a haven for pirates, freebooters, and smugglers into the late seventeenth century, and remained a frontier region even as indigo and sugar production picked up.[14] As a result, sugar plantations never quite reached the prominence and size they had in the north and west. Their owners were less wealthy and more likely to be resident than their counterparts elsewhere.[15] Further, this isolation accounted for the substantial political block of moderately wealthy planters of color. Up through the early 1760s, the shortage of marriageable white women led many planters to openly marry free women of color and fully recognize their offspring, including granting full inheritance rights.[16]

With the end of the Seven Years War in the 1760s, much changed, as France's military failures had it increasingly worried that colonists were keener on personal profit than patriotism and feared collaboration with other powers or colonial autonomism. In turn, many white planters embraced politics that stressed solidarity with the metropole. Suddenly, where once sufficient wealth and property had allowed a small group of free people of color to ascend the social ladder, policies and practices became more outwardly hostile to all people of African descent.[17] Further, white planters began to encourage increased white migration from France. Unable to afford the more expensive start-up costs of sugar plantations, the new migrants contributed to a burgeoning expansion of coffee plantations and to the growth of the white artisan and laborer class.[18] Always a prominent factor of colonial life, race rigidified and became a more pressing political concern.

Both the ideas and the shifting political terrain of the French Revolution brought simmering tensions between whites—planters, merchants, and artisans— and free people of color to a head. Emboldened by events in France, white merchants, artisans, and laborers formed Provincial Assemblies and lobbied Paris for political recognition as the true heirs of the revolution. In part responding to colonial pressure, the French National Assembly ordered the election of Colonial Assemblies which would in turn send voting representatives to Paris, overturning

Re-Framing the Haitian Revolution 173

a longstanding system of government by administrative decree. However, they intentionally left voting eligibility vague, trying to satisfy all parties, but effectively leaving this decision in colonial hands. Following established practice, whites elected the mandated Colonial Assembly, which immediately clarified that free people of color were ineligible to vote or serve. Responding both to the window of possibility offered by the vague eligibility law and to the rising current of white solidarity, free people of color began to organize and petition for full political rights.

Enslaved Mercenaries

In November 1790, inspired by an earlier unsuccessful revolt led by Vincent Ogé (a wealthy free person of color) and new decrees for full political equality won by free people of color struggling elsewhere in the colony, free people of color in the south rose in arms.[19] Their claim to political rights became a point of mounting tension and warfare between them and white planters. Both sides armed their enslaved people and promised them liberty in exchange for their military service.[20]

As David Geggus explains, the practice of arming enslaved people to put down insurrections had precedents, but the extent to which it occurred during the Haitian Revolution was completely unparalleled.[21] While the promise of liberty undoubtedly weighed heavily on the decision of many enslaved people to join free people of color, military service also carried with it opportunities for prestige and even material gain. Further, it offered "immediate freedom from plantation labor."[22] Many of the enslaved men armed by both sides were not as untrained as planters suspected; many would have been captured as prisoners of war during intra-African wars and sold to European traders.[23] Yet, the task of arranging these men into a coordinated fighting unit was difficult; Northern province revolt leaders Georges Biassou and Jean-François wrote that, rather than directing their followers, they were,

> entirely subject to the general will, and what a will that is, of a multitude of blacks of the coast who for the most part can scarcely make out two words of French but who above all were accustomed to fighting in their country.[24]

During the conflict between wealthy white planters and free people of color, enslaved mercenaries often served in particularly vulnerable and dangerous roles, and served as tempting targets for either side.[25] However, after the two groups had reached an accord favorable to free people of color, neither side kept their promises to their enslaved mercenaries. One colonist wrote that, in the experience of military service, the enslaved person "has lost the habit of working, and it is thus that he got accustomed to thinking."[26] The experience of armed struggle, accompanied by the new set of social relations it created both between enslaved people and colonists, and among enslaved people, created the opening for enslaved people to envision ever more vibrantly another set of possibilities. Many of the mercenaries refused to surrender their arms,

174   *M. Becker*

established (or joined an existing) a maroon community in the mountains, and demanded that their former masters fulfill their promises.[27]

Forming a Community of Struggle

Attempting to cut off communication between the rebels and other enslaved people in uprising at Trois-Rivières, the colonial militia found their best efforts met with only limited success. The maroons of Platons, many of whom had developed a close familiarity with the terrain of the province through previous *marronage*, knew secret passages and routes through the woods, gorges, and other difficult terrain that the militias thought unpassable and thus did not attempt to block.[28]

In July 1792, Armand and Maréchal, two maroon leaders, met individually with representatives from the colonial government to negotiate for the first time. The maroons demanded freedom for three hundred leaders, three free days per week for each enslaved person, and the abolition of the whip as a means of punishment.[29] It is striking that their demands addressed the condition of all enslaved people in the plain. Three free days a week would allow enslaved people more opportunities to tend their provision grounds, to participate in markets and the informal economy that might allow them to purchase their freedom, and to commit marronage to visit nearby family members. The abolition of the whip would remove one of the most brutal tools of slave discipline from legal use. These were not minor demands and would have required nerve and courage to present. Nonetheless, granting these demands was unthinkable to the colonists, fearful that to do so would inspire other rebels.

Following their respective meetings, the two leaders returned to their camps, and shortly afterwards, relocated to a central spot, the mountain of Platons, raiding and torching plantations along the way.[30] An uneasy peace fell over the plains for a few months while the new maroons attempted to grow their ranks and bide their time to make more substantive demands. For example, M. Gaujon, a planter who at first took refuge in Les Cayes during the initial stages of the revolt, recounts, after several nights of repeated disturbance, coming across a rebel named Joseph Cupidon "preaching revolt" in his slave quarters with a neighbor shortly after returning home.[31] Such visits were relatively common; the flight of many planters from the plains provided rebels with the opportunity to visit slave quarters undetected to explain their plans to struggle for their freedom and recruit enslaved people to their cause.[32]

By mid-July, enslaved people began to rise in arms across the southern plain. They returned to their most common offensive motion, raiding plantations to seize arms, food stores, and other supplies, to destroy plantation machinery and facilities that represented the master's power and authority, and to recruit enslaved people to join their ranks. This mission served a strategic aim: in destroying the productive power of the plantation, the rebels damaged the economic engine of the society as well as a principal instrument of their own exploitation. Further, these tactics of destruction served to strike terror into the colonists' hearts and their capacity to wage war.

Re-Framing the Haitian Revolution 175

Pleading for Peace, Preparing for War

Colonists had once appreciated the mountains separating them from the rest of the country, for fostering a degree of autonomy, but now increasingly felt they were a trap. It was both arduous and time-consuming for troops to cross over to provide much needed reinforcements and military supplies.[33] The colonists increasingly turned their hopes to Governor Blanchelande, who was touring the areas in rebellion. When he arrived in Les Cayes on July 23, he was confronted by a group of less established planters demanding he convene an expedition against the maroon stronghold. Their position was quickly countered by another group of particularly wealthy and conservative planters, who feared this tactic, even if successful, would result in more destruction due to the maroons' guerilla tactics.[34] Heeding the warnings of this second group, Blanchelande went with a delegation of planters to meet with Armand and Maréchal.

The leaders repeated their earlier demands, promising peace only if three hundred maroon leaders were granted their freedom and every enslaved person granted three days free from work. Blanchelande, eager to restore colonial order and unwilling to accept any of the maroons' terms, promised amnesty regardless of their property destruction and the deaths they had caused, provided they would only lay down their arms and return to their plantations. The maroon commanders asked for time to consider their response.[35]

Two days later, the maroons torched four plantations, signaling a clear answer. A few days later, they waged an attack on the Bérrault Plantation, where Armand had previously been enslaved and which served as a stronghold of the colonial militia. According to the planter Bérrault, Jean-Baptiste, his second *commandeur*, had recognized Armand among the rebels and asked him how he could bring himself to destroy his master's plantation. Armand allegedly responded, "At Le Cap, the slaves did not leave a single structure standing; the same must happen here in the Plaine-du-Fond!"[36] Armand's words, if a third-hand account can be trusted, show that he at least was conscious of the actions of enslaved people in other parts of the colony. Historians have often been tempted to suggest that enslaved people plotting uprisings early in the Haitian Revolution often operated in ignorance of each other. Armand's statement suggests that, if not working in collaboration with each other, enslaved people were at least aware of and inspired by struggles in other parts of the colony.

Blanchelande's Expedition to Platons

Finally convinced that negotiations would not succeed, Blanchelande organized a military expedition to Platons, devising a battle plan involving several columns that would surround the maroons. However, the commanders failed to coordinate with each other, messing up the detailed plan. The maroons were attentive to troop movements, and managed to catch the columns unaware and attack them from the brush with well-coordinated guerilla tactics.[37] Armand sent an envoy to Blanchelande to call for peace. Blanchelande, in turn, sent his aide-de-camp to wait at the edge of the woods for a negotiator from the maroon side. Instead, two hours later,

176   *M. Becker*

the maroons hoisted a head at the top of a pike (just as the colonists had often punished rebellious enslaved people) and began to chant in mockery, "Long live the King! Long live Blanchelande!"[38] As the governor finally began to receive news of how badly the columns had been defeated, he ordered a hurried retreat, leaving behind several cannons and other weapons and ammunition. Blanchelande was widely excoriated when he returned to Les Cayes as a collaborator, a friend of free people of color, and an incompetent and ignorant governor.[39]

Negotiating for Freedom and Sovereignty

To emphasize their strength in the expedition's aftermath, the maroons conducted several major raids, burning several of the largest plantations, before sending as envoy one of their new prisoners of war. The envoy reported a new demand: freedom for all the maroons at Platons and three free days for every person still in bondage. The Provincial Assembly sent a delegation to meet with leaders at Platons. Upon their return, the delegation reported that they had convinced the maroon leaders to accept the manumission of four hundred people, and, as a sign of good faith, to surrender nine hundred good rifles and to coerce the others back to their plantations. However, fearful of precedent, the Assembly remained reluctant to manumit any rebel. They did consider manumitting enslaved people who had fought alongside the white planters in the recent conflict, provided they agreed to help put down this new insurrection.[40]

Still in internal conflict, the Assembly sent another delegation to Platons, which returned with an even bolder demand: general emancipation and full territorial rights. During their visit, Armand attempted to appoint André Rigaud, a wealthy planter and free man of color, as their liaison with the Assembly. However, there was internal tension and vocal dissent among the maroons around the wisdom and efficacy of this choice. In part as a move to cement his authority and to placate his followers, Armand threatened to burn Les Cayes to the ground if the Assembly failed to respond by the following day.[41]

Under substantial pressure, the Assembly eventually agreed to grant 700 manumissions, for a force of 5,000.[42] Only about half of the intended recipients accepted the offer, and not all of those who accepted did so with the intention to abide by its provisions. Many accepted their freedom and service in Rigaud's companies, but used their position traveling throughout the province under the guise of military service to incite insurrection, spread news of revolts elsewhere, and share supplies with rebels.[43] These decrees represented a signal moment in the history of Platons. The maroons had battled against military and militia forces and had humiliated the sitting governor. Through armed resistance and negotiation, they had persuaded the Assembly to agree to some of their demands. Although what they received may seem limited, it was remarkable, and it had been achieved against tremendous odds. However, it also represented a moment of rupture, as a community forged through struggle fractured over the path forward.

In mid-October, maroon captains Armand, Bernard, Maréchal, and Jacques Formon wrote to M. Montesquiou Fezensac, new commandant of the province's armed forces. In tone, their letter was very humble; they assured the general of

Re-Framing the Haitian Revolution 177

their respect and asked that he honor them with his justice. Compared to accounts of previous communication, it suggested a new openness to negotiation and a recognition of their increasingly precarious position. However, the letter treated Fezensac as their equal and claimed for themselves the titles of "captain-commandants," audacious gestures in colonial eyes. Fezensac, affronted, responded that he would never recognize them as commanders, and insisted they should return to their masters and surrender their arms in hopes of mercy.

Fezensac's threat recognized the destruction that the maroons had already wrought across the plain. Entire municipalities, including Les Cotteaux, ceased to exist when all the planter and colonist inhabitants packed up their belongings and relocated to Les Cayes.[44] Those confined by the ongoing warfare to the city of Les Cayes were forced to rely on government rations. With their laborers in rebellion, their crops turned to ash, and their agricultural machinery destroyed, many planters accrued mounting debt, which they saw little hope of being able to repay. M. Siffet's situation epitomized that of the planter class: all of his buildings, from his house to the hospital were burned, his crops pillaged, most of his animals led away. He was only able to save two horses from his once vast wealth.[45] M. DeLanôzey, a plantation manager, offered M. Choiseuil Prarlin a more optimistic account: the windmill and several slave quarters torched, several other buildings damaged, some crops destroyed, and five escaped enslaved people. They were lucky.[46] Some planters, bankrupt, turned to selling their enslaved people at record low prices. In the rare circumstances that they were able to find buyers, planters accepted their payment and told their clients "Go find your blacks at Platons!"[47] The plantation system was in crisis, and dire straits called for drastic measures.

"This Land Has Not Been For You What It Has Been For Us"

Recognizing that the rebels' military tactics would continue to frustrate any attempt at a head-on assault, Fezensac instead established a cordon of military camps around the perimeter of Platons. He hoped to contain the rebels to a small portion of the province and gradually starve them from new recruits, munitions, and necessary supplies. The commandant was well aware that the success of the maroons depended upon their ability to pillage plantations in the plain for supplies and then retreat quickly toward the mountains, depending on guerilla tactics to pick off the militia. Establishing the cordon might compel them to fight an offensive battle, which Fezensac bet they would lose. In mid-October, the commandant's plans were strengthened by the arrival of reinforcements from France, primarily from L'Aubé, a poor rural province outside of Paris.[48]

As soldiers massed around them, the maroons of Platons labored to establish an alternative to the lives they had had in bondage. Efforts that had once been directed toward the profit and comfort of their masters were now exerted on their behalf. They built on land that had once been destined for coffee plantations; now, instead of coffee, they hoped to plant the seeds of their own freedom.[49] At its height, the settlement numbered 10,000–12,000 people and had 800–900 homes, divided into four to seven smaller camps.[50] Each camp was presided over by a different leader; four were probably Armand, Maréchal, Jacques Formon,

178   M. Becker

and Gilles Bénech. One colonist even reported the maroons had named their settlement the Kingdom of Platons and elected a king.[51]

Around the settlement's perimeter, near a precipice that dropped 3,000 feet, they constructed entrenchments of earth or rock.[52] They attempted to plant crops, soil permitting, and stockpile food supplies. In addition to constructing houses, they erected two infirmaries to quarantine the sick.[53] The roles that maroons were not prepared to fill themselves were assumed by captives seized during their raids. For example, M. Philbert, a doctor, was captured to tend to Maréchal's combat wounds.[54] Another captive was an armorer, tasked with repairing their weapons.[55]

Even despite the troops all around, the settlement boomed. Networks among enslaved people, forged in the cane field and on the coffee plantation, in the marketplace and in covert worship services, served to spread the news of Platons far and wide, fostering resistance and encouraging people to take refuge at Platons. With such a visible alternative within reach, conflicts and discomfort that previously would not have pushed enslaved people to action suddenly motivated escape. For example, Cézar, an enslaved man, fled his plantation after a quarrel with the overseer, which ended in him receiving two or three blows with a cord. "Cézar had been wavering for quite some time," the agent wrote to his master, seeing the quarrel as but the final straw. He also noted that Cézar's flight correlated with that of numerous domestics from Les Cayes—and knowing that many of them were friends of Cézar, assumed that they had fled together.[56] The burgeoning population of Platons suggests there were many Cézars.

The maroons regularly attacked the soldiers' camps on Sundays and holidays, while they were occupied with merry-making. Sometimes, they were successful in breaking through the cordon; more often, the soldiers held their line. However, the continual attacks had a chilling effect on the soldiers, who turned to blatant terror, like mounting the heads of dead maroons around their camp on pikes, to secure their advantage.[57] As they became increasingly desperate for munitions and supplies, the maroons improvised with the materials on hand. For example, they used their knowledge of herbs and other plants to create poisoned arrows that they shot at soldiers during their attacks.[58] As they attacked, they chanted lyrics designed to intimidate: "Coupé tete à li, coupé bras à li, coupè jambe à li, amaré li," or "Cut this one's head off, cut that one's arm off, cut this other one's leg off, tie him up!" They made drums out of calabashes filled with small stones that they shook to accompany their chant and create a frightening racket.[59] One soldier wrote to his mother:

> They [the maroons] come and treat us as if we were the brigands and tell us, "nous après tande zaute," which is to say, "we had expected you, and we will cut off your heads to the last man; this land has not been for you what it has been for us…"[60]

To Settle a Score

As the soldier observed, this struggle carried a different importance for the enslaved and the self-liberated than for the soldiers sent to crush their revolt. Platons, however imperfect, represented a space of relative freedom, which they had carved out in the midst of a society premised on their exploitation and dehumanization. If they were to lose their stronghold, they would almost certainly be executed as an example to others who might consider following in their footsteps. The maroons resisted valiantly, but as an epidemic began to spread throughout the region, they began to grow sick in large numbers, exacerbating their existing weaknesses.[61]

In the midst of this, Fezensac abandoned his post and fled to France.[62] Several bands of maroons took advantage of the resulting disorder to break through the militia's lines to reach plantations, intending to seize supplies that would allow them to hold out longer. One of the bands came across one of the few plantations where the master and other whites were still in residence and seized several captives, including a doctor. After the doctor had tended to their most serious wounds, the maroons sent him back into Les Cayes with letters to present to local officials.[63] In one letter, they called for all whites to vacate the plain for a short period of time, so that they could settle their score with the free people of color who had betrayed their promise to free their former mercenaries.[64]

It is possible that this letter spoke to a very real tension between the maroons and free people of color. As the letters soldiers later found at Platons revealed, free people of color had been partly responsible for providing the rebels with arms and munitions even after the April 4th decree, and maroons had turned to André Rigaud, a leader among free people of color, as their negotiator with the provincial government early in their struggle.[65] In recent months, however, whatever of the coalition had persisted seems to have begun to break down. Maroons had early on targeted white planters, overseers, and plantation managers; they had begun to target whites and free people of color in equal numbers.[66]

However, this letter was also a profoundly strategic gesture. If the colonists even temporarily removed the cordon containing the maroons at Platons, the maroons would be able to gather much needed supplies to continue their struggle. Given access to the plains, they might even have been able to surround the colonists in Les Cayes and lay siege to the city. As they wrote the letter, they probably harbored serious doubts that it would have the desired effect; the previous months had shown that colonists agreed to concessions only under extreme duress. It was a sign of the maroons' receding fortunes that colonists did not take this demand seriously, only calling for increased military force and complete destruction of the maroons. One planter emphasized a sentiment that others undoubtedly shared: "There can be no agriculture in San Domingo without slavery; we did not go to fetch half a million savage slaves off the coast of Africa to bring them to the colony as French citizens."[67]

In late December, newly appointed Commissioner Étienne Polverel arrived in Les Cayes, celebrated by free people of color for his April 4th proclamation which had recognized their political rights, and scorned by many planters, who saw his actions as a risk to the future of the colony.[68] Shortly after Polverel's arrival, the maroons made a final offer to negotiate, perhaps hoping to legitimate some of their victories at the moment that their stronghold was becoming weaker due to ongoing siege by the colonial troops and the attendant food shortage and illness. They may have heard of Polverel's reputation as the

180   *M. Becker*

representative of the French Revolutionary government and of his abolitionist sympathies, and thought that what was not achievable with previous authorities might be possible now.[69]

Polverel refused to negotiate, but promised the maroons that if they descended from the mountains in small groups and surrendered their arms, he would grant pardons. Even so, Polverel's proposal seemed too lenient to many colonists and the authorities of Les Cayes. They thought it would be effective in the short run, as many maroons would take advantage of the proffered clemency to escape Platons with their lives. However, they assumed it would only take a few more months and the departure of the French troops for enslaved people to once again take up arms.[70]

Facing political pressure, Polverel finally felt that he had no other option but to order another expedition, this time with a more organized and better prepared force, composed of members of the colonial militia, reinforcements from the French army, and volunteers from across the southern province. Among them also were 50 vicious attack dogs, intended to sniff out the secret hiding places of the maroons and foil ambushes intended to take the colonial troops by surprise.[71]

The Fall of Platons

The maroons, despite their weakness and limited supplies, tried to stave off the invaders as long as possible. They attempted to employ previously successful tactics, such as ambushes on the approaching troops, with limited success. They tried to stretch their munitions by mixing coal with gunpowder, and eventually even loaded one of their cannons not just with cannon balls, but grapeshot, cartridges, bullets, and whatever other projectiles they could find that might cause damage to approaching soldiers.[72] Yet, while they faced tremendous losses, the attacking troops lost only five men, and an additional 10 were wounded.[73]

By the evening of January 12, the maroons sensed that they could not hold out much longer. Their leaders proposed a plan. Throughout the night, they would evacuate Platons in small groups and retreat higher into the mountains to Macaya. They believed that through ceding their stronghold, many of them would be able to survive in order to fight another day. They allowed each of the maroons the choice to join them, return to their plantations and risk the reaction of their masters, or remain at Platons.[74] Several thousand escaped to Macaya, and more still returned to their plantations. About 600 people—including the aged, the sick, women, and children—who were unable to flee or who hoped for mercy and humanity from the approaching soldiers—chose to stay.[75] Soldiers massacred and brutalized all those who remained, sparing only a few of the youngest children.[76]

The soldiers were amazed by what they found. One exclaimed in surprise upon realizing that the maroons had constructed as many houses at the peak of Platons as existed in Les Cayes.[77] Others discovered an extensive collection of correspondence with planters and other prominent men in Les Cayes and the surrounding parishes. Although there is only limited information on the contents of these letters, they suggest that the maroons were actively engaged in negotiations not only with the colonial government, but also with individual planters

Re-Framing the Haitian Revolution 181

and landowners, both white and free people of color. Some of these correspondents appear to have been actively involved in supplying the maroons with munitions. Though no one has located the letters, second-hand evidence about their content suggests that the connection between the maroons at Platons and the free people of color who initially armed them may have continued at some level well after the maroons adopted their own agenda. While many of these secretive supporters likely cooperated with the maroons out of self-interest, rather than belief in the evils of slavery, their existence suggests that it may be too much to depict the struggle of maroons as one supported only by other enslaved people and opposed in unison by whites and free people of color.[78]

To be sure, the conquest of Platons represented a victory for planters, not to mention the colonial government. Yet, it was a victory won at great cost, after almost nine months of sustained resistance. It was not predestined. Rather, for much of the time colonial forces were encamped at Platons, it seemed quite feasible that the maroons would retain their stronghold or even triumph. It had also, and perhaps most importantly, rendered a substantial and irreversible transformation in the enslaved people who had joined in struggle for their freedom. Even as the militia burned the settlement to the ground, destroying a particular set of possibilities, each soldier and every colonist knew that it was impossible to return to things as they had been before.

Reverberations of Platons

On July 25, 1793, Commissioners Polverel and Sonthonax issued a joint proclamation offering freedom to enslaved people who would agree to take arms in service of the French republic and to coerce those enslaved people in rebellion to return to their plantations. They mentioned Armand, Maréchal, Jacques Formon, Gilles Bénech, and other leaders at Platons by name. The commissioners may have issued the proclamation in accord with their abolitionist sympathies, but they were compelled to do so by the struggles of enslaved people throughout the colony. By the time they acted, they were only giving official sanction to a right enslaved people had claimed for themselves.[79]

Many of the maroon leaders accepted the commissioners' offer, with differing levels of sincerity. Jacques Formon used his new position as cover to travel the colony, encouraging enslaved people to rise in rebellion, and eventually was executed by French forces after a short military trial. Armand and Gilles Bénech tried to dutifully fulfill their obligations, but were taken captive by their former comrades and held hostage for betraying their struggle.[80] The jail records of Les Cayes burgeoned with enslaved people unclaimed by their masters; many of them were likely maroons from Platons.[81]

On August 29, 1793, Commissioner Sonthonax issued a proclamation abolishing slavery in the Northern Province. Commissioner Polverel extended his proclamation to the Western Province in late September and to the South in early October.[82] These decrees, while immediately significant as official declarations against slavery in a world which had been structured by it, had not emerged on their own. Rather, they responded to a course of events. In this respect, what Commissioner Polverel

182 M. Becker

established in the Southern Province in October 1793 brought into being the demands that the maroons of Platons had made from the provincial government in August 1792, over a year in advance. Commissioner Polverel attempted to abolish slavery while maintaining a system of coerced agricultural labor. However, newly freed people instead adopted a set of practices around appropriating plantations to expand their provision grounds, toward collective ownership or toward their own purposes, around free mobility throughout the colony, and helping themselves to rations and supplies of the plantation.[83]

In the South, André Rigaud and allied free people of color cemented the political power they had achieved through joining with the white planters to chase the maroons from Platons. As the war dragged on, Rigaud became the effective governor of the south. However, the critical aspect of his military strength was in companies he organized with newly freed people, starting with the maroons of Platons. As was the case with enslaved mercenaries during prior struggles, they may have served Rigaud's ends but also had their own goals and ambitions. Maroon communities persisted in the Plaine-du-Fond, rising to political prominence again several years later.[84]

One can further see the reverberations of Platons in the maroon communities formed by Goman, Nicolas Régnier, and Gilles Bénech (himself a former leader of Platons) in the western part of the Southern Province that lasted, in one form or another, through independence, or the critical role that Armand, former Platons commandant, played in organizing a revolt of plantation workers during the war for independence following the deportation of Toussaint L'Ouverture.[85]

In closing, I would like to return to the challenge from Michel Rolph-Trouillot posed at the beginning of this chapter. He contended that historians at the time he wrote were unable to fully conceptualize the Haitian Revolution because the intellectual traditions within which they operated were still too closely tied to Western traditions of slavery, race, and colonization. Trouillot's argument hinges on the recognition that a historical narrative is always the result of choices to emphasize certain things and ignore others. This choice does not happen in a vacuum. Rather, historians make decisions based on particular epistemological frameworks that determine particular horizons of possibility, frameworks tied to the political and social realities of their day.[86] Revisiting Trouillot's question, I ask: What are the implications of our own narrative choices, the priorities which we signal through the stories that we choose to tell? What are the horizons of possibility of our own historical moment, those frontiers beyond which we find ourselves unable to imagine? What new frameworks might we need to adopt in order to better understand historical actors like the maroons of Platons? In what sort of world might their stories and the stories of countless others like them become more legible?

Notes

1 I completed the research for this chapter while an undergraduate at Brown University, with the funding support of the Brown International Scholarship Program, the Office of the Dean of the College, and the Center for the Study of Slavery and Justice. I owe a tremendous debt to Anthony Bogues, a creative and generous scholar with a rare

Re-Framing the Haitian Revolution   183

commitment to political struggle, who mentored me during the research process and in writing the thesis on which this chapter is based. Conversations with the other members of the Providence Africana Reading Collective and with a political education class at Direct Action for Rights and Equality were instrumental in sharpening my analysis and thinking about the broader implications of this work. The Center for Latin American and Caribbean Studies at Duke University provided partial funding to present an earlier version of this chapter to the 2014 Africa Conference at the University of Texas at Austin. Many thanks too to Malika Bennabi, Nathan Bergmann-Dean, Lucy Asako Boltz, Clare Boyle, Osman Chaudry, Carlo Célius, Isaac Curtis, Gavriel Cutipa-Zorn, Camellia Dao-Ling Lee, Radia Legouera, Anani Dzidzenyo, Tania Flores, Rachel Ama Asa Engmann, Françoise Hamlin, Masumi Hayashi-Smith, Eduarda Araujo, Marco McWilliams, Andrea Sterling, Patrick Sylvain, Corey D. B. Walker, and Mika Zacks.

2 Michel-Rolph Trouillot, *Silencing the Past: Power and the Production of History* (Boston: Beacon Press, 1997), 82.

3 Ibid., 74.

4 Among others, see Jean Casimir, *Pa Bliye 1804/Souviens-Toi de 1804* (Port-au-Prince: Imprimerie Lakay, 2004); Laurent Dubois, *Avengers of the New World: The Story of the Haitian Revolution* (Cambridge, MA: Belknap, 2004); Doris Lorraine Garraway, ed., *Tree of Liberty: Cultural Legacies of the Haitian Revolution in the Atlantic World* (Charlottesville: University of Virginia, 2008); David Patrick Geggus, ed., *The Impact of the Haitian Revolution in the Atlantic World* (Columbia: University of South Carolina, 2001); Malick Ghachem, *The Old Regime and the Haitian Revolution* (Cambridge: Cambridge University Press, 2012); Clinton Hutton, *The Logic and Historical Significance of the Haitian Revolution and the Cosmological Roots of Haitian Freedom* (Kingston: Arawak Publications, 2005); Maurice Jackson and Jacqueline Bacon, ed., *African Americans and the Haitian Revolution: Selected Essays and Historical Documents* (New York: Routledge, 2010); Jeremy Popkin, *You Are All Free: The Haitian Revolution and the Abolition of Slavery* (Cambridge: Cambridge University Press, 2010); Karol Weaver, *Medical Revolutionaries: The Enslaved Healers of Eighteenth-Century Saint-Domingue* (Urbana: University of Illinois Press, 2006).

5 Anthony Bogues, *Haiti and the Politics of an Impossible Revolution*, work-in-progress.

6 Maya Deren, *Divine Horsemen: The Living Gods of Haiti* (New Paltz: McPherson, 1983), 96–102.

7 Ibid., 98.

8 Vincent Brown, "Social Death and Political Life in the Study of Slavery," *The American Historical Review* 114, no. 5 (2009): 1232–1233.

9 Sidney Mintz and Michel Rolph-Trouillot, "Social History of Haitian Vodou," in *Sacred Arts of Haitian Vodou*, ed. Donald Consentino (Seattle: University of Washington Press, 2002), 126–129.

10 Carolyn Fick, *Making of Haiti: The Saint Domingue Revolution from Below* (Knoxville: University of Tennessee Press, 1990), 33–34.

11 Scott, "Common Winds," 43–47.

12 Fouchard, *Maroons*.

13 Ibid., 26; Julius Scott, "The Common Wind: Currents of Afro-American Communication in the Era of the Haitian Revolution," (PhD diss., University of Michigan, 1986): 23–24.

14 John D. Garrigus, *Before Haiti: Race and Citizenship in French Saint-Domingue* (New York: Palgrave MacMillan, 2006), 21–50.

15 David Patrick Geggus, "Sugar and Coffee Cultivation in Saint Domingue and the Shaping of the Slave Labor Force," in *Cultivation and Culture: Labor and the Shaping of Slave Life in the Americas*, eds. Ira Berlin and Philip D. Morgan (Charlottesville: University Press of Virginia, 1993), 78.

184   *M. Becker*

16 Garrigus, *Before Haiti*, 45.
17 Ibid., 110–114.
18 Ibid., 119, 137–139; Jean Fouchard, *The Haitian Maroons: Liberty or Death*, trans. A. Faulkner Watts (New York: E. W. Blyden Press, 1981), 274–275.
19 Garrigus, *Before Haiti*, 235–248.
20 Pauléus Sannon, *Histoire de Toussaint Louverture*, Vol. 1 (Port-au-Prince: Imprimerie Aug. A. Héraux, 1932), 102–103; Fick, *Making of Haiti*, 133.
21 David Patrick Geggus, "The Arming of Slaves in the Haitian Revolution," in *Arming Slaves: From Classical Times to the Modern Age*, eds. Christopher Brown and Philip Morgan (New Haven: Yale University Press, 2006): 209.
22 Geggus, "Arming of Slaves," 227.
23 John Thornton, "'I Am the Subject of the King of the Kongo': African Political Ideology and the Haitian Revolution," *Journal of World History* 4, no. 2 (1993): 201.
24 Quoted in Thornton, "African Political Ideology," 202.
25 Sannon, *Toussaint*, 102–103.
26 Dubourg to Caussé, December 23, 1792, Les Cayes, Document 395, Box 30, HCA.
27 Bernard Foubert, "Colons et esclaves du sud du Saint-Domingue au début de la Révolution," *Revue française d'histoire d'outre-mer*, LXI, no. 233 (1974), 202; M. LeRongac to Sophie Ladurentie, January 17, 1793, Document 394, Box 30, HCA; Reflections of M. d'Alers, inhabitant of Platons, Folder 621, Box 62, Series DXXV, ANF.
28 Réflexions de M. d'Alers, habitant des Platons, Folder 621, Box 62, Series DXXV, ANF.
29 André Rigaud to M. de Thiballier, June 26, 1792, Box 401, Series 30, HCA; Mémoire de l'Assemblée Provincale et des Municipalités Réunies du Sud à l'Assemblée Coloniale de la Partie Française de Saint-Domingue, June 26, 1792, Folder 638, Box 63, Series DXXV, ANF; M. Bérrault to M. Cordun, January 17, 1793, Les Cayes, Box 392, Series 30, HCA; Journal exacté, Folder 638, Box 63, Series DXXV, ANF.
30 L'Assemblée Provincale du Sud à l'Assemblée Coloniale, July 9, 1792, Folder 620, Box 62, Series DXXV, ANF.
31 Déclaration du Citoyen Gaujon, Box 401, Series 30, HCA.
32 Mémoire de l'Assemblée Provincale et des Municipalités Réunies du Sud à l'Assemblée Coloniale de la Partie Française de Saint-Domingue, July 26, 1792, Folder 638, Box 63, Series DXXV, ANF.
33 Extrait des pieces déposées aux archives de l'Assemblée Coloniale par l'Assemblée Provinciale et provisoirement administrative du Sud et l'Assemblée Coloniale, Les Cayes, July 19, 1792, Folder 619, Box 62, Series DXXV, ANF.
34 Blanchelande aux Négres Esclaves en Insurrection aux Anglais, Folder 620, Box 62, Series DXXV, ANF; Blanchelande to l'Assemblée Coloniale, Folder 621, Box 62, Series DXXV, ANF.
35 Blanchelande to l'Assemblée Coloniale, July 28, 1792, Folder 667, Box 66, Series DXXV, ANF; City of Les Cayes to M. Delaval, July 27, 1792, Folder 671, Box 66, Series DXXV, ANF.
36 Journal exacté, Folder 638, Box 63, Series DXXV, ANF; M. Bérault to M. Berault, jeune, January 17, 1792, Les Cayes, Box 392, Series 30, HCA; Blanchelande to the Colonial Assembly, Folder 621, Box 62, Series DXXV, ANF.
37 *La Gazette des Cayes*, No. 80–85, Box 392, Series 30, HCA; Mémoire de l'Assemblée Provincale et des Municipalitiés Réunies du Sud à l'Assemblée Coloniale de la Partie Française de Saint-Domingue, July 26, 1792, Folder 638, Box 63, Series DXXV, ANF.
38 Blanchelande to L'Assemblée Coloniale, Folder 621, Box 62, Series DXXV, ANF; Journal exacté, Folder 638, Box 63, Series DXXV, ANF.
39 Journal exacté, Folder 638, Box 63, Series DXXV, ANF; Puvouy to M. Rivierre, January 15, 1793, Box 392, Series 30, HCA; *La Gazette des Cayes*, No. 80–88, Box 392, Series 30, HCA.
40 André Rigaud to M. Roume, September 16, 1792, Les Cayes, Folder 23, Box 2, Series DXXV, ANF.
41 Journal exacté, Folder 638, Box 63, Series DXXV, ANF.

Re-Framing the Haitian Revolution 185

42 André Rigaud to M. Roume, September 16, 1792, Les Cayes, Folder 23, Box 2, Series DXXV, ANF; Demencour to Meunier, December 22, 1792, Les Cayes, Box 393, Series 30, HCA.

43 Demencour to Meunier, December 22, 1792, Les Cayes, Box 393, Series 30, HCA; Ferrano to M. Salenave the elder, September 30, 1792, Les Cayes, Box 393, Series 30, HCA; Rigaud to Polverel, August 22, 1793, Les Cayes, Folder 212, Box 21, Series DXXV, ANF.

44 Philibert to M. Desrouadierer, January 13, 1793, Les Cayes, Box 393, Series 30, HCA.

45 M. Siffet to M. Siffet (father), November 4, 1792, Box 393, Series 30, HCA.

46 M. DeLanôzey to M. Choiseuil Prarlin, January 17, 1793, Cayes Fond d'Isle à Vache, Box 393, Series 30, HCA.

47 G. Potain to A. Baudoiy, January 6, 1793, Les Cayes, Box 392, Series 30, HCA.

48 Gensterbloem to Mlle. Felicité Beaudrau, December 20, 1792, Camp Général, Box 393, Series 30, HCA; *La Gazette des Cayes*, No. 84–90, Box 392, Box 30, HCA; Foubert, "Colons et esclaves," 200.

49 Foubert, "Colons et esclaves," 207

50 Billard, son, to Mmes. Billard, Moreau and Amand Billard, January 16, 1793, Les Cayes, Box 394, Series 30, HCA.

51 B. Dubreil to LeJeune, January 19, 1793, Cayes St. Louis, Box 394, Series 30, HCA.

52 Ibid.

53 Billard, son, to Mmes. Billard, Moreau and Amand Billard, January 16, 1793, Les Cayes, Box 394, Series 30, HCA; Dubreil to citoyenne Piquot, January 17, 1793, Les Cayes, Box 395, Series 30, HCA.

54 M. Philibert to M. Desrouadierer, January 13, 1793, Les Cayes, Box 393, Series 30, HCA.

55 Puvouy to M. Rivierre, January 15, 1793, Box 392, Series 30, HCA.

56 M. Muzard to M. Lacaussade, January 18, 1793, Les Cayes, Box 392, Series 30, HCA.

57 Gensterbloem to Mlle. Felicité Beaudrau, December 20, 1792, Camp Général, Box 393, Series 30, HCA.

58 St. Martin to Duplessy, January 16, 1793, Les Cayes, Box 395, Series 30, HCA.

59 Gensterbloem to Mlle. Felicité Beaudrau, December 20, 1792, Camp Général, Box 393, Series 30, HCA.

60 Gensterbloem to his mother, January 16, 1793, Les Cayes, Box 393, Series 30, HCA.

61 Foubert, "Colons et esclaves," 204; Coinchoon to his father, January 15, 1793, Les Cayes, Box 395, Series 30, HCA; M. Souiesleuy to M. Pelerin de la Bucseiere, Box 392, Series 30, HCA.

62 *La Gazette des Cayes*, No. 95, December 2, 1792, Box 392, Series 30, HCA.

63 M. Deville to M. Pelities, son, December 7, 1792, Box 392, Series 30, HCA; Fortune de Perrigny to Mme de Perrigny, Box 392, Series 30, HCA; Léon de Perrigny to Messieurs Elie le Febvre the younger and the son, lawyers, January 3, 1793, Les Cayes, Box 392, Series 30, HCA; Ferrano to M. Salenave the elder, November 30, 1792, Box 392, Series 30, HCA; Philibert to M. Desrouadierer, January 13, 1793, Les Cayes, Box 393, Series 30, HCA.

64 M. Deville to M. Pelities, son, December 7, 1792, Les Cayes, Box 392, Series 30, HCA.

65 M. Cambert to M. Malvès the elder, January 16, 1793, Les Cayes, Box 392, Series 30, HCA.

66 M. Deville to M. Pelities, son, December 7, 1792, Les Cayes, Box 392, Series 30, HCA.

67 Gayes to Pelletan, November 17, 1792, St. Louis, Box 393, Series 30, HCA.

68 Rene Lambert to M. Malivers the elder, January 13, 1793, Les Cayes, Box 392, Series 30, HCA; M. Castelpers to Mlle. Castelpers, January 16, 1793, Fond d'Isle à Vache, Box 393, Series 30, HCA.

186   *M. Becker*

69 Letter to MM. Gamba and Archdeacon, December 20, 1792, Les Cayes, Box 395, Series 30, HCA.
70 Ibid.
71 B. Deville to Bayonne de Deville, Box 392, Series 30, HCA; Rene Lambert to M. Malivers the elder, January 13, 1793, Les Cayes, Box 392, Series 30, HCA.
72 Demaleval, Champel, and Bouffart to Mme. Leplicher, January 12, 1793, Cayes St. Louis, Box 393, Series 30, HCA; Caudron Beauzamy and others to J.-B. Lafosse, January 14, 1793, Les Cayes, Box 395, Series 30, HCA.
73 Bergeaud to M. Milhau, January 16, 1793, Les Cayes, Box 392, Series 30, HCA.
74 Billard, son to Mmes. Billard, Moreau, and Amand Billard, January 16, 1793, Les Cayes, Box 394, Series 30, HCA.
75 Demaleval to Champel, January 19, 1793, Les Cayes, Box 392, Series 30, HCA.
76 M. Cambert to M. Malvès the elder, January 16, 1793, Les Cayes, Box 392, Series 30, HCA.
77 Billard, son to Mmes. Billard, Moreau, and Amand Billard, January 16, 1793, Les Cayes, Box 394, Series 30, HCA.
78 M. Cambert to M. Malvès the elder, January 16, 1793, Les Cayes, Box 392, Series 30, HCA.
79 Proclamation du Polverel et Sonthonax du 25 juillet 1793, Le Cap, Folder 849, Box 97, Series DXXV, ANF.
80 André Rigaud to Polverel and Sonthonax, July 25, 1793, Le Cap, Folder 212, Box 21, Series DXXV, ANF; Rigaud to Polverel, August 22, 1793, Les Cayes, Folder 212, Box 21, Series DXXV, ANF.
81 État de ce qui est dû au citoyen L'Abbé, concierge, pour nourriture et frais de géolle des nègres ci-après nommés, lesquels ont été élargis du prison en vertu de la proclamation du citoyen Polverel..., Les Cayes, October 10, 1793, Folder 281, Box 27, Series DXXV, ANF.
82 Dubois, *Avengers*, 160–165.
83 Fick, *Making of Haiti*, 167–171.
84 Ibid., 225–226.
85 Ibid., 225–226, 230–235.
86 Trouillot, *Silencing the Past*, 70–107.

References

Archival Sources

DXXV Series. Archives Nationales de la France, Paris [ANF].
High Court of the Admiralty Papers, British National Archives, Kew [HCA].

Secondary Sources

Bogues, Anthony. *Haiti and the Politics of an Impossible Revolution*, work-in-progress.
Brown, Vincent. "Social Death and Political Life in the Study of Slavery." *The American Historical Review* 114, no. 5 (2009): 1231–1249.
Deren, Maya. *Divine Horsemen: The Living Gods of Haiti*. New Paltz: McPherson, 1983.
Dubois, Laurent. *Avengers of the New World: The Story of the Haitian Revolution*. Cambridge, MA: Belknap of Harvard University Press, 2004.
Fick, Carolyn. *Making of Haiti: The Saint Domingue Revolution from Below*. Knoxville: University of Tennessee Press, 1990.
Foubert, Bernard. "Colons et esclaves du sud du Saint-Domingue au début de la Révolution. " *Revue française d'histoire d'outre-mer*, LXI, no. 233 (1974): 199–217.

Fouchard, Jean. *The Haitian Maroons: Liberty or Death*, trans. A. Faulkner Watts. New York: E. W. Blyden Press, 1981.

Garrigus, John D. *Before Haiti: Race and Citizenship in French Saint-Domingue*. New York: Palgrave MacMillan, 2006.

Geggus, David Patrick. "Sugar and Coffee Cultivation in Saint Domingue and the Shaping of the Slave Labor Force" in *Cultivation and Culture: Labor and the Shaping of Slave Life in the Americas*, eds. Ira Berlin and Philip D. Morgan. Charlottesville: University Press of Virginia, 1993.

Mintz, Sidney and Michel Rolph-Trouillot. "Social History of Haitian Vodou," in *Sacred Arts of Haitian Vodou*, ed. Donald Consentino. Seattle: University of Washington Press, 2002.

Sannon, H. Pauléus. *Histoire de Toussaint Louverture*. Vol. 1. Port-au-Prince: Imprimerie Aug. A. Héraux, 1932.

Scott, Julius. "The Common Wind: Currents of Afro-American Communication in the Era of the Haitian Revolution." Unpublished PhD diss., University of Michigan, 1986.

Trouillot, Michel-Rolph. *Silencing the Past: Power and the Production of History*. Boston: Beacon Press, 1997.

10 Uprooted

African Americans in Mexico; International Propaganda, Migration, and the Resistance against US Racial Hegemony

Alfredo Aguilar

Long after the official demise of slavery, African Americans remained second-class citizens. Fortunately, African Americans had a possible ally. Mexico posited itself as a counter-weight to combat the racial United States hegemony, whereby granting African Americans the possibility of a heard voice. The relationship between the US and Mexico produced propagandistic motivations as ploys regarding African American interactions with Mexico during the nineteenth century and into the twentieth century. Mexico sought to exploit the position of African Americans in the United States and the US sought to exploit the paranoia surrounding African Americans' actions. The larger hegemonic battle between the United States and Mexico shaped their pivotal roles in the successes and failures of African American international endeavors with regard to Mexico. Mexico hoped to combat the United States' western hemisphere domination by assisting African Americans via colonizing efforts, political rhetoric, the denunciation of slavery, and possible international revolutionary alliances. The United States hoped to impede the spread of radicalism and loss of agricultural workers, to combat the international focus of their own racism and denote Mexico as inferior in the process. Overall, the United States hoped to establish their international hegemonic dominance over areas and people they deemed inferior.

The earlier abolition of slavery in Mexico and the welcoming environment Mexico presented to people of African and African American descent created a vivid testimony of anti-slavery sentiment in Mexico during the nineteenth century. The migration successes and attempts made by African Americans during the late portion of the nineteenth century and the early portion of the twentieth century seem unsurprising considering the social and cultural sentiments of Mexico toward blacks from earlier periods. Although some moves of criticism toward the United States regarding its position on slavery arose from conflicts between the two nations, Mexico typically reviled slavery and historically took positions against slavery during the nineteenth century. Mexico produced the equivalent of the international "Promised Land" for African Americans; at least it was presented and perceived that way. This optimistic view must consider the fact that during Mexico's primary wars with the United States in the nineteenth century, it made it a point to demonstrate its position on slavery, its view of US slavery, and its alleged hospitable environment to African Americans.

Nineteenth-Century International Conflicts

During the period of the Texas Revolution, abolitionists asked about the possibility of the emigration of blacks from the United States to Mexico. It is important to point out that early American abolitionists were not primarily concerned with black freedom but rather white freedom from blacks. Pursuing colonization efforts in lands further from the concentration of the American population is critical to understanding the motivation for doing so. The movements stemmed from the racist desire to rid America of the enslaved and to send them to an area where another nation could tailor to them, a nation that was seen as inferior to the United States: Mexico. This established United States racial hegemony early on. The then current Vice President Valentín Gómez Farías responded to the request of migration in 1833:

> If they [Negro slaves] would like to come, we will offer them land for cultivation, plots for houses where they can establish towns, and tools for work, under the obligation [that they will] obey the laws of the country and the authorities already established by the Supreme Government of the Federation.[1]

During the Texas conflict, the Mexican Secretary of War, José Maria Tornel, denounced the existence of slavery in his criticism of the United States. Simultaneously, Mexican officials used the criticism of slavery as a guise to construct their own moral virtue. United States and Mexico relations were at an unstable stage. Tornel "called attention to the 'astonishment of the civilized world' at the support given by the United States to the 'peculiar institution.'"[2] Furthermore, Tornel said that Mexico considered all men brothers, which were created by our common father.[3] Tornel's criticism was a propagandistic ploy of denouncing US activities to highlight the "receptive" nature of Mexico toward US blacks, although Mexico had its share of racial problems. Additionally, Tornel's purpose was to overshadow the views of Mexican racial hierarchies and shine light on America's racial inconsistencies. Antonio López de Santa Anna, who played a wide-ranging colorful role in Mexico, uniformly wrote:

> There is a considerable number of slaves in Texas also, who have been introduced by their masters under cover of certain questionable contracts, but who according to our laws should be free. Shall we permit those wretches to moan in chains any longer in a country whose kind laws protect the liberty of man without distinction of caste or color?[4]

Comments by Mexicans such as those by José Maria Tornel and Antonio López de Santa Anna can be viewed as opportunistic to give political and proactive support against slavery. However, this consensus existed nationally in Mexico prior to the Texas Revolutionary period and was reflected in the position of Tornel and Santa Anna. In 1810, at the start of the Mexican War of Independence from Spain, Miguel Hidalgo and Jose Maria Morelos (of partial African

190   A. Aguilar

descent) proposed the decree for the abolition of slavery. Guadalupe Victoria, the first President of Mexico, also reiterated this position on slavery.

African Americans attempted to seize the opportunity to sketch a new life in Mexico. For instance, Matamoros in the 1830s attracted a black expatriate population about the starting of a colony, but it never was formalized.[5] Former slaves interviewed in 1937, such as Felix Haywood who saw Mexico as a safe haven for slaves, stated, "there was no reason to *run* up north. All we had to do was to *walk* south, and we'd be free as soon as [we] cross[ed] the Río Grande."[6] Another former slave named Walter Rimm stated:

> All we had to do was *walk*, but walk south and we'd be free as soon as we crossed the Río Grande. In Mexico you could be free. They didn't care what color you were, black, white, yellow, or blue. Hundreds of slaves did go to Mexico and got on all right. We would hear about them and how they were going to be Mexicans. They brought up their children to speak only Mexican [*sic*].[7]

Mexico had its share of racial tensions present under President Vicente Guerrero, but his administration placed the country far ahead of its northern neighbor. These racial tensions were part of the old hierarchical system established by Spain during the colonial era. In 1832, the German, Carl Christian Becher, visited Mexico and viewed the new life that those of African descent gained in a post-Guerrero state. They, and other groups previously restricted under the former colonial government, were now exercising newfound rights.[8] Becher also compared Afro-Mexicans with African Americans and their social position in the United States, writing:

> These blacks, as is known, are free in the republic of Mexico; which is to say, they enjoy, intimately, the same rights as do the rest of the inhabitants of the state, which is not the case in the United States of North America, where, as a result of the laws, or for prejudices, the blacks are humiliated and pressed down to the category of the lowest level of men.[9]

Previously, another German, Karl Wilhelm Koppe "observed that legal rights seemed to energize the blacks and to result in widespread intermarriage of Africans and other races" in colonial Mexico.[10] The *casta* system, which was a hierarchical system of racial classification was being dismantled through miscegenation, and while racism still existed in Mexico, what was fundamentally different was that Mexico gave no legal basis to racial discrimination. The idea of intermarriage would also be presented from the American perspective. A United States official in Mexico noted,

> it is a very great mistake to suppose that they [blacks] enjoy anything like social equality even with the Indian population.... The Negro in Mexico ... is looked upon as belonging to a class a little lower than the lowest.[11]

Uprooted: African Americans in Mexico 191

The latter opinion is reflective of US and Mexico relations when it came to the issue of slavery. More so, it highlights the tactic of propaganda (possible misinformation) to deter African Americans from viewing Mexico as a place of relocation, as well as highlighting Mexico's racial problems. Mexico hoped their anti-slavery stance posed the possibility of disrupting life in the United States for African Americans. It also posed the possibility of being empty rhetoric used primarily as a tactic against the United States rather than being proactive in seeking African Americans. It seemed that the United States and Mexico were interchangeably voicing similar opinions of each other, especially in times of war.

As the Texas Revolution carried on, it eventually transformed into the Mexican-American War, where more propaganda was used by both the United States and Mexico concerning African Americans. At the height of the Mexican-American War (an extension of the Texas Revolution), slaves and free blacks were at the forefront of the American crises. Senator Robert J. Walker of Mississippi wrote an open letter which was circulated to millions of Americans in 1844.[12]

> Capitalizing on the ambivalence of northerners squeezed between expansionist and anti-slavery sentiment, Walker made a case for "self-destruction" in the nature of United States slavery, leaning heavily on Mexico and other Latin American countries as the ultimate happy haven for ex-slaves.[13]

Again, the case of abolition and freedom for slaves was not concerned with empathy, but rather to free themselves of African Americans. While this sentiment primarily addressed ex-slaves, slaves still in positions of forced toil had sought out countries like Mexico since they were brought to colonial America as well.[14] This attitude continued to exist beyond the existence of slavery where blacks in the United States remained in sub-par social and economic conditions.

While the debate of the annexation of Texas went to the US Congress, Sen. Walker argued that if Texas was annexed, blacks had the option of leaving for Mexico, thus solving the race problem in the South. This was primarily motivated by the idea to rid the US of blacks and motivate them toward migration. The annexation occurred in 1845 and Walker had set his slaves free earlier because of political pressure from Congress. Walker did not have a claim to slavery anymore; he however continued to have a racist view. Walker offered his approach:

> The sparse population occupying the land [Mexico] would welcome the Negroes and treat them as equals. The people of Latin America are overwhelmingly persons of color.... These people cherish no race prejudice against Negroes. The barriers of color, which in the United States would exclude Negroes forever from the privileges of equality, would not operate there. The Negroes would be integrated as equals in a society of equals and not always sullen inferiors in a despised caste.[15]

Walker's analysis provided insight into the "colored" propaganda he was using to stimulate the "options" the US could pursue. Walker placed emphasis on the

192   A. Aguilar

idea that "Latin America is overwhelmingly persons of color" and offered African Americans "equality" in Mexico. Walker and the majority of the US society viewed both groups as lower and he argued that they should be grouped together. Walker also argued that "The freed Negroes ... having no employment opportunities on exhausted soil, flow southward into Mexico, Central America, and South America, where an ideal climate similar to that of Africa, would provide abundant crops."[16]

International Colonization Endeavors

The American restrictions on African American movement post-Civil War reflect the racist hegemony white America hoped to continue post-emancipation. The rules, laws, and racial customs of America have been notably pointed out such as voter restrictions, tenant farming, sharecropping, debt peonage, Black Codes, and Jim Crow. The Civil War produced efforts to relocate African Americans to a colony established within the US periphery bordering Mexico. Also, during America's involvement in the Spanish-American War a colony was proposed to colonize the Philippines with African Americans.

Propaganda was used not only by both nations to influence the migratory efforts, but newspapers and people with direct participation with the efforts also played roles. The interactive and interlocking role of propaganda played a vital role to the success and failure of the African American migration and resistance endeavor. For example, during the Civil War on February 16, 1864 an "abolitionist" and US Senator James Lane from Kansas proposed a bill that would create a black colony that covered a southwest portion and argued that Mexico would not object because they tolerate racial difference and practice intermarriage.[17] Senator Lane's abolitionist sentiment was not driven by an egalitarian approach to life; it was driven by his staunchly racist view. For instance, he sponsored a black law in 1857 that proposed to make Kansas an all-white state. His abolitionist view was for the removal of blacks, so his colonization efforts were determined by his view of blacks and objection to them remaining in Kansas. Furthermore, another motivating factor in his endeavor was a creation of a buffer state between Mexico and the United States to fend off the often turbulent relationship with Mexico.

In his *Vindication of the Policy of the Administration*, Lane stated that the United States should create a buffer and proposed a "policy of the highest order [which] requires that we establish on our southern border an independent, self-sustaining and self-reliant people, loving liberty, and ready to protect it, whose first effort to illustrate the principles they have derived from us."[18] The key being "ready to protect it," meaning the United States under Lane's proposal was to place African Americans between Mexico and the United States as a possible buffer for war. Furthermore, Lane's view of Mexico's racial tolerance and intermarriage highlight the recognition of Mexico's anti-slavery stance but simultaneously offers his supposed foresight of another nation.

While racism was a huge key to Lane's efforts, some southerners would have been reluctant to allow this colonization endeavor to come to fruition because it

Uprooted: African Americans in Mexico   193

would surely have disrupted and depleted their labor force. In Kansas, Lane and his constituents did not depend on the black labor force. It also highlighted his view of Mexico and its people claiming that they would not object to the proximity of this proposed African American colony, or rather did not consider.

Similarly, during the Spanish-American War, the white supremacist Senator Ben Tillman also suggested the migration of blacks from the United States, this time, to the Philippines. Migration was encouraged not only through colonization efforts, but as a means to solve the high populations of African Americans. Sen. "Pitchfork Ben" Tillman of South Carolina sought out new methods to solve the race problem of the United States, urging that the "new territories be used as a racial safety valve to decrease lynchings by deporting troublesome blacks."[19] Tillman's pursuits also displayed the racism present in the United States by ignoring the ramifications of this plan for the people of the Philippines, as well as for African Americans. In a speech where Tillman was justifying the use of violence toward African Americans, he stated his racism and thoughts on relocation of African Americans. Tillman did not believe in equality of races, was fearful of their "lust," wished they went back to Africa, and regretted they were ever brought to America.[20]

Albert J. Beveridge, another US senator spoke about the Philippines' people and the justification of establishing US hegemony there through racist motivation and profiteering intent. Beveridge stated, "the common people in their stupidity are like their caribou bulls. They are not even good agriculturists. Their waste of cane is inexcusable. Their destruction of hemp fiber is childish. They are incurable indolent."[21] The United States placed African Americans on par with Mexicans and then with the people of the Philippines.

The US government was not the only government discussing proposed plans for African American colonization regarding Mexico. During the period of Tillman's comments, a Mexican named Guillermo Wodon de Sorinee pointed out the possibility of African American migration to Mexico. In a mix of racist and reluctant productive thought, written in 1900, Guillermo Wodon de Sorinee pushed for the immigration of African Americans to Mexico, but with a cautionary reservation about holding back an excess of migrants because it could potentially produce problematic social consequences. His view was that Mexico was not entirely committed to total migration of African Americans, which points out the flaws in the propaganda pushed by Mexico as it asserted its position to the United States. Wodon de Sorinne "believed that short infusions of blacks from the U.S. south could jump start the Mexican agricultural export sector."[22] This was in alignment with the same thought that African Americans had. For example in the 1880s, black Texans had approached Mexico with plans to launch a colony there to boost cotton production.[23] Wodon De Sorinne saw the potential for positive economic possibilities for Mexico, but simultaneously displayed Mexico's problematic racial issues.[24]

While these politicians were promoters of African American migration efforts, some took it upon themselves to attempt the move. A San Antonio entrepreneur named William H. Ellis sought out Mexico's opportunities with the William H. Ellis colony of 1895. Karl Jacoby, a borderlands historian, described

194   A. Aguilar

the effort of Ellis to set up a colony of African Americans in Mexico.[25] While generally viewed as a failure, the propaganda by both Mexico and the United States points out the underlying motivations behind the moves to speak out about the colony. Ellis wrote in 1889 in Mexico City that he had received word from the government of Mexico to bring in 20,000 African Americans from the US South into Mexico.[26] For the recruitment by Ellis he received financial compensation from the Mexican government in government bonds for every person.[27] Upon the failure of the colony, Juan Llamedo, the president of the Mexican Colonization Company that sponsored the effort spoke remorsefully of the event. He spoke about the loss of profit possibility and sympathy to the colonists. Llamedo stated:

> this Company has sustained great loss by the importation of the Negroes, and regrets that they have not met with the prosperity which in all sincerity we had hoped they would attain, while we have omitted no measure calculated for our mutual advantage.[28]

In the United States, several southern newspapers were quick to point out the colony's failure through racist means with the hope to mitigate the relocation of the much-needed African American labor force. The newspapers' methodology was used as a ploy of propaganda and written to demean the colonization efforts to Mexico by blacks. For example, one article, titled "Lassoed the Negroes," refers to a group of colonists who left the colony and went into the desert after its initial failure.[29] They had to be caught by horsemen. In the article, they also used such phrases as the "shipment of Negro labor" and as a "batch of colonists," which demonstrates the paper's view of them as trade goods or commerce.[30] In Alabama (where most of the colonists came from) the *Courier* stated, "this is the home of the Negro. He should accept the Southern sun and the cotton fields and make of himself a more useful citizen."[31] Furthermore, the racism permeated another newspaper: "They are happier among the white people who know them and are able to make allowances for their shortcomings," affirmed the *Tuskegee News*.[32] This also served as criticism of Mexico for its inability to work with them.

Two decades later in California, Mexico once more sought out African American colonizers. Juan Uribe, as a government representative for Mexico (also a lawyer representing a land company), visited Los Angeles in 1919 speaking to a group of African Americans about Mexico's view of them. Uribe stated, "I was impressed with the fact that the Colored American will not much longer be content with the menial positions in life."[33] Uribe's comment pointed out the sub-par condition of African Americans in the United States. It, however, also reflected a subtle Mexican criticism of the US and its racism. African Americans may have possibly known of the history with Mexico, and Uribe iterated the perceived positive sentiment Mexico had toward African Americans. Years earlier, writing to the NAACP in 1912, an official in Mexico corresponded from Torreon, Mexico to *The Crisis* that other groups that faced the difficulty of acceptance such as the Jews and the Irish had to migrate and leave home to solve economic and racial conflicts. And claimed prejudice did not exist in Mexico.[34] Uribe shared a similar sentiment toward African Americans and stated:

> I believe my Colored American friends in the United States have in their ranks talent of every kind and description.... My only regret is that it is not physically possible to immediately transport several millions [*sic*] of these fine people who are my brothers and sisters to my beloved Mexico, where the earth yields her riches, as nowhere else and where ... people are not disturbed by artificial standard of race and color.[35]

This features an underlying reason to suggest such a proposal. At this time, Mexico and the United States were at odds concerning oil. The same news article that ran Uribe's comments also referred to US companies obtaining Mexican oil, stated that

> these men who have taken millions out of Mexico in the form of oil in years past without paying any taxes are now resenting the fact that the Mexican government requires them to pay about half as much tax on a barrel of oil taken out of the ground in Mexico.[36]

This, as pointed out by Uribe, showed his understanding for American objection toward Mexico's nationalistic stance as he adamantly stated, "their protests however, are in vain and they will have to pay taxes."[37]

The United States was upset that Mexico was nationalizing their oil. In 1917, Mexico had established their Constitution after the Mexican Revolution. Article 27 of the Constitution stipulated that Mexico had primary ownership over natural resources, a sticking point with the United States.[38] Uribe discussed this in response to questions about the paranoia surrounding the possibility of the United States invading Mexico. He brushed this off as yellow journalism, but the threat, real or not, showed the tension between the two nations, as the oil crisis points out. Uribe backed a colonizing effort in Baja, California, which hoped to settle African Americans in Mexico. This had the potential to affect the labor force in America and Juan Uribe poignantly stated, "the acquisition ... is the finest step that the Colored American brothers have yet made for their economic and political freedom."[39] A point that subtly illustrated the lack of opportunities that had been offered in the United States. The colony, which proposed to move African Americans to Mexico from the United States, had the possibility of disrupting the economics of the black labor force.

Jack Johnson: A Man to Fear Inside and Outside the Ring

Another sticking point that involved Mexico and the United States dealt with a renowned figure of the 1910s. Mexico in particular took advantage of the situation. Jack Johnson, a Texan and famed African American boxer, reached a boiling point with the United States when he refused to abide by his sentence under the Mann Act as he crossed a state line with a woman, his partner. These

196 *A. Aguilar*

charges were motivated by racial bias, and under the restrictive laws, he was not permitted to cross artificial lines of boundary. Johnson, like other African Americans of the time, understood Mexico's position toward the United States and opted to move there in exile to circumvent the law. Johnson's example is one of many, he was a known athlete of this era, and had the means to exit the United States.

Yale scholar John Dollard, who studied the 1930s South, states:

> oftentimes, just to go away is one of the most aggressive things that another person can do, and if the means of expressing discontent are limited, as in this case, it is one of the few ways in which pressure can be put.[40]

The freedom of movement was aggressive but also liberating for Johnson and others. Isabel Wilkerson described post-emancipation America as "the first act of independence by a people who were in bondage in this country far longer than they have been free."[41] Jack Johnson moved to Mexico and established an alliance with the revolutionary forces and sought out ways not only to discredit the American racial system but also to speak to African Americans and the "possibilities" for them there. Mexico would not object.

In 1919, Jack Johnson, the famed pugilist, placed advertisements with messages about their "possible" Mexico in black newspapers in the United States. He announced in *Favorite Magazine* of Chicago

> If you want us, Mexico, we are ready to become your citizens and willing to do all that we can to make you a great power among the nations. If you want us, Latin America, we are ready to dwell among you and make you rich as we have made the southern white man rich.[42]

He claimed Mexico was "willing not only to give us the privileges of Mexican citizenship, but will champion our cause."[43]

His reference to Latin America however, struck a chord. Jack Johnson praised Mexico over the Central and South American countries. Johnson announced, "Brazil may have its opportunities, but there are far better ones in this city [Mexico City]."[44] He stated, "I believe this to be the best place in the world for our people.... The expense of coming here, especially from the southern states, is considerably less than going to South American countries."[45] Johnson said this after he had created a land company in Mexico.[46] The *Chicago Defender* stated Johnson is praised as an important figure in business and politics, an owner of a land company in Mexico, and hundreds are settling in Mexico because of Johnson's celebrity.[47] While he may have had some racial considerations behind better opportunities for his people, one must also consider the economic interests he had the chance to gain. After all, his personality historically was primarily concerned with himself.

In the *Messenger* for instance, "Jack Johnson's Land Company" extended the following enticing invitation:

Uprooted: African Americans in Mexico 197

Colored People. You who are lynched, tortured, mobbed, persecuted and discriminated against in the boasted "Land of Liberty" ... OWN A HOME IN MEXICO where one man is good as another and it is not your nationality that counts but simply you! The price is reasonable—$5.00 an acre and up—but best of all there is [no] "race prejudice" in Mexico and in fact, severe punishment is meted out to those who discriminate against a man because of his color or race. Neither is there censorship, espionage or conscription.[48]

While credit is due to Jack Johnson for standing by his convictions and proclaiming this about Mexico, the idea was not a new and radical one and neither was it entirely factual when considering Mexico's racial problems. Mexico, however, wanted to take advantage of Johnson's fame and boisterous voice as a criticism of the United States without directly pronouncing this. Mexico's motivation to criticize the United States indirectly dealt with tensions regarding the punitive expedition of General Pershing and the occupation of Veracruz. Pershing's incursion into Mexico in search of Pancho Villa from 1916–1917 and the 1914 Veracruz port occupation by US forces were not welcomed in Mexico. Johnson's land company's message concerning Mexican racial tolerances and promotion of inexpensive land sounds more like an advertisement of profiting rather than a liberating message. It still contained the possibility to pique interest for the readers of these magazines and journals and hope for blacks to settle in Mexico.

It also helped him politically as he hoped to stay in Mexico as his situation was better there than in the United States. Johnson had a great standing with the revolutionary regime in Mexico under President Venustiano Carranza. An American observation of Johnson confirmed this:

Johnson stands very high with the Carranza government and [there] are more Negroes now in Mexico City than ever before. Americans from there are of the opinion that the Carranza government are carrying out through Johnson quite propaganda in the United States. Some time ago Johnson gave an exhibition in Nuevo Laredo and had about twenty Negroes from different portions of the United States meet him there.[49]

The Walter Sanborn incident points out that the Mexican revolutionary forces sought to use Johnson and not allow him to be a victim of racism in Mexico. He, however, was still victim to a racist incident which quells the idea that Mexico was free of racial activities, granted it was an American who was the culprit of the act. The Carranza regime was using Johnson as a voice for criticism of the United States. American spies and government agents of the United States corroborated these claims further: "a spy who had infiltrated the Socialist Party in Mexico told his paymasters in Washington that 'Johnson wished to spread race propaganda and he was interested in socialist ideology.' "[50]

While a spy could be reporting the conclusion the United States government wanted to hear, many others also heard Johnson's radical ideas. At a speech

198   *A. Aguilar*

"given before a cheering crowd in front of the Vega Hotel in Nuevo Laredo, Johnson said that when and if the gringos invaded Mexico, American blacks would stand alongside their Mexican brothers."[51] Johnson understood the stance of the United States racist policy of hegemony and hoped to counteract it if African Americans and Mexicans united. Johnson boisterously exclaimed:

> the colored race are going to show them that when, or if the time ever comes when the Americans will attempt to come over there, the black man is your friend, and [is] with you, and will stand by you.[52]

Both groups had one enemy on their mind, the United States. However, Johnson" use of the phrase "when they come over there" displayed the provisional commitment he had toward Mexico as a temporary asylum using "there" instead of "here" as he was on Mexican soil.

The United States government was fearful of Jack Johnson and his anti-American sentiment in Mexico. The spread of radicalism is something the United States hoped to suppress. The paranoia was furthered when Jack Johnson visited Panama, an important route for American trade.[53] A.L. Flint, the General Purchasing Officer and Chief of Office in Panama reported that Jack Johnson "may come to the Isthmus in the near future from Mexico."[54]

Paranoia or Reality: International Collaboration

Jack Johnson illustrated the potent force of one African American and his alliance with Revolutionary Mexico. For the force of the Mexican Revolution had also reached all the way to New York and the African Blood Brotherhood and its leader Cyril Briggs.[55] The Mexican Consul in New York City acknowledged and appreciated the efforts this African American community had toward their colored brothers down south. The Mexican Consul reported "*radicales de este pais, haciendo una campaña energica en favor de Mexico* (Radicals of this country are forming an energetic campaign in favor of Mexico)."[56] Pancho Villa, a revolutionary Mexican, also pointed out this radicalization and called for allegiance between oppressed minorities under the white supremacist government of the United States.[57] Villa attacked Columbus, New Mexico and was chased by General Pershing, oddly with some African American soldiers. Villa's decree did not come without its motivational reasoning when considering Villa's contentious position with the US and its army. Villa similarly proclaimed, as Jack Johnson did, that "Negroes are all ready to side with us [Mexico]."[58] Villa's contempt for US racial hegemony was also considered by the United States during World War I, especially when considering that African Americans had the possibility of switching allegiances.

During World War I, German agitators sought out African Americans' alliance because of their peculiar position in the United States. Additionally, with the uncovering of the Zimmerman Telegram, which secretly sought out Mexico's alliance with Germany, the United States had more potential collaborations to concern them. The German agitators were especially keen on the American

Uprooted: African Americans in Mexico 199

South, as they knew this was the worst location for African Americans because of historically entrenched racism. Mexicans played a role with the Germans in the recruitment efforts of African Americans. The *New York Times* announced:

> Germans not only followed the Negroes into the cotton fields and mills, but also into the Army.... All of the Negro propaganda workers were Mexicans and half breeds and men that were brought to Mexico City and instructed and sent across the border and the wave of Negro propaganda work went from the Mexican border east, and embraced the states principally of Texas, Louisiana, Arkansas, Mississippi, Alabama, [and] Georgia. North and South Carolina were on the outskirts of the movement.[59]

The *New York Times* reported that the US government had:

> seized a white man and a black man at Birmingham after they toured Alabama, Louisiana, Georgia, the Carolinas, and Mississippi, "posing as Bible salesmen and ministers of the gospel" and urging black people to migrate to Mexico on specially designed trains.[60]

The migration attempt was not merely a humanitarian effort. The Germans were hoping to sway African Americans from their allegiance to the United States. The allegiance was hardly entrenched and Germany's action posed a threat to the United States. Whether Germany's intent was sincere or if it was merely using this as a way to disrupt the United States is also important to consider.

The *New York Times* was not the only newspaper publishing on the German clandestine operation in the United States. The black newspaper, the *California Eagle*, reported that the "German government has agents in the south promising blacks if they 'rise against the whites and government' that the Kaiser 'will then place them on par with the whites.'"[61] The idea may have appealed to African Americans as they combated white American racial values. This could have motivated Mexico to assist Germany as well.

Furthermore, the distribution of this idea infected North Carolina and had government officials alarmed. In Washington, North Carolina a meeting took place between "Negro" ministers. The official statement reported that:

> two of the most intelligent [men] have reported to [me] that at a place called Evergreen in Columbus County an old Negro man named Oliver, well known in that community, was approached a few nights ago by a German spy. He told him that he, the German, was visiting the colored people particularly to inform them that the Germans were their friends and that they fully expected to defeat the white people of this country and gain possession and that they colored people would not be molested under the new laws which the Germans would establish.[62]

Undoubtedly, for African Americans, being potentially considered on par with whites was an important issue. After all, equality had always eluded them.

200　*A. Aguilar*

Furthermore, the possibility for a prospective government to create laws on equal footing for all citizens was a system African Americans could be seen supporting. Germany and Mexico were not the only countries offering assistance to African Americans. Japan, a non-European nation, offered the opportunity for a nation to come in and promised equality through governmental action during tension with the United States. The "Japs [*sic*] are promising certain things to the colored people on this coast if they will join in with Japan and Mexico when the trouble is begun here in California."[63] The US South was not the only segment of the US plagued with the prospect of collaboration. It seemed Germany had the south and Japan had the west. Equality was promised by Japan as it was with Germany. George Holman, a government agent in Los Angeles, was told that Tokyo "had been making overtures to the Negroes to side with them and that in a year or so they would take California and that when they did the Negroes would be treated right."[64]

African Americans were placed in a predicament. If they enlisted in the US military and fought against Germany, it was as second-class citizens. Furthermore, if they fought against Japan, that enabled the continuation of "white dominance" in the globe. Tensions had increased between Japan and the United States post-World War I concerning racism against Japan by the US. This further confirms the US racial hegemony that they hoped to continue to push internationally. Cyril Briggs of *The Crusader* urged the African American in 1920 "not to fight Japan or Mexico." Briggs would go on to say that the "Negro who fights against either Japan or Mexico is fighting for the white man against himself, for the white race against the darker races and for the perpetuation of white domination of the colored races."[65]

A few years earlier a US congressman had verified the idea for American racist domination concerning Mexico. Oklahoma Congressman William H. Murray demonstrated the paranoia of losing the hegemony of the "white dominance" with regard to Mexico. Murray vehemently questioned, "whether Mexico is to become a white man's country or to [fall] under control and domination of Asiatic races."[66] He stated further, "it may ultimately determine not only the perpetuity of our own Republic but the civilization of the Aryan race."[67] This explained some attitudes from the US government toward radical action taking place within its sphere of influence, especially concerning Mexico and collaboration between African Americans and non-white races. Murray hoped to combat the "darker races" cooperatively, working together to uproot "white supremacy" by Murray through the "white colonization of Mexico" and ultimately argued "it does not violate our own interests to own every foot of land from here to the Panama Canal."[68] Whether the threat of a "darker race" conspiracy to overthrow the white supremacy of the United States was real did not matter. The thought itself was disrupting and the propaganda was dangerous.

The fear of international corroboration posed a possible danger, but there was also concern for revolutionary activity within the borders of the United States. The US government had concern regarding Mexican involvement in militant activity in the United States. Military propaganda proved to be a more serious allegation. There were intelligence reports in the United States that were cause

Uprooted: African Americans in Mexico 201

for alarm. It seemed African Americans were arming themselves. One report claimed that "over the entire south, particularly Texas, Louisiana, and Arkansas there are spread secret societies of Negroes for the purpose of aggressive action against the whites," as was reported in Texas by Texas Ranger Captain William M. Hanson.[69] This raised a more serious alarm than otherwise had been detected because some of these African Americans were also in the United States military. Captain Hanson pointed out that returning black soldiers were in possession of arms, and in a riot in Longview, Texas several African Americans had several thousand firearms.[70]

The Texas Rangers, who have a questionable history in Texas, discovered an alleged situation in Wharton, Texas where munitions were sought out by African Americans. The Texas Rangers discovered "unusual calls at the store for the purchase of high powered revolvers and rifle ammunition on the part of Negroes."[71] The Rangers were concerned that the "Mexican situation may appeal to [the] radical element among Negroes ... [and sought to] ascertain if about six Negroes speaking some Spanish [were] available for undercover work[,] particularly border points."[72] While the fear from their perspective was real the fact that the source of investigation was the Texas Rangers is concerning because of their racist history. They may have had a motive of spreading the possibility of African Americans counter-violence to invoke action.

Similar to the experiences of Captain Hanson in Texas, other West/Borderlands areas were inundated with revolutionary activity and collaboration with Mexicans. Since the revolutionary Mexican forces were in favor of equality amongst "colored people," the US needed to closely monitor collaboration. Furthermore, paranoia existed in white American society about the forming of non-white American revolutionary activity in a "society of colored anarchists."[73] Seventy miles from Clearview, Oklahoma the revolutionary Ricardo Flores Magon had a gathering in Lehigh in 1912 which embraced "American and Negro *compañeros*" who "spoke in favor of the Revolution."[74] This oration was not futile, for some African Americans had enlisted in the Flores Magon forces, one in particular named Lieutenant Roberts.[75] The Flores Magon brothers also had connections to San Antonio, Texas. In Houston, these types of meetings were also taking place. A government report stated that there were:

> secret meetings among the Negroes in Houston.... It is stated [that] both Negro and Mexican speakers are disseminating anti-American and anti-white propaganda. The Negroes are being told that trouble is about to arise between Mexico and the United States, and that the Mexicans are better friends to the Negroes than the Americans and that, therefore, the Negroes should join forces with the Mexicans in the conflict.[76]

Further south in Nuevo Laredo, Mexico, a correspondence was uncovered between two brothers that called for recruitment of African Americans to Bolshevism. Maximo Alcocer of Nuevo Laredo sent a message to his brother Catarino Alcocer who was in San Antonio, Texas. Maximo wrote to Catarino, "my beloved Negroes are those whom we need in our party as they are the most humiliated. They should be most brave."[77] The letter represented the fear that the US had of radical Mexicans and their alleged recruitment of African Americans. Government officials claimed "Bolshevists are now planning an active propaganda among the Negroes in America" and they feared that they "will come through the Mexican border."[78] William F. Buckley Sr. of Texas warned, "Bolshevism in this country came from Mexico" and was advised that "you will have to eradicate it from Mexico before you will be able to fight it successfully here."[79]

African Americans did not make the situation easy for those attempting to quash any black agitation. Hanson reported, "much difficulty will be encountered in obtaining Negro informants, as in the present situation none could be trusted."[80] Furthermore, "efforts are thought to be under way by the Carrancista government to get Negroes into Mexico in order that they may assist the army, many of them having already been trained in our own service."[81] According to another intelligence report, Jack Johnson was "publicly in favor of race riots in [the] U.S." and furthermore was one of the "promoters of the Carranza propaganda in the U.S."[82] Allegedly, Johnson was also "fermenting racial feelings with blacks and Mexicans against whites."[83] Whether it was true or not, the allegations showed that the US government feared collaboration between the Mexican government and African Americans.

Uprooted People and Ideas

The United States feared collaboration, especially if it could disrupt the racial hegemony the US had long established and fought to continue. The real dilemma was whether there was a real threat or if it was created out of sheer paranoia. One thing was certain, minorities, immigrants, and lower class people sought to gain a steady hold of equality and "White America" did not want that. In fact, "White America" wanted to uproot the possibility for equality, and minorities like African Americans, sought to uproot the racist hegemony that had long existed in the United States. With the assistance of Mexico, another group of people that was marginalized by the United States, African Americans fought to dethrone the racist system that was reaching out internationally.

There needs to be a reiteration, a reexamination if you will, of the international relationship between Mexico and African Americans in the context of United States racial hegemony. African Americans played a direct and indirect role regarding the relationship between Mexico and the United States during conflicts. This history had an effect on the United States approach to African Americans, the development of the relationship between African Americans and Mexico, and shaped US policies. Mexico and the United States were at odds during the nineteenth and early twentieth centuries and the relationship had an effect on African Americans. Furthermore, both nations attempted to use this to their advantage by either promoting the possibility of a relationship or by attempting to deter the relationship. The United States, Mexico, and individual parties implemented propaganda use as they vied for different initiatives regarding African Americans. The question was whether a particular party was uprooted or whether the fight would continue well into the twentieth century.

Uprooted: African Americans in Mexico 203

Notes

1 Relacionados con Texas, L-E 1057, III, Reservado Number 2, Secretary of Relations to J.M. Castillo y Lanzas, August 20, 1833, *Secretario de Relaciones Exteriores, Archivo Histórico, México City.*

2 Rosalie Schwartz, *Across the Rio to Freedom* (Texas Western Press, 1974), 24.

3 José María Tornel y Mendivil, "Relations between Texas, the United States of America and the Mexican Republic," in Carlos E. Castaneda, ed., *The Mexican Side of the Texan Revolution* (Dallas: P.L. Turner Company, 1928), 327–328.

4 Antonio López de Santa Anna, "Manifesto Relative to his Operations in the Texas Campaign and his capture," in *Mexican Side of the Texas Revolution,* 65.

5 Benjamin Lundy, *The Life, Travels and Opinions of Benjamin Lundy, Including his Journeys to Mexico; With a Sketch of Contemporary Events, and a Notice of the Revolution in Haiti* (New York: New York University Press, 1969), 113–114.

6 Ronnie C. Tyler and Lawrence R. Murphy, *The Slave Narratives of Texas* (Austin: Encino Press, 1974), 68.

7 Ibid., 68.

8 Theodore Vincent, *The Legacy of Vicente Guerrero* (Gainesville: University of Florida Press, 2001), 152.

9 Becher quoted in Pobblet, Martha. *Cien Vajeros en Veracruz: cronicas y relatos* 4 vol. (Xalapa: Gobierno de Veracruz), 231.

10 Vincent, *The Legacy of Vicente Guerrero,* 153.

11 Ruth R. Olivera and Liliane Crete, *Life in Mexico under Santa Anna: 1822–1855* (Norman: University of Oklahoma Press, 1991), 21.

12 Robert J. Walker, *The Letter of Mr. Walker of Mississippi Relative to the Annexation of Texas: In Reply to the Call of the People of Carroll County, Kentucky, to Communicate his Views on that Subject* (Philadelphia: Mifflin and Parry, 1844).

13 Schwartz, *Across the Rio to Freedom,* 29.

14 Ibid., 28–31.

15 Frederick Merk, "A Safety Valve Thesis and Texas Annexation," *Mississippi Valley Historical Review,* XLIV, 1969, 416–419.

16 Schwartz, *Across the Rio to Freedom,* 29.

17 Ben Vinson III, *Flight: The Story of Virgil Richardson, a Tuskegee Airman in Mexico* (New York: Palgrave Macmillan, 2004), 146.

18 James Henry Lane, *Vindication of the Policy of the Administration Speech of Hon. J. H. Lane, of Kansas, in the Senate of the United States, February 16, 1864, on the Special Order, Being Senate Bill No. 45, to Set Apart a Portion of the State of Texas for the Use of Persons of African Descent* (Washington D.C.: Gibson Brothers, 1864), 9.

19 James Leiker, *Racial Borders* (College Station: Texas A&M University Press, 2002), 109.

20 "Speech of Senator Benjamin R. Tillman, March 23, 1900," *Congressional Record, 56th Congress, 1st Session,* 3223–3224. Reprinted in Richard Purday, ed., *Document Sets for the South in U.S. History* (Lexington, MA: D.C. Heath and Company, 1991), 147.

21 "Speech of Senator Albert Beveridge, January 9, 1900," *Congressional Record, 56th Congress, 1st Session,* 704–712.

22 Vinson, III, *Flight,* 154.

23 Leiker, *Racial Borders,* 115.

24 Vinson, III, *Flight,* 154.

25 Jacoby, Karl, *Between North and South: The Alternative Borderlands of William H. Ellis and the African American Colony of 1895,* in Samuel Truett and Elliot Young eds., *Continental Crossroads* (Durham: Duke University Press, 2004).

26 Clipping, November 19, 1889, C192, *Charles Turner Scrapbook* A, Charles Turner Scrapbooks, Missouri Historical Society, St. Louis.

204   *A. Aguilar*

27   Ibid.
28   U.S. 54 Congress, 1 Session, 1895–1896, *House Doc.* 169, "Failure of the Scheme for the Colonization of Negroes in Mexico," pp. 24–26. The United States National Archives and Administration, Washington, D.C.
29   *The Watchmen and Southron*, August 21, 1895.
30   Ibid.
31   *Alabama Courier*, August 8, 1895.
32   *Tuskegee News*, September 26, 1895.
33   *California Eagle*, September 13, 1919.
34   *The Crisis*, 5 (Number 5, March, 1913), 248.
35   Ibid.
36   *California Eagle*, September 13, 1919.
37   Ibid.
38   The Political Constitution of the Mexican United States, Article 27.
39   *California Eagle*, September 13, 1919.
40   John Dollard, *The Early Sociology of Class: Caste and Class in a Southern Town*, Vol. 6 (New York: Taylor and Francis, 1998), 301.
41   Isabel Wilkerson, *The Warmth of Other Suns: The Epic Story of America's Great Migration* (New York: Random House Press, 2010), 10.
42   *The Favorite Magazine* (Chicago), circa November 1919.
43   Ibid.
44   *Chicago Defender*, June 7, 1919.
45   Ibid.
46   Gerald Horne, *Black and Brown* (New York: New York University Press, 2005), 31.
47   *Chicago Defender*, July 12, 1919.
48   See 1919 advertisement from *The Messenger* in Theodore Vincent, ed., *Voices of a Black Nation: Political Journalism in the Harlem Renaissance* (San Francisco: Ramparts Press, 1973), 260.
49   William M. Hanson to Judge Kearful, October 11, 1919, Folder 177, William F. Buckley Papers, University of Texas, Austin.
50   Horne, *Black and Brown*, 35. Randy Roberts. *Papa Jack: Jack Johnson and the Era of White Hopes* (New York: Free Press, 1985), 212.
51   Roberts, *Papa Jack*, 212.
52   Horne, *Black and Brown*, 35. Roberts, *Papa Jack*, 212.
53   Horne, *Black and Brown*, 36.
54   A.L. Flint, Chief of Office, Panama, to Attorney General, February 19, 1920, Record Group 60, Department of Justice, Straight Numerical Files, File No. 164211, National Archives and Records Administration, College Park, Maryland.
55   Horne, *Black and Brown*, 140.
56   Memorandum from Mexican Consul, September 8, 1919, 17–18–143, Secretario de Relaciones Exteriores, Archivo Histórico, México City.
57   *California Eagle*, April 8, 1916.
58   Friedrich Katz, *The Life and Times of Pancho Villa* (Palo Alto: Stanford University Press, 1998), 526.
59   *New York Times*, December 15, 1918.
60   *New York Times*, April 7, 1917.
61   *California Eagle*, April 4, 1917.
62   Sprunt, J. to Hall, D. April 2, 1918, Box 26, II, World War I Collection, North Carolina State Collection, Raleigh.
63   Report by George Holman, October 24, 1919, Reel 13, #0072, Surveillance Papers. Department of Justice—Bureau of Investigation of Surveillance of Black Americans, 1916–1925. National Archives and Records Administration RG 65, Washington, D.C.
64   Report by George Holman, October 24, 1919, Reel 13, #0072, Surveillance Papers.
65   *The Crusader*, December 1920, 12.

Uprooted: African Americans in Mexico 205

66 Remarks of the Hon. William H. Murray of Oklahoma in the House of Representatives, November 7, 1913, Box 6, Series 501, Thomas Catron Papers, Center for Southwest Research, University of New Mexico, Albuquerque.
67 Ibid.
68 Ibid.
69 Captain Hanson of Texas Rangers to Director of Military Intelligence, October 15, 1919, Reel 21, #824, Surveillance Papers. National Archives and Records Administration RG 165 War Department: General and Special Staffs—Military Intelligence Division, Washington, D.C.
70 Ibid.
71 Report, July 2, 1920, Reel 13, #547, Surveillance Papers. Department of Justice—Bureau of Investigation of Surveillance of Black Americans, 1916–1925. National Archives and Records Administration RG 65, Washington, D.C.
72 Report, December 4, 1919, Reel 5, #404, Surveillance Papers. Department of Justice—Bureau of Investigation of Surveillance of Black Americans, 1916–1925. National Archives and Records Administration RG 65, Washington, D.C. Horne, *Black and Brown*, 78.
73 Mark Ellis. *Race, War, and Surveillance: African-Americans and the United States Government During World War I* (Bloomington: University of Indiana Press, 2001), 54.
74 Benjamin Heber Johnson, "Sedition and Citizenship in South Texas, 1900–1930," PhD dissertation, Yale University, 2001, 86.
75 Lowell L. Blaisdell, *The Desert Revolution: Baja California, 1911* (Madison: University of Wisconsin Press, 1962), 119.
76 Report, March 10, 1920, Reel 17, #491, Surveillance Papers. National Archives and Records Administration RG 59 Department of State, Washington, D.C.
77 "Confidential" report, circa 1921, "For the period August 1, 1920 to January 31, 1921, " "General Intelligence Affairs," Box 71, Folder 16, Albert Fall Papers, Huntington Library, San Marino, California.
78 Report, July 21, 1920, Reel 17, #580, Surveillance Papers.
79 Report "from: No. 16," "Source: Pedro del Villar," November 4, 1919, Folder 177, William Buckley, Sr. Papers, University of Texas, Austin.
80 Captain Hanson of Texas Rangers to Director of Military Intelligence, October 15, 1919, Reel 21, #824, Surveillance Papers. National Archives and Records Administration RG 165 War Department: General and Special Staffs—Military Intelligence Division, Washington, D.C.
81 Ibid.
82 Memorandum, October 15, 1919, Reel 109, M1194, Name Index to Correspondence of the Military Intelligence Division of the War Department General Staff, 1917–1941, National Archives and Records Administration, College Park, Maryland.
83 Memorandum, August 11, 1919, Reel 109, M1194, Name Index to Correspondence of the Military Intelligence Division of the War Department General Staff, 1917–1941, National Archives and Records Administration, College Park, Maryland.

References

Primary Sources

Clipping, November 19, 1889, C192, Charles Turner Scrapbook A, Charles Turner Scrapbooks, Missouri Historical Society, St. Louis.
Confidential report, circa 1921, "For the period August 1, 1920 to January 31, 1921," "General Intelligence Affairs," Box 71, Folder 16, Albert Fall Papers, Huntington Library, San Marino, California.

206 A. Aguilar

Flint, A.L. Chief of Office, Panama, to Attorney General, February 19, 1920, Record Group 60, Department of Justice, Straight Numerical Files, File No. 164211, National Archives and Records Administration, College Park, Maryland.

Flipper, Henry O. to Senator Albert Fall, February 25, 1914, Box 80, Folder 20, Albert Fall Papers, Huntington Library, San Marino, California.

Hanson, Captain William M. to Judge Francis J. Kearful, October 11, 1919, Folder 177, William F. Buckley Papers, University of Texas, Austin.

Hanson, Captain William M. of Texas Rangers to Director of Military Intelligence, Washington D.C., October 15, 1919, Reel 21, #824, Surveillance Papers. National Archives and Records Administration RG 165 War Department: General and Special Staffs—Military Intelligence Division, Washington, D.C.

Interview, Alva M. Stevenson to Gerald Horne, May 23, 2001 (in possession of Gerald Horne).

Interview, David Westerfield, May 17, 2001 (in possession of Gerald Horne).

James Henry Lane. *Vindication of the Policy of the Administration Speech of Hon. J. H. Lane, of Kansas, in the Senate of the United States, February 16, 1864, on the Special Order, Being Senate Bill No. 45, to Set Apart a Portion of the State of Texas for the Use of Persons of African Descent* (Washington D.C.: Gibson Brothers, 1864).

López de Santa Anna, Antonio. "Manifesto Relative to his Operations in the Texas Campaign and his Capture," in Carlos E. Castaneda, *The Mexican Side of the Texas Revolution* (Austin: Graphic Ideas, 1970).

Memorandum, August 11, 1919, Reel 109, M1194, Name Index to Correspondence of the Military Intelligence Division of the War Department General Staff, 1917–1941, National Archives and Records Administration, College Park, Maryland.

Memorandum from Mexican Consul, September 8, 1919, 17–18–143, *Secretario de Relaciones Exteriores, Archivo Historico, Mexico City.*

Memorandum, October 15, 1919, Reel 109, M1194, Name Index to Correspondence of the Military Intelligence Division of the War Department General Staff, 1917–1941, National Archives and Records Administration, College Park, Maryland.

Relacionados con Texas, L-E 1057, III, Reservado Number 2, Secretary of Relations to J.M. Castillo y Lanzas, August 20, 1833. Secretario de Relaciones Exteriores, Archivo Historico, Mexico City.

Relacionados con Texas, L-E 1091, XXXVII, Notice published in English, "The President of the Mexican Republic to the Troops engaged in the Army of the United States of America," August 15, 1847. Secretario de Relaciones Exteriores, Archivo Historico, Mexico City.

Remarks of the Hon. William H. Murray of Oklahoma in the House of Representatives, November 7, 1913, Box 6, Series 501, Thomas Catron Papers, Center for Southwest Research, University of New Mexico, Albuquerque.

Report by Mexican consul in Calexico, December 19, 1919; Memorandum to Mexican consul, January 19, 1920, IV-736-10, Secretaria de Relaciones Exteriores, Archivo Historico, Mexico City, Mexico.

Report by Gus Jones, July 8, 1922, Box 84, Folder 16, Albert Fall Papers, Huntington Library, San Marino, California.

Report by George Holman, October 24, 1919, Reel 13, #0072, Surveillance Papers. Department of Justice—Bureau of Investigation of Surveillance of Black Americans, 1916–1925. National Archives and Records Administration RG 65, Washington, D.C.

Report, "from: No. 16," "Source: Pedro del Villar," November 4, 1919, Folder 177, William Buckley, Sr. Papers, University of Texas, Austin.

Uprooted: African Americans in Mexico   207

Report, December 4, 1919, Reel 5, #404, Surveillance Papers. Department of Justice—Bureau of Investigation of Surveillance of Black Americans, 1916–1925. National Archives and Records Administration RG 65, Washington, D.C.

Report, March 10, 1920, Reel 17, #491, Surveillance Papers. National Archives and Records Administration RG 59 Department of State, Washington, D.C.

Report, July 2, 1920, Reel 13, #547, Surveillance Papers. Department of Justice—Bureau of Investigation of Surveillance of Black Americans, 1916–1925. National Archives and Records Administration RG 65, Washington, D.C.

Report, July 21, 1920, Reel 17, #580, Surveillance Papers. National Archives and Records Administration RG 59 Department of State, Washington, D.C.

"Speech of Senator Albert Beveridge, January 9, 1900." Congressional Record, 56th Congress, 1st Session, 704–712.

"Speech of Senator Benjamin R. Tillman, March 23, 1900," Congressional Record, 56th Congress, 1st Session, 3223–3224. Reprinted in Richard Purday, ed., *Document Sets for the South in U.S. History* (Lexington, MA: D.C. Heath and Company, 1991).

Sprunt, J. to Hall, D., April 2, 1918, Box 26, II, World War I Collection, North Carolina State Collection, Raleigh.

Tornel, Jose Maria y Mendivil, "Relations between Texas, the United States of America and the Mexican Republic," in Carlos E. Castaneda, ed., *The Mexican Side of the Texan Revolution* (Dallas: P.L. Turner Company, 1928).

U.S. 54 Congress, 1 Session, 1895–1896, House Doc. 169, "Failure of the Scheme for the Colonization of Negroes in Mexico." The United States National Archives and Administration, Washington, D.C.

Wilson, Woodrow. "7th Annual Message," December 2, 1919. Online by Gerhard Peters and John Woolley, *American Presidency Project.* www.presidency.ucsb.edu/ws/?pid=29560.

Secondary Sources

Blaisdell, Lowell. *The Desert Revolution: Baja California, 1911.* Madison: University of Wisconsin Press, 1962.

Casasús, María Luisa Herrera. *Raices Africanas en la Poblacion de Tamaulipas.* Victoria, Universidad Autónoma de Tamaulipas, Instituto de Investigaciones Históricas, 1998.

James, Clifford. *Routes: Travel and Translation in the Late Twentieth Century.* Cambridge, MA: Harvard University Press, 1997.

Dailey, Maceo C. and Kristine Navarro. *Wheresoever My People Chance to Dwell: Oral Interviews with African American Women of El Paso.* Baltimore: Black Classics Press, 2000.

Dollard, John. *The Early Sociology of Class: Caste and Class in a Southern Town.* New York: Taylor and Francis, 1998.

Ellis, Mark. *Race, War, and Surveillance: African-Americans and the United States Government During World War I.* Bloomington: Indiana University Press, 2001.

Gallichio, Marc. *The African American Encounter with Japan and China: Black Internationalism in Asia, 1895–1945.* Chapel Hill: University of North Carolina Press, 2000.

Hales, Douglas. "The Cuneys: A Southern Family in White and Black," PhD dissertation, Texas Technical University, 2000.

Hart, John Mason. *Revolutionary Mexico: The Coming and Process of The Mexican Revolution.* Berkeley and Los Angeles: University of California Press, 1987.

Hart, John Mason. *Empire and Revolution: The Americans in Mexico Since the Civil War.* Berkeley and Los Angeles: University of California Press, 2002.

208   A. Aguilar

Horne, Gerald. *Black and Brown: African-Americans and the Mexican Revolution, 1910–1920.* New York: New York University Press, 2005.

Jacoby, Karl. "Between North and South: The Alternative Borderlands of William H. Ellis and the African American Colony of 1895," in Samuel Truett and Elliot Young, eds., *Continental Crossroads.* Durham: Duke University Press, 2004.

Johnson, Benjamin Heber. "Sedition and Citizenship in South Texas, 1900–1930," PhD dissertation. Yale University, 2011.

Katz, Friedrich. *The Life and Times of Pancho Villa.* Palo Alto: Stanford University Press, 1998.

Leiker, James. *Racial Borders.* College Station: Texas A&M Press, 2002.

Livingston, David W. "The Lynching of Negroes in Texas, 1900–1925," MA thesis, East Texas State University, 1972.

Lundy, Benjamin. *The Life, Travels and Opinions of Benjamin Lundy, Including his Journeys to Mexico; With a Sketch of Contemporary Events, and a Notice of the Revolution in Haiti.* New York: New York University Press, 1969.

Merk, Frederick. *A Safety Valve Thesis and Texas Annexation.* Mississippi Valley Historical Review, XLIV, 1969.

Odum, Howard. *Race and Rumors of Race: Challenge to American Crisis.* Chapel Hill: University of North Carolina Press, 1943.

Olivera, Ruth R., and Liliane Crete. *Life in Mexico under Santa Anna: 1822–1855.* Norman: University of Oklahoma Press, 1991.

Pobblet, Martha. *Cien Vajeros en Veracruz: cronicas y relatos* 4 vol. Xalapa: Gobierno de Veracruz.

Redkey, Edwin S. *Black Exodus: Black Nationalist and Back-to-Africa Movements, 1890–1910.* New Haven: Yale University Press, 1969.

Roberts, Randy. *Papa Jack: Jack Johnson and the Era of White Hopes.* New York: Free Press, 1986.

Rogers, Joel A. *Sex and Race: A History of White, Negro, and Indian Miscegenation in the Two Americas* 2 Vols. New York: Helga Rogers, 1967.

Schwartz, Rosalie. *Across the Rio to Freedom: U.S. Negroes in Mexico.* El Paso: Texas Western Press, University of Texas at El Paso, 1974.

Shankman, Arnold. "The Image of Mexico and the Mexican-American in the Black Press, 1890–1935," *Journal of Ethnic Studies* 3, no. 2 (Summer 1975): 43–56.

SoRelle, James Martin. "The Darker Side of 'Heaven': The Black Community in Houston, Texas, 1917–1945," PhD dissertation, Kent State University, 1980.

Sprague, William Forrest. *Vicente Guerrero: Mexican Liberator; a Study in Patriotism.* Chicago: R.R. Donnelly and Sons Company, 1939.

Tyler, Ronnie C. and Murphy, Lawrence R. *The Slave Narratives of Texas.* Austin, Encino Press, 1974.

Vincent, Theodore, ed., *Voices of a Black Nation: Political Journalism in the Harlem Renaissance.* San Francisco: Ramparts Press, 1973.

Vincent, Theodore. *Black Power and the Garvey Movement.* Oakland: Nzinga Books, 1988.

Vincent, Theodore. "Black Hopes in Baja California: Black American and Mexican," *Western Journal Of Black Studies* 21, no. 3 (1997): 204. *Academic Search Complete,* EBSCO*host* (accessed July 31, 2013).

Vincent, Theodore. *The Legacy of Vicente Guerrero, Mexico's First Black Indian President.* Gainesville: University of Florida Press, 2001.

Vinson III, Ben. *Flight: The Story of Virgil Richardson, a Tuskegee Airman in Mexico.* New York, Palgrave Macmillan, 2004.

Uprooted: African Americans in Mexico   209

Vinson III, Ben. and Restall, Matthew, eds. *Black Mexico: Race and Society from Colonial to Modern Times (Dialogos)*. Albuquerque: University of New Mexico Press, 2009.

Washington, Booker T. *Up From Slavery: An Autobiography*. Garden City: Doubleday and Co., 1907.

Welsome, Eileen. *The General and the Jaguar: Pershing's Hunt for Pancho Villa*. Lincoln: University of Nebraska Press, 2006.

Wilkerson, Isabel. *The Warmth of Other Suns: The Epic Story of America's Great Migration*. New York: Random House Press, 2010.

Woodson, Carter G. *A Century of Negro Migration*. Public Domain Books, 2004.

11 Re-Membering Samson Other*Wise*

Resistance, Revolution, and Relationality in a Rastafari Reading of Judges 13–16

A. Paige Rawson

What designates scholarship as distinctively African/a? What defines African diasporic (biblical) hermeneutics? And is it possible for a queer Anglo-wo/man, such as myself, to employ a hermeneutic rooted in and inflected by the African diaspora? In this essay, I attempt to engage and embody these inquiries through the interpretation of a popular folktale (found in the Hebrew Bible) with sacred symbolic significance for the Rastafari movement: the story of Samson and the Philistines. Within the history of its reception the character Samson has become a cultural icon of sorts; the biblical tragicomic (anti)hero of excessive strength, unbridled passions, insatiable appetites, and capricious (not to mention violent) outbursts is indubitably a figure of considerable ambivalence whose personhood is portrayed always *as* and *in relation to* an Other. Samson's effective physical prowess and affective mortal weakness have left his readers and audience— much like Delilah and the Philistines—bewildered and frustrated in their attempts to "pin him down" or contain him.

While most biblical scholars situate Samson and his story neatly within the genre of folktale, no scholar to date has actually considered how Samson has been (re)appropriated *as* folktale—a much more precarious project indeed.[1] As yet, no scholar has explored the meaning of Samson within post-biblical communities whose social structures are characterized by orality within contexts of imperial domination, in order to speculate about the story's significance and function within (its so-called) or(igin)al contexts. Ultimately, then, engaging the work of Bakhtin (Carnivalesque-Grotesque), Glissant (Relationality), and Halberstam (Failure), I endeavor to make a so-called postcolonial and queerly affective reading of Samson, ruminating on the potentiality of his meaning and signification for the post-exilic Persian community of Yehud qua the Rastafari movement through a (poststructuralist) Rastafari re-membering of Samson— where the events of his life and death as well as his relationship(s) to and with the Philistines have radical revolutionary implications for all life lived (in the) Other*Wise*.

In the interpretation of Samson (or any biblical character) to ask *who* (a question of identity) is to implicitly ask *whose* (i.e., the interpreter of that *who*): "Who's/Whose Samson?"[2] The preservation of the ambiguity resident in this inquiry is critical to (poststructuralist theory and to) my project, for whether

Re-Membering Samson OtherWise 211

explicitly acknowledged or not, asking the former elicits the latter. To adequately "answer" the former (*Who is Samson?*) is to always already acknowledge/accent its contingency upon the latter (*Whose Samson?*) and to accept the impossibility of a definitive origin or source for either.[3] Therefore, I query in an effort to get us reflecting upon the ways in which the character Samson—through the re-membering and the re-memory of his folktale—has been interpreted, appropriated, and deployed by many diverse communities for vast and varied purposes.[4] In the current iteration of this project, however, I focus solely upon the Rastafari appropriation of Samson and venture an entirely avant garde interpretation of the final scene of the folktale through Rastafari biblical hermeneutics.[5] At heart, then, my interest in Samson, his reception history or narrative (legacy) and his rhetorical and, therefore, always already political reappropriation—Samson's re-membering and [re]deployment by interpretive bodies—*is* to be found (like any other hermeneutic entanglement) in *what is at stake in the encounter*. Why does Samson *matter*, to *whom*, and *how* does he function.[6] It is my hypothesis that Samson's is a (textual) body that matters affectively to and for social bodies—both ancient and contemporary—in the (political) performance and (re)production of communal ethics and identities.[7]

In attending to these analyses one may only conjecture about the function of Samson as folktale within the post-exilic community of Yehud—the context in which this narrative would have emerged in its [not so] "final" form. Might the oral performance of such a grotesque enfleshing of (a failed) ritual embodiment *not only* reflect more acutely (and accurately) the precarity and complex religious and political negotiations of a marginalized community of bodies under empire *but also* more effectively function to empower those bodies than a totalizing myth of absolute strength and sovereignty in the face of that oppression? Here contemporary discourse on Queer and Affect Theory inflect a Rastafari biblical hermeneutic as I read Samson's story in Judges 13–16 for its disruptive ambivalence as Carnivalesque-Grotesque. The folktale's affective power, however, is not merely evinced in our ambivalent reactions to the narrative or traditional interpretations which bifurcate its protagonist—what I understand to be an affectual effect of the dialectic of disgust and desire. The affective fecundity of this tale is most visceral and, therefore, evident in the way in which Samson has become a biblical specter of great ubiquity, who seems to symbolically stand on his own.[8] It is, then, understandably difficult to imagine Samson OtherWise; that is, as other than *either* Samson of great strength who ultimately defeats himself (surrendering to temptation at the hands of the wicked woman Delilah) *or* Samson the sacrificial servant of YHWH (who kills himself in order to defeat the evil Philistines and bring "salvation" to the Israelites).

Even as Samson is "repulsed by and attracted to the Philistines" (and they to him),[9] so too are readers caught in an interpretive web of liminal ambivalence—for this is a tale which surely *pulls* its audiences in even as it *pushes* us away (and not only from its protagonist).[10] Upon my interpretation and, therefore, re-membering through an embodied biblical hermeneutic at the intersections of orality and affect, Samson of Judges 13–16 is a cypher for "Israel" (Yehud) and through him this ancient communal body becomes an intra-historical affective

212   *A. P. Rawson*

body engaging *other* bodies across temporo-spatiality.[11] There are therefore, profound political and relational implications both in the text's "original" contexts (Judah and Yehud) and for contemporary interpretive bodies—perhaps no more palpable than the Rastafari movement, who re-member Samson as the original lock bearing Rasta.[12] In the dialogical process of interpretation, as the postmodern reader engages the text as folktale (originally performed orally), penned by a diasporic (post-exilic) people, alongside the Rastafarian Samson, these representations converge, even as they diverge, as assemblage in the event of a sort of trans-temporal *cross-cultural poetics* (Glissant), emerging as something altogether new—firmly rooted in the past yet perpetually transmuting.[13] In this way, then, the making of Samson within its ancient context and the re-membering of Samson in contemporary Rastafari biblical hermeneutics is an embodied encounter with the Other outside (and inside) ourselves—with the potential to affect (transform) and be affected (transformed) by the bodies involved in each particular performative (re)iteration. Inspired by this dialogical intra-temporal or cultural-relational poetics of interpretation, I consider each of these theoretical and political pieces and then move to interpret Judges 16:25ff in order to expose the innumerable interpretive events whereby Samson can only ever be other than *either (good)/or (bad)* ... and is always already embodied in/as his *re-membering OtherWise*.

A Rastafari Politics of Failure? Re-Membering Judges 13–16 as Carnivalesque-Grotesque and Samson as (Queer?) Creolized Caribbean Chronotope

In *Poetics of Relation*, Glissant describes Creolization as transformation that signals the end of (the pursuit of) myths of origin,

> We realize that peoples who are most "manifestly" composite have minimized the idea of Genesis. The fact is that the "end" of the myth of Genesis means the beginning of the use of genealogy to persuade oneself that exclusivity has been preserved. Composite peoples, that is, those who could not deny or mask their hybrid composition, nor sublimate it in the notion of a mythical pedigree, do not "need" the idea of Genesis, because they do not need the myth of pure lineage.... The poetics of creolization is the same as a cross-cultural poetics: not linear and not prophetic, but woven from enduring patience and irreducible accretions.... Creolization is the unceasing process of transformation...[14]

The Rastafari claim Samson as their biblical Nazirite forebearer in a lineage of Rasta resistance to Western imperial cultural domination (Babylon). To claim such ancestry, however, is to also claim hybridity. For while Samson's defiance has historically been interpreted as his resistance to change or growth and cast as either strength or weakness, upon a closer look Samson appears to be in a constant state of flux—betwixt and between poles even to his death. It is his fluidity, ambivalence, and ambiguity, I contend, which evinces the grotesque quality of the folktale more even than its morbid, hyperbolic events. And there is no scene that betrays Samson's slipperiness (and, therefore, the indefinability and vulnerability of Israel in relation to the so-called Philistines) more than the folktale's final scene. From birth, however, Samson's life is couched in conflict and narrated in relation to the Philistines. Born to a barren mother, who though nameless is visited by a divine messenger and given orders to consecrate the child to God through the Nazirite Vow—an oath which affords Samson divine strength and requires that he, among other things, abstain from cutting his hair.[15] Throughout the story, Samson is challenged by the Philistines and each time, by his superior fortitude, he overcomes. As the story draws to a close, we find Samson bound by the Philistines, but this time the price of his liberation is fatal. To honor his livity, Samson must take his life and the lives of the Philistines as well.

Rather than interpreting this as the final, and only absolutely successful, iteration in a series of defiant acts against the Philistines—where Samson is fighting to overcome once and for all his ambivalent relationship to and with the Philistines—when read according to Rastafari *I-n-I* philosophical theology, the pericope might as easily be interpreted as a (seismic) shift in the protagonist's understanding of his relationship to/with the tale's antagonist. In fact, in my re-membering, Samson's last words serve as the consummate confirmation of his vulnerability to the Philistines and theirs to him, as well as one of the axial tenets in Rastafari teaching—one which has yet to be explicitly addressed in Rastafari depictions of Samson. While Rastafari interpretations of Samson harness his strength and defiance for its political efficacy—rather than focusing on his flaws or failures—there is great potential within this final scene for an even more profound and politically efficacious Rastafari re-membering.[16]

Most often represented as a prolific monster of a man, depictions of Samson often appear to miss the irony of the text. Samson's size can only be inferred, since the text is almost entirely silent on the subject. In other words, instead of a massive muscled meaty man or even a giant bumbling oaf, what if the part of Samson was in fact performed by a wiry-weasely, scrawny awkward fellow? (Think Dave Chapelle rather than Dwayne Johnson.) Would that not only ensure that Samson's hyperbolic strength be unequivocally interpreted as dangerously divine, but also that the folktale functions even more effectively as Carnivalesque-Grotesque? Bakhtin famously asserted that Carnivalesque-Grotesque is both a literary modality and a political strategy.[17] In *Folk* festivals, as in folktales, we find the carnivalesque spirit in which "common folk" manipulate the socially sanctioned norms of the *Official* order that organize "regular" time and they do so through inversion (as a *WUD: World-Upside-Down*), which results in their subversion. For Bakhtin the WUD as such is perhaps nowhere more palpable than in and through the oral performance of Carnivalesque-Grotesque folktales.[18] It is not merely oral traditions and performance of such folktales Bakhtin emphasizes, but the very culture and conditions out of which such folktales emerge—and here Bakhtin and Glissant intersect most clearly.

In *Caribbean Discourse* Glissant, like Bakhtin, argues that (the cultural valence of) folktale is contingent. In other words, that the very ways in which a

214   *A. P. Rawson*

folktale instantiates as embodied oral performance and cultural performativity—the way it quite literally *matters*—varies according to context (and performative and interpretive bodies). It is, in fact, *only* in situations of imperial domination and severe segregation and (class) stratification that Carnivalesque-Grotesque folktale has value and import as a necessary cultural critique with political ramifications.[19] While Glissant himself has embraced such a spirit of Carnivalesque, the Rasta movement has publically decried Carnival.[20] Rastafarians have distinguished themselves in their rejection of "Official" social mores and the refusal of the West Indian tradition of Carnival, since both represent—according to a Rastafarian epistemology—an acquiescence to the rules and roles of the Master's House.[21] The seeming contradiction begs the question: *If* Samson's is a Carnivalesque-Grotesque folktale, but the Rastafari movement as a whole rejects Carnival—deeming anything aligning them with Empire (much less its entertainment) as dehumanizing downpression—and *yet* this diverse community appeals to Samson, *then*, how is it possible that Samson is both Dread(ed) Rastaman and Carnivalesque-Grotesque...? The difference that blurs the dichotomy, I contend, is in the distinction Rastafari would identify between the modern embodiment of Carnival (as entertainment and performance) and Carnivalesque-Grotesque folktale (as an epistemology and a politics). For the former appeals to humor and inversion of hierarchy constructed and perpetuated by the colonizer and is a primarily *Official* festival within Caribbean contexts while the latter is a modality for and means to political resistance (to the *Official*) by colonized *Folk*.

Carnivalesque, for Bakhtin, is a socio-political performance while Grotesque is a literary modality and their intersection materializes in the lived experience of real bodies.[22] Carnivalesque-Grotesque, then, is a performative vehicle of ritual embodiment for the solidarity and identity of particular communal interpretive bodies.[23] The Rastafari movement—an oral way of being (livity) and a socio-political strategy—is the very lived experience of *Folk* resistance to *Official* institutions of hegemonic colonial discourse. Folktales themselves are Carnivalesque-Grotesque and in the Rastafarian movement they function as an important socio-political and cultural medium, playing an instrumental role in performing and reproducing communal identity and solidarity. It is not necessarily the *Official festival* performance of these tales, but their *oral* performative re-membering within communal bodies of *Folk* that constitutes strategy and consolidates identity. Even as Carnivalesque-Grotesque requires a Mouse to make a Lion, the Rastafari movement demands the slave liberate herself (and the master).[24]

In his work, Glissant is articulating strategies for a popular revolution in Martinique through what he deems *a cross-cultural poetics*, appealing to the very political potentiality with which the spirit of Carnivalesque is pregnant.[25] It is "creative disorder" and what Glissant sees as "part of the 'tradition of oral festivity' and corporeal rhythms [and] ... an essential component in a Caribbean sensibility."[26] Glissant states: it is "the camouflaged escape of the carnival, which I [*sic*] feel constitutes a desperate way out of the confining world of the plantation;"[27] in its *creative excess*, Carnival represents the very antithesis of the regimented and regulated space of the plantation *and* the Garden of Genesis.[28] Carnival becomes, for Glissant, a revolutionary esthetic that is embodied in

Creolization as Caribbean folk appropriating the pejorative label imposed by French colonizers. Carnival, however, only holds such profound possibility in its repossession, since Carnival was itself "appropriated by the official media as a kind of local eccentricity." Rooted as it is in a valuation of both the individual and collective bodies, Carnival is for Glissant "a form of revolution permanente ... of ceaseless change," a "demonstration of a cross-cultural poetics [and] a joyous affirmation of relativity."[29] Glissant writes:

> If we speak of creolized cultures (like Caribbean culture, for example) it is not to define a category that will by its very nature be opposed to other categories ("pure" cultures), but in order to assert that today infinite varieties of creolization are open to human conception, both on the level of awareness and on that of intention: in theory and in reality...[30]

It is the reappropriation of Carnival and its cross-cultural (poetic) relevance, which become the example of and impetus for radical political transformation and critical to the conceptualization of Samson as both Carnivalesque-Grotesque folktale and socio-political symbol for the Rastafari.

David Hart, in his essay "Caribbean Chronotopes," also takes on the political implications of folktale, capitalizing upon other intersections between Bakhtin's chronotope and Glissantian orality and Caribbean folklore. Hart articulates Caribbean chronotope (time-space), which opens up a bloomspace for my own engagement of Glissant's poetics—through the Carnival mentality as the creation of *endless somethings* from a history of/as "nothings" (Walcott)—and Rastafari politics as (oral) relational poetics and radically embodied hermeneutics, reading the folktale of Samson Other*Wise*.[31] It is particularly "the 'time-space' flux of the chronotope [that] is especially useful in the Caribbean folklore ... [as] authors often look to the past for agency in the present."[32] How much more so the folktale of Samson—a story appropriated by the Rastafari from their freighted encounter with the Bible, the European *republica christiana*, Western biblical interpretation, and all that entails.[33] Therefore, as a Carnivalesque-Grotesque folktale of Caribbean chronotope with critical implications for Rastafari identity and politics Samson's story demands that we read it as an oral, embodied performative cultural myth, penned for posterity and the production and preservation of a particular (and) present communal body.

In his reflections on the chronotope, Bakhtin proposes that it manifests when in a folktale, narrative, or novel time "thickens, takes on flesh, becomes artistically visible [and], likewise, space becomes charged and responsive to the movements of time, plot and history."[34] According to David Hart, the chronotope "brings together time and space in a critical moment of flux with an imbued power that may produce either a debilitating or a strengthening change in the protagonist."[35] The *moment of flux* (which might also be understood in terms of the Deleuzian *event*) is integral to queer theory—as in this fleshy time-space of potentiality, non-normative or queer bodies disrupt officially sanctioned intelligibility through the appropriation and re-membering of the very concept of the (ideal/human) body.

216   *A. P. Rawson*

Interpreting Samson accordingly allows contemporary readers the opportunity to at least begin to conceptualize (and contextualize) the narrative disruptions embedded in the poetic bodies of the text, which disturb the very differentiation between those bodies (both *interpreted* and *interpreting*)—as *either* good/positive/us/Self *or* bad/negative/them/Other—and are always already mapped onto corporeal bodies. Interpreting Samson as Carnivalesque-Grotesque through Orality, Queer and Affect Theory succeeds in exposing and exploding these binaries in a way that *pulls* down partitions and *pushes* (Derridean) Deconstruction to confront real "live" bodies. For in this profoundly performative and excessively affective (bloom)space,[36] the bodies *behind the text* blend into those between its lines and those *before the text* blend into those *beneath* it. In this way, then, the hierarchal binaries of interpreter/interpreted, author/reader, master/slave, order/chaos, male/female, life/death, speech/writing, and so forth, dissolve. This becomes an interpretive event wherein each re-membering body is placed beside its innumerable constitutive Others, exclusivity is undone by queer multiplicity, and difference *as duality* is rendered hilarious because preposterous … for these diverse bodies are "doomed to fail" dichotomous delineation.[37]

I know of no other more thorough exploration of the potential of such failure than Jack Halberstam's critiques of (re)productive time and his reclamation of "Low Theory" and the reframing of *Failure* (as queer art form). I turn to Halberstam in order to contend that the political gravity of his theoretical assertions lies in the constitution of *agency* vis-à-vis the (strategic) failure of the "agent" to replicate the master's discourse.[38] Halberstam's endorsement of so-called Low Theory reappropriates just this sort of failure in the service of a distinctively queer politics.[39] The notion of *failure* might be characterized most succinctly by a *resistance to mastery*, which invests in (finding) "counterintuitive modes of knowing such as failure and stupidity" as alternatives to hegemonic colonial discourse.[40] While Halberstam's notion of failure is in relation to the (academic) institution and its tyrannical appropriation of epistemology, I contend that one might read a similar movement in Glissant, Bakhtin, and in a Rastafarian re-membering of Samson.[41]

Halberstam contends, "conversation rather than mastery seems to offer one very concrete way of being in relation to another form of being and knowing without seeking to measure that life modality by the standards that are external to it."[42] Through his notion of Creolization and the role of writer as a *forcer de langage*, Glissant similarly advocates for and champions the avant garde and what I consider *a politics of failure* whereby so-called Creolized bodies intentionally frustrate Western European epistemologies through the esthetic incarnations of a distinctively *Caribbean discourse*.[43] If, as Halberstam argues, we must first opt for relation vis-à-vis conversation, and thereby *resist mastery*, his strategy is precisely what Glissant and Bakhtin argue for in their representations of literature, a *poetics of relation* and *heteroglossia* respectively. Each acknowledging the unavoidable and, therefore, politically profuse frustration of the (constructed as) "common sense" of hegemonic authorized discourse through the unfinalizability of the wisdom of foolish failures that plague the very notion of identity as origin.[44]

Re-Membering Samson OtherWise   217

[It] takes us not simply through the looking glass but into some negative spaces of representation, dark places where animals return to the wild, humans flirt with their own extinction, and worlds end.... To live is to fail, to bungle, to disappoint, and ultimately to die; rather than searching for ways around death and disappointment, the queer art of failure involves the acceptance of the finite, the embrace of the absurd, the silly, and the hopelessly goofy. Rather than resisting endings and limits, let us instead revel in and cleave to all of our own inevitable fantastic failures.[45]

In the end, Samson dies. At the conclusion of a frustrated and fractured life, not even (a noble) death can save Samson (or the bodies re-membering him) from failure.[46] Samson is doomed to perpetual and unfinalizable failure due to an end, which although overdetermined,[47] is not altogether unambiguous. However, it is not only the content of the folktale that betrays Samson's unfinalizability, but also its always already imperfect repetition and reiteration of innumerable re-memberings by illimitable (interpretive) bodies who (knowingly or unknowingly) perform Samson's failure as genealogical critique. For even as Samson signals—both in the Hebrew text and in its (re)interpretation(s)—an unfinalizable and, therefore, infinitely open end, he simultaneously frustrates all appeals to origin, essence, and identity. As Samson's inaugural annunciation indicates, Judges 13:5 may be interpreted variously as (n)either *the first to deliver* or *begin to save Israel from the Philistines* and could also signify that Samson is the first *to save Israel by the hand of the Philistines*—thereby confirming his ambiguous inception, intention, and identification.[48] The text as the character is enigmatic, even incoherent.

According to Halberstam, the art of failure—and I would argue a politics of failure—should "*privilege the naïve or nonsensical* (stupidity) ... [and] argue for the nonsensical or nonconceptual over sense-making structures that are often embedded in a common notion of ethics."[49] The *naïve* or *ignorant* might actually lead to a different set of epistemological practices altogether, whereby—as in Carnivalesque-Grotesque—what is perceived as Folly is Wisdom and the character traditionally "read" as Fool (and/or Foil) is instead the Wisest of all. Carnival is, according to Derek Walcott, a Caribbean ritual that is "a mass art form which came out of nothing," and a creative mentality that "seriously, solemnly dedicates itself to the concept of waste, of ephemera, of built-in obsolescence ... [not] of manufacture but of art ... this regeneration of perpetually making it new."[50] Failure is the very bloomspace of (re)generation. It is just this sort of errantry for which Glissant advocates, embodied in the (Other)Wisdom of strangers such as Samson.[51]

I would argue that the wisdom of orality as (affective) embodied cognition is a queer epistemology, which *means* with the body and *inscribes* upon the soul. In the words of Jack Halberstam:

Queerness offers the promise of failure as a way of life ... but it is up to us whether we choose to make good on that promise in a way that makes a detour around the usual markers of accomplishment and satisfaction.[52]

218   *A. P. Rawson*

Samson signals the detour. And, like any other (biblical) character, each time he is re-membered through the critically different repetition of his story (as *différance* abounds), Samson is (re)generated in/as the possibility of signifying anew. In particular, however, Samson's failure creates the partial openness—or *open futurity*— that is always already (the [re]vision) of his tragicomic) death. Samson's ending is the very crack by which he is (re)appropriated and (re)created over and again— though not because the Wild/Chaos/Monster is destroyed, but because s/he *cannot be* and so haunts any effort at absolute annihilation of the Other. It is, then, within the various (re)iterations or (re)incarnations of Samson's re-memory that the manifold potentialities for the (in-breaking) event emerge amidst "the limits and the risks of resignification."[53] It is in these spaces betwixt and between that a Rastafari re-membering—not rooted in land or origin but in its own relational poetics— reminds us of our own uncertain origins, our unfinalizable endings, and the fleshy affective entanglements that threaten us with the cognizance of our own profound perpetual potentialities.

(Re)Reading Samson as Israel/Other Undoing Empire(Racism):[54] Revolutionary Rastafari Re-Membering in the Khora-ography of Rhizomatic Relational Identity

It is in this hyphenated chronotopic bloomspace—where the activity of creation is unrelated to origin and identity is exploded by its impossibility—that the amorphous shape, or *shapelessness*, and manifold fecundity of the rhizome replaces the root (as metaphor of becoming). In *Poetics of Relation*, Glissant differentiates between the varieties of identity by placing them in two distinct categories: *Root Identity* and *Relation Identity*. *Root identity* is defined by its foundation on a myth of origin and is "sanctified by the hidden violence of a filiation" that inheres in this myth.[55] Root identity grounded "the thought of self and of territory and set in motion the thought of the other and of voyage," claiming legitimacy to land (as territory) through the proclamation of entitlement, it is preserved through conquest and its authorization.[56] *Relation identity* on the other hand is not attached to a cosmology but "to the conscious and contradictory experience of contacts among cultures" and emerges within "the chaotic network of Relation" as opposed to filiation. It does not derive legitimacy from entitlement but "circulates, newly extended," conceiving of land as a place "where one gives-on-and-with" rather than territory to be possessed—"Relation identity exults the thought of errantry and of totality."[57] It is for the totality of this errantry that in its more recent iterations, Glissant has begun to consider relation identity in terms of the Deleuzian rhizome.

In *A Thousand Plateaus*, Deleuze and Guattari's exposition on the rhizome as assemblage resonates with(in) Glissant's relational poetics. The philosophers assert

> unlike trees or their roots, the rhizome connects any point to any other point, and its traits are not necessarily linked to traits of the same nature.... It is composed not of units but of dimensions, or rather directions in motion.[58]

Re-Membering Samson OtherWise   219

Ruminating upon the implications of the DeluezoGuattarian rhizome, Glissant identifies its appeal for/as relation identity: "The single root is that which kills around it while the rhizome is the root that extends to meet other roots."[59] It is a poetics of Relation, *the chaos-monde in relation (to itself)*, a khora-graphy of sorts.[60] "It has neither beginning nor end, but always a middle (*milieu*) from which it grows and which it overspills ... between things, interbeing, *inter-mezzo*."[61] Concluding their introductory reflections on the rhizome Deleuze and Guattari write;

> The tree is filiation, but the rhizome is alliance, uniquely alliance. The tree imposes the verb "to be," but the fabric of the rhizome is the conjunction, "and ... and ... and ..." This conjunction carries enough force to shake and uproot the verb "to be." Where are you going? Where are you coming from? What are you heading for? These are totally useless questions ... establish a logic of the AND, overthrow ontology, do away with foundations, nullify endings and beginnings.[62]

The queer(er, clear) connections between rhizome and relation are palpable—each is characterized by errantry, orality, and affect, inviting us to an embodied radically relational (biblical) hermeneutics inspired by the wisdom of the *chaos-monde*.[63]

Glissant's writing *speaks* of the frustration of root by relation and/in the immanence of the past, perpetually interrupting the present.[64] Our re-memory is both a conscious activity and a subconscious event as we come to acknowledge our incapacity to order the chaos that orchestrates our world and relations therein.[65] Therefore, Glissant's errant poetics, like Bakhtin's carnivalesque chronotope, in relation to the Rastafari expose the ways in which folktales are (re)appropriated, represented (orally), and re-membered so as to become part of the communal consciousness of a collective body as an intra-temporo-cultural assemblage.[66] I understand Glissant's errant poetics of relation to be politically revolutionary *because they are* radically (intra)relational and, as a result, have profound implications for an embodied (biblical) hermeneutics; that is, affectual, sensual, transnational, and intertextual interpretation.[67]

Judges 13–16, then, becomes radically relational as Samson is Israel, but always already other than Israel and/as Israel's (Philistine) Other.[68] A cypher for Israel Samson also represents YHWH God (Jah),[69] but if not read as embodying and exceeding Israel Samson's revolutionary ruin goes unrecognized, his fecund failure forgotten—a rebel buried beneath the rubble.[70] For like the rays of the sun (for which he was named) Samson is never (only) One,[71] diffuse in effect/affect and experienced directly though never directly perceived. Samson slips and slides his way through the folk narrative worlds of Judges 13–16, touching, feeling, and sticking to bodies. Betraying his Nazirite vows and normative gender scripts,[72] Samson is wo/man, but also wise folly and humanity indistinguishable from divinity. Samson is the haunting hyphenation that disrupts difference as hierarchal binary. At various times and affective registers Samson (dis)appears as prostitute/pimp, mother-father, martyr-monster/maiden-murderer,

220   A. P. Rawson

penetrator/penetrated, feminine/masculine, enslaved-master/free-bonded, judge/
convict, hero/villain-saint/sinner-suicidal-savior, s/he is failure/victor, warrior/
trickster, and more. Any attempt to read Samson as Other than Other*Wise* is to
fail (to re-member) Samson.

It is precisely Samson's perpetual borderline (schizophrenic) crossings that
haunt readings and representations such as that of the so-called Deuteronomistic
Historian, of biblical scholars such as Greg Mobley, and/or any solidified notion
of nationhood for Israel or those who are invested in *nationhoodness*. And
Samson threatens not only the borders between nations, but also the very trust
we have in the definitive difference between *you* and *me*, "us" and "them." It is
an OtherWisdom, a Wisdom of the Other, that *scares us to death* because it
signals death. For Samson's "stranger danger" is his re-membering within the all
too permeable boundaries of our skin. The threat of this proximity haunts interpretation, identity, Nationhood, body, and text (as oraliture).[73]

When one considers Samson's liminality, transience, and mercurial behavior
in light of Israel's political, cultural and ethnic negotiations (particularly within
Yehud), not only does Samson signal Israel, but the failure of a system obsessed
with the need to establish primacy (vis-à-vis genealogy) and authorize its own
intelligibility. The end of such ideology, then, marks the beginning of conscientization (an always already open futurity) and the ecstatic interdependence of all
life: a sign of the affectual bloomspace of (the in-breaking event) as continually
operating OtherWise. Whether Samson's perpetually erratic behavior in relation
to the Other-Philistines is read as predictable or always already initiating a new
moment, Samson certainly signifies difference as *différance*. Samson (as Israel)
incessantly wandering,[74] embodying the raw wildness of the *nephesh*, the
"bundle of desires,"[75] that is life…even as he signals the instability of agency
and/as the threat of impending death—of the Philistines and the "I."[76]

Upon my Rasta re-membering, the progression in Samson's last three state-
ments reveal Samson's conscientization. In the penultimate scene Samson is
once again in a bind at the hands of the Philistines, this time however unable to
free himself from bondage. Unaware that his hair has been cut and/or that
YHWH has left him—the text is ambiguous—what is entirely apparent is that
Delilah has weakened him, so when Samson struggles to break free, he fails.
Seized, taken to Gaza and shackled, Samson is imprisoned and made a mill slave
by the Philistine lords. Alas, all is not lost, for 16:21b holds a small detail with
profound consequence: during Samson's enslavement, the hair on his head
begins to grow back. Samson's head, in fact, holds great import for my re-
membering and the Rastafari, going back to take a closer look at 16:17 reveals
its relevance and reframes the entire pericope.

Before he is bound, Samson states, "No razor has ever touched my head."[77]
Rethinking his terminology renders an alternative translation in support of a Rastafari re-membering. First, the word *rosh*, translated *head*, represents a broad
spatio-temporal semantic range in Hebrew and English signifies a head (of a
body, river, politik, etc.), the male member, as well as a beginning, and/or
Wisdom. I read *rosh* as Wisdom and translate the verse accordingly. Therefore,
morah—translated "razor" (or "shearing knife")—is also the root of *moreh*:

Re-Membering Samson OtherWise   221

"master teacher" or "teacher of lies."[78] *Morah* is followed by the particle of negation and the verb *alah*—a spatial verb prevalent in Judges and typically translated "to go up" or "to ascend."[79] Due to the assumed context, *alah* alongside *morah* here seems to indicate shaving and has been ubiquitously translated as such. However, *alah* can also mean to cover, to rise (in importance), to take possession, and/or to do of one's initiative.[80] Ergo, if or(igin)al audiences were thinking neither literally nor literarily, but orally, aurally, and therefore more broadly and affectively *and* we read the Masoretic text rather than the BHS, the text could instead be read, "No master/teacher of lies will rise above and/or take possession of my Wisdom." In other words, as statement asserting the very OtherWisdom of the Nazirite/Rastafari commitment not to cut or comb one's hair/dreads: Because no Master rules me, my feral locks are proof of my (overstanding) OtherWisdom.

Samson is summoned by the Philistine masters to "entertain them" and is then shackled between the pillars (*amudim*) of their Temple (16:25). The scene and dialogue are undoubtedly affective: a blinded and baldheaded Samson is dropping leg for the Philistine lords and thousands of onlookers. When he is led by a young boy to stand between the pillars, he asks to be released so that he might *feel* the pillars.[81] The text proceeds without complication, but as a Carnivalesque-Grotesque folktale, one can safely assume Samson is up to something—especially when in the next breath, the narrator describes the temple and its inhabitants. Samson feels the pillars, leans against them, our eyes follow him, whose eyes scan the crowd of thousands whose eyes are all on him. And then it happens. Samson cries out to Jah one last time (*pa'am*), and one last time Jah responds with his [*sic*] *ruach*. In verse 28 Samson begs Jah to "Re-Member" him by giving him strength *once more*—to be avenged. While Samson emphatically proclaims he wants revenge, he does not state that he be avenged for the Philistines' shearing his locks, enslaving, and/or ridiculing him. He wants vengeance "if only ... for (one of) his *two eyes*."[82] That is, *I-an-I*.

It, however, his third and final statement, which is the paramount example of a Rastafari I-n-I epistemology, Pan-Divinity, as the oneness of God alive in all humans.[83] Just before Samson pulls the pillars and obliterates the edifice upholding the system under which he stands, he screams out: "Let me die with the Philistines!"[84] While Samson's statement appears self-evident, it might actually have greater relational and political consequence. For in Samson's final stand is a performative speech act that signals just the opposite of what the audience expects: not only the destruction of the Temple but the annihilation of the very discourses/institutions/apparatus that produce and perpetuate it. In other words, the power of Samson's performance is not merely that he eradicates the Philistine Other (as/and self), but that he pulls down the pillars upholding the structure, which defined and differentiated Samson and/from Philistine.[85]

The intentions and implications of Samson's actions, however, are not merely evinced in the words he speaks just before the Temple collapses, but also in the text's depiction of the event. In an effort to resolve any ambiguity the TNKH translates Judges 16:30, "Samson cried, 'Let me die with the Philistines!' and he pulled with all his might." While the TNKH is (unintentionally) highlighting

222   A. P. Rawson

affective ambivalence—as the protagonist *pulls* the pillars toward himself—the Hebrew word here, *natah*, conveys greater polysemy than the translation indicates.[86] The semantic range of this verb is relatively broad and signifies extension (*pushing*) as often if not more than retraction (*pulling*). I emphasize the ambiguity in the meaning of this word to foreground the ambivalence of Samson's activity and, I would argue, his affect. For this movement, whether pushing or pulling (has no object and) could very easily encompass his *b'coah* as strength *and* vulnerability, so powerful that the effect (of affect) is the collapsing of the Temple and all the Philistines with it.[87] Might it then be, that by leaning so forcefully (*b'coah*) on the pillars—either intentionally or unintentionally—that he exposes the instability of the pillars (and faulty foundation) of the structure and, therefore, of the system itself...?

The great irony of this scene is that Samson now blind (at the mercy of the Philistines) sees more (with *I-n-I*) than in all the story, through his wandering and wondering, that in this mo(ve)ment he is not just killing "Philistines" one more time (*pa'am*). This time he is, in fact, eradicating the very structure (the Master's House) that has constructed difference in terms of polarity in hierarchical dualism—whereby one is always already Master (since the construction is "founded" on genealogical claims) and, therefore, the Other must perpetually be enslaved. As evinced in his final words, Samson asks Jah for strength to do what he was sent to do but not in the way he has ever done it before. Samson's action, therefore, is not simply for the emancipation of enslaved bodies, but in order to *emancipate* [I-n-I]*selves from mental slavery*. That is, Samson and the Philistines who are themselves subjects/objects of this hierarchal dehumanizing system—not only one class of people, but divided according to intelligibility in and amongst, over and against themselves.

Samson's is the critical mo(ve)ment of a conscienticized being, who in *touching-feeling*[88]-seeing (with/as *I-n-I*) that we are all equally enslaved in the system, heretofore makes the decision not to perpetuate the system through unconscious mimicry (of the rules of the Master's house), but instead to pull down the very pillars (tenants) upon which it stands, the barriers that separate, the poles that isolate, the bars that subjugate. In so doing, Samson not only speaks that *I-n-I* are the same ... he enacts it. Therefore, when Samson destroys the Temple, he succeeds in his mission even as he fails, because he defies the "Law" imposed on him by the Master, who is mastered by the System. For while Samson's body is in chains, his mind is liberated and never more than in Judges 16:25–30—Samson's last stand, which is simultaneously his fall. Here Samson reveals that all bodies within the structure, regardless of vantage, are enslaved by the system. It is not just Samson who was bound, but the Philistines who sought to bind him. The critical shift for Samson happens in the final scene. Like the Rastafari resistance to Carnival, no longer would Samson "entertain" the Master. He asks to be released and the young boy—who symbolizes the unconditioned mind—lets him go as *feels* the pillars and the pain of the incarcerated, both oppressor and oppressed. Political action as revolutionary event can only be realized through radical relationality—what I consider ecstatic interdependence— such as we find in the re-membering of Samson's last (over)stand through the

Re-Membering Samson OtherWise   223

embodied, oral interpretation of Rastafari biblical hermeneutics. In this eventalbody-space we come face-to-face with the possibility of re-membering not only Samson but also ourselves, OtherWise.

Reading with a hermeneutics inflected *because affected* by Rastafari theology reads to tear down the hierarchal dualisms that construct lived experience and difference as dichotomous.[89] Rastafari "cite up" the Bible in ways that privilege the experiences of particular bodies and when interpreted universally by a community of critical interpretive bodies thinking OtherWise, the biblical text may be utilized not to merely perform and preserve identity, but for the political survival and thriving of all bodies as incarnations of divine multiplicity.[90] It is with real "live" bodies in mind, that Samson (and all other biblical characters) must be perpetually re-membered through Rastafari biblical hermeneutics—where the Hebrew Bible meets and is transformed by real "live" bodies, interpretive bodies affected by those (affective) bodies in the text. Is it possible that Samson is, in fact, using God in order to undermine and (because he is now able to truly) *overstand/stand over* the very (super)structure by which YHWH is himself [*sic*] being established—over and against Other gods...? An affective Rastafari re-membering of Samson as Carnivalesque-Grotesque reminds us to read orally, to resist Official memory, to wander chorically, to appeal to rhizomatic relationality over root identity, to push to pull down (phallogocentric) systems of oppression, and acknowledging our permeability to the Other within (our own skin) to reinterpret Samson OtherWise—a reading for and by the bodies of those who themselves live (in the) OtherWise. The Wisdom of those Others who are the bodies in-between whose own experience as Other-ed has given them the OtherWisdom to re-member Samson with critical *différance*.[91] How does one know the difference? How can one identify Wisdom? *I-n-I* will know it when *I-n-I* sees it, as *one* that is always already *we*—multiple and multiplying in the embodiment of OtherWisdom re-membering. Biblical hermeneutics can only be revolutionary when they are radically relational, honoring the affective (rhizomatic) event(ing) of real "live" (interpretive) bodies in every mo(ve)ment.[92] And so, in accordance with my interpretive proposition, the story of Samson becomes a folktale of failure where Samson's *last stand* is the articulation of his overstanding of/in/as *I-n-I*.

Notes

1 Specifically, Susan Niditch, Carole Fontaine and Colleen Camp, as well as Edith Davidson.

2 For the *El DeBarge* fans in the audience, you might recall their chart topper "Who's Johnny?" released in 1986, which exemplifies the ambiguity in the inquiry due to the contraction of *who* and *is*.

3 That is to say that while both appear to inquire about the location, root, cause, or identity of a character, thinker, or thought, neither question can guarantee such a thing. I am here appealing to Austin's speech act theory and Althusser's interpellation, which have both enjoyed illustrious careers in the hands of Foucault, Barthes, Derrida, de Man, and Judith Butler.

4 The distinction between re-membering and re-memory while slight is nevertheless significant. The distinction is apparent in the work of Gerald West on the former and Toni Morrison (and Avery Gordon) on the latter.

224   *A. P. Rawson*

5 Implicit in my question *Whose Samson?* (i.e., *Which* face/story of Samson are we seeing/hearing?) are two other questions: "*How* has Samson been (re)appropriated?" and "*Why?*" or "For what purposes?"

6 The term "interpretive bodies" is my personalizing of Stanley Fish's "interpretive communities" (1980) in order to emphasize the embodied, communal, and affective nature of the collectives who re-member stories and texts in ways particular to their identity and perpetuation on the level of material corporeality.

7 See Butler 1993.

8 See Gunn 2005. David Gunn relates that Samson's reception—from early Jewish commentators' through Christian and popular history—has been "mixed" and his own mapping of the text betrays this same affective ambivalence. Referencing Revisionist Zionist Vladimir Jabotinsky's version of Samson, his language betrays the subjective and affective implications Gunn understands to be implicit in the interpretive endeavor; identifying Jabotinsky's rendering as "his Samson," this is one of innumerable times Gunn uses the possessive pronoun to speak of particular representations of Samson throughout (primarily) Western history.

9 Gunn (2005): 190.

10 Ahmed (2004): 81ff. A web, then, with the potential for (un)becoming an Other*Wise* affective bloomspace (Seigworth and Gregg).

11 What I consider a "Touching Feeling Backwards" Reading, a term which is my own "mash-up" of Eve Sedgwick's notion of *Touching Feeling* (Queer/Affect), Heather Love's concept of *Feeling Backwards* (Queer/Cultural), and Judith McKinlay's "Reading Backwards" (Feminist/Biblical)—particularly apt because othered bodies (queer, "strange," or non-literate) are commonly labeled "backwards." Not only so, but to the Euro-Western eye, Hebrew is written "backwards" and reflecting upon or studying the past is often referred to as "looking back(wards)."

12 A claim so ubiquitous for the Rastafari that it requires no source. I focalize upon the Rastafari movement as case study en route to my own re-membering.

13 I am, of course, conjuring Glissant's notion of Creolization, which is a poetics of relation.

14 Glissant (1989): 141, 142.

15 Which appears to be the only vow he keeps—until Delilah, that is.

16 Samson's vulnerability is most often portrayed universally in conjunction with temptation and according to lust, specifically for Delilah (who becomes another iteration of the *ishah zarah*).

17 Bakhtin (1984): 5ff.

18 Glissant (1989): 141, 142. Glissant, likewise, is juxtaposing these two forms of festival and discourse in his work.

19 Influenced by the socio-political context in which both wrote, Bakhtin and Glissant's interests in the political efficacy of such esthetic strategies, created and appropriated within contexts of imperial domination: Bakhtin in the 1920's in Russia and Glissant in and around Martinique in the twentieth century.

20 See Glissant 1996. Glissant appeals to narratives of the past not as stories "to pass on" but to reactivate.

21 While none of the literature on Rastafari hermeneutics correlates Carnival to the Philistine lords' demand that Samson "entertain" them, there are pertinent connections and potential for further engagement and critique.

22 Bakhtin 1981; also see Clark and Holquist 1984.

23 Bakhtin explicates it is neither a festival (for the entertainment of the elite) nor a literary genre.

24 When considered in the context of Israel's narrative tradition and the exorbitant tales told about the people in their communal imaginative re-memberings, we are reminded of David in Saul's oversized armor and Joseph donning a crown two times the size of his own. Likewise, Bob Marley himself was only 5'8" but his footprint and his *Legend* expand across the globe.

Re-Membering Samson OtherWise 225

25 Glissant (1989): xli. In the Introduction to *Caribbean Discourse*, J. Michael Dash summarizes Glissant's vision:

> Caribbean Discourse presents the Caribbean in terms of a forest of becoming in the untamed landscape, in the human carnival, in the interplay of linguistic and aesthetic forms. Unfettered by an authoritarian language or system, the human forest of the carnival becomes an exemplary Caribbean space. Individual and community, tree and forest, parole (individual utterance) and langue (collective expression) interacts as old hierarchies are dismantled and old associations erased.

26 Ibid.
27 Ibid.
28 Ibid., xli–xlii.
29 Ibid., xlii, xliii.
30 Glissant (1989): 140, 141.
31 Ibid. 263–264. Glissant's *Poetics of Relation* as orality and creolized errantry instantiates reverberating rhizomatic force and when supplemented by Bakhtin's carnivalesque-grotesque chronotope (what I understand to be the poetic [as always already political] frustration of hierarchy and binary epistemologies) and the embodied hermeneutics of the Rastafari movement holds revolutionary political consequence.
32 Hart, 1. In his article "Caribbean Chronotopes: From Exile to Agency," Hart draws upon Glissant's Creolization, Bakhtin's "chronotope" ("the flux of 'time-space' in popular folk tales"), and Homi Bhabha's "dissemination" to think cultural agency in Caribbean postcolonial contexts.
33 See Murrell 2000.
34 Bakhtin 1981: 84. The chronotope, or spatial/temporal frame of a narrative, is a concept that Bakhtin defined to study literary narratives (also see Todorov 1984). According to Bakhtin, the spatial and temporal frames of a narrative are closely integrated (space as a trace of time and time as a marker of space) and make up one unique "spatial-temporal" frame (chronotope); the spatial/temporal frame of a narrative plays a key role in the production of meaning, as the matrix of situated meaning-making, roles, identities, values, boundaries and crossings, cultural classes of discourse and tools (Deleuze 2006); the chronotope of the narrative relates its interpretation by a reader, a spectator, or a researcher with the broader historic, socio-cultural setting in which it is interpreted.
35 Quoting Hart, Meerzon writes,

> This exilic chronotope constitutes the "backward glance" to the past, which affirms the onlooker's "exile from the present".... It is a peculiar spatial and temporal moment of exchange in Caribbean literature through which, paradoxically, *exile becomes a solution of exile*. Caribbean authors thus subvert the exile of the present by looking to the past (Hart 23).

36 See Seigworth and Gregg "An Inventory of Shimmers."
37 See Barthe's "Death of the Author" (1967).
38 See Butler 1990.
39 While Judith Butler's *Gender Trouble* is recognized as the "seminal" text of Queer Theory and a manifesto on the subversion of normative gender scripts, Halberstam's *Female Masculinity* is a more explicit affront to the institution of (heteronormative male) masculinity and a LGBTQ cult(ure) classic for its critical ruminations on non-conforming bodies, performativity, mimicry, appropriation, and subversion (by Folk).
40 Halberstam, 11. According to Halberstam it is also refusal as the critique of "all-encompassing and global theories" (Foucault). Stupidity plays a key role in the way failure is understood and, referring not simply to "lack of knowledge but to the limits of certain forms of knowing and certain ways of inhabiting forms of knowing" (12).
41 Ibid., 11. Appealing to Moten and Harney's "Seven Theses," Halberstam understands his project to "join forces with their 'subversive intellectual' and agrees to steal from

226   *A. P. Rawson*

the university, to, as they say 'abuse its hospitality' and to be 'in it not of it.' " It bears noting that while Halberstam here seeks to speak seditiously against the institution and for the amateur, Halberstam does so safely seated in the security of a tenured position within the academy.

42 Halberstam, 12. *Resistance to mastery* is, in fact, the first of the seven theses Halberstam expounds upon in her exploration of the import of failure for queer communities.

43 Braithwaite, xxx. According to Kamau Braithwaite, the very word "Creole" seems to have originated in the combination of the Spanish words *criar* (to create, imagine, establish, found, settle) and *colono* (a colonist, founder, settler) into *criollo*: "a committed settler, one identified with the area of settlement, one native to the settlement though not ancestrally indigenous to it." The notion of *creole* and *creolization*, then, explicitly exposes the constructed nature of identity as such.

> "Creole," in the context of this study, presupposes a situation where the society concerned is caught up "in some kind of colonial arrangement" with a metropolitan European power, one the one hand, and a plantation arrangement on the other; and where the society is multi-racial but organized for the benefit of a minority of European origin. "Creole society" therefore is the result of a complex situation where a colonial polity reacts, as a whole, to external metropolitan pressures, and at the same time to internal adjustments made necessary by the juxtaposition of master and slave, elite and labourer, in a culturally heterogeneous relationship.
>
> (xxxi)

44 Halberstam, 17. Halberstam's own musings echo the disruption of Official discourse:

> Accordingly, *hegemony*, as Gramsci theorized it and as Hall interprets it, is the term for a multilayered system by which a dominant group achieves power not through coercion but through the production of a system of interlocking ideas which persuades people of the rightness of any given set of often contradictory ideas and perspectives. Common sense is the term Gramsci uses for this set of beliefs that are persuasive precisely because they do not present themselves as ideology or try to win consent.

45 Halberstam, 186–187. What Halberstam asserts of animated film, I would likewise contend is true of biblical narrative:

> While many readers may object to the idea that we can locate alternatives in a genre engineered by huge corporations for massive profits and with multiple product tie-ins, I have claimed that new forms of animation, computer-generated imagery in particular, have opened up new narrative opportunities and have led to unexpected encounters between the childish, the transformative, and the queer.

The "dark side of animation" could easily be the "dark side of the Bible." Halberstam concedes:

> Of course in animation for children they never do quite end, and there is usually a happy conclusion even to the most crooked of animated narratives.... But along the way to these "happy" endings, bad things happen to good animals, monsters, and children, and failure nestles in every dusty corner, reminding the child viewer that this too is what it means to live in a world created by mean, petty, greedy, and violent adults.

46 Is Samson's possibility enacted in his suicide? At risk of glorifying suicide, I would like to make explicit the distinction I am making between literal and literary (metaphorical) suicide.

47 Visible "on-stage" violence and explicit commentary on Samson's death (marks of Carnivalesque-Grotesque) announce his final failure, but Samson's life was a failure due to his inability to honor or adequately perform his Nazirite vows.

Re-Membering Samson OtherWise   227

48 The lack of consensus among scholars reflects the various ways in which the verbs, substantives, and multiple prepositions in this verse might signify. Therefore, translations abound, reinforcing Samson's as an entirely opaque and inaccessible origin (of *salvation for Israel*), which may be interpreted as a series of false starts and innocuous attempts toward an unrealizable end.

49 Halberstam, 14.

50 Walcott, 261. Also see Loichot 2000.

51 In my dissertation, I argue that this errant OtherWisdom is also manifest in Plato's χωρα—the wandering womb of the cosmos—a correlation that highlights the creative and/in the chaotic.

52 Halberstam, 186–187. But, he reasons,

> Indeed while Jamaica Kincaid reminds us that happiness and truth are not the same thing, and while numerous anti-heroes, many of them animated, quoted in these pages have articulated a version of being predicated upon awkwardness, clumsiness, disorientation, bewilderment, ignorance, disappointment, disenchantment, silence, disloyalty, and immobility, perhaps Judith in the movie version of *Where the Wild Things Are* says it best: "Happiness is not always the best way to be happy."

53 Butler (1997): 38. Also see Deleuze 1992.

54 *Empiracism* is neologism I've coined to signify the racism implicit in empiricism (and, of course, empire).

55 Glissant (1997): 143–144.

56 Ibid.

57 Ibid. 144.

58 Deleuze (1992): 21.

59 See Glissant, "Sliding Island."

60 See Derrida and Caputo 1997.

61 Deleuze and Guattari (1992): 21, 25.

62 Ibid.

63 *Chaos-Monde* and ecstasis in Glissant (1989) are the relation of the oral and the written, the ecstatic *cri* (cry) and the static *corps* (body). Ecstasy for Samson is khoragraphy—being [hurled] outside the socially constructed self into the divine manyone (Keller).

64 A defining characteristic not only of Glissant but of Africana theory and African-American literature is the rumination on the presence of those unseen who are still very present.

65 See Loichot 2007.

66 See Deleuze and Guattari 1987.

67 Though (Rastafari) re-membering of Samson might appear to have been an appeal to root identity, it may be read OtherWise: as a manifestation of rhizomatic force for a revolution of errantry.

68 Similarly, the multiple Other(ed) characters multiply in meaning, further contributing to this boundary blurring.

69 Gunn, 249–250. Though Gunn himself never states that Samson *is* Israel, he infers as much. In Gunn's intertextual interpretation of Judges 13–16 alongside Isaiah 40–55, Samson is Israel, the nations beyond Israel, Cyrus, YHWH, etc.—a fluidity that likely reflects Samson's function for/within the folktale's original contexts.

70 Jeanba, 48.

71 See Crenshaw 1978.

72 See Derks 2015.

73 Jobling, 274–280. Jobling utilizes Derridean hauntology (1993) to disrupt Marx's discrepancy between Ghosts and Spirits and *living with the lost ideal*. Also see Glissant 1989.

74 Again, as khora, the wandering womb of the cosmos.

228   *A. P. Rawson*

75 Danna Nolan Fewell's translation of the Hebrew word for the *life breath* given to humans by *Elohim* (Gen. 1).
76 Gadamer (1997): 302. It is continually on the horizon as fusion of meaning.
77 The prohibition is only found in two places: 13:5 when the messenger speaks with Samson's mother and 16:17 when Samson shares his vow with Delilah. "The hair of his *rosh*" is only mentioned in two other places: 16:19 when his seven locks are cut and 16:22, when his hair is growing back.
78 HALOT, 560–561.
79 Ibid.
80 See HALOT, 828–829.
81 Samson's first words to the *na'ar* leading him by the hand are literally, "Let me go and let me *feel* the *amudim*" (16:26). While it seems to echo the request/command for release of the Hebrew people in Exodus 9:1, the roots are not the same.
82 Judges 16:28.
83 See Nettleford in Murrell *et al.* 1998: 311–325. Also see McFarlane (107–121). I-n-I is not only a theology, philosophy, and epistemology, but a subjectivity. In my dissertation I refer to it as a *theopoetics* (of relationality).
84 TNKH Judges 16:30.
85 The binary of dominant Master/subordinate Slave is but one iteration of an insidious paradigm constructed to resolve the inescapably ambiguity that perpetually haunts identity by establishing order and intelligibility (once and for all) as essential and originary.
86 See HALOT, 692–694.
87 Who are, incidentally, never mentioned again in the book of Judges and do not reappear until 1 Samuel 4 (if we are reading the books chronologically).
88 See fn. 12.
89 See Nettleford in Murrell *et al.* 1998.
90 Murrell and Williams, 343, 344. The embodied, emergent, evental reading of the biblical text in the hands of Isaiah Shembe, in the hands of a young HIV positive widow in the Siyaphila Support Group, in the hands of the Rastafari, and even in my hands … this is, *we*—these bodies, our bodies, reading and reciting scripture aloud—*are* an ever present reminder of the reality of the multiplicity of interpretation and the orality that is divorced from the written text.
91 To be clear, these are not folk who would necessarily identify themselves in poststructuralist terms. I do so, however, to emphasize the ways in which these goodly folk—reading in the fray because occupying the fray—are fleshy radically present bodies, always haunted by the many pasts sharing this bloomspace, and actually practically enact what may otherwise only be theorized.
92 For an explication on the event in both Badiou and Deleuze, see Faber, Kripps, and Pettus 2010.

References

Ackerman, Susan. "What if Judges Had Been Written by a Philistine?" *BibInt* 8 (2000): 33–41.
Ahmed, Sarah. *The Promise of Happiness*. Durham: Duke University Press, 2010.
Ahmed, Sarah. *The Cultural Politics of Emotion*. New York: Routledge, 2004.
Ahmed, Sarah. *Strange Encounters: Embodied Others in Post-Coloniality*. New York: Routledge, 2000.
Bakhtin, Mikhail. *Problems of Dostoevsky's Poetics*. Minneapolis: University of Minnesota Press, 1984.
Bakhtin, Mikhail. *Rabelais and His World*. Translated by Hélene Iswolsky. Bloomington: Indiana University Press, 1984. (Translated from Tvorchesivo Fransua Rable, Moscow: Khudozhestvennia literatura, 1965.)

Bakhtin, Mikhail. *The Dialogic Imagination*. University of Texas Press, 1981.

Britton, Celia. *Edóuard Glissant and Postcolonial Theory: Strategies of Language and Resistance*. Charlottesville: University of Virginia Press, 1999.

Butler, Judith and Athena Athanasiou. *Dispossession: The Performative in the Political*. Malden, MA: Polity Press. 2013.

Butler, Judith. *Frames of War: When is Life Grievable?* London: Verso, 2010.

Butler, Judith. *Precarious Life: The Powers of Mourning and Violence*. New York: Verso, 2004.

Butler, Judith. *Undoing Gender*. New York: Routledge, 2004.

Butler, Judith. *Excitable Speech: A Politics of the Performative*. New York: Routledge, 1997.

Butler, Judith. *Bodies That Matter: On the Discursive Limits of "Sex."* New York: Routledge, 1993.

Butler, Judith. *Gender Trouble*. New York: Routledge, 1990.

Campbell, Horace. *Rasta and Resistance: From Marcus Garvey to Walter Rodney*. Trenton, NJ: Africa World Press, Inc., 1987.

Chevannes, Barry. *Rastafari: Roots and Ideology*. Syracuse, NY: Syracuse University Press, 1994.

Crenshaw, James. *Samson: A Secret Betrayed, A Vow Ignored*. Atlanta: John Knox, 1978.

Davidson, Edith. *Intricacy, Design, and Cunning in the Book of Judges*. Bloomington, IN: XLibris, 2008.

Davidson, Steed. "Leave Babylon: The Trope of Babylon in Rastafarian Discourse." *Black Theology* 6 (2008): 46–60.

Dash, J. Michael. *Edóuard Glissant*. Cambridge: Cambridge University Press, 1995.

Deist, Ferdinand. "'Murder in the Toilet' (Judges 3:12–30): Translation and Transformation." *Scriptura* 58 (1996): 263–272.

Deleuze, Gilles. *The Fold: Leibniz and the Baroque*. Minneapolis: University of Minneapolis Press, 1992.

Deleuze, Gilles and Felix Guattari. *A Thousand Plateaus: Capitalism and Schizophrenia*. Translation and foreword by Brian Massumi. Minneapolis: University of Minneapolis Press, 1987.

Derks, Marco. "If I Be Shaven Then My Strength Will Go from Me: A Queer Reading of the Samson Narrative," *Biblical Interpretation* 23, 4–5 (2015): 553–573.

Derrida, Jacques and John Caputo. *Deconstruction in a Nutshell*. New York: Fordham University Press, 1997.

Fewell, Danna Nolan. "Imagination, Method, and Murder: Un/Framing the Face of Post-Exilic Israel." In *Reading Bibles, Writing Bodies: Identity and the Book*. Edited by Timothy K. Beal and David M. Gunn. New York: Routledge (1997): 132–152.

Fontaine, Carole. "'Be Men, O Philistines' (1 Samuel 4:9): Iconographic Representations and Reflections on Female Gender as Disability in the Ancient World." In *This Abled Body: Rethinking Disability and Biblical Studies*. Edited by Hector Avalos, Sarah Melcher, and Jeremy Schipper. Atlanta: Society of Biblical Literature, 2007.

Fontaine, Carol, and Claudia Camp. "The Words of the Wise and Their Riddles." In *Text and Tradition: The Hebrew Bible and Folklore*. Edited by Susan Niditch. Atlanta: Scholars (1990): 127–151.

Gordon, Avery. *Ghostly Matters: Haunting and the Sociological Imagination*. Minneapolis: University of Minnesota Press, 2008.

Glissant, Edouard. *Poetics of Relation*. Translated by Betsy Wing. Ann Arbor: University of Michigan Press, 1997.

Glissant, Edouard. *Caribbean Discourse: Selected Essays*. Charlottesville: University of Virginia Press, 1992.

230   *A. P. Rawson*

Gregg, Melissa and Gregory J. Seigworth, eds. *The Affect Theory Reader*. Durham: Duke University Press, 2010.

Gunn, David M. *Judges*. Malden, MA: Blackwell, 2005.

Gunn, David M. "Samson of Sorrows." In *Reading Between Texts: Intertextuality and the Hebrew Bible*. Edited by Danna Nolan Fewell. Louisville: Westminster/John Knox, 1992.

Halberstam, J. *The Queer Art of Failure*. Durham: Duke University Press, 2011.

Halberstam, J. *In a Queer Time and Place: Transgender Bodies, Subcultural Lives*. New York: New York University Press, 2005.

Hart, David. "Caribbean Chronotopes: From Exile to Agency." *Anthurium: A Caribbean Studies Journal* 2, 2 (2004).

Jackson, Melissa. *Comedy and Feminist Interpretation of the Hebrew Bible*. Oxford: Oxford University Press, 2012.

Jobling, David. *Berit Olam: 1 Samuel*. Collegeville, MN: The Liturgical Press, 1998.

Klein, Lillian R. *The Triumph of Irony in the Book of Judges*. Sheffield: Almond, 1988.

Koosed, Jennifer L., and Tod Linafelt. "How the West Was Not One: Delilah Deconstructs the Western." *Semeia* 74 "Biblical Glamour and Hollywood Glitz" edited by Alice Back (1996): 167–181.

Kristeva, Julia. *Powers of Horror: An Essay on Abjection*. Translated by Leon S. Roudiez. New York: Columbia University Press, 1982.

Meerzon, Yana. *Performing Exile, Performing Self: Drama, Theatre, Film*. New York: Palgrave Macmillan, 2012.

Mobley, Gregory. *Samson and the Liminal Hero in the Ancient Near East*. New York: T & T Clark International, 2006.

Niditch, Susan. *Judges: A Commentary*. Louisville: Westminster/John Knox Press, 2008.

Niditch, Susan. "Samson As Culture Hero, Trickster, and Bandit: The Empowerment of the Weak." *CBQ* 52 (1990): 608–624.

Niditch, Susan. *A Prelude to Biblical Folklore: Underdogs and Tricksters*. San Francisco: Harper & Row, 1987.

Morrison, Toni. *Beloved*. New York: Random House, 1987.

Murrell, Nathan Samuel, William David Spencer, and Adrian Anthony McFarlane, eds. *Chanting Down Babylon: The Rastafari Reader*. Philadelphia: Temple University Press, 1998.

Raphael-Hernandez, Heike, and Shannon Steen, eds. *AfroAsian Encounters: Culture, History, Politics*. New York: New York University Press, 2006.

Rowlett, Lori. "Violent Femmes and S/M: Queering Samson and Delilah." In *Queer Commentary and the Hebrew Bible*. Edited by Ken Stone. New York: Sheffield Academic Press (2001): 106–115.

Scott, James C. "The Uses of Disorder and 'Charisma.'" In *Two Cheers for Anarchism: Six Pieces on Autonomy, Dignity, and Meaningful Work and Play*. Princeton: Princeton University Press (2012): 1–29.

Scott, James C. *Domination and the Arts of Resistance: Hidden Transcripts*. New Haven: Yale University, 1990.

Scott, James C. *Weapons of the Weak: Everyday Forms of Peasant Resistance*. New Haven: Yale University, 1985.

Sedgwick, Eve Kosofsky. "Melanie Klein and the Difference Affect Makes." In *After Sex? On Writing Since Queer Theory*. Edited by Janet Halley and Andrew Parker. Durham: Duke University Press (2011): 283–301.

Sedgwick, Eve Kosofsky. *Touching Feeling: Affect, Pedagogy, and Performativity*. Durham: Duke University Press, 2003.

Taylor, Patrick. "Sheba's Song: the Bible, the Kebara Nagast, and the Rastafari." In *Nation Dance: Religion, Identity, and Cultural Difference in the Caribbean*. Edited by Patrick Taylor. Bloomington: Indiana University Press (2001): 65–78.

Thompson, Stith. *The Motif Index of Folk-Literature*. Bloomington: Indiana University Press, 1958.

Thompson, Stith. *The Folktale*. New York: Holt, Reinhart, and Winston, 1946.

Vickery, John B. "In Strange Ways: The Story of Samson." In *Images of Man and God: Old Testament Short Stories in Literary Focus*. Edited by Burke O. Long. Sheffield: Almond (1981): 58–73.

Walcott, Derek. "The Caribbean: Culture or Mimicry?" *Journal of Interamerican Studies and World Affairs*. Vol. 16, No. 1 (February 1974): 3–13.

Weitzman, Steven. "The Samson Story as Border Fiction." In *BibInt* 10/2 (2002): 158–174.

Yee, Gale A., ed. *Judges and Method: New Approaches in Biblical Studies*. 2nd edn., Minneapolis: Augsburg-Fortress, 2007.

Index

African Blood Brotherhood 198
African Diaspora Program (ADP) 76, 77
African National Congress (ANC) 110, 111, 113, 120
African Nationalism 113
African Union 34, 75, 76, 77n21, 79
American Committee on Africa (ACOA) 111
apartheid 1, 7, 11n29, 109, 111, 112, 115, 116, 119, 120, 122n10, 124
Awolowo, Obafemi 66

Bantu World 109, 114–22, 123n23, 123n24, 123n25, 123n28–123n 67, 124, 125
Bolshevism 201, 202; bolshevists 202
Bokwe, R.T. 110

Carnivalesque-Grotesque 210, 211, 212, 213–16, 217, 219, 221, 222, 223, 224n21, 225n25, 225n31, 226n47
Church Missionary Society 96, 105n87, 162
Coloured 11n29, 85, 86, 87–101, 115, 120, 104n40; Coloured Community 90, 91, 94–5, 97, 99, 100, 101; Free Coloureds 85, 87, 89, 92–3, 95, 97, 101, 103n40
Council on African Affairs (CAA) 110–11, 115
Creoles 86

Drum 112–14, 115, 122, 122n11, n12, n13, 123n14, 123n15, 123n16, 123n17, 123n18, 123n19, 123n20, 124
DuBois, W.E.B. 110, 111, 115, 118, 122n9, 124, 183n4, 186n82

Glissant, Edouard 210, 212, 213–16, 217, 218–19, 224n13, 224n14, 224n18, 224n19, 224n20, 225n25, 225n30,

225n31, 225n32, 227n55, 227n59, 227n63, 227n64, 227n73, 229

Hausa 154

Igbo 152, 153, 154, 157, 158, 159, 160, 161, 162, 164, 165n4, 165n19, 166n57, 166n69, 167, 168
International Covenant on Economic, Social, and Cultural Rights (ICESCR) 35, 62, 67, 69, 73, 80
International Criminal Court (ICC) 26, 28

Jim Crow 25, 109, 111, 117, 119, 120, 192
Johnson, Jack 195–8, 202, 204, 205n74, 208

Kaunda, Kenneth 66

Legba Revolution 170

maroons 170, 174, 175–82, 183n12, 184n18, 187; maroon community 9, 174
marronage 171, 174
Matthews, Z.K. 110, 113, 121, 123n17
Millennium Development Goals (MDGs) 33, 38, 43, 46, 72, 75, 79n70, 81
missionary 96, 162; education 162; groups 162; stations 98; work 96
Mexican Revolution 195, 197, 198, 207, 208

NAACP 109, 110, 112, 120, 194
Nelson, Mandela 112, 115
Nkrumah, Kwame 66, 77n16, 80

Overseas Development Institute (ODI) 38, 43n5, 44n9, 44n26, 45n33, 45, 46
Owens, Jesse 116

Index 233

poverty reduction 32, 33, 67, 68, 71, 77n10, 78n45, 78n51, 79n54, 80, 81

Rastafari 10, 210–16, 218–19, 220–1, 222–3, 224n12, 224n21, 225n31, 227n67, 228n90, 229, 230, 231
relationality 59, 210, 222–3, 238n83
Relation Identity 218–19
reproductive rights 3, 4, 8, 10n9, 11n13, 13, 47, 48–50, 53, 55, 58
Responsibility to Protect (R2P) 28, 6
Robeson, Paul 109, 110, 111, 117–18
Robinson, Jackie 118
Robinson, Sugar Ray 116, 118
Root Identity 218, 223, 227n67

Sen, Amartya 18, 24, 28n4, 31, 77n6, 81
Senghor, Leopold 66
Sisulu, Walter 110, 115
social protection 8, 32–6, 37–8, 40–3, 43n2, 43n3; 43n5, 43n6; 43n8, 44n9, 44n10, 44n11, 44n12, 44n22, 44n23, 44n26, 44n28, 44n29, 45n31, 45n33
Sustainable Human Development (SHD) 32, 71

Tambo, Oliver 110
Texas Rangers 201, 205n69, n80

Texas Revolution 189, 191, 203n4

United Nations 2, 19, 26, 33, 35, 46, 64, 68, 69, 71, 73, 75, 77n3, 77n5, 78n46, 78n30, 79n52, 79n67, 81, 110, 119
Universal Declaration of Human Rights 10n5, 13, 26, 27, 35, 67, 78n43

Villa, Pancho 197, 198, 204n58, 208, 209
vodou 170, 171, 183n9, 187

Warrant Chief 152, 153, 154; System 154
Washington, Booker T. 115, 118, 120, 209
West and Central African region (WCA) 38, 39
Women's War of 1929 151, 152, 153, 154, 163–4, 164n2, 165n3, 165n5; 165n8, 165n12, 165n14, 165n15, 165n18, 166n37, 167, 168
World Bank 33, 44n27, 46, 72, 76, 77, 79n56, 81, 110
World Health Organization (WHO) 3–4, 11n11, 13, 72, 75, 78n34, 79n53, 79n57, n69, 81

Yoruba 154, 157, 158–9, 162, 165n25, 166n41, 166n42, 166n43, 67n85, 168, 169

Taylor & Francis eBooks

Helping you to choose the right eBooks for your Library

Add Routledge titles to your library's digital collection today. Taylor and Francis ebooks contains over 50,000 titles in the Humanities, Social Sciences, Behavioural Sciences, Built Environment and Law.

Choose from a range of subject packages or create your own!

Benefits for you
- Free MARC records
- COUNTER-compliant usage statistics
- Flexible purchase and pricing options
- All titles DRM-free.

Benefits for your user
- Off-site, anytime access via Athens or referring URL
- Print or copy pages or chapters
- Full content search
- Bookmark, highlight and annotate text
- Access to thousands of pages of quality research at the click of a button.

REQUEST YOUR FREE INSTITUTIONAL TRIAL TODAY

Free Trials Available
We offer free trials to qualifying academic, corporate and government customers.

eCollections – Choose from over 30 subject eCollections, including:

Archaeology	Language Learning
Architecture	Law
Asian Studies	Literature
Business & Management	Media & Communication
Classical Studies	Middle East Studies
Construction	Music
Creative & Media Arts	Philosophy
Criminology & Criminal Justice	Planning
Economics	Politics
Education	Psychology & Mental Health
Energy	Religion
Engineering	Security
English Language & Linguistics	Social Work
Environment & Sustainability	Sociology
Geography	Sport
Health Studies	Theatre & Performance
History	Tourism, Hospitality & Events

For more information, pricing enquiries or to order a free trial, please contact your local sales team:
www.tandfebooks.com/page/sales

 Routledge | The home of Routledge books

www.tandfebooks.com

Printed in the United States
By Bookmasters